EDUCATION OF A FELON

ALSO BY EDWARD BUNKER

The Animal Factory

No Beast So Fierce

Dog Eat Dog

Little Boy Blue

EDUCATION OF A FELON

A Memoir

EDWARD BUNKER

Introduction by
WILLIAM STYRON

St. Martin's Press
New York

Design by Judith Stagnitto Abbate/Abbate Design

Library of Congress Cataloging-in-Publication Data

Bunker, Edward.
Education of a felon : a memoir / Edward Bunker ;
introduction by William Styron— 1st ed.
p. cm.
ISBN 0-312-25315-X (hc : alk. paper)
1. Bunker, Edward. 2. Criminals—California—
Biography. 3. Prisoners—California—Biography. I.
Title.

HV6248.B7733 A3 2000
364.1'092—dc21
[B]   99–055061

First Edition: March 2000

10 9 8 7 6 5 4 3 2 1

This one's for my son. I waited many years so I could deal him a better hand than I had. I'm sure he'll play his cards better than I played mine.   e.b.

CONTENTS

INTRODUCTION

E DWARD B UNKER IS one of a small handful of American writers who
have created authentic literature out of their experiences as criminals and
prisoners. Now sixty-five years old, Bunker has been out of prison since 1975,
but before that time he spent nearly all of the years of his life, except those
of his earliest childhood, behind bars. That is to say, until his early forties
Bunker was far better acquainted with incarceration as a way of life than he
was with even limited freedom. That this career, so practically devoid of any of
the normal inducements toward education and self-realization, could have
produced writing of any kind is most unusual; that it yielded not only *No Beast
So Fierce* but three other novels of genuine literary achievement (so far) is as-
tonishing, placing Edward Bunker among the tiny band of American prisoner-
writers whose work possesses integrity, craftsmanship, and moral passion in
sufficient measure to claim our serious attention. In order to understand the
nature of Bunker's extraordinary accomplishments, it is necessary to recount
some of the details of his life, which was one of deprivation and violence, indeed, an existence so close to nihilism—at least in the mind of the bourgeois
reader—as to make almost totally implausible any idea of creativity or the
eventual blossoming of a literary career.

Bunker was born and reared in, of all places, Hollywood, California. Unlike the majority of American criminals, he was born white. His father was a
stagehand in legitimate theaters around Los Angeles and occasionally found
employment in the movie studios—he once worked for the Hal Roach organization during the filming of the famous *Our Gang* comedies. His mother was a
professional dancer and performed as a chorus girl in Busby Berkeley movies.
Alcoholism drove Bunker's father into a state hospital and the couple was divorced when Eddie was four. Exacerbated by the hard times of the Great

Depression, the boy's life followed the pattern of so many others that are the product of alcoholism and broken families. He was in and out of foster homes and military schools, from which he began to run away with determination augmented by an obstinate antiauthoritarian streak well developed even at that early age. At eleven he was committed briefly to Camarillo State Hospital for observation, and a year later he was sent to the juvenile reform school at Whittier. He made his escape, and when caught was sent to a much tougher school designed for unruly boys four or five years older. Here he spent a year or so and at fourteen was paroled. Twenty-nine days into freedom he was caught trying to rob a liquor store and was shot (though not seriously wounded) by the owner. This crime gained Bunker a sentence to the youth prison at Lancaster, even though he was considerably younger than the legally mandated age of eighteen to twenty-five. Throughout this period, Bunker was consistently thrown into an environment with older criminals. After having stabbed a guard at Lancaster, he was taken to the Los Angeles County Jail, where at fifteen he was placed in the tank reserved for notorious cases. His companions included several murderers awaiting the death penalty. Because of his age, and because his lawyer, the celebrated Al Matthews, who took the case pro bono, was able to show that correctional officers had abused Bunker on prior occasions, the judge deemed him too young for San Quentin and gave him a county jail sentence with probation. Proceedings were suspended. He was set free.

It was while he was briefly at large that Eddie was befriended by Mrs. Hal Wallis, wife of the renowned film producer (*Casablanca, Becket,* and many others) and herself a onetime comedienne in Mack Sennett's *Keystone Comedies.* Louise Fazenda Wallis made efforts to steer Eddie in the direction of probity and worthiness, but her concern came to naught. His friends, except for Louise Wallis, were reform school graduates and confirmed professional criminals. Bunker, now sixteen, began selling marijuana and was enthusiastically engaged in boosting (professional shoplifting) and learning to play short con games such as "The Match," "The Strap," and "Laying the Note." He was delivering some marijuana when a pair of detectives flagged him down. A wild chase ensued through Los Angeles streets; the automobile he was driving caromed off three cars and hit a mail truck head-on before he was captured. The judge was still unwilling to send a sixteen-year-old to San Quentin and gave him a year in the county jail and more probation. He promptly escaped.

At this point Bunker's luck ran out. Rather, the calendar said he was seventeen—still not eighteen, but old enough. For the escape and the assault on the Lancaster guard, he was sentenced to two concurrent six-month-to-ten-year terms, and he was sent to San Quentin.

It was during the four-and-a-half-year stay at San Quentin that Bunker discovered books and began to read and write. Louise Wallis sent him a Royal portable typewriter and a subscription to the *New York Times* Sunday edition and *Book Review.* In his excited exploration of literature, he became a voracious reader, absorbing four or five books a week, ranging from a two-volume

Military History of the Western World to collections of short stories from *The New Yorker* to novels by Thomas Wolfe, Faulkner, Dreiser, Hemingway, and Dostoevsky—and others equally or less celebrated. He also wrote a novel, which he later regarded as very bad, and many short stories, all unpublished.

When released on parole, he returned to the outside world with serious intentions of going straight, and once again he was taken under the wing of Louise Wallis, who obtained a job for her protégé at a nearby boys' home, where she was the foremost benefactress; there he was employed as a combination chauffeur of boys, pool supervisor, study hall tutor, and counselor. Unfortunately, his protector began suffering severe depression and became dysfunctional, and Bunker lost his only anchor in a precarious world. Now twenty-three, he tried to obtain such legitimate jobs as story analyst or reader at various movie studios, but because of his criminal record he had no luck. Realizing that he had been not only locked up, but locked out of society, he resolved, as he has said, "to get by on my wits," which at first meant selling used sports cars as a front while planning crimes in the back. He conceived schemes for robberies that were executed by others. "These guys were heisting liquor stores on impulse," he recalls. "I laid things out so they could make some money." He also planned to organize Hollywood call girls by extorting the pimps and madams to pay him protection. He lived this way for four years. By then he had drifted away from his relationship with Louise Wallis. Finally, caught in a forgery and check-passing scheme, he was sentenced once again to San Quentin for an indeterminate term of six months to fourteen years. This was Bunker's longest imprisonment, and one that did not terminate until he had served seven years. During this period he continued to read widely and to write with passion and amazing industry, producing four unpublished novels and many short stories. Lacking the money for postage, he often sold his blood to make up the needed amounts to send the stories to magazines. He recalls this interlude as one of near madness—so long was the sentence in terms of the crime, forgery usually being considered a minor felony. Worst of all, the sentence was meted out a year at a time, so he never knew whether he would be paroled in six months or six years, or anything in between.

Bunker's work deals largely with the rage and frustration one feels when, on release from prison, he faces at best the indifference—and at worst the hatred and hostility—of the outside world. One of the sharpest memories Bunker retains of that time is how, after years of wearing the ample prison brogans, his new dressout shoes caused severe blistering of his feet. He wrote over two hundred letters in application for legitimate jobs—but received not a single answer, his prison record acting effectively as his curse. Such is the fate of most ex-convicts in America, for whom the expiation of sin through incarceration does not usually serve, in the eyes of society, as meaningful redemption. A true outcast, Bunker fell once again into crime. One night, after having burglarized a floor safe in a bar, he was arrested following a high-speed automobile chase.

At the moment of arrest, he feigned insanity, claiming he was born in 1884 and that he had warned Roosevelt about the Japanese attack on Pearl Harbor. During the arraignment, he told the judge that the Catholic Church was trying to put a radio in his brain. Proceedings were suspended pending a psychiatric hearing. The psychiatrists who examined Bunker found him to be an "acute, chronic schizophrenic paranoid with auditory hallucinations and delusions of persecution." So successful was this ruse that he was sent to the prison at Vacaville, where he was deemed a high-security risk, a threat Bunker was at pains to exploit by taking every opportunity he could to loudly babble at the walls.

Eventually returned to Los Angeles for trial on the safe burglary charge, he made bail and remained free for a year. While on the streets, he shuttled back and forth between Los Angeles and San Francisco, managing what he now refers to as a "little drug empire." At this point, to augment his income, he decided to rob a prosperous little Beverly Hills bank. The ensuing series of coincidences might have possessed comic overtones had the outcome not been so dire. Unknown to him, Bunker's car, at the time he set out to rob the bank, had been secretly wired with a radio device by narcotics agents, who expected the "beeper" to allow them to trail their dupe to a drug transaction. Bunker, however, armed and prepared to commit a robbery, and now followed in his car not only by motorized agents but also by a helicopter, led the officers to the very door of the bank, where pandemonium ensued as the thwarted robber was suddenly recognized, pursued, and, after a long chase by car, caught at gunpoint and severely beaten. This time the outlook was truly grim. He tried suicide. A three-time loser, Bunker was sentenced to five years for the bank robbery and six years for drug conspiracy, the terms to run concurrently.

There our story might have ended—that of another wretched misfit swallowed up in the living death of institutional retribution—were it not for the saving grace of art. For it must be remembered that even during his life of crime Bunker had toiled at being a writer. His first novel, *No Beast So Fierce*, was accepted for publication while he was awaiting trial.

He was now in the federal penal system because of the bank robbery and narcotics charges, and found himself packed off to serve his time at the McNeil Island federal penitentiary in Puget Sound, Washington. While there, he once again displayed his antiauthoritarian rage and refused to let himself be housed in a ten-man cell. For this revolt he was transported to the most fearsome prison in America, the hulking lockup at Marion, Illinois, which supplanted Alcatraz as the fortress where the nation confines its worst felons, a place in which six hundred guards oversee three hundred inmates. Still, while imprisoned in this place, Bunker continued to write. His second novel, *The Animal Factory*, was completed there. (A third novel, *Little Boy Blue*, appeared in 1982, and a fourth, *Dog Eat Dog*, in 1996.) Meanwhile, and most importantly in terms of his writing career and his eventual fate, the year 1973 saw the publication of *No Beast So Fierce*; it was received with excellent reviews and considerable attention. It should be pointed out, however, that by this time

Bunker was already a prison legend and his fame had extended to the outside world. He had written angry articles for *The Nation*. A searing essay he had penned concerning the racial crisis in American prisons had been featured in *Harper's Magazine* and announced prominently on its cover; its thesis—that the irreconcilable enmity between blacks and whites in prison would certainly lead to catastrophe—was a warning that evoked wide concern. This article and the publication of *No Beast So Fierce* were instrumental in gaining his parole in 1975. He has serenely remained outside prison walls in the years since.

Bunker presently lives with his wife in Los Angeles, where he continues to write fiction and where he has obtained notable success as a screenwriter. In 1978, *No Beast So Fierce* was made into a film entitled *Straight Time*, starring Dustin Hoffman. The film was not a commercial success and suffered critical neglect, rather mysteriously, since it is a taut and exceedingly well-made work which explores the themes of crime and punishment with great insight. In 1985, Bunker was coauthor of the screenplay of *The Runaway Train*, a gripping drama about escaped felons from an Alaska prison; it was a critical and commercial hit and gained Oscar nominations for its stars, Jon Voight and Eric Roberts. Now, in 1999, filming has been completed for Bunker's *The Animal Factory*. Bunker has adapted well to civilian life after his many years of violence and desperation. His attitude and demeanor bespeak the composure of a man who is at peace with himself after a lifetime of existential dread such as the average law-abiding citizen can only distantly imagine. Of medium height, compact and muscular, he still has a tough and streetwise expression, the face of a man who has known cruelty and suffering; but his eyes twinkle; the initial appearance of ferocity is softened by a quality both wise and benign. Reserved, almost shy in manner, he can become animated and powerfully articulate; his intellectual ability, which possesses scope as well as nimbleness, is all the more impressive for being the product of passionate self-education. The letters he writes—and he writes dozens out of the habit formed in the loneliness of prison cells—are splendid models of the epistolary art, shrewd, discursive, witty, beautifully expressed, and often profound. Edward Bunker was dealt a rotten hand at the beginning of his life, and his days thereafter were largely those of a victim in society's brutalizing institutions. That he emerged from these dungeons not a brute but an artist with a unique and compelling voice is a tribute to his own invincible will, besides being a sweet victory by the artist himself over society and its contempt for the outcast. In his work readers will be able to discover urgent truths about crime and punishment—and therefore about our ultimate concern with freedom—set down by a vigorous and important writer.

—William Styron

EDUCATION OF A FELON

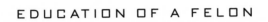

1

NO HEAVEN,
NO HELL

IN MARCH OF 1933, Southern California suddenly began to rock and roll to a sound from deep within the ground. Bric-a-brac danced on mantels and shattered on floors. Windows cracked and cascaded onto sidewalks. Lathe-and-plaster houses screeched and bent this way and that, much like matchboxes. Brick buildings stood rigid until overwhelmed by the vibrations, then fell into a pile of rubble and a cloud of dust. The Long Beach Civic Auditorium collapsed, with many killed. I was later told that I was conceived at the moment of the earthquake and born on New Year's Eve, 1933, in Hollywood's Cedars of Lebanon Hospital. Los Angeles was under a torrential deluge, with palm trees and houses floating down its canyons.

When I was five, I heard my mother proclaim that the earthquake and storm were omens, for I was trouble from the start, beginning with colic. At two, I disappeared from a family picnic in Griffith Park. Two hundred men hunted the brush for half the night. At three, I somehow managed to demolish a neighbor's backyard incinerator with a claw hammer. At four, I pillaged another neighbor's Good Humor truck and had an ice-cream party for several neighborhood dogs. A week later I tried to help clean up the backyard by burning a pile of eucalyptus leaves that were piled beside the neighbor's garage. Soon the night was burning bright and fire engine sirens sounded loud. Only one garage wall was fire-blackened.

I remember the ice-cream caper and fire, but the other things I was told. My first clear memories are of my parents screaming at each other and the police arriving to "keep the peace." When my father left, I followed him to the driveway. I was crying and wanted to go with him, but he pushed me away and drove off with a screech of tires.

We lived on Lexington Avenue just east of Paramount Studios. The first word I could read was *Hollywoodland*. My mother was a chorus girl in vaudeville and Busby Berkeley movie musicals. My father was a stagehand and sometimes grip.

I don't remember the divorce proceedings, but part of the result was my being placed in a boarding home. Overnight I went from being a pampered only child to being the youngest among a dozen or more. I first learned about theft in this boarding home. Somebody stole candy that my father had brought me. It was hard then for me to conceive the idea of theft.

I ran away for the first time when I was five. One rainy Sunday morning while the household slept late, I put on a raincoat and rubbers and went out the back door. Two blocks away I hid in the crawl space of an old frame house that sat high off the ground and was surrounded by trees. It was dry and out of the rain, and I could peer out at the world. The family dog quickly found me but preferred being hugged and petted to sending forth an alarm. I stayed there until darkness came, the rain stopped, and a cold wind came up. Even in Los Angeles, a December night can be cold for a five-year-old. I came out, walked half a block, and was spotted by one of those hunting for me. My parents had been worried, of course, but not in a panic. They were already familiar with my propensities for trouble.

The couple who ran the foster home asked my father to come and take me away. He tried another boarding home, and when that failed he tried a military school, Mount Lowe in Altadena. I lasted two months. Then it was another boarding home, also in Altadena, a five-thousand-square-foot house with an acre of grounds. That was my first meeting with Mrs. Bosco, whom I remember fondly. I seemed to get along okay, although I remember hiding under a bed in the dorm so I could read. My father had built a small bookcase for me. He then bought a ten-volume set of *Junior Classics*, children's versions of famous tales such as "The Man Without a Country," "Pandora's Box," and "Damon and Pythias." I learned to read from these books.

Mrs. Bosco closed the boarding home after I had been there for a few months. The next stop was Page Military School, on Cochran and San Vicente in West Los Angeles. The parents of the prospective cadets were shown bright, classy dorms with cubicles, but the majority of the cadets lived in less sumptuous quarters. At Page I had measles and mumps and my first official recognition as a troublemaker destined for a bad end. I became a thief. A boy whose name and face I forgot long ago took me along to prowl the other dorms in the wee hours as he searched pants hanging on hooks or across chair backs. When someone rolled over, we ducked and froze, our hearts beating wildly. The cubicles were shoulder-high, so we could duck our heads and be out of sight. We had to run once when a boy woke up and challenged us: "Hey, what're you doing?" As we ran, behind us we heard the scream: "Thief! Thief!" It was a great adrenaline rush.

One night a group of us sneaked from the dorm into the big kitchen and used a meat cleaver to hack the padlock off a walk-in freezer. We pillaged all the cookies and ice cream. Soon after reveille, we were apprehended. I was unjustly deemed the ringleader and disciplined accordingly. I was also thereafter marked for special treatment by the cadet officers. My few friends were the other outcasts and troublemakers. My single legitimate accomplishment at Page was discovering that I could spell better than almost everyone else. Even amid the chaos of my young life, I'd mastered syllables and phonetics, and I remembered many of the exceptions to the rules. It is trivial, yet because I could sound out words, I could read precociously—and soon voraciously.

On Friday afternoons nearly every cadet went home for the weekend. One weekend I went to see my father, the next to my mother's. She now worked as a coffee shop waitress. On Sunday mornings I followed the common habit of most American children of the era; I went to the matinee at a neighborhood movie theater. It showed double features. One Sunday between the two movies, I went to the lobby, where I learned that the Japanese had just bombed Pearl Harbor. Earlier, my father had declared: "If those slant-eyed bastards start trouble, we'll send the U.S. Navy over and sink their rinky-dink islands." Dad was attuned with the era, where *nigger* appeared in the prose of Ernest Hemingway and Thomas Wolfe and others. Dad disliked "niggers," "spics," "wops," and the English with "their goddamn king." He liked France and Native Americans and claimed that we Bunkers had Indian blood. I was never convinced. Claiming Indian blood today has become somewhat chic. Our family had been around the Great Lakes from midway through the eighteenth century, and when my father reached his sixties his wrinkled leather skin, in addition to his high cheekbones, made him look like an Indian. Indeed, as I get older, I am sometimes asked if I have Indian blood. I really don't know— or care.

At Page Military School, things got worse. Cadet officers made my life miserable, so on one bright California morning, another cadet and I jumped the back fence and headed toward the Hollywood Hills, three miles away. They were green, speckled with a few red-tiled roofs. We hitchhiked over the hills and spent the night in the shell of a wrecked automobile beside a two-lane highway, watching the giant trucks rumble past. Since then that highway has become a ten-lane interstate freeway.

After shivering through the night and being hungry when the sun came up, my companion said he was going to go back. I bid him good-bye and started walking beside a railroad right-of-way between the highway and endless orange groves. I came upon a trainload of olive-drab U.S. Army trucks that waited on a siding. As I walked along there was the rolling crash as the train got under way. I grabbed a rail and climbed aboard. The hundreds of army trucks were unlocked so I got in one and watched the landscape flash past as the train headed north.

Early that evening, I climbed off in the outskirts of Sacramento, four hundred miles from where I had started. I was getting hungry and the shadows were lengthening. I started walking. I figured I would go into town and see a movie. When it let out, I would find something to eat and somewhere to sleep. Outside Sacramento, on a bank of the American River full of abundant greenery, I smelled food cooking. It was a hobo encampment called a Hooverville, with shacks made of corrugated tin and cardboard.

The hoboes took me in until one got scared and stopped a sheriff's car. Deputies raided the encampment and took me away.

Page Military School refused to allow me to return. My father was near tears over what to do with me. Then we heard that Mrs. Bosco had opened a new home for a score of boys, ages five through high school. She had leased a twenty-five-thousand-square-foot mansion on four acres on Orange Grove Avenue in Pasadena. It was called Mayfair. The house still exists as part of Ambassador College. Back then such huge mansions were unsalable white elephants.

The name MAYFAIR was affixed to a brass gate post. The house was worthy of an archduke, but a nine-year-old is unimpressed by such things. The boys were pretty much relegated to four bedrooms on the second floor of the north wing over the kitchen. The school classroom, which had once been the music room, was off the vast entrance hall, which had a grand staircase. We attended school five days a week, and there was no such thing as summer vacation. The teacher, a stern woman given to lace-collared dresses with cameos at the necks, had a penchant for punishment. She'd grab an ear and give it a twist or rap our knuckles with a ruler. I already had a problem with authority. Once she grabbed my ear. I slapped her hand away and abruptly stood up. Startled, she flinched backward, tripped over a chair, and fell on her rump, legs up. She cried out as if being murdered. Mr. Hawkins, the black handyman, ran in and grabbed me by the scruff of my neck. He dragged me to Mrs. Bosco. She sent for my father. When he arrived, the fire in his eyes made me want to run. Mrs. Bosco brushed the incident away with a few words. What she really wanted was for my father to read the report on the IQ test we had taken a week earlier. He was hesitant. Did he want to know if his son was crazy? I watched him scan the report; then he read it slowly, his angry flush giving way to a frown of confusion. He looked up and shook his head.

"That's a lot of why he's trouble," Mrs. Bosco said.

"Are you sure it isn't a mistake?"

"I'm sure."

My father grunted and half-chuckled. "Who would have thought it?"

Thought what? He later told me the report put my mental age at eighteen, my IQ at 152. Until then I'd always thought I was average, or perhaps a little below average, in those abilities given by God. I'd certainly never been the brightest in any class—except for the spelling, which seemed like more of a trick than an indicator of intelligence. Since then, no matter how chaotic or nihilistic my existence happened to be, I have tried to hone the natural abilities they said I had. The result might be a self-fulfilling prophecy.

I continued to go home on weekends, although by now my mother lived in

San Pedro with a new husband—so instead of switching off every weekend, I spent three of four with my father. Whichever one I visited, on Sunday afternoon I would say good-bye, ostensibly returning straightaway to Mayfair. I never went straight back. Instead I roamed the city. I might rent a little battery-powered boat in Echo Park or go to the movies in downtown Los Angeles. If I visited my mother in San Pedro, I detoured to Long Beach, where the amusement pier was in full swing.

Late in the evening, I rode a big red Pacific Electric streetcar back to Pasadena, where I had to walk about a mile to Orange Grove Avenue and Mayfair. I went up the rear drive. A balcony at one end could be reached by climbing a slender tree and scrambling onto the balcony. Directly across from the balcony door was the room I shared with two other boys. Nobody ever missed me or noticed when I arrived as long as I was on hand Monday morning.

One Sunday night when I crossed the balcony, turned the doorknob, and pushed the door opened a few inches and stopped. Something was blocking it from the other side. Leaning against it hard, I managed to force the upper part open enough to squeeze through, stepping on what seemed to be a body next to the door. Crouching, I felt around the blackness and touched a face. A bolt of fear shot through me. The face was cold. It was the face of death. I think I let out a cry, but nobody heard me.

Not wanting my after-midnight arrival to be discovered, I undressed and climbed into bed. Lying there, I knew I couldn't just ignore the situation. Not wanting to step on the body in the darkness, I went through the bathroom to the next bedroom, where four boys slept, and from there into the hallway. I woke up Mrs. Bosco and told her what I'd found.

She put on her robe and brought a flashlight, took me to my room, and told me to go to bed, then locked the door. I went to bed and managed to fall into a light sleep, although I came awake when I heard muffled voices and saw light under the door.

A few minutes later, I heard the key unlock the bedroom. In the morning the body was gone. It belonged to Frankie Dell, a pale, frail boy who was a severe hemophiliac with a rheumatic heart. He had simply collapsed and died in the hallway. He might even have been going for help.

Mrs. Bosco's was the only home I ever liked as a child. She treated me more like a teenager than a nine-year-old. During weeknights I was allowed to go alone into downtown Pasadena. I went to a movie, of course. I learned geography from the two big maps affixed to the wall in my room: Europe, including the Mediterranean and North Africa, was on one map, the Pacific plus Asia on the other. I had pins of various colors to mark battles, troops, and the front lines of the war that was going on. Finding the Solomon Islands to mark Guadalcanal took my eye to Australia and New Zealand. The star on the map told me that Canberra was the capital of Australia.

Mr. Hawkins, the black handyman whose apartment was over the immense garage, had once been a prizefighter, and he taught me how to throw a left jab.

The jab I learned wreaked havoc on the nose of Buckley, the home bully. We started to fight in the upstairs hall. I backed up, one step at a time, down the length of the long second-floor hallway, sticking a jab in his nose whenever he seemed coiled to charge. One of Mrs. Bosco's pretty daughters, a USC coed, came out of her room and broke it up. Buckley had two rapidly swelling eyes and a bloody nose. I was unmarked. About the same time, I learned the value of the Sunday punch, which was simply striking first. In reform school I would study experts on the Sunday punch and hone my own ability. Fistfighting is a useless skill in boardrooms and business meetings. It will not get you the girl. Most middle- and upper-class white men go through adult life without ever having a single fistfight. But where I spent youth and young manhood it is a useful skill, especially since I hadn't been given strength, speed, or stamina. My reflexes were mediocre. I do, however, take a good punch without falling. I have beaten bigger, stronger men, who were faster and in better shape, including a U.S. Marine karate instructor, simply by punching first and continuing to punch with both hands before they ever got started. Occasionally, someone overcame that first onslaught and beat my ass, but not usually. In later years I leaned to pace my attack so a few punches accomplished what had taken many wild ones long ago. On the chin and most go down, and once down they should never be allowed to get up and continue. But I've digressed. Back to my childhood in Mayfair on Orange Grove Avenue, nicknamed King's Row because of the many great mansions, including the famed Wrigley mansion.

ONE SUNDAY NIGHT IN DECEMBER, it was past midnight when I got off the streetcar on Fair Oaks and Colorado in downtown Pasadena and began my walk. The last street was a narrow lane with tiny frame houses for servants that ran parallel to Orange Grove a block away. The lane and tiny houses are long gone, but back then they were fronted by huge trees that overhung the street. A lighted Christmas tree was in one home window and a candle in another. They calmed my fear at walking through the shadows where wind and moonlight made weird moving shapes. It was enough to make an imaginative nine-year-old whistle his way through the dark.

I turned into the rear gate of Mayfair. Up the slope loomed the dark outline of the great house set among tall pines. They suited its Bavarian hunting chalet architecture. The house had once belonged to an American general who apparently had invested heavily in Germany after World War I. I found the certificates between the walls. I was now familiar with the great house as I circled to the slender tree next to the balcony.

The tree actually grew three feet from the balcony, but as I climbed, my weight bent it over, and I disembarked by throwing both arms over the rail and pulling my legs away from the tree. It snapped back straight and erect.

On the balcony I always felt a pang of anxiety: had someone locked the balcony door? Nobody ever had, so far, although I was prepared to break the glass and reach inside if it ever became necessary. Nobody would know who or why; the broken glass might even go unnoticed for days. No need for that on this night. The door opened as usual.

The hall was totally dark, again as usual. I immediately smelled something I couldn't recognize. It was definite but not overpowering. I reached for the room door. It opened. I went in.

The room was pitch-black. From memory I crossed the darkness to my bed in the corner. It was gone. Where was my bed?

I reached out, feeling for the bed next to mine. Nothing.

My heart jumped. I was scared. I went to the door and flipped the light switch.

Nothing.

I felt along the wall. Empty space. Something weird was going on. I wanted to yell, but that would expose my postmidnight arrival. With my fingers touching the wall, I moved to the door. Before reaching it, my shoes crunched on broken glass.

My heart raced. What was happening? I nearly choked, because no rational possibility came to mind. I knew better than to think it was magic or the supernatural, but the idea was inescapable for a moment. Just then, in the blackness, something brushed against the calf of my leg, triggering instant terror. I jumped up in the air, came down, and tore open the door. I can't remember crossing the hall to the balcony. In the darkness I climbed on the rail and jumped for the tree. It was three or four feet out. I got both hands on it, and it bent away from the balcony, pulling my upper body with it. My feet were still on the balustrade. For a moment I was a human bridge; then my feet came free.

The limb I held snapped with a loud crack. I fell through, breaking limbs that grabbed and scratched me, and finally landed flat on my back. Every bit of air was smashed out of my lungs. I knew I was going to die. I could not breathe. Even while dying from my inability to breathe, I drew up my legs and rolled over to rise. I wanted distance from the huge mansion. I wasn't thinking. I was running on automatic fear.

When the first tiny breath kicked in, I was limping across the parking area toward the shrubbery. There was an acre of greenery, much of it half-wild, right here—and I knew every inch of it. I hit the wall of shrubbery with both of my hands folded over my face. I plowed through with the branches tearing at my clothes and face.

I veered right, behind the garage, and hit the ground in a space beneath a giant elm whose limbs covered the ground. We had put a flattened cardboard box in there, as boys do.

My exhaustion modified my fear. It was crazy. I knew there were no ghosts. (Years later, while I was telling this story, a listener said, "I'll bet it was a cat's tail that brushed your leg." I think he was right. Mrs. Bosco had a black cat that roamed the house and brushed against legs. What else could it have been?) I spent the night in that space beneath the tree, sometimes shivering with the chill, sometimes dozing off for a few minutes.

By first light my entire body ached. My back really hurt and would turn into the largest black-and-blue mark I've ever seen.

I dozed and came alert to the sound of rattling garbage cans. Mr. Hawkins was hoisting them onto the back of a pickup truck. He was working in the space beside the garage where the cans were kept.

"Mr. Hawkins!" I called.

He stopped work and peered, closing one eye to focus the other one. "Is that you?" he asked. He knew me better than the other boys. Beside the jab, he had taught me how to tie a Windsor knot. He may have been poor, but he dressed sharp on his day off.

I stepped out of the shrubbery but kept the edge of the garage between myself and the house. "What's going on, Mr. Hawkins?"

"You ain' seen Miz Bosco yet?"

"No."

"She called your daddy Sunday afternoon. He said you'd be here las' night 'bout six. She's been worried sick."

"What happened? Where is everybody?"

"We had a fire in the attic late Saturday . . . early Sunday 'fore it was light. Look there." He pointed at the roof. Sure enough, there was a hole about four feet across. Its edges were charred black from fire.

"It was the wiring," he said. "They moved the beds to the school auditorium over yonder." He gestured with a finger. "It's just until she can get all the boys picked up."

A maroon 1940 Lincoln Continental flashed into sight. It went past us around the circular drive and pulled up at the mansion's front door. The car stopped and Mrs. Bosco came down the walk to greet the couple who emerged.

"That be Billy Palmer's folks," Mr. Hawkins said. "Gotta get those bags." He pulled off his work gloves and abandoned the garbage cans, heading toward the house. I backed up into the bushes.

A few minutes later, Mrs. Bosco and Mr. Hawkins came into view. They were heading right toward my hiding place. I backed farther into the bushes, tripping down on my butt. That galvanized me. I got up, turned, and ran. Mr. Hawkins called my name. He thought I was still where I had been. I was rapidly adding distance between us.

I went over the wrought-iron front fence and ran across the wide boulevard, then crossed a lawn and went down a driveway to a backyard the size of a baseball diamond. Several people in white—I would think of the scene years later when I read F. Scott Fitzgerald—were playing croquet. I flew past their periphery. One or two looked up; the others saw nothing.

By noon, I got off a big red streetcar at the Pacific Electric Terminal on Sixth and Main Streets in downtown Los Angeles. The sidewalks teemed. Uniforms of all the armed services were abundant. There was a long line outside the Burbank Theater. the burlesque theater on Main Street. Two blocks away was Broadway, where there were several movie palaces on each block, their marquees flashing bright in the gray December light. I would have gone to a movie, for movies always let me forget my troubles for a few hours, but I knew that this was a school day and the truant officers routinely patrolled the downtown movie houses for truants.

On Hill Street near Fifth was Pacific Electric's subway terminal. The streetcars left for the sprawling western communities and the San Fernando Valley to the northwest through a long tunnel in the hillside and come out on Glendale Boulevard. I took a streetcar to Hollywood, where my father worked backstage at Ken Murray's *Blackouts,* a variety review with chorus girls and comics in a theater on a side street off Hollywood Boulevard. I was familiar with this area. I wanted to be where I knew my way around.

Hollywood Boulevard was new, bright, and crowded. Thirty years earlier it had been a bean field. Now servicemen were everywhere. They came from training camps and military bases all over Southern California. They were drawn to Hollywood and Vine and especially to the Hollywood Canteen, where they might just dance with Hedy Lamarr or Joan Leslie, or they could stroll the boulevard and see if their feet fit the imprint of Douglas Fairbanks or Charlie Chaplin outside Grauman's Chinese Theater. Sid Grauman had built three great palaces to honor the movies. The downtown Million Dollar Theater was the first, but he realized the city's wealth was moving west, so he built two on Hollywood Boulevard, the Chinese and Egyptian. The latter had a long walk from the box office to the lobby that was lined with images of ancient Egypt and giant kitsch statues of Ramses II and Nefertiti or somebody with a head like an animal. That first night on my latest runaway, I went to the plush Hawaiian, farther east on the boulevard, which was showing the original *Mummy,* with Boris Karloff, and a new sequel, *The Mummy Returns.* It scared away my troubles for a few hours.

When I came out, a cold wind had risen. No rain was falling, but the sidewalk and street were dark where it had come down while I was inside. I turned up Gower. The Hollywood Hills started a block north of the theater. Beyond Franklin Avenue was Whitley Heights. It was "old" Hollywood and looked as if it belonged in either Naples or Capri. It had once been fashionable enough for Gloria Swanson, Ben Turpin, and Ramon Novarro. In the war years it was still nice, although since then it has lost favor as Hollywood's surrounding streets became infested with poverty and poverty's handmaidens: crime, drugs, and prostitution.

Rain began to fall. I tried to find shelter. I could get out of the rain but not away from the wind. It was time to go to where my father worked. I walked along Franklin and turned back down Ivar. The marquee had been turned off, and the box office was closed. I wasn't going there anyway. I went down the alley beside the building to the stage entrance. I didn't know the old man on the door, but he knew my father and remembered me from an earlier visit. "We were working the Mayan downtown. It was *Abie's Irish Rose . . .* or maybe *Song of Norway.*"

I remember *Abie's Irish Rose* at the Mayan, but not the old man. It was immaterial; he motioned toward me. I shook my head.

"When's curtain?"

"Ten-fifty-two . . . 'bout half an hour."

"I'll be back."

"Here's your dad now. Hey, Ed!"

My father, wearing the white bib overalls of a stagehand, was crossing backstage. He turned his head, saw me, and hardened his expression. As he walked over, his jaw muscles pulsing, I wanted to turn and run. I was sure he wouldn't show his anger here, but I knew the fury of his exasperation. He was never mean, but frustration sometimes overcame him. He looked at me. "Just like a bad penny," he said.

What did that mean? Bad penny? I'd never heard the phrase and had no idea what it meant. Still, the tension of the situation made it imprint on my memory, so years later I remembered this moment whenever I heard the phrase.

My father took his keys from his pocket. "Go wait in the car," he said. "It's around the corner on Franklin."

I took the keys and went out. His car, a '37 Plymouth with the first streamlined ship as hood ornament, was easy to find. The white stood out in an era when dark colors, especially Henry Ford's black, still dominated. On the windshield was a decal "A," which meant the car was allowed the basic ration of four gallons of gas a week. Gas coupons were issued and handed over in the gas station. Stealing and selling gas coupons would become my first monetary crime.

I unlocked the car and got in to wait, listening to the rain hit the roof, watching it bounce on the ground. It was hypnotic, soothing, and I must have dozed off. I hadn't really slept the night before. I closed my eyes with cars parked all around. When I opened them again, the other cars were gone and my father was knocking on the window.

I opened the door lock and slid over to make room. I was wary, for although my father was generous and loving, once or twice he had lost his temper and cuffed me around, yelling in frustration, "What in God's name is wrong with you? You can't do what you do. You'll . . . you'll end up—" His anguish stifled his words. I could feel his torment. It never rose to anything near abuse, but it made me feel terrible to upset him, and I invariably promised reform.

This time he avoided looking at me as he pulled out and headed for the Cahuenga Pass. (The Hollywood Freeway was almost a decade in the future.) As he drove, he grunted and shook his head, reacting to the turmoil in his mind. I thought we were going to the residential hotel where he lived, but he drove past that intersection and went up into the hills. The clouds were breaking up, allowing a little moonlight to come through. Soon we were at the summit, looking down on Lake Hollywood, which was really a reservoir. The view overlooked the western half of the City of Angels, a sprawl of glittering lights with patches of darkness in between. In another ten years, the lights would fill all the LA Basin to the sea—and deep into the desert going the other way.

My father shut off the engine and gave a long, agonized sigh. When it was over he sagged visibly. "What do I do now? Mrs. Bosco is closed down. She didn't have a permit for those two crazies upstairs."

Mrs. Bosco had kept two truly demented boys or young men up there. No doubt she had been paid handsomely to keep them out of sight. One I remember was just slightly gaunt and freckled. The other was named Max. He had thick black hair and heavy black facial hair. You would say he was bearded, but it was really that he had gone unshaven for a month or more. Max used to come down to unload the station wagon when Mrs. Bosco returned from buying provisions. He was strong. He was obsessed with rending his clothes. They hung in rags across his torso and in strips down his legs. He would rip up a new pair of Levi's if he was goaded. All you had to do was stare at him and tell him, "Max, bad boy! Bad boy, Max!" and he would start passionately rending his clothes.

She had no permit for these two. And the fire had illuminated their presence to the authorities. Even if she managed to finance roof repair, she was closed down. It was the only place I'd gotten along, even marginally.

I wanted to say, "Let me stay with you," but the words were choked back. What I wanted was impossible and only agitated him when I brought it up. His standard reply was that he had to work nights, there was nobody to look after me, and I was too young to look after myself.

He turned and looked at me closely. "Are you crazy?" he asked.

"I don't think so."

"You sure act crazy sometimes. I thought everything was great with Mrs. Bosco—"

"It *is* great, Pop."

"No, it isn't . . . not when I find you've been roaming the city all night. You're nine years old, for Christ's sake."

"I'm sorry, Pop." It was true; my sorrow for his anguish was painful.

"You say that, but . . . it only gets worse. . . . Sometimes I think about starting the car with the garage door closed."

I knew what that meant, and from some source within me came a Catholic canon: "If you do that, you'll go to hell, won't you?"

Even in his despair, he swelled with scorn. "No, I won't. There's no hell . . . and no heaven, either. Life is here. Reward is here. Pain is here. I don't know very much . . . but that much I know for sure." He paused, then added: "You'll remember this, won't you?" He held my arm above the elbow and stared at me.

I nodded. "I'll remember, Pop."

I have remembered, and although I've searched everywhere for a refutation, the facts of existence affirm the dismal truth of his declaration. The only way to deny it is to make a leap of faith across the chasm of reality. That I cannot do. Whatever else I've done, flagrantly and repeatedly and without apology, violating every rule that blocked whatever it was I wanted, I have tried to sift kernels of truth from tons of chaff bullshit. Truth is the distilled meaning of facts, for any truth refuted by a fact becomes a fallacy.

I am an apostle of Francis Bacon, the messiah of scientific objectivity, which leads inexorably to secular humanism and relativism and contradicts the notions of kneeling in prayer before one totem or another, be it a cross, golden calf, totem pole, or African fertility god with a giant phallus.

2

STATE-RAISED

IN

CALIFORNIA

EVA SCHWARTZ, NÉE BUNKER, was my father's only sibling. Two
years older than her brother, she had married Charles Schwartz, who wasn't
Jewish despite the name. He owned a small movie theater in Toledo, beside
Lake Erie, where my fur trading ancestors had settled in the eighteenth century. *Bunker* is Anglicized French from the original *Bon Coeur,* or "Good
Heart." Childless herself, she had raised a cousin's daughter. When her husband died, Aunt Eva moved west to take care of her brother's son.

Now, for the first time I could remember, I had a home. It was a tiny bungalow they rented in Atwater Village, an area between Glendale and the LA
River. I had a dog, a small tricolor bitch of mongrel pedigree, and a girlfriend,
a blonde named Dorothy who lived next door. I showed her mine and she
showed me hers. Her father owned a cocktail lounge on Fletcher Drive near
the gigantic Van de Kamp bakery. The dog, named Babe, was my best friend
and constant companion. Every day in the fierce summer of '43, we trudged a
mile or so along the concrete-lined riverbank, and crossed a footbridge into
Griffith Park. It had a huge public swimming pool. Nearby were several stables
where a horse could be rented to ride through the miles of trails in the park.
Off Riverside Drive was the big steak house owned by Victor McLaglen, the
only actor who both won an Academy Award (as best actor for *The Informer*)
and fought Jack Dempsey.

I was a habitual wanderer by then. I always wanted to see what was over
the next hill or down the road around the next corner. Sometimes I went north
beside the river into Burbank, sometimes south beside the railroad tracks. In
Burbank I climbed the fence into Warner Brothers' back lot and played among
permanent sets of island lagoons and jungle villages. My dog always waited
outside the fence until hell froze or I returned. We also explored Lockheed,

easily bypassing the ring of antiaircraft-gun emplacements. Once the army bivouacked several thousand soldiers in part of Griffith Park. Rows of tents, lines of olive green trucks. They disappeared as magically as they had appeared.

The railroad tracks ran between the factories, shops, and Van de Kamp, a huge commercial bakery. A nearby pottery factory was later declared a major environmental hazard and was fenced off for years. I climbed over the sagging fence several times to see if I could find adventure on the other side. I played in a mount of white powder that might have been asbestos. It never seemed to bother me; it would be decades before anyone declared asbestos was dangerous.

Along the street nearest the railroad tracks were little houses. About a mile from there the single lane of tracks entered the main railroad freight yards and became dozens of tracks. This area was across the tracks in terms of status and "bohemian" in lifestyle. An impish and precocious little Irish girl named Dorothy lived there with her hard-drinking, heavy-smoking mother. Whenever I arrived, Dorothy's mom had a cigarette in her mouth and a glass of beer close by. At least she wasn't drinking from the bottle. It was far different from my aunt's stern Calvinistic demeanor and demands. Dorothy's mom once mentioned how rationing made it hard to get gas. After she had said that, I remembered a cigar box full of clipped gas coupons in a Texaco gas station close to the Gateway Theater on San Fernando Road. The Gateway was where I saw *Citizen Kane*. Walking home the following Saturday afternoon, I stopped at the Texaco for a Coke. I watched the attendant clip the coupons from a customer's ration book and carry them past me and put them in a cigar box on the desk in the office. The Irish girl's mother would pay a dollar apiece for gas coupons. A dollar would buy a cheeseburger, a milk shake, and ticket into a first-run movie theater downtown. The following Saturday afternoon, I delivered far more coupons than she could pay for. She gave me ten dollars, and during the next few days she sold the rest to her friends. I made forty dollars, which is what a unionized stagehand made for a week's work. It was my first successful money caper.

This period of my life was happy for me. Alas, it was disillusioning for my aunt. She was totally unable to rein me in. I was the neighborhood hellion, but I was a well-spoken hellion. In quick succession I was caught shoplifting from the local Woolworth, seen throwing a rock through a window (to impress Dorothy; although we got away, they caught my dog and traced me through his collar), and eventually caught by a gas station attendant with my hand in the cigar box of gas ration coupons. I was spanked and put to bed, and I promised my father and God that I would change my ways and be a good boy. I was sincere.

Of course I always felt different or forgot my promise the next day. I woke up in a new world every morning. When summer ended, I went to public school for the first time—the Atwater Avenue elementary school. Because they had no transcripts and because I'd been in three military schools and half a dozen boarding homes in five years, they tested me. Despite the chaos of my childhood, I scored two full years ahead of my age group in reading skill, although I was below average in mathematics. I don't know any more now, fifty years later, about math than I did then. I think my weakness in math was because it must be taught in sequence; one thing laid down a foundation for the next. My peripatetic life had not been conducive to that.

The principal split the difference and put me two semesters ahead of my age. I would go to middle school the next semester, a couple of weeks after I turned eleven.

A month after school started, however, my aunt and father sat me down and solemnly told me that the house we were renting was being sold. We had to move, but because of the war they could find nothing. I would have to go to another foster home or military school. I was devastated, but I agreed to go if my father promised to remove me if I disliked it. Dislike was a certainty, decided even before he delivered me to the Southern California Military Academy on Signal Hill in Long Beach. The rules forbade visits for a month. The commandant wanted newcomers to get over homesickness before they could go home for weekends.

My father said he would visit as soon as the month passed. I counted the days.

The fateful Friday arrived without my father's appearance. At recall, the ranks were thin because most boys went home for the weekend. Instead of going to the cadets' dining room, I went out the back door of the dormitory and scaled a back fence. Adventure beckoned, new experiences, and, most important of all, freedom. My escape would also punish my father, who had lied to me. He had given his solemn word and broken it.

From Long Beach, I caught a red car to downtown Los Angeles. It took about forty minutes. I planned to catch a yellow #5 or "W" car to the Lincoln Heights district, where my aunt had moved into a tiny apartment in a four-unit building. Downtown, however, had flashing movie marquees. I stopped to see a movie based on Agatha Christie's *Ten Little Indians,* with a quality cast, including Barry Fitzgerald as the villain. He had me fooled, faking his own death to turn suspicion away.

It was late when I came out of the movie. The old yellow streetcar was almost empty. The few passengers were in the center section, which had glass windows. I preferred to ride in the back section, where the windows were open. I liked the cold air. It invigorated me then and it still does.

Aunt Eva's lights were on, and my father's car was parked in front. I passed on by. Since I was wearing my military school uniform and my regular clothes were in my aunt's apartment, I decided to come back the next day when she was at work.

Several blocks away, beside a railroad bridge across the Arroyo Seco Parkway (now the Pasadena Freeway), was Welch's Industrial Laundry. I took an armload of torn, discarded bed sheets and overalls from a bin beside a loading dock and carried them to a scrap yard where old machines were turning to rust. I found a huge extractor on its side, and pushed in the rags and climbed in. It was a small space and I was unable to completely extend my legs if lying down. At least I escaped the cold night wind. Hours later I heard a humming in the ground, a sound that grew into an earth-shaking crescendo. A train was coming and seemed as if it would run over my hideout, its waving headlight coming through every crack with blinding power. It passed about twenty feet away.

When the morning sun warmed the world, I climbed out. Every muscle in my body was cramped. One night of living on the street and my khaki uniform with the stripe down the leg was dirty enough to turn heads.

I walked to a Thrifty Drug Store, planning to eat breakfast at the fountain counter. As I neared the entrance I saw a newspaper stand. The newspapers had a black border, the headlines reading: ROOSEVELT DEAD.

The news stunned me. Roosevelt had been president for my entire life. He had saved America during the depression. "He saved capitalism from itself," my father once said, which I couldn't understand back then, yet I was awed by the accomplishment. He was commander-in-chief in the war that still continued, although Allied armies were now marching through Germany. His voice was familiar from his Fireside Chats. Mrs. Roosevelt was America's mother, and Fala, for all his Scottish blood, was America's dog. The news brought tears to my eyes. I changed my mind about breakfast.

An hour later I rang Aunt Eva's doorbell to make sure she was gone. Then I went around the corner of the building where a little door opened into a compartment for the garbage can. Behind the garbage can was another little door into the kitchen. Decades would pass before bars on the windows of the poor and security systems in the homes of the wealthy became common. I opened the outer door, pushed the inner one open, and squeezed through. I called out, "Aunt Eva!" just in case. Nobody answered. I then went about my business.

A closet had a box with my clothes. I found a pair of Levi's jeans and a shirt. In the bathroom I began filling the tub. While the water ran, I went into the kitchen to find something to eat. The refrigerator yielded a quart of milk and loaf of bread. I moved to the toaster on the sink counter. Through a window I looked out at the house next door.

At that moment a policeman scurried across my line of sight and ducked behind a tree.

Crash! I dropped the glass and sprinted down the hall to the bathroom. I wore only shorts and a T-shirt. Frantic, I pulled on the jeans and the shoes, not bothering to button the former or lace the latter.

Above the bathtub was a window. I opened it and pushed out the screen. The narrow window was twelve feet above a passage between the apartment building and the garages. As I climbed up into the window frame, a policeman came around the corner below me. I jumped over his head onto the garage roof and ran to the other side. The garage ended over a brush-covered forty-foot embankment. I leaped off the roof and rolled down through weeds and bushes to the bottom.

A policeman appeared above me, looking down.

I jumped up and went over a fence beside the slanted concrete of a storm drain channel. The channel became a torrent when the rains came, but today it was a trickle three feet wide and four inches deep. I splashed through it. On the other side was another concrete wall with a far steeper angle. At its top was a fence bordering the freeway. Several feet below the fence was a storm drain outlet, now dry. I'd previously tried to run up the angled wall to the hole and had always fallen short. This day, though, I went up it like a mountain goat, disappearing into the storm drain beneath the freeway and into the city.

Half an hour later, I was two miles away on Mount Washington, huddling in a shallow cave. Rain began to darken the earth. It was a lonely moment in my young life.

Late that night, I found a bundle of the next morning's newspapers outside the door of a neighborhood market. When the morning rush began, I was on the corner of North Broadway and Daly, peddling newspapers for a nickel apiece. Twenty-five cents was enough to eat and go to a movie. Late at night, I made my way back to Welch's Industrial Laundry and burrowed into the rags beside the track. By the third day I was so filthy that eyes followed me when I entered the market where I'd stolen the newspapers for two nights. On the third night they weren't there. I had enough to buy milk and a candy bar, meanwhile slipping several more inside my shirt.

When it started to rain again, I climbed the slope behind my aunt's apartment building. The rain cleared the street. This time nobody was looking out a window as I pushed through the little door into the kitchen. I called out, "Aunt Eva! Aunt Eva!" No answer. The apartment was empty.

I wanted to get in and out quickly. Again I ran the bath and dug clean clothes from the box. I bathed quickly, the water turning gray from the grime in my hair and on my ankles, face, and hands. I pulled on the clothes while still wet. When dressed, I felt a little more secure—and I was hungry.

I found some canned tuna in a dish and put two slices of bread into the toaster for a sandwich. As I ate it, I went to see if she had some change lying around. In her bedroom I spotted the envelopes on the dresser. Some were bills; one had an SPCA return address. It had been opened. I pulled out the letter. It was a receipt for putting my little dog to sleep. When I realized what they'd done, I think I screamed. I've had many things happen to me, but I think that was the greatest anguish I ever experienced. It welled through me. I choked and gasped; my chest felt crushed.

I rocked back and forth and sobbed my utter and absolute torment. Thinking of it more than half a century later still forms tears in my eyes. My aunt and father had told me she had a home in Pomona. Instead they had given her over to be killed because she was too much trouble. I believe that this was the moment the world lost me, for pain quickly turned to fury. How could they? She had loved them and they had murdered her. If I could have killed both my aunt and my father I would have—and although a child's memories are quickly overlaid with evolving matters, I never forgave them.

Three days later, a Friday morning, I came again for a bath, clothes, and food. This time my father waited in the shadows. He blocked the door so I couldn't run. He had to call the juvenile authorities. "Nobody else will take you. God knows I don't know what to do."

"Why don't you kill me like you killed my dog?"

"What?"

"You know what! I hate you! I'm glad I made you old."

Using the number on a business card, he started to dial the phone. I started toward the bathroom, planning to go out the window again. He put the phone down. "Stay right here."

"I gotta go to the bathroom."

Perhaps sensing my plan, he put the phone down and accompanied me. As I stood at the toilet, I saw a heavy bottle of Listerine on the shelf over the toilet. I grabbed it, whirled, and swung at my father's head. He managed to duck. The bottle gouged a hole in the plaster.

Twenty minutes later, two juvenile detectives arrived and took me away. By evening I was at the juvenile hall on Henry Street, in the shadow of the general hospital. It was past my bedtime when they finished processing me. A tall, gangly black counselor with a loose-limbed gait escorted me through locked doors and down a long hallway to Receiving Company. The hallway floor gleamed with polish. At the end of the hallway, where another hallway crossed it like a T, another counselor sat at a desk illuminated solely by a small lamp. The black counselor handed my papers to the man at the desk. He looked them over, looked at me, then picked up his flashlight and ushered me down another hall to double doors into a ten-bed dormitory. He used the flashlight beam to illuminate the empty cot.

The clean sheets felt smooth and cool. Despite my exhaustion, sleep came hard. The bright floodlights outdoors illuminated the heavy mesh wire on the windows. I was caged for the first time. When sleep finally took me, in my dreams I cried for my dog and for myself.

I awakened among boys in a world somewhat reminiscent of John Barth's *Flies*. Around me were boys from Jordan Downs, Aliso Village, Ramona Gardens, and other housing projects. Others came from the mean streets of Watts, Santa Barbara Avenue, East Los Angeles, Hicks Camp, and elsewhere throughout Los Angeles's endless sprawl. Most came from families without a father on hand, back then called a broken home. If a man was around, his job was probably going to buy the heroin with the money the mother made selling herself. If she went, she could expect they would sell her lactose for heroin or, if they didn't have that, might just take her money and cut her throat as an afterthought. It was a *quid pro quo* relationship between two junkies. It worked for them but wasn't conducive to raising a thirteen-year-old who was already marked with blue tattoos and the values of *vatos loco*. This was a mishmash of young testosterone and distorted *machismo* and hero worship of an older brother already in *la pinta*.

Until now, whatever my problems may have been, I had been entitled to the privileges of the bourgeois child. Now I was swimming in the meanest milieu of our society, the juvenile justice system. Hereafter I would be "state-raised." Its values would become my values, mainly that might makes right, a code that accepts killing but forbids snitching. At first I was an outsider, the precociously educated white boy with the impeccable grammar. I was picked on and bullied, although that was brief because I would fight, even if I was slower and less strong. I could sneak up and bash a tough guy with a brick while he slept or stab him in the eye with a fork in the mess hall. My perfect grammar and substantial vocabulary quickly changed to the patois of the underclass. For a while when I was fourteen, my English had a definite Mexican accent. I had an affinity with Mexicans or, rather, with Chicanos, with their stoic fatalism. Instead of wearing the Levi's jeans that were *de rigueur* among suburban white teenagers, I preferred the Chicano-styled surplus marine fatigues, with huge baggy pockets along the side. Often dyed black, they were worn loose on the hips and rolled up at the bottom. That way the legs were very short and the torso was extra long. I wore a ducktail upswept along the sides, so thick with Three Flowers pomade that running a comb through it brought forth globs of grease. Pomade wasn't allowed in juvenile hall, so we stole margarine and used that. It had a rancid stench, but kept the ducktail in place.

I went all the way. My shoes had extra-thick soles added on, horseshoe taps on the heels, and other taps along the sides and on the toes. Running was difficult, but stomping someone was easy. My pants were "semi," which meant semidrape or semi–zoot suit. A zoot suit was "full drape," but they had lost favor before I became concerned about style. The music I liked wasn't on the "Hit Parade." It wasn't Perry Como and Dinah Shore that thrilled me, but the sounds and the funk known along Central Avenue and in Watts: Lonnie Johnson, Bull Moose Jackson, Dinah Washington, Billy Eckstine, Ella, Sarah, and Billie, Illinois Jacquet, and Big J McNeeley on sax, with Bird as the icon of everyone who was hip.

In the four years following my arrival at juvenile hall, I moved swiftly and inexorably through the juvenile justice system. I was in juvenile hall eight times and twice went to the state hospital for observation. I talked sanely but behaved insanely. The hospital officials weren't sure about me. I escaped at least half a dozen times, living as a fugitive on the streets. I could hot-wire a car in less than a minute. Once when I escaped from the Fred C. Nelles School for Boys in Whittier, I stole a car. Halfway into Los Angeles, I stopped to urinate behind a Pacific Outdoor sign. When I got under way again, I failed to turn on the headlights. In San Gabriel a police car parked at a corner flashed his headlights. I knew it wasn't a command to pull over, but I had no idea what it was. They pulled in behind me. I watched in the mirror. When the red lights flashed, I punched the gas. During the ensuing chase, they fired a couple of shots. I could feel the heavy slugs hit the car. One came through and made a spiderweb pattern in the windshield. I ducked way down, my head below the dash. I opened the driver-side door and followed the white line in the middle of the street, confident that anyone ahead would see flashing lights and hear the screaming siren and get out of the way. When I glanced ahead, I looked over the dashboard. *Oh shit!* I was coming upon a T corner. I had to turn right or left. I hit the brakes and tried to turn. The car jumped the curb and was on a wet front lawn. It might as well have been ice as it skidded sideways and crashed through a front window into a living room. They had their guns trained on me before I could crawl from the wreckage.

Back at Nelles, they put me in the punishment cottage. It was run with the harsh discipline of a marine disciplinary barracks. The Man took a dislike to me. One morning he thought I was shirking work, so he threw a dirt clod that hit me in the back of the head. It flew to pieces and gave no injury, except to my ego. I looked at him and the anger showed. "You don't like it, Bunker?" he challenged. With him he had two other counselors and three "monitors," boys used as goons against their own.

I maintained control but seethed inside. When we went in for lunch (part of the punishment was having the same menu seven days a week; every lunch was stew) and the Man went by my table, I called his name. He turned and I threw the bowl of stew in his face. Up jumped the monitors. I'd recently lost a fight to just one of them. Against three, plus the Man, it was no contest. They dragged me from the mess hall, down three staircases, and along a hallway to the isolation cell at the rear, kicking and punching me all the way. When I was locked in the cell, the Man turned a fire hose on me through the bars. The bars diminished some of the force, but it was still enough to cut my legs out from under me and slide me up against the wall.

An hour later, the Man came to gloat at my battered face and drenched body. "You look like a wet cat." His lip curled in a sneer. "You won't be throwing things for a while."

Down low, hidden by my body, I held a flattened roll of wet toilet paper with a pile of shit on top. While his sneering declaration was still in the air, I hurled the roll of toilet paper and the shit against the bars. It broke apart and splattered his clothes and his face and the wall behind him. He was insane with rage, so much that another man would not open the gate.

That night they took me out the back door, put me in a car, and sent me to Pacific Colony State Hospital, near Pomona. Pacific Colony was primarily for the mentally retarded, but it took some ninety-day observation cases from the youth authorities. Its one locked ward was the most brutal place I've ever been. Even that far back, if the savage realities of the place had been exposed, it would have been a scandal. Most of my time was spent in the dayroom sitting on the benches that lined three sides. Each bench had four names written on tape. We sat in silence with our arms folded. Any whispering and an attendant walking on crepe soles behind the benches might knock you off to the floor. The fourth side of the dayroom had cushioned wicker chairs. Four of them were on a raised dais where the attendants sat. Their goons used the chairs at floor level.

For entertainment, the attendants staged fights between patients. Disputes were settled that way, or else the attendants acted as matchmakers. The winner got a pack of cigarettes.

One favored punishment was "pulling the block." The "block" was a slab of concrete that weighed about a hundred pounds. Wrapped in layers of old wool blanket, it had two eye hooks that fastened to a wide, flat canvas harness about ten feet long. The composite tile floor in a long side hall was smeared in thick paraffin wax. The blanket-wrapped block was pulled up and down the hall twelve hours a day. One Chicano from La Colonia in Watts was on the block for thirty days for getting high on phenobarbital.

The most brutal punishment was hanging someone by the hands from the overhead ventilation ducts. The miscreant wasn't actually lifted off the floor, but he had to stand on the balls of his feet or let the weight fall on his arms and wrists. After ten minutes it was torture. In fifteen the victim was usually screaming. The attendants preferred old-fashioned beatings. Maybe they liked the workout it gave them. Seeing the situation and knowing that I only had a ninety-day observation case, I tried to remain inconspicuous. One night about two months into my sojourn, I was standing at my window while looking across the grounds. A hundred yards away was a female ward. A youth named Pee-Wee in the next room was yelling out the window to his girlfriend. The attendant in charge at night was named Hunter, but he was called the Jabber. Unknown to me, he was hurrying from door to door, peering through the little observation window to catch whoever dared to yell across the nuthouse grounds at night.

I turned from the window at the sound of the door being unlocked behind me. The Jabber came in with the shivering energy of a badger. Without a word, he punched me in the face with both hands, short punches from someone accustomed to using his fists. Both hit me flush, one in the mouth, one against the jaw. I tasted blood from my lip being cut by my teeth, and from my jaw a bolt of pain announced its dislocation. He rocked on the balls of his feet, hands up, leering: "I'll teach you to yell, you little scumbag."

He danced in and punched again. I ducked and went down on the bed, leaning away and covering up. It was hard for him to get at me with his punches, so he began to stomp and kick my calves and thighs, muttering angry curses. I knew that fighting back might get me killed.

They could get away with anything. I'd seen brutalities that would never happen in reform school, or even a prison for that matter, where there are procedures for hearings. This was a *hospital*. We were patients being cared for.

The Jabber left after that. I could feel my eye swelling shut. In the process, my bedding had been torn off. I pulled the cot away from the wall and began to straighten the blankets.

My door opened again. The Jabber stood there, rocking back and forth on the balls of his feet in a facsimile of Jimmy Cagney. He was twirling his key chain like an airplane propeller. Behind him were a big redheaded attendant and a patient with special status because he did some of their dirty work. The Jabber came around the bed to where I stood and began to punch me around again.

I'd been choking back my fury. He was in my face, his eyeglasses sparkling. He sneered at me and bunched his muscles to strike again. This time I punched first. My fist smashed his glasses. The glass cut him above one eye and across the bridge of his nose. Blood poured down his starched white shirt with its black snap-on bow tie. Because his knees were backed against the bed, the force of the punch sat him down. I tried to hit him again. The red-headed attendant got an arm around my neck from the rear and pulled me back. My fingers were tangled in the Jabber's shirtfront, which tore away from his body, leaving the shirt collar and the bow tie.

As the redhead choked me, the patient goon lifted my feet off the ground. Someone got on the bed and jumped down on my stomach. Someone else smashed a fist into my face six or seven times. They were full-force punches by a grown man.

When they all left, I could barely breathe. Anything more than a tiny sip of air sent a bolt of pain through my chest. My right eye was completely shut. I was spitting out blood from my lip, which had been cut wide open against my teeth.

At midnight, when the shift changed, my door opened again and two graveyard-shift attendants came in. One of them was named Fields, a name I still remember after fifty years. He had played football for a small local college. Now the smell of liquor was on his breath. The rules required me to stand up when the door opened. I managed to rise. He then knocked me down and kicked at me until I managed to crawl under the bed. He tried to pull the bed away so he could get at me. In his drunken rage he might have kicked me to death if the other attendant had not finally restrained him: "Knock it off, Fields. You'll kill him. He's just a kid."

The next morning the ward doctor, a little man with an accent, came to my room and clucked like a chicken as he poked at my swollen and disfigured face. It was in terrible shape. My closed eye stuck out like an egg. "I don't think you'll strike another attendant, will you?" he asked. I shook my head and thought, *Not unless I could kill him.*

I was kept locked in my room for the rest of the observation period. After I was certified as sane they returned me to reform school.

Three weeks later, after getting back to reform school, I escaped with a black kid from Watts named Watkins. We stayed with his mother and sister on

103d near Avalon. His father was in the navy. The family had a little yellow frame bungalow that had a chicken coop in the backyard. The juvenile officers came around at night, trying to catch us sleeping there. We knew better and slept in a shed between the railroad tracks and Simon Rodia's Watts Towers. The towers were vaguely reminiscent of pictures I'd seen of Angkor Wat in Cambodia. You could always see the towers against the sky when you rode the red car that stopped at the Watts station. After Watkins spent a couple months running the streets, they caught him. I got away and lived several more months in a barrio called Temple. I slept in an old Cord automobile that was on blocks in a backyard and ran around with the *vatos loco.*

I got caught because of my first love, an Italian girl. I met her through her brother, whom I knew from juvenile hall. Her younger sister told her parents that I was sleeping in the shed at the rear of their house. They called the police, who came early one morning. I woke up to a pistol in my face.

Instead of being returned to the reform school in Whittier, I was sent to Northern California, outside Stockton, to the Preston School of Industry. It was for boys sixteen and seventeen, with a few who were eighteen. I had barely turned fourteen.

When I arrived at the Preston School of Industry, I was pulled aside and given the warning I was always given: "Okay, Bunker, try any of your bullshit here, we'll make you wish you hadn't. This isn't a playpen. We know how to handle punks like you."

Fourteen months later, they expelled me from reform school to freedom. They had tried the discipline of juvenile hall and Whittier, plus a few other tricks such as shooting tear gas in my face and, once, putting me in a strait-jacket for twenty-four hours. I will concede that they stopped short of what had happened in the state hospital. Had they not done so, they might have driven me to murder or suicide.

Preston followed a practice still used fifty years later. Big, tough youths were made "cadet officers." They received extra privileges and parole credits for using their fists and feet to maintain order through force and fear. Each company had three: one white, one black, one Chicano. They had to be both tough and tractable. One cadet officer was Eddie Machen, who would be a top heavyweight contender a few years later. Any one of them alone could whip me. After one of them kicked me for being out of step while marching to the mess hall, I waited until he was seated to eat; then I walked up behind him and stabbed him in the eye with a fork. He was rushed to Sacramento, where they saved his eye, but his vision was never the same in that eye. I was assigned permanently to G Company, a unit with a three-tier cell block. It was dark and gloomy and a carbon copy of a prison cell block. Six mornings a week, we ate in our cells, then marched forth with picks and shovels on our shoulders. We cleared weeds from irrigation ditches or shoveled pig shit, which smells fouler than anything else in the world. Sometimes we poured concrete for new pig-pens. At noon we marched back, ate in our own little mess hall, showered, and went to our cells until the next morning. Most others chafed in torment over so much cell time, but I much preferred the cell because there I could read.

Some nameless benefactor had donated a personal library of several hundred books. Most of them seemed like they were from the Book of the Month Club, but many others had once been gifts, if the inscriptions were any indicator. After the hard covers had been removed, they were stored in disorder in a closet. We showered three at a time and could trade two or three books then. The Man would turn on the closet light and let us search through the books until we finished with our showers. I always hurried to be first out of the water and dry so I could get an extra minute or two trying to find a book that I might like better than another. I had no critical faculty. A book was a book and a path to distant places and wonderful adventures. I did develop an early preference for the historical novel, which was extremely popular throughout the forties. I looked for authors, and I soon recognized some names of the best-selling writers, like Frank Yerby, Rafael Sabatini, Thomas Costain, Taylor Caldwell, and Mika Waltari. I remember Hemingway's *For Whom the Bell Tolls,* Richard Wright's *Native Son,* and a single volume with several tales by Jack London: *The Sea Wolf, Call of the Wild,* and *The Iron Heel.* One novel was in the form of a memoir about a revolution in America. For several chapters I thought I was reading a true story, but when it narrated a civil war in 1920 I knew that had never happened. Still, much of what the author wrote about society resonates with truth today. It was in G Company that I realized that novels could be more than stories that entertained and excited. They could also carry wisdom and look into the deepest recesses of human behavior.

By code or administrative policy or some rule, they were not allowed to keep a youth under sixteen in a lockup cell for more than twenty-nine days at a time. They really liked having me in G Company; I wasn't causing them any trouble, no fights, no assaults on personnel. I wasn't spitting on them or stuffing the toilet and flooding the cell house, agitating insurrection, or planning an escape. So on the thirtieth morning, they took me out of G Company after breakfast. I checked into the regular company and went to lunch. After lunch they took me back to G Company. I was glad to return to the half-read book I was reading, *The Seventh Cross,* by Anna Seghers.

After being incarcerated for three out of four years—I'd spent the other year in a series of escapes—I was paroled to my aunt by the youth authorities. She would have preferred that I parole elsewhere, but there was no elsewhere. My mother, whom I hadn't seen since my first trip to juvenile hall, was remarried and had a daughter. Neither my mother nor her husband wanted me around, and I felt the same. My father, now sixty-two, had a bad heart and was prematurely senile and in a rest home. He didn't recognize me when I went to see him.

My aunt met me with love, but she and I saw the world differently. On the one hand, she saw a fifteen-year-old boy who had gotten into trouble, but who should have learned his lesson by now. She thought I should behave as a fifteen-year-old boy is supposed to behave.

I, on the other hand, saw myself as a grown man, at least with the rights of an eighteen-year-old. I'd lived on the streets on my own since I was thirteen. I wasn't going to be home at 10:00 P.M. if I didn't want to be, or at midnight either for that matter. As for school, when I went to check in, my records came up. The registrar looked them over and told me to return on Monday.

On Monday, the woman behind the counter handed me the letter. On Los Angeles Unified School District stationery and signed by the superintendent and the chief psychiatrist, it notified all concerned that Edward Bunker was not required to attend school. A phone number was included if anyone had questions. The letter had a seal of some kind. Nobody I know has ever heard of this happening to anyone else in Los Angeles. It was great, for although I loved learning, I loathed school. I already knew that true education depends on the individual and can be found in books.

The night streets beckoned. Pals from reform school, most older than me, were on the streets and into things. It was exciting to make the after-hours joints along Forty-second and Central, where booze was sold in teacups under the table and you could get great ham and eggs and grits and hear some music and nobody asked for identification. I had some if needed. It stretched things, but what the hell, who cares?

My aunt disliked my hours and prophesied that I'd be back in trouble again. She was right. I would have disputed it. Then again, I lived entirely in the time being. I never planned more than two days ahead. I woke up in a new world every morning. The differences between my aunt and me and how we saw the world began to poison our relationship.

I came upon a little less than two thousand dollars by helping a Chicano named Black Sugar from Hazard dig up a bunch of head-high marijuana plants that were being grown between rows of corn up in Happy Valley. It was a nice score. Nobody would know. Nobody would go to the police.

I emancipated myself from my aunt and my parole officer. For three months I was having fun. I rented a room, bought a '40 Ford coupe for $300, and was on my own. Then I got arrested when I was visiting two buddies out of reform school who had been sticking up supermarkets. Eighteen years old, they lived in a house on the east side of Alvardo just south of Temple Street. Someone's mother owned the house, but the room under the back porch was where "anything went." It was a clubhouse for incipient convicts. It was a great place to hang out waiting for something to happen, someone to come by, someone to call, someone to think of something. It was also a great place to raid. And they did. They found some pistols, some illegal pills, and some pot. It was enough to get everyone booked until it got sorted out. They mainly wanted to take all of us to lineups for robberies. Nobody picked me out, but my fingerprints came back with an outstanding parole violator warrant issued by the youth authorities.

THE SUPERINTENDENT OF THE PRESTON SCHOOL of Industry threatened to quit if I was returned to his institution, or so I was told by the man who drove me from the LA County Jail to the prison for youthful offenders in the town of Lancaster. It was on the edge of the vast Mojave Desert but still in the county of Los Angeles. Built during World War II as a training base for Canadian fliers, it was now operated by the California Department of Corrections. They'd built a double fence topped with rolled barbed wire around the buildings. Every hundred yards was a gun tower on stilts. Presto! A prison.

Except for a couple dozen skilled inmate workers brought from San Quentin or Folsom (surgical nurse, expert stenographer/typist for the associate warden, and so forth), the convicts of Lancaster were between eighteen and twenty-five. Ninety percent of those were between eighteen and twenty-one. When the transporting officer removed my chains in Receiving and Release, I was fifteen years old.

While I was being processed, a sergeant arrived to take me to the captain. Wearing white overalls and then walking across the prison with the sergeant, I felt self-conscious. Heads turned to scan the newcomer. One or two knew me from other places and called out, "Hey, Bunker! What's up?"

Inside the Custody Office, which was somewhat reminiscent of an urban newspaper's city room, was a door with frosted glass and "L. S. NELSON, Captain" stenciled on it. The captain commanded all uniformed personnel. Nelson was in his thirties and had red hair. Later, when the red was mixed with sand and he was warden of San Quentin, everyone called him Red Nelson. He was one of the legendary wardens, a man known to be hard but fair. He had a strong jaw and sunburned face. His eyes were hidden behind a pair of aviator-style dark glasses. He wore them for the tough impression they conveyed. As he leaned back in his swivel chair and webbed his fingers behind his neck, there was the vaguest hint of a sneer in his voice. "Shit! You don't look like a holy terror to me. You're too light in the butt to be *that* tough. You'll be lucky if somebody around here doesn't break you down like a shotgun."

"I'm not worried."

"Me, either. But I thought I'd tell you how it is. You've made a little name for yourself in those kiddie joints. This isn't a kiddie joint. This is a prison. Start any shit here and you'll swear the whole world fell on you. I'll stomp your brains out. Got it?"

"Yes, sir," I said. "I wanna do my time and get out as soon as I can." My words were true, but I also resented the threat. Everywhere I'd been—military school, juvenile hall, reform school, nuthouse—they all had promised to break me. All had inflicted severe physical and emotional pain on me, but here I was. If going into the general population had been less important to me, I would have dumped his desk over on him and taken the ass kicking—so he would know that I wasn't intimidated by his words.

"Okay, Bunker . . . hit the yard. Any trouble, I'll bury you so deep in segregation they'll have to pump in the air." He dismissed me with a jerk of the thumb. I turned and the waiting sergeant opened the door.

Assigned to Dorm #3, I was making up my bunk when buddies of mine from reform school and juvenile hall began streaming in, grinning and horseplaying. Someone jumped on me and I bumped into a bunk that skidded loudly across the floor.

"Take that horseplay outside," yelled the dorm guard from his desk. We went outside down the road to the handball courts. Ahead of us was a crowd. We came up from behind. In the center stood two young Chicanos, lean as hawks; each had a big knife. One of them I recognized from reform school without remembering his name. Off to the side was the object of their dispute, a petite white queen called Forever Amber. She was wringing her hands together. The Chicano I recognized gestured to the other, plainly signaling "come on . . . come on. . . ." His denim jacket was wrapped around his forearm. Both wore white T-shirts.

What then happened bore no resemblance to a movie knife fight. They came at each other like two roosters in a cockfight, leaping high and flailing, stabbing and being stabbed. The one without the jacket took a blow that opened his forearm to the bone. Then he stabbed back. His long shiv penetrated the other's white T-shirt and sank to the hilt. Both grunted, but neither gave way. In seconds, both were cut to pieces. The one with the jacket suddenly muttered, "Dirty sonofabitch. . . ." He sank to his knees and fell forward on his face, his knife falling from his dying fingers while his blood spread in a pool soaking the dry, hard earth.

The other Chicano turned and walked away, blood spraying from his mouth. It reminded me of a blowing whale. Forever Amber ran after him, still mincing and all femininelike. About fifty yards down the road, the "winner" suddenly stopped, coughed up a glob of blood, and fell. He tried to rise but stopped on his knees, his head down. Several convicts rushed forward and carried him to the hospital, but they returned thumbs down. He, too, had died.

It took a while after "lights out" for the dorm to settle for the night. Silhouettes in skivvies moved through the shadows to the washroom and latrine. They carried their toothbrushes in their teeth or in their hands, with towels wrapped around their necks. Down the dorm, two figures seated on adjacent bunks put their heads together as they whispered. Sudden laughter. The guard grunted, "Knock it off down there." Silence.

I was on my back, fully dressed except for my shoes, and I pulled a towel over my eyes. I had no enemies; no need for caution. Coughing. Bedsprings squeaking, the *shhh-shhh* of slippers moving along the aisle. The dorm windows were empty frames, holes in the wall really, the shape of windows. The double fences with rolled barbed wire, the lights, and the gun towers made window security superfluous. The desert wind that rose at every dusk was hot and hard tonight. It made the rolled barbed wire vibrate and the chain-link fence roll along its length, like an ocean wave rolling along the beach. In my mind, I saw the swift and deadly knife over and over, each moment almost frozen in time. I now recognized death. It had been delivered by the right hand, half sideways and half upward in a motion that looked defensive rather than attacking. The other guy was left-handed—or at least he had his knife in the left hand. He had it extended and was slicing at his opponent's face. When his left arm was extended, the soft spot just under the left side of the ribs was exposed. It was there his opponent's knife sank to the hilt. It must have cut a heart valve.

Bang! He was dead. With a snap of the fingers! He was history, too. That night after the lights were out, I lay on my upper bunk, listening to the night sounds, creaking bedsprings, wordless whispers, and choked laughter—and I thought about those two dead young Chicanos. They had died fighting over a sissy and pure *machismo*. To many in the world, my behavior was chaos for the sake of chaos. You probably could have gotten good odds that I would not live into my sixth decade, much less reach my seventh. Now I'd seen a double killing and it was a serious shock. Although I made no conscious decision and my behavior would continue to be wild and erratic, thereafter I always had something that stopped me on the brink of the precipice. I would never and have never gone *mano a mano* with knives. I wanted real victory, not a Pyrrhic version.

FOR THREE MONTHS I MANAGED to avoid the hole, and I had just two fistfights. One was with an Indian named Andy Lowe, whom I'd known since juvenile hall. We were in the dorm, body punching. Body punching is a bare-knuckle boxing match except no punches are aimed at the head. Andy could whip me when we were young, but no longer. When he tensed to punch, I rammed my left jab in his chest, stopping him so I could pivot away. He was missing every time he punched. He didn't appear to be angry, so when a fist slammed against my head I thought it was a slip. Such things do happen.

Then two more bony fists thudded into my face—and there was no "sorry." When he tried again, instead of putting the jab in his chest, I rammed it into his nose. The fight was on.

Someone yelled, *"The Man!"* We immediately broke apart and the spectators dispersed to their bunks. The guard sensed something amiss but was unable to decide what it was.

The other fight was with a Chicano, Ghost de Fresno. I'd once had a fight with his younger brother in Preston. Ghost took up the cudgel. Cottages that had once been bachelor officers' quarters for the Canadian air force were now privileged housing, three to each cottage, and that was where we went to fight. Although I was getting the best of it, I could feel my stamina fast slipping away. That was always my weakness. Luckily someone again yelled, *"The Man!"* I dived under a bunk, but Ghost tried to get away. The cottages were out-of-bounds unless assigned. He was taken to the holding cell for investigation. They never found out who had been his opponent. Because there had been several inmates stabbed since the double killing, they didn't want to risk returning Ghost to the general population. At twenty-one, he was older than average, plus he had been committed by the Superior Court after a valid conviction, so he could be transferred to San Quentin. And that is what happened. They put him on a bus and sent him north, which was fine with me.

Because I had nobody to send me twelve dollars a month, the amount then allowed for cigarettes and other amenities, I had to find some sort of income. I went into the home brew business. Each gallon required a pound of sugar, a pinch of yeast, and any of several things for mash to ferment: tomato puree, crushed oranges or orange juice, raisins, prunes, even chopped-up potatoes. Mixed together, they start to ferment immediately. You have a drink that tastes like beer and wine poured together that has about 20 percent alcohol. Yeast and sugar were bought from a thieving culinary worker, despite the facts that the free cooks watched closely and that the bread all came out flat. The difficult part of the whole process was finding places to hide the brew while it fermented. It was bulky and it smelled. It could not be airtight because the fermenting process made it swell. I used one hiding place that I would use again: the fire extinguishers. Each was fitted with a rubber line sewn from an inner tube by a convict in the tailor shop. Each would hold about four gallons. A quart of brew cost five packs of Camels, and customers ordered ahead of time. In about a month I had five fire extinguishers continually fermenting, and I was rich by prison standards. Actually, all I had was a whole lot of tobacco, although it would buy whatever else was for sale within the fences.

Three months went by. I'd never gone a single month without going to the hole since my first day in juvenile hall. My bubbling fire extinguishers were everywhere—on the Quonset hut gym wall, two in the dormitory, one in the library, one in the hospital corridor. I spent my time either gathering the ingredients, mixing the concoction, and putting it up or taking it down and wholesaling it by the gallon. It made time go faster.

Then one day, a library wastebasket caught on fire. The librarian reached for the fire extinguisher and got a foul-smelling home brew. Captain Nelson was red-hot. He told the library clerks to snitch or ride the bus to San Quentin. One of them snitched me off. After count but before dinner release, two guards came to the dormitory door, spoke to the guard, and came down the center aisle between the sagging cots. I knew they wanted me the moment they came in, although I waited for the crooked finger to make it official.

I grabbed a jacket, a pack of cigarettes and matches, and the book I was reading, *Gone With the Wind*. I knew I was going to the holding cell. It wasn't *the hole*. The holding cell was where you went until the disciplinary hearing. It was five in the afternoon. The lights would be on until ten-thirty or eleven. What was I supposed to do all night? Read *Gone With the Wind*, that's what.

At ten the next morning, I was taken to a disciplinary hearing. Captain Nelson was the hearing officer. I'd been hoping for the associate warden, who shared the duty. If I didn't have bad luck, I'd have no luck. Half a dozen other young inmates were standing in a line, also pending disciplinary court. The guard took me past them, tapped on the door, and opened it a few inches to peer inside. He must have gotten the nod, for he opened the door wide for me to enter.

Capt. L. S. "Red" Nelson was behind the desk. It was our first conversation since my arrival. I'd seen him on the yard a couple of times, and I veered away to avoid his sight.

"Here you are, Bunker. I knew I'd see you. I see you went into wine making."

I said nothing. What was there to say? Moreover, I had no wish to gossip with Captain Nelson even in the best of times.

". . . think you're a tough guy," he was saying. "You wouldn't be a pimple on those guys' asses." He was talking about Alcatraz, where he'd worked before coming to the California Department of Corrections. He told me about being locked in a cell with six other guards while three badass bank robbers from Oklahoma and Kentucky emptied a .45 into the cell. Nelson had survived without a wound. This had somehow made him fearless.

"Anyway," he said after he finished his reminiscences, "You're charged with D twelve fifteen, inmate behavior. On or about September twenty-third, you put four gallons of homemade alcoholic beverage in the library fire extinguisher. How do you plead?"

"Not guilty. Nobody caught me with any home brew."

"We don't have to. Both library clerks said it was yours. So I find you guilty. You are sentenced to ten days' isolation, plus I'm raising your custody to maximum and putting you in administrative segregation. Review your status in six months."

Six months! In segregation. It was lockup twenty-three hours a day. The difference between isolation and segregation was that segregation had some privileges—books and canteen and other trivial things that become important when there is nothing else. I could handle it, but six months was out of proportion to my little transgression. Making home brew was minor in the scheme of things. Segregation was long-term lockup for stabbing someone or trying to escape.

Nelson was looking at me with a sneer, as if to say, "You don't like it, punk?" I restrained the urge to turn his desk over. He waved me out. The guard opened the door for me. "One to isolation," Nelson said to the guard in the hallway.

The guard in the hallway had me sit down as they prepared the lockup order.

The buzzer sounded and the guard beckoned the next inmate. When he came out, the inside guard announced, "Thirty days' loss of privileges."

The buzzer sounded again. The hallway guard turned to open the door for inmate number three. In the moment that the guard's back was turned I stood up and walked out until I made the corner and turned. I expected a voice to yell, "Hold it, Bunker!" Nobody said anything.

Outside the Custody Office, I headed for the big Quonset hut gymnasium where I knew a knife was stashed. It was too small to be called a shiv. The blade was only two inches long, and it had a round point. It would cut but not stab at all.

After picking up the knife, I went toward the library, planning to attack one or both of those who had ratted on me. Five guards with night sticks came around the corner as the public-address system began calling me for a visit. That was absurd. I never got visits.

I would never reach the library, but I would play the hand out. I turned the corner between dormitories and headed for the yard. Close behind me came the crunch of footsteps on gravel. I started to turn and was instantly hit by a tackle worthy of an NFL linebacker. I was on my back and he was on top of me. He grabbed at the knife and got the blade. I jerked it away and sliced his palm open. Something hit me in the head; it was a sharp blow. I thought it was a rock. When it came again, I saw it was the fat sergeant's sap.

Guards piled on, snatching, punching kicking. Around them a circle of inmates had formed. Someone yelled, "Get off him, you cowardly—"

"Not here! Not here!" yelled a voice of authority, wanting no witnesses.

They dragged me by the legs, my back scraping on gravel and asphalt, across the prison to "the block," a small building of ten cells used as the hole. Once inside, they went crazy. I was lucky there were ten, for they encouraged one another as they each rained kicks and punches down on me, getting in one another's way. Three would have been better for them. I coiled my knees high, my forearms covering my face. They cursed and stomped. An attack on one was an attack on all. Kill a convict and nobody got angry, but assaulting a guard was sacrilege.

One guard made a mistake. When he bent over, looking for a place to put his fist in my face, it brought him closer. I lunged up with both feet, uncoiling my body for added force, and hit him flush in the face. It sat him down.

They grabbed my legs, one on each, two more grabbed my upper body, and they lifted me high and slammed me down on the concrete floor. It made me cry out. "Again," someone said. They did it several times.

Finally, they tore off my clothes and dumped me in an empty cell. One paused to leave me with the comment: "I'll bet you won't assault another officer."

My retort was silent but true: *I've just begun to fight.*

Without a mirror, I had to use my fingers to assess the damage. There was a big lump on the back of my head where it had hit the floor. My scalp had a gash from the sap. Blood ran down my cheeks and neck and caked on my shoulders and chest. It had been a savage beating, but not as bad as at Pacific Colony. All things considered, I was in good shape—and not ready to quit.

An hour or so later, an inmate was mopping the walkway outside the cells. I had him give me the mop. I put the handle in the bars and snapped it off in the middle, took off the mop head, and bent the frame prongs out so it vaguely resembled a pick or a mattock. Then I reached around the bars and stuffed splinters of wood in the big lock.

Soon a guard peeked around the corner. "You don't quit, do you?"

"Not yet."

He gave a "tsk-tsk" and shook his head. Then I heard him making a phone call but could not make out what he said. Half an hour later, he peeked around the corner again. "The captain's on his way and he's got something for you."

I heard the outer door open and Captain Nelson's voice. He and a small-boned sergeant named Sparling came around the corner. Both of them had gas masks around their necks. Captain Nelson had a tank strapped to his back and a wand-sprayer in his hand. It looked as if he were going to spray plants with insecticide. "Hand it over, Bunker."

"Come and get it."

"Okay." He smiled and pulled the gas mask over his face. Sergeant Sparling did the same. The captain raised the wand and sent forth a wet spray. What the . . .

When spray touched my bare skin, I felt on fire, as if the spray were gasoline set afire. I later learned it was liquid tear gas. At the time, I thought it was killing me. I threw away the mop handle, rolled on the floor, and tried to run up the wall. I behaved like a fly hit with bug spray. My eyes burned and ran. It was terrible. Inmates in nearby cells were screaming their torment.

Nobody could be left for more than a few minutes in such a concentration of tear gas. They started to unlock the cell, but the wood splinters in the lock stopped them. It was hard for them to see from behind the gas masks. By the time they got the door open, the worst of the gas had settled. It still burned, but far less.

"Raise your hands and back out," Captain Nelson said. He stood to one side of the gate, the sergeant to the other.

I backed out with my hands up. As soon as I cleared the gate, I reached out with my right hand and pulled the sergeant's mask off and punched him with my left hand. Down he went.

Captain Nelson jumped on my back, trying to choke me down, but I managed to lunge and spin around and slam him into the bars.

The sergeant scrambled up and ran outdoors where a squad of guards without gas masks was waiting. Meanwhile, Captain Nelson and I were throwing punches in the corridor outside the cells, both of us running snot from our noses and tears from our eyes. His gas mask was askew, and he looked ridiculous.

A herd of guards cursed me with the tear gas burning their eyes. They dragged me outdoors. Behind us the other convicts were yelling for respite. I was naked in the burning desert sun. I stood under a gun tower and they took up positions surrounding me at a distance of ten feet or so. The asphalt was so hot that I had to dance from foot to foot. It must have been a weird sight, a naked fifteen-year-old dancing in front of guards with watering eyes. Before he left, Captain Nelson had someone get me a towel to stand on. I had a tan over most of my body, so I didn't burn—but my ass had never been exposed to the sun, much less the afternoon desert sun.

An hour or so later a station wagon pulled up. A lieutenant got out and handed me a set of khakis. When I was dressed, they handcuffed me, put me in the screened-off backseat, and drove me out the back gate. I asked where we were going. They wouldn't tell me, but when they took a right turn instead of a left I knew we were heading toward the LA County Jail.

THE LA COUNTY JAIL was on the tenth through fourteenth floor in the Hall of Justice at the corner of Broadway and Temple Street. When the correctional lieutenant handed me over to the booking officer, he gave him a sheet of paper. The report said that I had been arrested under Section 4500 of the California Penal Code. Section 4500 states that any inmate serving a life sentence who commits an assault liable to cause great bodily harm is to be sentenced to the gas chamber. There was no alternative. The life sentence, according to California Supreme Court decisions, also includes indeterminate sentences—one year to life or five years to life. Actually, I came under Section 4500, subsection B. The subsection wasn't mentioned on the papers. The booking officer asked me how old I was. I told him I was nineteen. With a shrug, he assigned me to "10-A-1," also known as "high power." It was the special security tank for men facing the gas chamber, cop killers and notorious murders.

Most prisoners are moved in groups or sometimes sent places in the jail on their own, but high power inmates are moved under escort one at a time. Being in high power gives one a certain cachet in the topsy-turvy world of underworld values. It usually takes from eight to twelve hours to get through the booking process. In groups, everyone has to wait for all the others to finish each step of the procedures before moving on. I was moved ahead of everyone else. First the booking office, next to the Bertillion Room, where they took mug photos and several sets of fingerprints. Copies were sent to Sacramento and to the FBI in Washington. I was showered, sprayed with DDT (this was before *Silent Spring*), and given jail denim to dress in. A medical technician had me "skin it back and squeeze it down" to see if I had gonorrhea. He quickly looked at my bruises, then pronounced me fit. After gathering a blanket and a mattress cover, inside of which was an aluminum cup and spoon, a deputy led me through the maze of the jail to the tenth floor next to the Attorney Room, where high power was located by itself. During the walk, we passed walls of bars, inside of which were walkways outside cells. The jail was crowded. Most cells had four or five occupants. Even the tank trusty in the first cell had three. The cell gates were open, and the men were out on the runway, walking or playing cards. As I went by one tank someone said, "Who'd he kill? He's just a kid."

The tanks were racially segregated for the most part. One exception was the "queens'" tank. With towels wrapped like turbans around their heads, jail shirt tails tied at the bottom like blouses, makeup ingeniously concocted from God knows what, jeans rolled up and skin-tight, they were all flamboyant parodies of women. Spotting me, as I walked with the guard along the length of their tank, they hurried along beside us: "Put him in here, Deputy! We won't hurt him."

The deputy snorted and quipped, "All we'd find is his shoelaces."

"What's your name, honey?"

I didn't reply.

"Who'd you kill, kid?"

"If you go to the joint, I'll be your woman—and kill anybody that fucks with you."

I said nothing. It was a loser to exchange quips with queens; their tongues were too sharp, their wit too biting. Needless to say, I had no worries about anyone fucking me. I was no white-bread white boy. If someone said something wrong or even looked wrong, my challenge would be quick, and if the response was less than swift apology, I would attack forthwith without further words.

When we were past the queens' tank, we continued through a maze of steel stairs and bars, past pale green tile walls, past white tanks, black tanks, Mexican tanks. We came to a tank with a nearly empty runway. A bridge game was in progress on the floor, a folded blanket serving as a table. The escorting deputy handed the tank deputy my booking papers and a name tag that went into a slot on a board. "You're in Cell Six," he said, beckoning me toward the gate into the tank. He had to first unlock the steel door of a control panel beside the gate. "Fish on the line!" He yelled. "Cell Six."

He unlocked the tank gate and pulled it open, and I stepped inside. The bridge players looked up; a few heads appeared in open cell doors to look me over. One was black. Everyone was segregated in the jail except fruiters and killers. That seemed to have some irony.

I walked down the tier. It was narrow and I had to step across the bridge game, excusing myself as I did so. I reached Cell Six. It already had two men on the two bunks. I'd known the jail was crowded, but somehow I had expected that each man on trial for his life would have a cell to himself. I hesitated. "Come on in," said the man on the top bunk. He was small and muscular, in his late thirties, with gray sideburns. The man seated on the bottom bunk wore a tank top undershirt that bulged at the gut. He looked to be Italian.

From the front the jailer shook a lever that made all the cell gates vibrate loudly. "Grab a hole, A-One! Grab a hole!"

The card game broke up. The two or three other men out on the runway made for their cells. The tier started to clear. I stepped inside. I had some fear. I was being locked in a cell with two grown men facing trial on the most serious felonies imaginable. From the front the jailer yelled, "Watch the gates! Coming closed!" All the cell gates slammed shut with a horrendous crash of steel on steel.

Throughout the jail, gates were vibrating and slamming shut. It was a general lockup. The heavyset man on the bottom bunk moved over. "Sit on down. How old are you?"

"Nineteen," I lied.

He shook his head and grunted. His name, I would learn, was Johnny Cicerone, and he was a real Mob guy, or the LA version thereof. The Mob, I would learn, has little enclaves around Southern California, but it doesn't carry the power here that it wields in the East. Johnny controlled a bookmaking operation in several factories and the general hospital; plus he was the muscle for the Sica brothers, Joe and Freddy; Jimmy the Weasel Fratianno; and Dominic Brooklier, the *capo de regime* on the West Coast. Legend had it that they made their bones taking out Bugsy Siegel.

"How'd you get in high power?" asked the smaller man, whose name was Gordon D'Arcy. "Who'd they say you killed?" (In jail or prison, I would learn, you never ask anyone what he did but, rather, what the authorities alleged he did. That way you could answer without admitting anything.)

"Nobody. I stabbed a bull in Lancaster." I kept silent about how superficial it was.

"Stabbed a hack! Damn!" His surprise was evident. He gestured toward my bruised and battered face. "Looks like they fucked you up."

"Yeah, they danced on me a little. It's no big thing." The stoicism valued in the underworld was already part of me. Never snivel. Try to laugh, no matter what.

D'Arcy grinned. In the upcoming days I learned that he was a professional armed robber facing a life sentence for kidnap/robbery. It was a technical kidnap: he'd moved a supermarket manager from produce to the rear office to open the safe. Moving someone from room to room triggered the "Little Lindbergh" law. If the victim had suffered any injury, D'Arcy would have faced the gas chamber. As it was, he only faced life if convicted. The victim said he could identify D'Arcy solely by his eyes. The perpetrator had worn a ski mask over his entire face, so the defense attorney put five men in identical clothes and ski masks and paraded them in front of the witness and jury. The witness instantly pointed to D'Arcy. He screamed, then fainted. The jury deliberated in less than three hours before finding him guilty. Now he was on appeal.

Cicerone riffled a deck of playing cards. "C'mon, Gordon, lemme get my money back."

"Get your ass up here and get whipped."

Cicerone grabbed a pencil and a tablet already marked with the scores of previous games. "Go ahead and stretch out on my bunk," he said to me. "We don't eat for about half an hour or so."

"Thanks. Say, where do I sleep?"

"There's a mattress under there." He pointed under the bottom bunk. "We pull it out at night. You're lucky you're not in some other tank where they've got five to a cell."

I pulled out the mattress. It was more of a pad than a mattress, and it was coated with a sheen from hundreds of sweating bodies. I was too tired to put on the clean mattress cover they'd given me. I pushed the mattress back under the bottom bunk and stretched out on the bunk. It was like a little cave. What a day—and it wasn't over yet. What was going to happen? No doubt they would take me to court in a few days and rule me unfit to be tried as a juvenile. Then I would begin the process of trial in the Superior Court. What then? I'd personally known one young man, Bob Pate, who had tried to escape from Lancaster. He had been a Juvenile Court commitment, and they had brought him here. He was eighteen or nineteen, and they had given him six months. I would turn sixteen in four months. Would a judge send me to San Quentin? One thing, at least I'd be an adult in the eyes of the law.

While I mused, I heard the gate at the front of the tank and a rattle as metal bowls and coffee cans and other things were pushed inside. A khaki-clad trusty soon appeared outside the bars. He counted out nine slices of bread and put them on the bars. After him came another trusty carrying a huge water can with a long spout.

D'Arcy jumped down off the bed and grabbed several cups that he put on the floor inside the bars. The trusty hesitated until D'Arcy gave him a quarter. He then filled all of them and continued down the tier. Everything was cheaper back then.

My cell mates ended their game to drink the hot beverage. A sweet tea with a taste I'll never forget, it was served every night.

"Chow time!" bellowed a voice at the front. I heard the *click-clack* of a gate being opened at the rear. An obese Asian shuffled past in slippers. "Who's that?" I asked.

"Yama shit or somethin' like that," Cicerone said. "He's been here since forty-five . . . or maybe forty-six. Sentenced to death for being a traitor."

"A traitor? What happened?"

"You tell him," Cicerone said, motioning to D'Arcy.

"He's an American citizen. He joined the Japanese army in either Japan or in the Philippines. He was in on the Bataan Death March. I don't think they'll top him. He'll get a reversal or a commutation or something."

"Motherfucker deserves a gassing," Cicerone said. "If anybody does."

When the fat Japanese-American came back, another gate opened and another man came by. He was Lloyd Sampsell and he nodded to D'Arcy while going by. They knew each other from the Big Yard in San Quentin. Sampsell was one of the "Yacht Bandits," so-named because after they took off big payroll robberies they would sail up and down the California coast on a yacht. He had escaped from prison and killed either a security guard or an officer in a robbery and was sentenced to die. He had been brought from death row for some kind of court hearing.

The next man was also headed for death row. He was big, with a hawk nose that had been broken more than once. He was Caryl Chessman, the Red Light Bandit. I'd heard about him. He was supposed to be very smart. A detective once compared me to him. He passed and returned to his cell. Next was a small man with a sharp ferret face and scar tissue that stretched the flesh around his right eye. I was standing at the bars. He did a double take and stopped when he saw me. "God damn! Who're you?"

I recognized the underlying message. My face turned fiery.

"Move it, Cook!" yelled the guard up front.

Cook winked at me and continued to the front for his food. When he came back, I was at the rear of the cell, sitting on the toilet. He was looking for me. When he saw me, he blew a kiss. I didn't know who he was. I didn't care who he was. I jumped up. "Fuck you! You fuckin' punk motherfucker."

"Aww, baby, don't be so mean."

"Get in your cell, Cook!" yelled the jailer again. "Grab a hole!"

When Cook was gone, I asked my cell partners, "Who's that motherfucker?"

"Billy Cook," D'Arcy said. "He killed a family in Missouri and dumped them down a well. Then he killed some other people while he was coming west. They caught him in Mexico and threw him back across the border. He killed some guy that picked him up here in California. He got sentenced to death yesterday."

I vaguely remembered hearing about the case. "He's got an eye that won't close, right?"

"Yep. When they nabbed him, they didn't know if he was awake or asleep because of that eye."

"Front section . . . comin' open!" yelled the jailer. "Watch the gates!"

The gates of all the other cells began to vibrate; then they came open.

"Come on," D'Arcy said.

I followed him and Cicerone onto the runway where about a score of men were lining up at the front while khaki trusties scooped spaghetti with a red sauce into a combination plate and bowl. It had the width of a plate and sides like a bowl.

"How come we come out together and those other guys come out one at a time?"

"They're full-fledged monsters. We're only half-monsters."

"The ones already sentenced to die, they keep them apart—or if they think they might cause trouble."

The cells were left open while we ate; then we were locked up while trusties swept and mopped the run. When the floor was dry, the gates in the front section were opened again. D'Arcy took a folded blanket and spread it outside the cell doorway and plopped down two decks of Bee playing cards. Other prisoners gathered and sat down on the runway around the blanket. "You in?" D'Arcy asked Cicerone.

"Uh-uh. My lawyer's comin' tonight. I gotta write some shit down for him."

It was a poker game. Lowball, where the lowest hand wins and the best is ace through five. It is also, as I would learn over time, the poker game that requires the most skill to play well. Lying on the bottom bunk, I watched the game without being in anyone's way.

After dinner, the jail was quieter, though never silent. On the walkway outside the tank, little bells dinged and little red lights flashed. These were signals for "prowlers," the guards who walked on quiet feet along the tanks. Cicerone was called out. While he was gone, the game broke up for count. We had to line up on the runway in ranks of three, so the two jailers walking along outside could count us by threes. "Count's clear!" yelled a deputy when he reached the end.

"Want some tea?" D'Arcy said.

"Yeah. But I'd rather have a cigarette."

"You don't have any cigarettes? Here." He dumped several from a pack of Camels and handed them to me. I hesitated, as I wanted no obligations. It was one of the primary unwritten rules of jail and prison: don't get obligated. "Go ahead," he insisted, so I kept the cigarettes.

"Have any money?" he asked.

I shook my head.

"Family?"

I shook my head.

He shook his head. "It's a tough life if you don't have nobody."

He took a roll of toilet paper, unrolled and loosely rerolled a bunch of it, then tucked the bottom up through the hole in the middle, put it on the rim of the toilet bowl, and set it afire. It burned in a cone, like a burner, and lasted long enough to make a metal cup of hot tea. He poured half into another cup and handed it to me. It was good, especially with a cigarette. He told me about Johnny Cicerone. The so-called gangster squad of the LAPD was after him. He was collecting a $2,000 debt from a "wanna-be" who had stiffed him. In the course of the collection, he had slapped the guy and taken him to a cocktail lounge in a bowling alley on Vermont that the debtor owned. That was where the money was. Cicerone had gotten paid, but the LAPD was trying to bury him. Because Cicerone had slapped the stiff with a pistol they had charged him with kidnap/robbery with intended violence. It was the same offense that had gotten Caryl Chessman on death row. Even if a death sentence was unlikely, a life sentence was not. . . .

"What's going to happen to him?" I asked.

D'Arcy indicated that he had no idea. (A couple of years later, I would discover that Cicerone had plea-bargained to something else and served about three years in Soledad.)

The front gate opened and Cicerone came down the tank and into the cell. "Any tea left?"

"Yeah. I saved you a cup. Gotta heat it."

From elsewhere in the jail, through the walls came the vibration of the gates as they slammed shut.

A minute later, our deputy yelled, "Grab a hole, A-One!"

The men on the runway headed for their cells. One of them stopped at our gate. "Here," he said, handing me a folded note. "Cook sent it."

I opened the note, reading only a few words before I threw it in the toilet. He would see me when the tank went to showers. D'Arcy and Cicerone were looking at me with sympathy. "He's a sicko," D'Arcy said.

"Yeah." I half-hoped that my cell partners would help me, even though I knew it unlikely. They had just met me and had their own very serious troubles. Their sympathy ended with sympathy, not intervention. Besides, in the cage he who cannot stand alone must certainly fall.

"Fuck him," I said.

"What're you gonna do?"

"I'm not gonna let him fuck me . . . and I'm not gonna run to the Man. When do we shower?"

"Tomorrow."

"He wants to see me in the shower."

"Jesus."

"Got any old blades and a toothbrush?"

"In the milk carton." Cicerone glanced over at a milk carton on the shelf at the rear. It had one side cut away so it served as a box for odds and ends as well. Old rusted razor blades, pencil stubs, a toothbrush whose bristles had been used to clean something besides teeth. Using the flame from half a book of matches, I set the toothbrush on fire. When it was soft I twisted off the bristles and lit more matches, and when it was burning and soft I blew out the matches and pushed half a razor blade into the plastic, squeezing the plastic around it. I'd seen a Chicano in juvenile hall open a guy's back from shoulder to hip with one slice. A hundred and twenty-five stitches. As deadly weapons go, it wasn't much, but it was the best I could devise under the circumstances. My cell partners watched me with impassive faces. Only when Cicerone patted me on the back and said, "You've got guts, youngster," did I know positively that they were on my side.

Despite total exhaustion, I found it hard to sleep that first night in the county jail. High power was an outside tank. It had the wall of bars, beyond which was the jailer's walkway—but then there were small windows, through which came the sounds of the city at night, autos and streetcars on Broadway ten floors below. The streetcars rang two bells before moving from each stop. The sound stirred the same inchoate feelings as a train whistle in the night. Why was I so different? Was I crazy? I didn't think so, despite my sometimes seemingly insane behavior. There seemed to be a fore-ordained chain of cause and effect. In the morning I planned to attack a maniac who had killed at least seven times. What else could I do? Call out for a deputy? Yes, they would protect me this time, but the stigma of cowardice and being a stool pigeon, which is how my peers would see it, would haunt me forever. It would invite open season on me. I did have one advantage. He would never expect me to attack without warning, not the skinny little kid he saw. He would assume his string of bodies would paralyze me.

Despite the storms in my mind, my exhaustion was so complete that I fell fast asleep.

IN THE MORNING, BEFORE GOING to the showers, we had to strip our mattresses, fold up the covers and blankets, and line up all our personal property on the floor against the cell wall. We were only allowed to wear underwear and shoes and carry a towel. While we were showering, a dozen deputies would search the tank for contraband. I folded my towel around the toothbrush handle, confident it would pass unnoticed as I went through the gate in the crowd.

Several deputies passed our cell. The gates of the rear section popped open. The men already sentenced to die went first. Billy Cook looked at me and winked as he passed. I was expressionless although my stomach felt hollow.

Seconds later, a jailer called, "Bunker, property slip and jumper!" In those days, before riveted wristbands, we carried property slips for identification and, because jail prisoners kept their civilian shirts, a denim jumper stamped LA COUNTY JAIL was required when out of the tank. I pulled on my pants and the denim jumper. I couldn't take the toothbrush with me.

"Give it here," D'Arcy said.

I handed it to him.

"Cell Six! Coming open! Watch the gate!" yelled the jailer.

The gate vibrated and popped open. I walked down the tier, past the faces behind the bars. Where was I going? Had somebody snitched that there was going to be trouble?

An escort waited. "Where'm I going?" I asked.

"Bertillion Room."

Bertillion Room? That was where mug photos and fingerprints were taken. Bertillion was the nineteenth-century man who had used skull and bone measurements to identify criminals, a useless procedure that was replaced by fingerprinting. The name remained. What did they want me for?

It was for a thumbprint for a youth authority detainer. That took but a minute; then the deputy escorted me back through the jail. Billy Cook was on my mind. If showers were over, it would be another week until we confronted each other. Anything could happen in a week. He might be moved to death row at San Quentin. He had already been sentenced.

We came to a corner. Straight ahead was the route to the tank. The deputy turned; we were heading for the shower room. Showers were still in progress.

The dice had thrown me snake eyes. My stomach sank. For a moment I wanted to blurt out: "I've got trouble with Billy Cook." I couldn't do it. Whatever happened . . . let it happen.

We turned another corner. A score of deputies filled the corridor outside an open grille gate, beyond which were a short hall and a room full of benches and steam. The showers were beyond that.

"Here's Bunker," the escort said to the tank jailer. "Back from Bertillion."

"Go on; get wet," the jailer said, gesturing to me for emphasis.

The shower room beyond was almost empty. There were a few vague figures in the steam, men who had already finished and were drying themselves. The benches were full of underwear and shoes. Everyone was in the showers—where it was really steamy.

D'Arcy appeared. "Here." He handed me a towel. I could feel the toothbrush inside the folds. "He's in the back of the first row."

I clenched the meager weapon through the towel. Fear tried to sap my strength. Shutting it off, I set my mind on frenzy.

Without undressing, I headed for the archway with the steam pouring forth. Inside were several waist-high partitions. Down each were half a dozen showerheads. Two or more naked men shared each shower, some soaping while others rinsed. As I squeezed along the wall, avoiding naked bodies, I stared into the thick steam, holding the toothbrush tight and ignoring the water wetting my pant legs.

Alone in the last shower, he had shampoo in his hair and his face was turned up into the stream of water. His skinny little white body was pitted with acne, his arms covered with blue jailhouse tattoos. He was two steps away, and I hesitated for one moment. When he turned his head, the white shampoo foam rolling down, his eyes were open and he saw me. His eyes widened, and he started to smile; then he saw the weapon, or something in my face. He turned to reach for a towel that had been thrown across the half-wall separating the rows of showers. I was sure it held a weapon. He would have gotten it if he hadn't slipped on the wet floor. One foot shot out, and he went down on one knee.

Before he could recover, I pounced, swinging the toothbrush handle with the protruding razor blade. It got him high on the back, near where the neck begins, and sliced down about six inches before his movement carried him out of the blade's arc. I chopped again, this time so hard that the razor blade snapped and flew away. His ducking plus the force of the blow threw him on his knees with his back to me. He was naked. I was fully clothed. Killer or not, at the moment Billy Cook was at my mercy and he was yelling for help. Naked prisoners were rushing to get out. I jumped on his back, grabbed his hair from the rear, and slammed my fist against the side of his head. Pain shot up my arm, but his cry made it worthwhile. I was soaked with water and blood.

Someone came up behind me. Fingers dug into both cheeks and my eyes and tore me loose, gouging out flesh as I was hauled back. I saw the olive green of uniform legs.

The deputies dragged me out of the shower room and moved me through the maze of the jail, passing all the curious eyes behind bars. They opened a steel door and pushed me into a room with three smaller doors of solid green steel.

"Strip 'em off," was the order. Half a dozen deputies stood around me, young, strong ex-marines. They vibrated with the desire to dance on me. I followed the order.

When I was naked, someone threw me a pair of cotton long johns and I put them on. Another deputy handed me a round cardboard container, a quart of water. One of the three doors was open. The windowless room was eight foot square and had solid-steel walls and concrete floor. In a corner was a hole for body waste. The room had no furnishings. Someone said, "Five days," and I understood that was how long I was to be here. Five days. I stepped inside and the door slammed shut, steel crashing on steel. I was in the blackness of the grave. From outside a key banged on the steel. "When you hear *that,* you answer up. If you don't answer and we have to open the door, you'd better be dead, because if you're not dead, or damn near it, you'll wish you were. Got it?"

I heard muffled laughter, then an outer door closed and I was alone. Would I go crazy? What difference would it make? I'd simply be crazy by myself in the blackness. Nobody would care. Imagine the darkness of the blind in an eight-by-eight steel-walled cage. What would you do?

You meditate on everything you know. You sing all the songs you might recall in whole or in part. You jack off—rough sex on the concrete floor. You think about God—is there one or many—and why does he allow so much pain and injustice if he is the Joe Goss? My mother said God was real; everyone accepted him without question. I, too, had assumed that God was real—*until* I really thought about the facts in support or against. *Maybe* there was something spiritual in the universe, but God seemed to have stopped paying attention a few centuries ago.

I heard noises through the walls and floors, many gates crashing shut. Dinging bells signaled "prowlers." I had no idea what the various signals meant.

Once a day they unlocked the door, exchanging the cardboard container of water and leaving six slices of white bread. Bread and water. On the third day they inserted a paper plate piled high with macaroni. My stomach had shriveled and my appetite had dwindled. It was a huge ration—so I ate about a third and put the rest inside the six slices of bread. I made big fat sandwiches. I wrapped them in toilet paper. One for tonight, two for tomorrow. Then I figured I would have one day left.

A little later I heard a scratching sound. When I reached out for the sandwiches, my hand touched the greasy body of a rat. *Yoooo!* I leaped up and almost fainted from the sudden rush of blood.

Goddamned rats had come up through the shithole. No wonder they survived. Some suckers in India worshiped them. I'd read that in a *National Geographic* somewhere along the line.

I found the sandwiches. The rat had torn through the toilet paper and gnawed a good hunk out of one of them. I tore off the part he'd bitten and threw it down the hole. Then I ate all the rest. Fuck a rat. He had his chance. He got no second shot.

The gouges on my face from the deputy's fingernails scabbed over. So did my busted scalp. One thing I had to say: I could take a beating with the best of them. I thought of Billy Cook crying like a bitch as I kicked his ass. "He won't fuck with me no more, what you bet?" I said, then brayed laughter like a jackass into the blackness.

It was time to do push-ups. Several times a day, I did four sets of twenty-five. I spent a lot of time masturbating. Jesus Christ, I screwed many a goddess of the silver screen in the privacy of my mind. At other times I played a game with a button torn from my long johns. I threw it against a wall at an angle so it would bounce. Then I would make a ritualized search, using one finger, poking it down every few inches rather than sweeping the floor with my hand. That would have been too easy.

Six or seven times a day the outer door opened and, a few seconds later, a heavy key clanged against the door. "All right in here!" I called back, and the outer door closed, leaving me alone.

THE FIVE DAYS SEEMED AN ETERNITY when facing them, but when they were finished they were nothing. When the door opened and I stepped out, the light made me turn my eyes away. I was dizzy and fell against a wall when I started putting on my pants. "Hurry up," said a deputy. "Unless you wanna go back in there until you're ready."

"No, boss, I'm ready."

When we got back to the high power tank, I was assigned to one of the rear cells. In fact, it had been Billy Cook's cell. He had gone to the Death House at San Quentin the night before. I would never see him again, but in a couple of years I would talk to him through the ventilators between condemned row and the hole two nights before his execution. The cells were back-to-back, with a service alley of pipes and conduits between them. The night before the execution they would take him away and down to the overnight condemned cell. I yelled at him: "Hey, Cook, you baby-killing motherfucker! How long can you hold your breath? Ha, ha, ha. . . ." In my youth my heart was hardened to my enemies. Billy Cook was one I found despicable even without my personal grudge. He had slaughtered a family of five, including children, and dumped them down a well.

When the jailer told me they were putting me in the back for "protection," I protested with vehemence: "I don't need any protection."

The reply was, "We're protecting them from you." It was a lie, but it soothed my indignation.

As I walked down the runway to the rear section, one of the faces that looked out between bars was that of D'Arcy. "Hey! Wait a second," he said.

I stopped, ignoring the yelling deputy as D'Arcy went to the pillow slip hanging from a hook where he kept the commissary. He pulled forth a few candy bars and a couple packs of Camels.

"Bunker! Move it!" yelled the deputy from the gate, banging his key on the bars for emphasis. I held up a hand so he'd know I wasn't ignoring him.

"One second, boss."

D'Arcy handed me the cigarettes and candy. "You sure nailed that fucker."

"*Bunker!* Move it!"

"You better go."

"What's he gonna do? Put me in jail?"

Despite my bravado, I headed toward the cell I could hear being opened. As I walked past other cells, the faces seemed friendly and approving. Before stepping in, I noticed that I was next door to Lloyd Sampsell. He nodded, but his face was inscrutable. I stepped into the cell. "Watch the gate!" yelled the deputy. It began to shake. "Comin' closed!" It crashed shut.

"Hey, Lloyd!" called D'Arcy down the tier.

"Yeah, what's up?"

"Look after my pal down there."

"Oh yeah! Anybody'd nail that piece of shit is aces with me!" Sampsell yelled back, then said to me in a conversational tone: "Hey, Bunker, you got smokes over there?"

"Yeah. D'Arcy gave me some."

"You need anything, you lemme know. Okay?"

"I need something to read."

"Whaddya like?

"I dunno. Whatever."

"I got a whole bunch. You might like *Knock on Any Door*."

I remembered the movie with Humphrey Bogart. If a book became a movie, it was probably pretty good, or so my logic went at the time. "Send it over," I said.

Sampsell handed the fat, worn paperback through the bars. Before I could get into it, the morning cleanup finished and the cells in the front were unlocked. The accused kidnappers and murderers and other notorious criminals (but apparently less notorious than Sampsell or me) were allowed to roam the runway outside the cells. The daily routine was for D'Arcy to bring out a gray blanket and spread it on the floor outside Sampsell's cell so the perpetual poker game could crank up. On Wednesday, the day that the money man delivered the allotment of cash that could be drawn from a prisoner's account, there were more players than room—but as the week passed the losers disappeared and the game got down to the four or five best players: D'Arcy and Sampsell and Cicerone were always left. D'Arcy had no money on account, nor any visitors. He lived on the poker game. Sampsell played with his hands through the bars. The others sat cross-legged on the floor or leaned on elbow and rump. The game was lowball, of course. Poker isn't chess, where the inferior player never wins a game. In the short run the neophyte may be dealt unbeatable hands and sweep all before him, but over several hours or days the hands even up. The skilled player will minimize what he loses on losing hands and maximize those he wins. It could be said that he who says, "I bet," is a winner and he who says, "I call," is a loser.

Day after day, ten hours of each of them, I watched the game through the bars. D'Arcy sat to Sampsell's left, right by the corner of my cell, and began to flash his cards to me. He showed me if he bluffed (not often) and got away with it. The bluff, he told me, was really an advertisement to promote getting called when he had a powerhouse hand. It was nice to bluff successfully, but getting caught was also useful. If you never bluffed, you never got called when you had a good hand. In lowball more than any other poker game, how one plays a hand depends on his position relative to the dealer. Raised bets and reraises are frequent before the draw, and although there is a wager after the draw and sometimes it is raised, an axiom of lowball is that all the action is before the draw. D'Arcy gave me another poker axiom: be easy to bluff, for it is far cheaper to make a mistake and throw a hand away than to "keep someone honest" and call.

One afternoon they summoned D'Arcy to the Attorney Room. The other players moaned because he was the big winner and they weren't going to recoup their losses with him gone. On impulse and because winning thirty or forty dollars has scant importance to a man facing "natural life" in San Quentin, D'Arcy gave me a wad of money and told me to play for him.

With a pounding heart I reached through the bars and picked up the five cards spinning across the blanket toward me. I was both excited and scared. I wanted to win. Even more, I didn't want to lose D'Arcy's money.

D'Arcy was gone about half an hour. I'd played three or four small hands, winning one, and was just about even when he came in the gate—and I was involved in a big pot with an old man named Sol, who was awaiting trial for killing his business partner. The main evidence was plenty of motive: the partner was stealing from the company and sleeping with Sol's wife. The hand started with my having a pat eight, five, ace, deuce, trey. That's a good hand, especially pat. Ahead of Sol, I raised the pot. Sol raised behind me. I called his bet. The dealer asked how many cards I wanted. If I stayed pat without reraising Sol's raise, he would know that I had either an eight or a nine. With a seven or better I would have surely raised him again before the draw. His raise of my raise indicated the likelihood of his having a pat hand to maybe an eight, maybe even a nine, but very possibly a seven or better. Should I throw away the eight and hope for a seven, a six, or a four or even the joker? If I knew he was going to draw a card, I would surely stand on the eight. I didn't know that. "One," I said, holding up one finger. The card came across the blanket. I covered it without looking.

"One card," Sol said, turning over the queen that he had discarded. *Damn,* I cursed in my mind; he had outplayed me, made me break my hand and chance.

I looked at what I'd drawn. A five. I had a five already. Now I had a pair of them, and a shitty hand. "I check," I said. By then, D'Arcy had arrived and was standing next to my cell.

"Ten dollars," Sol said.

It was a big bet in a poker game in jail, where all one could draw was twelve dollars a week. Yet somehow, intuitively or perhaps with ESP, for which I have been subsequently tested and found to have under the Duke University standards established by their famous experiments, I knew Sol was bluffing. He bluffed all the time anyway. Even though I was sure he was bluffing, I could not call the bet. I had a pair, a big pair. I might have called with a jack or even a queen—but a *pair!* I couldn't call with a pair. He couldn't have a bigger pair. Then I remembered something D'Arcy had done once.

"I raise," I said. "All I have here." I started counting out the money D'Arcy had left me. It was about thirty dollars.

When I was up to eighteen dollars, Sol threw his cards away as if they were on fire. "Fuckin' kid sandbagged me! Checked and raised!"

To check, then let someone else bet and then raise is the coldest trap in poker. Some card parlors don't allow players to check and raise. If someone checks to me and then raises, I throw my hand in without thought unless I have a real powerhouse.

"Can I see?" D'Arcy asked. Sure. It was his money. I handed him my cards while I dragged in the substantial pot. I was aglow inside.

D'Arcy looked at the cards without changing expression.

"Lemme see, too," Sol said.

"No, no," D'Arcy said. "You gotta pay." He winked at me and threw the cards on the blanket.

Sol reached for the cards. D'Arcy, who was standing, stepped on Sol's hand, pinning it and the cards to the blanket.

"Hey . . . what the fuck," Sol said, pulling his hand free but leaving the cards facedown. "What the fuck do you think you're doin'?" Sol, sixty pounds heavier than D'Arcy, coiled to get to his feet.

"If you stand up, I'm gonna try to cut your head off," D'Arcy said, his usual congenial good manners replaced by the rattle of a sidewinder.

Sol folded back on his rump and raised both hands in surrender. He was intimidated and chose to put a humorous face on things. "I'll bet he had a six," Sol said. "Did he?"

D'Arcy winked, as if confirming Sol's supposition, then took off his denim jumper and sat down to play and conversation resumed.

"Who was it? Matthews?" Al Matthews was *the* criminal defense lawyer of choice. He had been the chief trial attorney of the public defender's office and had recently gone into private practice. Matthews was "hot" with those who knew how to select a lawyer for a criminal trial. At this point he had never lost a client to the gas chamber, and he had represented a lot of indigent capital defendants in Los Angeles.

"Yeah, Matthews," D'Arcy said, then grunted and turned a thumb down in the classic Roman gesture.

Meanwhile the cards came skidding across the blanket.

"What's that mean?" Sampsell asked.

"They revoked my stay."

"You'll be traveling."

"It'll take a few days for the paper; then I'll catch the train. What the fuck, they eat better up there." He picked up his cards and glanced quickly. Someone else opened; D'Arcy threw the cards away. Then he glanced over his shoulder at me behind the bars. "He's gonna call you down in a couple of days. You tell the deputy you want to see him?"

Before Al Matthews called me to the Attorney Room, whoever did such things had me taken to the Juvenile Court with Judge A. A. Scott presiding. A little over three years earlier Scott had committed me to the youth authorities. The People of California were petitioning the Court to have me tried as an adult. It was not contested. I had no attorney and I cannot remember being asked to say anything. I might as well have been a passenger on a train. The journey took ten minutes, and when it was over, they took me to a department of the Municipal Court and filed a complaint charging me not with Section 4500 but with 245 Penal Code, assault with intent to do great bodily harm. A date for a preliminary hearing was set. Bail was set at $20,000. Of course bail was unattainable while the youth authorities had a detainer on me. I knew all of this was going to happen, as I had been learning something about court procedures from the men around me. I wondered if the change in the complaint might get me placed in another tank, but there seemed to be minimal communication between the sheriff's department, which ran the jail, and the courts. There were routine procedures for routine things, releases and court appearances, but nobody would notify the jail about this difference. The court had no reason to know I was in high power.

I was learning other things, too. When the poker broke up for meals or count or at lights out, there was always a lot of conversation from cell to cell. D'Arcy was too far away, but Sampsell was next door. He told me about heisting the payroll at Lockheed sometime back in the thirties or forties; I don't remember which. He had an analytical mind and a slight country twang. He got excited when he told his heart-stopping adventures in crime. He recalled legendary tales of San Quentin, including his own escape from inside the walls of Folsom. I heard other stories, too, of crazy Bugsy Siegel, who disliked being called Bugsy although he let some people call him that because they didn't care how crazy he was. I learned that behind bars it was good to have the reputation of being as violent as anyone but not crazy, not unpredictable. You didn't want fear, for fear can make even a coward dangerous. In a world without civil process or appeal to established authority, one needed others to think they had the ability to protect themselves and their interests.

Al Matthews came to see me. I had no money, but he said he would handle my preliminary hearing and have it expedited to the Superior Court. There he would seek to be appointed by the judge in lieu of the public defender's office. He said he could try to waive a jury trial and have the case tried in front of the judge without the jury.

It was just as Matthews planned. He made no attempt to refute the charges, although the victim said he had a few stitches and didn't even miss a day of work. What Matthews did was to reverse things and put on trial what they had done to me. He showed the mug photo taken of me when I was booked into the county jail. Then a guard who had quit the Department of Corrections gave graphic testimony about how they had stomped me. The judge found me guilty, but what had been done was planted in his mind. A date for a probation hearing and sentencing was set. Al Matthews moved the judge to appoint Dr. Marcel Frym of the Hacker Clinic to examine me and file a report. The judge granted the motion.

Dr. Frym, an Austrian Jew with jowls that vibrated and an accent that reeked of intelligence, came to see me. In Vienna he had been a defense lawyer who had studied under Freud. Frym was a renowned expert on the criminal mind. In Vienna, which operated under the inquisitorial system, based on the Napoleonic Code, rather than the adversarial system used by nations under England's sway, the accused's mental condition was extremely relevant. The charge of the public prosecutor was not to convict but to find and present the truth to the judge. The philosophical underpinning is finding truth, not defeating an adversary. All questions must be answered. There is no Fifth Amendment. The defendant must answer the questions. The tangled mind is also part of the search. America's law is an outgrowth of trial by combat, with lawyers as champions and judges making sure the rules of combat are followed. Each system has its virtues and its flaws, but I do think the Napoleonic Code more efficient and fairer, and as a result it produces more truth. As for justice, who knows what that is? I have violated many laws, but if there was a god of justice I am unsure what would happen if he put what I did on one end of the scale and what was done to me on the other. At the sentencing the judge suspended proceedings and placed me on five years' probation, with the first ninety days to be served in the county jail. A condition of the probation was that I undergo psychiatric treatment under Dr. Frym at the Hacker Clinic in Beverly Hills.

Hip, hip, hooray! In spring I would walk from the Hall of Justice onto Broadway. I would be free, and we would see what was writ on life's next page. I wasn't about to start fretting over liabilities, real or fancied, societal or psychological. I lived in the momentary impulse.

A day or two after my sentencing, while I was waiting for the sheriff's department to classify me, word came from the booking office: "Chessman's down from the row for a hearing." The news excited the ex-cons and professional criminals in the tank. His quixotic battle through the courts, which had just started, added to his already-substantial underworld legend. His book, *Cell 2455, Death Row,* had not been published yet, but he was already famous, or infamous, in San Quentin and Folsom and in all of the Southern California newspapers. Within the hour, a deputy came down the tier, pushing a handcart on which were several cardboard boxes, Chessman's legal materials. He had "orders" from the Court, and the sheriff's department got heightened blood pressure when a Court ordered them to do anything. He had been sentenced to the gas chamber for a series of small-time robberies and sexual assaults along Mulholland Drive. Dubbed the Red Light Bandit because victims were pulled over with a red light. It was probably just red cellophane over the spotlight that many cars had back then. He claimed, and most criminals believed, that the LAPD had framed him or at least messed with the evidence while knowing he was innocent. He had been a thorn in their side for many years. He had once heisted illegal casinos and bordellos that the sheriff's department let operate in the hills above Sunset Strip. It did seem unlikely that someone who did that would turn around and commit nickel-and-dime robberies and vicious rapes. I believed him innocent. Had I thought otherwise, I would never have talked to him. My moral code didn't allow fraternization with rapists and child molesters.

Chessman had been called down for a hearing on the veracity of the trial transcript, the document used by the California Supreme Court—and all subsequent courts—to determine exactly what went on moment by moment in the long trial, where he had represented himself. Al Matthews was appointed as his adviser. The court reporter had used shorthand, not a machine, which was immaterial as long as he prepared the transcript. Alas, he died partway through the job and Chessman complained that the reporter who took over made errors critical to the appeal. That one issue would keep Chessman alive a dozen years, but he never got another trial. Back then, a direct appeal to the California Supreme Court took about a year to eighteen months between the judgment and the cyanide, sometimes less. At two years, Chessman was already beating the averages.

The crimes he supposedly committed went as follows: A car with a red light pulled up to a parked couple looking out at the clusters of lights in the bowl of the San Fernando Valley. A figure got out. He came over to the car. He had a gun. He robbed them and then made them perform sexually. In viewing the situation, I couldn't imagine getting it up if I was either victim or criminal. When I robbed a bank, my penis usually shriveled up nearly out of sight.

I was told, never having personally read the transcript, that Chessmen put himself on death row when he asked a female victim in Camarillo some kind of ignorant question that opened the door to damning testimony. With a decent trial attorney he would have gotten life, which in those days made you *eligible* for parole in seven years. I never heard of anyone with a first-degree murder conviction doing less than fourteen, but he had no murder and many with comparable crimes did a dime. In those days and in most places around the world, ten years is a long time to serve in prison, but nowadays, at least here, ten years is the sentence for misdemeanors, or what should be misdemeanors.

I thought they had deliberately manufactured a case against Chessman, something I don't believe now. He was guilty. He did it even though it still seems illogical. His legacy to the justice system is that he is considered the "jailhouse lawyer." Before Chessman, a convict carrying legal documents around the yard was either a dingbat or a con man selling lies to fools. Some prisoners once forged a Supreme Court opinion and sold copies on the yard for a carton of cigarettes each—although that was *after* Chessman. The truth is that far fewer would be imprisoned and/or executed if everyone had one-fourth of the prosecution's resources. We say our system is the best—by what criteria? Do we free the innocent and punish the guilty better than others? We do all right unless the guilty are rich, as nobody manages to punish the rich very much. Thank God the poor commit so many more crimes.

Chessman seemed to swagger when he walked, but actually his stride was the result of an injury in childhood. His hawklike nose had been broken; now he had a bent beak. He looked tough but not menacing. I could hear him unpacking the boxes of papers.

Sampsell: "Chess, you get your typewriter?"

"They got it. They gotta look it over. You know how that goes?"

"Sure do."

Chessman: "Say, next door."

That was me. "What's up?"

"What'd they say you did?"

"They say I stabbed a guard in Lancaster."

"Oh yeah! I heard about you. You beat the fuck outta Billy Cook, right?"

"I did the best I could."

"He deserved it . . . fuckin' turd. . . ."

I heard the thud from the heel of a hand hitting the wall, and Sampsell's voice, softer than usual, said, "Hey, Bunk."

"Yeah."

His hand appeared, reaching out between the bars and in front of the corner of my cell. He had a kite folded tight. (A "kite" is an unofficial note between convicts.) I reached out and took it.

"For Chess," he said.

I pounded on Chessman's wall. "Hey!"

"Yeah."

"Reach out."

I handed the note to Chessman. I have no idea what it said, but within a minute Chessman called, "Yeah, Lloyd, that's a good idea! I'll tell him when I see him! You got any smokes over there?"

"Sure. Hey, Bunk."

"Yeah."

"Take a couple packs and pass this along."

It was a carton of Camels with one pack missing. I took two and passed the rest to Chessman. Being accepted by men sentenced to die was bizarrely gratifying. In this dark world there is nothing more Promethean than attacking a guard. The powers that be take worse umbrage than merely having an eagle eat the transgressor's liver. When I said I'd stabbed a guard, the image conveyed to listeners was far different from the reality.

"You like to read?" Chessman once asked me.

"Oh, yeah. I'd rather read than eat."

"Me too. Maybe for a little while. Anyway . . . here. Pass 'em along if you're not interested."

Around the bars he passed two paperback books, Jack London's *The Sea-Wolf* and George Santayana's *The Last Puritan*. I remembered reading Jack London's *Iron Heel* in the Preston School of Industry. It had stood out. I immediately began to read the tale of Wolf Larsen, who lived by beating and stomping and clubbing his way past any who opposed him, except for his brother, who was more feared, and more fearsome, than he. Their ships prowled the Pacific. When the tank lights went out, I said, "What a great fuckin' book."

"*The Sea-Wolf?*"

"Uh-huh."

"Jack London was great. They love him in Russia."

"In Russia!"

"Yeah. He was a communist . . . or at least some kind of socialist. He was also a way-out racist. It seems almost a paradox . . . a racist commie. Weird, huh?"

"Who's your favorite writer?" I asked.

"You mean this week. That's how much it changes. You'll get to read a lot of books in the joint."

"I'm not going to the joint." For a moment I thought he'd forgotten what I'd told him about the probation and jail sentence.

"Oh, not this time, but you went to juvenile hall at ten, reform school at thirteen, and at sixteen you've been convicted as an adult. Someday you're going to prison. I just hope you don't wind up next door to me."

"I'm next door right now."

"I mean next door on death row."

The Death House. I saw Cagney's sniveling shadow as he was dragged to the electric chair. It was a time when executions were so common that nobody kept count, but it seemed all too possible to me—far more back then than now. Murder is perhaps the easiest serious felony to get away with. Only the most stupid and the most impulsive are apprehended and convicted. Only a fraction of the poorest and most ignorant are among those who go to the Death House. Fear of the death penalty would not make me hesitate one second now that I'm old and harmless, my fires of id burned down to ashes. But back when my rage and defiance always burned near explosion, I was afraid of the gas chamber.

"It scares me," I told Chessman.

"Shit, it scares me, too. How about you, Lloyd?"

"Yeah," Sampsell said laconically. "But it's too late now."

"You got a chance at reversal?" Chessman asked.

Sampsell's reply was a laugh.

"Me, I think I've got a shot. How can I have a fair appeal without the right transcript? They hired this reporter after the other one died . . . and where he couldn't decipher the shorthand, he asked the fuckin' prosecutor to clarify what was said."

"The prosecutor! How could he do that?"

"Because the judge said he could."

"Fricke?"

"The one and only."

"Does he ever get reversed?"

"I've never seem him reversed. Fricke's *California Criminal Law* is the *numero-uno* textbook. How can they reverse the guy that wrote the book they learned from?"

I listened to them in the jail night after night, two men who would both be put to death in the small green octagonal chamber where the cyanide pellets were dipped into acid beneath the chair. They reminisced about the legends of San Quentin. They told me about Bob Wells, a black man who was on death row for knocking a Folsom guard's eye out with a spittoon. Wells had started with a car theft and parlayed it all the way to death row. Chessman told me, "In the joint the best thing is to avoid trouble if you can . . . but if you get jammed and you gotta take somebody out, if you want to avoid the gas chamber or life make sure you stick him in the front—not in the back. In the front you can make a case for self-defense. Another thing: don't ever go over to his cell house or his job. You'll be out-of-bounds . . . where you're not supposed to be."

Theirs was good advice for 1950. Twenty years later it was impossible to be convicted of a prison murder without at least one guard as eyewitness. In the fifties, most convicts felt such helpless defeat that they usually confessed after a few days, or weeks, or even months, in the dungeon, which was what they called a certain row of cells in Folsom's #5 Building. Nobody even thought a convict might have the right to a lawyer. Bob Wells only ever saw his lawyer in the courtroom.

Another piece of advice I remembered from Sampsell: "Two guys are the perfect robbery mob. With one guy, you know you won't get snitched on . . . but one guy can only watch one person while getting the money. With two guys, one covers the room and the other sacks it up. One guy can cover a lot of people. And if somebody snitches, there's no doubt who it was. . . ."

I listened and remembered, but without saying so, I was not inclined to armed robbery. Indeed, I had no plans to be a criminal. Neither did I make a vow to God, or anyone else, that I would not be one. I was going to be penniless when the gate opened. All my friendships had been born in one cage or another, juvenile hall, reform school, jail. Whatever happened, I would keep on. Solid convicts would say, "When it gets too tough for everybody else, it's just the way I like it." That's an expression I've used often in my life.

ABOUT A WEEK AFTER MY SENTENCING, the jail bureaucracy transferred me to the Wayside Honor Rancho, where I lived in a dorm and worked pushing a Georgia buggy full of pig feces during the day. Nothing known to man smells worse than pig feces. All evening and on weekends, I played lowball poker. An old dope fiend confidence man taught me how to hand muck (palm cards) and deal from the bottom of the deck. Over the years I found that when I could cheat I didn't need to, because I was a better poker player than that. When the other players were so good that cheating would have helped, they were also so good that they, too, knew the moves. Nothing illegal was seen, but there were telltale ways of holding one's hand or framing the deck. The primary thing was being able to spot a card mechanic. When I did, I would give him the signal known to con men around the world, a clenched fist on the table. It signals he must play it on the up and up. A flat palm means go ahead and work. There are also standard signals for con men who play the

Match and the Strap and for boosters and till tappers and other members of the
vanishing breed of professional thieves who go back at least as far as Eliza-
bethan England.

At Wayside Honor Rancho, which was the county farm, I slept next to a
young pimp named J.M. He wore extremely thick glasses and had a sharp
mind. Every Sunday one of his whores brought him enough pot for a few joints.
After the evening count, we sat outside the dorm and got high. My poker game
suffered when I was high on grass. J.M. was serving thirty days for drunk driving and a string of unpaid parking tickets. He came in after me and went out
before me. As he was rolling up his gear for the bus ride to downtown Los Angeles, which was where prisoners were released, he wrote out a telephone
number and told me to get in touch with him when I got out. A Jewish bookie
named Hymie Miller, an associate of Los Angeles's preeminent mobster of the
era, Mickey Cohen, likewise took a shine to me. Miller could be contacted
through a cocktail lounge in Burbank that was owned by the Sica brothers,
both notorious LA gangsters of that time.

During my sojourn on the county farm, I got into one fistfight. It happened
during the poker game, although I cannot recall what precipitated it. The opponent was a big man, and what added to that was fat. He was boisterous and
arrogant, traits that have always grated on me. We were playing with a cot as
the card table, six of us—one seated at each end of the bunk and two along
each side. He was straight across from me. Whatever the dispute, he slammed
down his cards, said something like "fuckin' little punk," and started to rise.
He outweighed me by at least a hundred pounds, but he must have been nearly
fifty years old. Before he got all the way to his feet, I dove across the cot and
crashed into him, one hand trying to tear his testicles through his pants, my
teeth looking for an ear or nose to bite off.

Those things were unnecessary, for my body toppled him back and down
into the metal side rail of the adjacent bunk. My hundred and fifty pounds
came down on top of him.

He screamed. The others pulled me off him. I'd broken his shoulder. They
took him away to the general hospital, and I never saw him again. His name,
however, was Jack Whalen, and those who know about the gangster days in Los
Angeles, of Bugsy Siegel, Mickey Cohen, the Shannon brothers (who were born
the Shaman brothers), and others, know that Jack Whalen was the most feared
hit man and thug in the LA underworld. I didn't know that until after I had broken his shoulder.

Needless to say, nobody else caused me any trouble during the rest of my
time at the Wayside Honor Rancho. The days dwindled down, eight, seven, six,
five. I would be a free man soon.

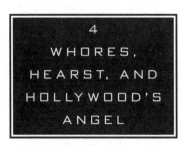

4

WHORES,
HEARST, AND
HOLLYWOOD'S
ANGEL

FREEDOM! MY FINGERS WERE ALL THUMBS and I was half-dizzy as I stripped off county jail denim and waited for my street clothes. The trusty came out of the racks of hanging clothes and pushed mine across the counter: deep-pleated and full-cut doeskin gabardine slacks and a jacket with big shoulder pads and a brown suede front. The look was stylish. When they brought me from Lancaster I was dressed in U.S. Army surplus khakis, but one morning when I returned from court the man ahead of me took off and hung up the doeskin slacks and suede-fronted jacket. I switched tags—and here they were. They fit as if tailored for me. Except for the high-topped jail brogans, I was going forth dressed in the fashion of 1950.

From the jail bathroom, where releases were dressed out, I was then sent up corkscrew steel stairs into a cage. It had a now-empty bench along one wall, while the other was like a barred cashier's cage. At the end away from the stairway was an electrically controlled barred gate.

A deputy sheriff stepped up to the cashier's window. "Who're you?"

"Bunker."

He looked through a pile of releases, found the right one with its attached documents, and motioned for me to step up. "What's your mother's maiden name?" he asked.

"Sarah Johnston."

"Where was she born?"

"Vancouver, British Columbia."

"Gimme your thumb."

He took a thumbprint and, while I used a hanging rag to wipe off the ink, compared it with a thumbprint taken when they booked me. Satisfied, he yelled around the corner to the elevator operator, "One out!" and pressed a button and the gate buzzed. I pushed it open, stepped out, and let it crash shut behind me.

Around the corner an old elevator operator was holding the door. I stepped in, the doors slid closed, and we dropped ten floors swiftly. The doors opened into the teeming main corridor of the Hall of Justice. Lawyers, cops, witnesses, litigants, defendants, bail bondsmen, and trial spectators swarmed rapidly about. Ahead of me was a big glass door. Beyond that, Broadway. I pushed out.

On the sidewalk, I stopped. Now what? Pedestrians swirled around me. The morning was sunny and warm. A pretty young woman in a bright print dress went by on high heels. I smelled her for a moment. She had tanned legs and her hair bounced around her neck. She was headed south on Broadway, toward the taller buildings and the many movie marquees. Al Matthews's office was in the old Law Building. It was south, too. I followed the young woman, looking at her legs and imagining them above the hemline. She moved with verve.

I continued to imagine as we crossed Temple Street. She turned into the first building, the old Hall of Records. Good-bye, pretty lady, good-bye. Could you be Laura, passing in the misty light? Oh well. The Law Building was across the street.

MATTHEWS & BOWLER, 11th Floor

The Law Building was shabby but still striving for gentility. One or two of the better criminal defense lawyers were still there. Joe Frano had a fancy office, as did Gladys Towles Root, she who came to court with purple hair—or green or blue or whatever else matched her clothes. Her trademark hats made bystanders duck. Feathers flew and blew everywhere. In the conservative world of the courts, she was flamboyance personified. She was a pretty good trial lawyer when she wanted to be. Some thieves swore by her. Like many jaded defense lawyers, she took every case, whether she could give it proper attention or not. It was a common joke that she had her own tier of clients in Folsom.

The elevator creaked, and when I entered the Law Offices of Matthews & Bowler the carpet was threadbare. Still, the place had a certain somber respectability, with leather-bound law books in cases around the walls and heavy leather furniture in the outer office. A birdlike woman, quick and petite, Emily Matthews, Al's wife, was behind the receptionist's desk. She came around the desk, smiling broadly, shook my hand, and told me who she was. Al had mentioned her to me. "Al's in court," she said. "But let me introduce you around."

A man was gold-lettering MANLEY BOWLER on a door. Bowler was Al's new partner. Emily knocked, and we entered. He was a slender, patrician-appearing man who shook hands and eyed me critically. "You're going to stay out of trouble this time?"

I replied with candor, "I sure hope so. But . . ." I ended with a shrug. I'd been in trouble as far back as I could remember, so how could I categorically declare I'd never get in trouble again? That would slap the face of probability.

"Well, let's hope you make it." He was friendly, but his eyes had a different look from Al's. Bowler's partnership with Al Matthews was short-lived, although their friendship continued. Manley had a prosecutor's view, and he soon returned to that side of the table, where his career flourished.

The outer office phone rang. Emily hurried to answer it, and Manley excused himself; he had work to do. I went to the reception area and started to tell Emily that I would return tomorrow. Still on the phone, she shook her head and gestured for me to wait. When she hung up, she said, "Stick around. Al wants to see you. Go sit in his office. Read something. I've got to answer these phones."

Al's office was spacious, the wood old and dark. Glass-fronted bookcases were along the walls from floor to ceiling. Rows of numbered volumes, *51 Cal App Rpts*, and *52, 53, 54*, etc. Two fat blue volumes: *Corpus Juris Secundum*. A couple of worn smaller books: *California Criminal Law,* Fricke; *California Criminal Evidence,* Fricke. Fricke was the guy Sampsell and Chessman had been talking about. *Black's Law Dictionary*. I think I believed that these books had incantations that were almost magical. If I knew them, I would be a wizard of law.

I went around the desk and sat in Al's chair. The desk was clear except for a photo of Emily and a boy about twelve years old. Under the edge of the green desk blotter was tucked a hand-written note. It said: *Eddie . . . Mrs. Wallis????* Did that refer to me? If it did, I would find out at the right time.

I began browsing. The first book I took down had a slip of paper serving as a page marker. Opening to the marker, I found a California Supreme Court opinion affirming a death penalty conviction. Emily came in. "You might as well go. Al isn't coming in until late this afternoon."

"What time?"

"It's hard to know . . . whenever the trial judge calls it a day. Some of them go late."

As I started to leave, she added, "The best time to catch him is in the morning . . . between nine and nine-thirty . . . before he goes to court."

That was fine with me. I wanted to roam free. We went from the office to the reception room.

"Where are you going to stay?"

"I thought I'd rent a furnished room." Back then, a furnished room cost nine or ten dollars a week. Called piss-in-the-sink rooms, they usually had a sink and faucet, with the bathroom down the hall.

"You got some money?"

I hesitated half a second before nodding. Actually, I had about forty dollars in ones and fives. A five was the largest denomination a prisoner was allowed in his possession. I'd been red-hot in a poker game during my last week.

The hesitation sent Emily to her purse. She extracted three twenty-dollar bills and tucked them in my breast pocket. "Nice outfit, by the way," she said.

When I departed with $100, I felt good. That could be two weeks' take-home for a factory worker. I was flush.

Back out on Broadway, I continued south. The sidewalks were filled with well-dressed shoppers. Yellow streetcars clanged up and down the middle of the street with barely room for a car to pass on the right. In the shadowed canyon of buildings, the movie marquees sparkled. I could see from Second to Ninth Street. Here, too, were Los Angeles's big department stores—the Broadway, May Company, Eastern Columbia, J J Newberry, Thrifty Drug Stores—and the local stores, Victor Clothing being the most well-known.

I looked in the display windows of the men's stores. The style of the hour was double-breasted suits with wide shoulders, wide lapels, pants with deep pleats, relaxed knees, and tapers to the cuff. It was a modified zoot suit, the first time the style of the underclass had been assumed by the fashionable people. The basic style had been in vogue since I began caring about clothes. I assumed, back then, that the same style would be sharp throughout my life.

The display window also reflected my image. I was moderately tall and slender and very average-looking, with lots of freckles. The years of mixing with precocious youths from East Los Angeles and Watts had molded my style. I walked like a hip Chicano from East Los Angeles.

Continuing my walk down Broadway, I thought of things I had to do. Foremost among them was visiting my father in the home for old folks. He was in his early sixties, which was much older then than it is now. He'd already had one severe heart attack, and my Aunt Eva had written that he was showing some *dementia*—the word the doctor used, she said. Thinking of him gave me a hollow ache in my stomach. He'd done all he could for me, a son he never understood. True, what he could do had never included a home and he had put my beloved dog to sleep, but even if there was no home, he had sacrificed to pay for good boarding homes and expensive military schools for me. I felt responsible for his aging so fast. I hated that he was in a retirement home, but I lacked the power to do anything about it. Maybe if I made enough money . . .

I'd have to visit Aunt Eva, too, but I hoped that I wouldn't have to ask her if I could stay. The last time had been tough on both of us. Maybe I would stop by this evening after she got off work, but that was hours away. What should I do right now? Maybe catch a #5 streetcar through Chinatown across the bridge to Lincoln Heights. Lorraine, my first girlfriend, lived there with her older brother and two younger sisters.

A car horn bleated. "Bunker!"

I looked around. An emerald-colored convertible with the top down was at the curb. The platinum blonde in the passenger seat was waving to me. I didn't know her, but I went over to see what she wanted. Behind the wheel was J.M., the pimp who got the pot on visiting day.

The blonde opened the door and slid over. Cars were honking behind us. The blonde smiled and gave them the finger.

I got in and we pulled away.

"Hey, Bunker, good to see you. Meet Flip."

"Hi, Flip."

"This is the guy I told you about . . . the one that fucked up Billy Cook."

Flip turned, her face close. "Congratulations. Let me shake your hand." Her fingers were slender, her flesh smooth, and her eyes were green and cat-like. With dye and makeup and stylish clothes, she was the most beautiful woman I'd seen outside a movie screen.

"Want to get high?" he asked.

"Does a bear shit in the woods?" I replied.

THE PARK WILSHIRE HOTEL was across the street from MacArthur Park. Financed by a union in the late twenties, the hotel was originally planned to be a first-class joint. Its architecture was striking, and the lobby had a grand staircase suitable for a Russian palace. Alas, the location was too far west of downtown Los Angeles to attract business travelers and too far east to get business from the movie studios. I was unaware of that as we waited for the elevator. To me it looked as palatial as the Waldorf-Astoria. Flip pushed the elevator button several times. Nobody is in a greater hurry than a junkie going to fix.

The elevator had an operator. As we were going up, he eyed me in a manner that asked my companions a silent question. "He's okay," was J.M.'s answer. "What's up?"

"A friend of mine's got a girl who wants to work," said the elevator man.

"She ever worked before?"

"No. But she's game."

"Bring 'er over tomorrow morning."

"*Late* tomorrow morning," Flip added. "After eleven."

"Yeah, late in the morning," J.M. agreed. "But don't be surprised if she changes her mind. A whole lotta young chicks *think* they wanna turn tricks. They can get big money for doing what comes naturally—layin' down first and gettin' up last—but when it gets right down to the reality of it with some pot-bellied old man who's drunk and mean, they can't handle it."

"That's why a lot of them turn into junkies. It covers their torment."

"Yeah, it does take away all pain," J.M. agreed. "Physical and mental."

"What it doesn't take away, it makes not to matter," Flip finished.

"I get it. I'll bring her by."

As we walked down the hallway, I smelled Flip's perfume. It was intense after the various odors of jail: sweat, piss, and disinfectant. She sure knew how to walk, long strides with her ass moving from side to side. She looked like a stripper strutting her stuff with her clothes on. J.M. put his arm possessively around her hip and said something I couldn't hear, and they both laughed. What did he have that would make her sell her body and give him the money? It wasn't his looks. He was dissipated, gaunt, and a little effete. I'd seen him naked in the shower at the county farm. He had blotchy skin pitted with acne scars. How could he have a chick who belonged on a calendar? Was he some kind of sexual genius? No. Somehow I knew his control had nothing to do with sex.

J.M. was unlocking the room door when another door opened farther down the hallway. A fat man in undershorts and over-the-calf stockings came out. His face was red, his body fish white. He kept one foot in the door so it couldn't close and lock him out. It was both awkward and comedic. "Where is she? Where'd she go?"

"Where'd who go?" J.M. asked.

"That whore . . . Brandi?"

"We didn't see anybody," Flip said. "Did we?"

I shook my head.

"Bullshit! She just came out. I heard a door out here." He was glaring at us. "You had to see her."

"Take it easy, mister," J.M. said, holding up his hands in a pacifying gesture.

Meanwhile, I stepped clear. If the fat man got too loud and threatening, I was going to sock him with a left hook to the stomach. It would quiet him. I was sure of that. Flip saw my move and used her eyes to tell me not to hit him.

Tears suddenly came to the man's eyes. He knew how stupid he looked.

"What happened?" J.M. asked.

"She took my wallet . . . and my pants. I was in the john when I saw her go out. It was just—" He snapped his fingers to indicate how quick things had happened. "What am I going to tell my wife? I'm gonna call the police."

I was half between a laugh and pity for him.

"Take it easy, mister," J.M. said. He walked toward the man and pushed his door all the way open. "Go in and wait. I'll see if I can help you."

The man's lips trembled; he looked at each of us, uncertainty on his face.

"Go on," Flip said. "You can't run around in your skivvies. It's going to be all right."

The trick squinted at us, then did as he was told. J.M. closed the door and came back to where we waited. As he turned the key in the door he was muttering curses.

Brandi, the missing whore, was waiting inside. She'd been listening through the door. "Look," she said, holding up a fat sheaf of currency. "Eight bills and change." She seemed nervous, and she had reason to be nervous. J.M. tried to backhand her. She ducked away and he kicked at her. She deflected some of it with her hand and took some of it on her thigh.

Flip quickly moved between them. "Take it easy. Don't bruise her. She won't be able to work."

J.M. checked himself, then he snatched the money. "Where's his wallet and his pants?"

"I threw them out."

"Out where?"

"The air shaft."

Flip looked down the air shaft in the building's center. "I can see them."

"Get your ass down there and get 'em," J.M. said to Brandi.

"Do I have to?"

"*Do I have to?*" he mocked. "Goddamn right you have to. He still might scream copper and get us closed down."

"You pay the patch, don't you?"

"What's that got to do with anything?"

"I thought he covered this kind of stuff."

"Yeah, he does—but not if there's a buncha complaints. I told all you silly bitches not to steal from a trick. Didn't I?"

Brandi's nod was grudging.

"I guess that's why you're a whore. . . . You're fuckin' dumb." He turned and handed Flip the money. "Go back over there and cool him out."

"You want me to give him the money back?"

"Yeah. And tell him we're getting him his pants and wallet."

Flip went out. J.M. reached for the telephone and told the front desk that he'd accidentally dropped his pants down the air shaft and a girl was coming down to search for them. Still on the phone, he gestured for Brandi to go. As she headed for the door, he hung up the phone and took one final kick at her rump with he side of his shoe. It lifted her on tiptoe for a moment. "Dumb bitch," he muttered when the door closed. He shook his head and chuckled, obviously enjoying the display of his power, a power that was an enigma to me. Why would beautiful women take being so demeaned? Flip and Brandi could use their bodies to subjugate many men. "Siddown. Make yourself comfort-able." I sat down and he began searching through drawers, then went into the bathroom. Through the open door, I could see him feeling around under the sink. What was he looking for?

Flip returned. "It's cool," she said. "Where's Brandi?"

"She went to get his pants back. Say, where's the outfit?"

"Out in the hallway in the fire hose. I'll get it." She went out, leaving the door ajar, and returned within seconds carrying a dirty handkerchief bundled around a bent and blackened teaspoon and an eyedropper with a baby pacifier on the bulb end and a hypodermic needle on the other. A gasket of thread around the eyedropper end tightly fastened the needle. It was a junkie outfit, circa 1950. Junkies didn't use syringes back then.

She put the unfolded handkerchief and its contents on top of a dresser. J.M. came out of the bathroom with a glass of water.

"We need some cotton," Flip said.

"Got it." J.M. sat on the bed, took off his shoe, and pinched a tiny ball of cotton from the bottom of the shoe tongue. He dropped it in Flip's palm as he put his shoe on. She added it to the paraphernalia lined up on the dirty handkerchief. "Look out the window," he said to me. "And see if she got those pants and wallet."

I raised the window into the air shaft and looked down. Brandi was carrying the pants back to the window she'd used to reach the bottom of the air shaft. "She's got 'em and just comin' back in."

"Fuck all that," Flip said. "Let's get fixed. That's what I want." She extended her hand toward J.M. and snapped her fingers.

He produced two #5 caps of white powder. They looked small to me. She pulled one of them apart and tapped the contents into the spoon. Drawing water from the glass into the eyedropper, she then let several drops fall into the spoon so it covered the powder, which immediately began to dissolve, although not entirely. She lit several book matches in a cluster and jiggled them under the spoon. The liquid turned clear. She quickly cooled the spoon bottom by touching it to the top of the water in the glass, rolled the tiny bit of cotton between thumb and forefinger, and dropped it into the liquid. She drew the liquid through the cotton and the needle into the eyedropper and then carefully measured a portion back into the spoon. My presence was forgotten.

J.M. rolled up his sleeve and wrapped an old necktie around his upper arm and pumped up a big vein.

Flip stood beside him and, bracing the eyedropper between thumb and index finger, tapped the needle into the vein.

A tendril of blood shot into the eyedropper. The needle was in the vein. She squeezed off a portion of the eyedropper's content and stopped. He waited, then nodded. She squeezed off the rest.

While he cleared his throat and savored the flash of heroin going through him—no sensation in the world compares to it—she ran water through the needle and drew up another portion in the spoon. She sucked the cotton dry, then squirted back three small drops as she winked at me.

Carefully she put the outfit down and wrapped the necktie around her biceps, holding one end of the necktie in her teeth. At the inner aspect of her elbow were bluish scars and tiny scabs. They were covered with makeup but showed through. The scars traced the veins and were vaguely reminiscent of a bird's tracks. And no wonder, for it took her several tries to register blood that meant she was in the vein.

"Chicks always have trouble," J.M. said, "especially when they're hooked real good. It makes their blood pressure drop or something."

She pumped in the heroin. Her distended pupils turned into pinpoints. I'd never seen it before, but once I learned to recognize it I could tell if someone was high on heroin across a crowded room if I could see his or her eyes.

"Ahhhh . . . God's medicine," she said, humming.

"Or the devil's," J.M. said.

She squeezed water through the needle to clean it, then sucked up the last few drops. "This is for you," she said. Her voice had the gravelly slur that comes from opiates, as I would learn.

I was scared. Mixed with my fear was a hypnotic fascination. It wouldn't kill me. What kind of sucker would I appear if I refused? And Charlie Parker liked it. What the hell. . . .

I rolled up my sleeve and took the necktie. "You fix me," I said to Flip.

She drowsily scratched the tip of her nose and nodded, came close, and took the outfit. Our bodies brushed together. I could feel her warm breath and smell its sweetness. I almost missed the prick of the needle. The blood registered immediately.

"Good pressure," she said, pausing momentarily to again scratch the tip of her nose. Then she squeezed the pacifier and the liquid disappeared into my body.

I waited for several heartbeats. Then came the indescribable warmth that spread through my entire being, erasing all pain. Good God! It was . . . wonderful. . . . Then, suddenly, came the nausea rising from my gullet to my throat.

I ran for the bathroom, hand over my mouth. The torrent splattered into the toilet. Thank God I hadn't thrown up on the floor. Then I would have felt the fool.

I stayed bent over the toilet awhile until nothing came as I dry-heaved. My shirt was soaked with sweat, and it was running from my forehead into my eyes. I wiped my face with a towel and exited the bathroom. The paraphernalia was gone. Brandi had returned and was giving J.M. some money. She looked up as I entered.

"What happened?" I asked.

"She tricked him," Flip said, then laughed. "A man with a hard dick is the biggest fool in the world."

I took a couple of steps. My movement stirred up the nausea again. Flip saw it on my face.

"Lie down," she said. "Don't move and you'll be cool."

I followed her suggestion and found that she was right. As long as I was quiet, so was my stomach. The bliss washed over me, the absolute euphoria and utter insulation from every torment, mental and physical. I felt wonderful when I closed my eyes and savored the glow. I hadn't known what to expect. It was different from the perception-distorting high of marijuana and the almost electric energetic charge of amphetamines. It made me drowsy yet did not dull my brain like Seconal or Nembutal. I simply felt *good*.

It seemed like only a few minutes had gone by, but when I looked at the window the sky was dark and the city's lights glowed.

The hotel's top floor was a whorehouse. J.M. had an arrangement with the night manager and with cabdrivers and bartenders. Pimps brought their whores there. One wanted a tiny piece of sponge; her period was nearly over, and the sponge absorbed the last traces of blood so she could work. Next came a black pimp who wanted to know if J.M. had any heroin. The black man's old lady was sick from withdrawal and couldn't work.

J.M. turned to Flip, who was at a mirror trying on earrings. "You've got the connection," he said.

"You want *me* to go to Temple Street?" She said it in a challenging tone; the message was obvious. Temple Street was somewhere she should avoid. It was notorious at the time; a pool hall and Traveler's Café on Temple Street were where drug dealers and thieves connected. Once on an escape from Whittier, I had slept for a week in the abandoned hulk of a '37 Cord parked on Beaudry Street, which intersected Temple half a block from the pool hall.

"I'll go with you, baby," the black pimp said.

"You're gonna throw us out a fix, right?" J.M. asked.

"Sure, man. Damn . . . you know that."

Flip looked at me on the bed while putting on her coat. My head and shoulders were braced against the headboard so I could survey the comings and goings. "How do you feel?" she asked.

"Shit! I feel great!" My voice had an added rasp, and I did feel great. The only problem was that if I moved around, it jiggled my stomach and the nausea returned. What the hell, I didn't have anywhere I had to go. This was great. I was seeing all kinds of things and people.

Everyone departed, Flip and the pimp on the errand, J.M. to pay the patch. The patch was a kind of bagman. All the street hustlers, pimps, confidence men, whores, gamblers, and boosters, who paid off the vice and bunco details, gave their payoff to a patch, and he dealt with the police bagman. The patch right now was a bartender in a cocktail lounge on West Eighth Street.

It didn't matter that I'd been left alone. In the argot of the junkies, I was coasting on the nod.

The door opened. Brandi came in with a *café-au-lait* black girl. "Hey, baby," Brandi said. "Where's Flip?"

"She went to score."

"Oh, shit! Say, we've got a hundred-dollar trick and we need a room."

"So?"

"This is the only one. We'll give you twenty."

I swung my feet to the floor. "Forget it. Where do you want me to go?"

"Go right there. The closet."

"The closet? What kinda shit is that?"

"Shhhh. He's out in the hallway."

I went into the closet. It was large, had an overhead light, and was empty except for some lingerie on a hook. Before I could say anything, Brandi turned off the light and closed the door.

Instantly I saw the light coming through the wall. It was a peephole. They had done this before. Voices came through the door. I accepted the invitation to play the voyeur and peeked through the hole. The hotel room was now bathed in green light, a catalyst I guess to erotic fantasy. It does smooth the wrinkles and make flab look firm. Brandi stood in the middle of the room in a garter belt, mesh stockings, and high heels. The black girl was in thigh-high rubber boots with long metal heels and an open-faced brassiere made of hard rubber. She had a twelve-inch ruler in one hand and was slapping it into the palm of her other hand. The sound was sharper than one might have imagined. Whooaaa . . . this I had to see. . . .

The whores played with the trick as if they were cats and he were a trapped mouse. It was a game the trapped mouse seemed to enjoy. He took off his expensive suit coat, unsnapped gold cuff links, and removed his shirt. As he stood there in his baggy shorts, with his flabby white legs and knobby knees, garters holding up his socks, he went from being a captain of industry to a trick with the speed of an erection. I expected to be aroused by the show, but instead I found myself biting my fist to keep from laughing, especially when he was on his knees cleaning the floor. The black girl stood over him, her pussy inches from his face, and gave him orders. He sneaked a look at her pussy. For punishment she swatted him on the butt with the ruler. "Ouch! Ohhh . . . that feels soooo good."

I'd heard a lot of jailhouse tales of whores, pimps, and tricks but this was something else entirely. Later when I became friends with call girls I was told that many men who buy sex do so because they are both a little kinky and a little priggish, so they pay for fantasies with a hooker that they would be ashamed to ask their wives to participate in.

Brandi turned on the light and laughed at me. "How was that?"

"Weird."

The *café-au-lait* hooker obviously felt bad. She sagged as she sat and sniffled. "Where the fuck is she?"

As if that were a signal, the door opened. Flip, J.M., and the black pimp came in.

"We be first, man," the black pimp said. "She gotta get to work."

"Sure. You paid for it."

I stayed in the background, watching the scene. No wonder they were called dope fiends. There was a glazed eye fever as they waited for their turn. It was as if it were some kind of sacrament. They carefully counted drops and divided them between spoons. The black pimp tapped in the needle, and the eyedropper turned red with his blood. He squeezed off some and stopped. "Shit! It's plugged." He pulled it out, took the needle from the eyedropper, and put the remaining fluid back in the spoon. "Oh God! I forgot. I had hep—"

"You did!" J.M. said. "Whaddya think, Flip. This guy had hepatitis and he put some of his blood back in the spoon."

"That's okay," she said. "I love hepatitis. Don't you?"

"Oh yeah." J.M. fitted the needle back on the eyedropper, drew up water, and squirted it through. It wasn't plugged. He drew up the fluid in the spoon and handed it to Flip. As I watched, I thought they were all crazy. In Preston

I'd known a boy who came down with acute hepatitis. When his skin turned yellow, so did the whites of his eyes, and his urine was like black coffee. He died a few days later.

Then I realized that they were sure the claim of hepatitis was a sham. The pimp virtually confessed when he shrugged. He'd hoped they would be afraid and he could have the rest.

"Gimme that hepatitis," Flip said. "It makes the flash better."

All the action slowed after 2:00 A.M. when the bars closed and the cabbies brought the last of the tricks. At 3:20, the Park Wilshire released five whores, three pimps, and a white boy delinquent. It had all been an adventure for me. For everyone else it was just another night of work. Now they were ready to eat. We piled into a taxi and J.M.'s car. I rode between J.M. and Flip, and the car motion jostled me against her. We headed downtown to The Pantry, a rough-and-ready steakhouse. It stayed open twenty-four hours a day, 365 days a year. The door was without a lock. It couldn't close.

When we flamboyant whores and flashy pimps entered, heads turned, including those of two uniformed policemen at the counter. I felt immediate fear, for technically I was still under the curfew law. Had I not been in the forefront of the group, I would have turned and walked out. That, however, would have invited suspicion, so I kept walking behind the waiter. He took us to two big tables they had pulled together at the rear. I was just sitting down in the corner when a voice called, "Lookit Sambo with the white ho'!"

One of the black pimps turned and called out, "The dog that said that's got a mama that sucks donkey dicks, and he gets fucked in the ass by big black dicks!"

"Ohh, shit," J.M. muttered, reaching for the pimp's sleeve. The pimp shook off the hand as a big redneck got up.

The policemen at the counter were also quick. The redneck's back was to them; he had not been aware of them until one of them grabbed his arm. "Get outta here," the cop said.

"I'm not finished with my coffee."

"Yes, you are . . . unless you wanna take it to Lincoln Heights with you."

"Yeah, okay." The redneck sneered at the black pimp over the cop's shoulder.

The black pimp started forward. The other cop blocked him with his nightstick. "Easy, boy!"

"Boy! I ain't your boy, man."

"Okay. I'm not your man, either. Just take it easy."

Beside me, Flip muttered, "Stupid fuck."

"Are you goin'?" the cop asked the redneck.

"Yeah." He threw some change on the table and went out, muttering something about "nigger-loving motherfuckers."

Both cops faced the black pimp. "C'mon now; don't bite off more'n you can chew."

The *café-au-lait* whore stood up and tugged her man's arm. "C'mon, baby; sit on down. Don't be parlayin' nothin' into somethin'."

Grudgingly the black pimp sat down, muttering, "Fuck it," as he did so.

The two policemen returned to the counter. The waiter came to take our order. Although a New York steak cost only seventy cents, nearly everyone ordered bacon and eggs. It took a few minutes for the tension to recede. Finally the pimp said, "That fool was lucky I didn't kick his ass." Everyone laughed.

We were eating when the front door opened. In came two more uniformed officers and two detectives. They went over to the officers at the counter, then looked toward our table at the rear.

I was next to the wall. "Here," Flip said. "Ditch this." From her purse on her lap she extracted a snub-nosed .38 wrapped in a handkerchief.

I took it, let my arm hang down, and curled my leg so when I dropped it my ankle broke its fall and eased the noise; plus I coughed loudly. Using my foot, I pushed it behind the table leg. By then the detectives and uniformed cops were filing down the aisle.

"On your feet . . . everybody."

"What for?" asked a whore.

"'Cause I say so, Miss Coupe de Ville."

Coupe de Ville! What a nickname.

"Outside . . . outside," said a cop.

I quickly headed for the door, as far from the pistol as possible. One cop noticed me trying to slip behind the others using their bodies as shields. He crooked a finger. "How old are you?" he asked.

"Twenty-two."

"You got any identification? A driver's license?"

"No driver's license. All I got is this." I handed him two business cards stapled together, one from my probation officer with an appointment day and time written in, the other from Al Matthews.

"Matthews is your lawyer, huh?"

"Yessir."

"Get outta here."

"What?"

"Start walking. Put it on the road."

Over his shoulder through the window I saw a uniformed cop at our table. He was bending over. I didn't wait to see what he had picked up. "Thanks," I said, pivoted, and walked away. About fifty feet from the door was an alley. As soon as I reached it and turned, my walk became an all-out sprint. I reached the next street and turned. What is now the Harbor Freeway was then a row of several old frame houses. I went partway down a driveway and ducked into the bushes. If the pistol had them looking for me, I would stand out walking around downtown at 4:00 A.M.

It was late spring and dawn came early. When the street lamps went out, cars began to appear and the first light of day peeked over Los Angeles's low skyline of the time. I came out of the bushes and began to walk east and north. It was about a mile and a half to Al Matthews's office. As I walked, I wondered if the police were looking for me. I doubted it. They had no way to prove the pistol belonged to me. The handkerchief had kept my fingerprints off it. While I walked and watched the stars fade, I wondered if something was wrong with my mind. Social scientists of the era thought crime was *prima facie* evidence of mental disorder. But wasn't that just demon possession by another name? On the one hand, I sure as shit did things that might seem crazy. On the other hand, I'd never heard voices or seen anything that wasn't there. Dr. Frym thought I had some paranoid traits. Why wouldn't I have paranoid traits, living as I had lived? As my life went on, my miniparanoia would save my life more than once.

WHEN AL AND EMILY MATTHEWS ARRIVED at the office, I was waiting in the downstairs lobby. From their eyes more than their words I could tell that my appearance worried them. I wasn't quite as neat as the day before. I wondered if my pupils were still pinpoints. I told them that I'd spent the night in the YMCA, which rented out rooms. Emily called Al aside. When she came back, she asked if I wanted a job for the day, painting a fence at their house. My reply was an enthused affirmative. I wanted the money enough to ignore my exhaustion.

My youth carried me through the morning while I splashed whitewash on a picket fence, but after lunch I sat down in the sunroom. I could hear music from the radio in the kitchen. I closed my eyes while listening to Billie Holiday singing "Crazy He Calls Me" and fell asleep. My next recollection was of Emily shaking me awake. It was twilight and we had to go back downtown to pick up Al at the office.

When we reached the office, Al wanted to see me alone. As soon as the door closed, he turned on me. "Why'd you lie?"

"About what?"

"About where you were last night?"

"I didn't lie."

"About four this morning you were with some pimps and whores. Sergeant O'Grady called me. There was a gun."

"I didn't have anything to do with a gun."

"If Judge Ambrose heard about what happened, gun or not, you'd be in jail on a probation violation."

I shrugged. My resentment of authority, and especially of any threat, was quickly ignited. Had the accusatory tone been from anyone else, I would have told him to kiss my ass . . . and fuck the judge in his ass. With Al, however, I checked myself, although he could see my attitude. He changed his: "Please stay out of trouble." He opened the door and beckoned Emily. "Mrs. Wallis called," he said. "She's interested in meeting Eddie."

"That's great," Emily said, then turned to me. "Eddie, we know a woman. She was in silent movies, and her husband is one of the biggest movie moguls in town. She wants to meet you tomorrow morning."

"She's got some work for you," Al said. "Emily, Geffy can take him after he drops us off." Geffy was Al's driver, investigator, and bodyguard. In the thirties Geffy had been a top-ranked welterweight.

Emily told me, "Be here tomorrow about nine."

"I'll be here."

"What are you going to do tonight?"

"I'm going to see an old girlfriend."

Al grinned. "You can't have any *old* girlfriends. Emily, did you pay him for his work today?"

"Not yet."

"Here." He extracted a twenty-dollar bill from his wallet and gave it to me. At that time, minimum wage was fifty cents an hour. I was very happy with the twenty.

As I went out, I thought about Mrs. Wallis. I was no reader of movie credits, but I did know the name of Hal B. Wallis. I'd seen it too many times to not recognize it, and especially so because it was on the movies I liked best, black-and-whites from Warner Brothers about gangsters and hard times, mainly starring Bogart, Cagney, Edward G. Robinson, and George Raft. They were not just actors to me; their characters were my role models.

A L   M A T T H E W S   O W N E D   A   S E A   G R E E N   C A D I L L A C   convertible. It was the first year with the trademark tail fins. This Cadillac was beautiful, and the first one in which I'd ridden. Cadillac's only competition was Packard; Mercedes was still a pile of bombed-out ruins; Mitsubishi was the Japanese junk plane that our Corsairs shot down by the bushel. In 1950, the United States made 80 percent of all the cars in the world and Cadillac reigned supreme.

The Hollywood Freeway was still a long ditch with exposed steel rods and concrete being poured. The route to the San Fernando Valley was either along Riverside Drive around Griffith Park or through Hollywood's Cahuenga Pass. Geffy took the latter route. The city already had memories for me. We passed a movie theater where I used to sneak in and sleep while a fugitive from reform school living on the streets. The men's room was behind the screen next to the emergency exit into the alley. When Joe Gambos and I would knock on the door in the alley, one of the winos who frequented the theater would let us in. One night, however, I knocked, the door came open, and a policeman charged out swinging his nightstick. Joe was standing behind me, so when I turned to run I bumped into him. The cop caught me across the backbone with the nightstick. The blow knocked me down, and the bolt of pain made me scream. I was writhing on the ground and the cop kicked me a few times before telling me to get going. I went. The next morning my entire back was black-and-blue. It was numb for weeks. I've never hated cops, but I knew then that they were frequently not what Norman Rockwell painted for *Saturday Evening Post* covers.

Geffy turned up Cahuenga Boulevard, passing the Hollywood Bowl. Across from the Bowl was an outdoor theater where the life of Christ was put on every summer. My father had worked there for several years.

The San Fernando Valley's orange groves were falling quickly to the developers' bulldozers. Tract homes were rising to house the greatest immigration in human history, which was then in full swing. Never before had so many people moved to one place in so short a time.

Geffy knew very little about Mrs. Wallis except that she had been a silent film comedienne in Mack Sennett's Keystone comedies. "Her name was Louise Fazenda. I remember her when I was a kid. She wore pigtails like a trademark. She was funny. I haven't heard anything about her for . . . twenty years, I guess."

We turned off Riverside Drive onto Woodman. The area was still all orange groves and alfalfa. Half a mile north of Riverside, at Magnolia, there was a ten-foot wall, whitewashed to resemble adobe. It was a long wall. Geffy turned into a short driveway with a solid green gate. There was an intercom with a button. The address was 5100 Woodman.

Geffy pressed a button and the intercom crackled. "Who is it?"

"We're from Al Matthews's office."

The gate swung open, controlled from the house. We drove in and the gate closed behind us. Flowers bordered the road, agapanthus and trellised roses on the right and a huge lawn on the left. The lawn sloped from the Monterey Colonial house, with trees close around it, to a swimming pool and bathhouse. Behind the bathhouse was a tennis court. The house itself was smaller than the mansion on Orange Grove Avenue in Pasadena, but the grounds were far better maintained. They radiated the serenity of a cloister.

The road kept going toward the rear, but a circular drive around a fountain ended at the front door. It opened as we arrived. Mrs. Hal Wallis was in her fifties and clad entirely in white. She hurried to greet us. She had very blond hair and a big mouth with a huge smile and was one of those persons that you warm to the moment you meet them. She told us to come in, but Geffy said he had to get back and take Al to court in Pomona that afternoon.

"Give him and Emily my love," Mrs. Wallis said, and turned to me. "Come on. Follow me." She took my hand and led me inside. The hallway was dim after the bright sunlight. She led me past a very formal living room, then through another room with blue chintz–upholstered chairs and down a hallway with Chippendale and polished brassware into the kitchen, which was sunny. There she introduced me to a snowy-haired woman named Minnie, who had been with the Wallises for a long time.

Mrs. Wallis looked me up and down. I was too dressed up to do the work she had in mind. She asked Minnie if Brent had any old jeans that I could use. Minnie wiped her hands and went to look. While Minnie was gone, Mrs. Wallis explained that her property went to a back street where there was an old house that nobody lived in. A mound of trash had accumulated over the years. She wanted it moved and dumped in a large pit. Did I know how to drive a truck, she asked.

"Depends on how big it is?"

Minnie returned with a pair of Levi's and a T-shirt. Mrs. Wallis held the pair of jeans to my waist. "He's a little heftier than you, but they'll probably fit."

The fit was adequate for the situation, although I wouldn't have worn them in public. My vanity was substantially greater at sixteen than it is at sixty. Indeed, the whole society put a greater premium on appearance in 1950.

"Follow me," she said, leading me out the back door toward the rear of her property. In a weathered shed was an old stagecoach. Nearby was a row of horse stalls, although there were no horses. There were a couple of small cottages, one used by her gardener, who came around the corner, saw us, and quickly ducked out of sight. "Who was that?" I asked.

"He doesn't know you. He's the gardener, poor man. He was in a car accident and his wife and daughter were killed. He went out of his mind. He was in Camarillo. He needed a special environment . . . privacy . . . seclusion. I was glad I could give him a job."

We came upon an area that looked like the storage yard of a farm. I'd noticed a large field behind the cottages. Mrs. Wallis said it had been a walnut orchard until a few years before. As I recall, some kind of flood had killed the trees. The property was still called Wallis Farms, which was printed on the many checks she would give me over time.

In a building that resembled a cross between a barn and an open-faced garage was an old stake bed truck. It was bigger than anything I'd ever driven, which was actually limited to a few stolen cars. "Can you handle it?" she asked.

"Sure." Why not? It wasn't as if I were driving it to Oklahoma City on Route 66.

We both got in and I got the motor running. She was going to show me the route. We started off, bouncing along a dirt road toward a paved street. It was Magnolia, which ran at right angles to Woodman.

"Turn here," she said. She meant the street. I thought she meant the space between rows of orange trees. The truck turned, but the bounce got worse, and the sides of the truck bed began snapping tree limbs.

"Oh my God!" she said, then dissolved into laugher as the truck hit a tree and stopped.

"Nobody's perfect," I said.

"My attitude precisely. Back up and try again."

I reached Magnolia and went around the block. The Wallises owned all the property in between, including several newer garden apartment buildings.

We turned into a driveway beside a house quite old by Southern California standards. In the overgrown backyard was a mound of the standard effluvia of a wealthy society: a mattress and bedsprings, boxes of trash and a refrigerator with the door torn off, boxes of discarded clothes, and scraps of lumber.

Mrs. Wallis told me where to dump what I loaded. "I'll walk back," she said, cutting straight across her property instead of going out to the street and walking around the block.

I began throwing things on the truck. It was late morning and the marine layer of clouds common to Southern California was rapidly burning away under the bright sun. The hard labor common to reform school and the county farm had instilled resentment in me. It was hot, dirty work. Sweat was running into my eyes. Then I got a sliver under a fingernail. By the time I'd finished with filling the truck the first time, I was telling myself that I wasn't coming back tomorrow. Many men take pride in hard labor, swinging a pick or wrestling a jackhammer. That attitude is planted in adolescence by family and culture and has myriad names: Protestant work ethic, the macho manhood of Hispanic societies, the competition of Japanese Bushido transformed to the mercantile world. I still recalled Whittier when I had to do hard labor and I hated it. I was not alone in that view. It was a group attitude, perhaps akin to what slaves feel. Repartee expressed the subcultural view: "'Manual labor' sounds like some kind of Mexican to me." "Work is for fools and mules, and you don't see long ears on me."

I drove the truck to the dump and pushed the trash off in a cloud of dust. On the way back for another load, I found Minnie waiting on the road. "Mrs. Wallis says to come in to lunch. Take the truck back to the garage."

In the kitchen, a place mat, silverware, and a napkin in a ring awaited me. Minnie had corn chowder and a ham-and-cheese sandwich with lots of mayonnaise waiting for me. It's strange how clearly I remember such details after so many decades.

As I finished, Mrs. Wallis entered. By now the San Fernando Valley, which would have been a desert if not for the Northern California water (what a wonderful story of chicanery *that* is), was a full-midday blast furnace. "It's too hot to work," she said. "Why don't you take a swim? There's lots of bathing trunks in the pool house."

"That's a great idea," I said.

"I thought you'd agree. One thing, though. If some men in collars show up, don't pay any attention to them. I let the brothers from Notre Dame High School swim in our pool. They almost never come until late afternoon, but . . . just don't be surprised."

"Okay."

I went out the kitchen door and around the back of the house, en route passing a large rose garden in full spring bloom. Mrs. Wallis would tell me later that Hal had a special affection for roses.

As I crossed the vast lawn dotted with shady maples and an occasional tall pine, birds sang. No wonder the Catholic brothers came here. It was as bucolic and peaceful as a seminary garden. Off to the side a whirling sprinkler cast sparkling drops through the sunlight. I went around the swimming pool to the bathhouse and found some swimming trunks that fit.

I walked out and dived into the pool. It was the first time I'd been in a private swimming pool or in any pool by myself, and it was great. I dived and swam until I was tired and then lay on the hot cement and let the sun dry me. I've always thought that lying on the warm cement beside a swimming pool is one of the most pleasurable sensations I've ever experienced.

Soon I saw Mrs. Wallis coming across the lawn. She'd changed clothes, but it was still all white. She always wore white, I never discovered why. She strutted in a parody of a zoot suiter, leaning backward, exaggerating her arm swing, a haughty expression on her face. She carried a tray with two ice-filled glasses and a pitcher. "Lemonade?" she asked.

"Sounds good."

She put the glasses on a wrought-iron table and poured the lemonade. As she handed me one, she said, "You've got a pretty good tan . . . at least from the waist up. I thought everybody in jail was pale . . . unless they're colored or Chicano."

"They let us take off our shirts to work out at Wayside."

"I used to be on the county parole board."

"I didn't even know the county *had* a parole board."

"They do . . . or at least they did . . . once upon a time."

She was a most likable woman, radiating a good-natured garrulousness. She was also curious about me and asked me a lot of questions. My replies were more wary than candid. Why should she be concerned about me? It was obvious that she had wealth surpassing the dreams of the average person. What did she want from me? She could sure do better than me for a gigolo. Although I was wary, I nonetheless found myself grinning and laughing. She was warm and funny.

A young woman in shorts and an immense straw hat, with two children ambling around her, appeared coming across the lawn. While they were still some distance away, Mrs. Wallis said that she was a neighbor, ". . . who used to be my son's girlfriend even though she's four years older. . . . Is that strange?" Over time I would learn that Mrs. Wallis often asked questions like that, in a deliberately conspiratorial manner of speech. It was not malicious. It was her way to draw you closer to her. "Her husband's directing a movie at Warner Brothers. If *they* knew she was coming *here* . . . *oi vey*, they'd be displeased."

They! What *they* was she talking about?

The children blew by and hit the water like two small bombs, and the young woman extended her hand as Mrs. Wallis made the introductions. I can't even remember her name or who she was, except that she was about twenty-five and quite pretty, with a full mouth of teeth showing as she smiled during the introduction. The best part was that it saved me from the velvet interrogation. When she was seated and they started to talk, I went into the water to play with the children, a boy and a girl—older than six, younger than ten. I was (and continue to be) poor at determining the ages of children, except for my own, who hadn't gotten that far yet. We threw a big light rubber ball around the water. They swam like seals. Why not? They were Southern California children of the upper middle class. Swimming was in their genes.

Minnie came out to tell Mrs. Wallis that "Miss Wallis" was on the phone. "Miss" Wallis was Hal's sister, Minna Wallis of Famous Artists and agent to Clark Gable and others. Over time I would learn that she was a sucker for poker and a merciless bitch at negotiation.

After Louise Wallis was gone for some minutes, I decided it was time to leave. The white sun of midday was tinged with orange as it came at a lower angle through the many trees, which were starting to move to the music of the rising evening breeze. The young woman called her children. "It's getting chilly," she said. I gave her a wave as I climbed from the pool at the far edge. It was closest to the bathhouse.

When I finished toweling myself and getting dressed, the young woman was gone. Reaching the house from the bathhouse would necessitate going around the swimming pool. As I walked along the short side of its rectangular shape, I failed to see the step from the deck down into the water. I took a step and my foot came down first on air and then in a foot of water. However, it pitched me sideways into the swimming pool. Chaplin could not have taken a better pratfall.

I arrived at the back door dripping water and thoroughly mortified. Minnie called Mrs. Wallis, who thought it was hilarious.

Wearing one of Hal's monogrammed terrycloth robes, my clothes a soaked pile on the rear stoop, I followed Mrs. Wallis upstairs to her son's bedroom. He was attending one of the Claremont Colleges and came home on the weekend. The room had a wall of books and the various photographs, pennants, and athletic equipment one would associate with a youth in America at the time. The acoustic guitar there was a little ahead of its time. The rage of the age was the saxophone. Mrs. Wallis went through drawers and closet, plucking me Levi's jeans (what we call 501s were all they made in '50), a knit polo shirt, and a short windbreaker of pig suede. While she was at it, she said he had more than he needed and made me a CARE package. She found a bag in which to carry them.

"Now we have to get your money," she said, leading me to her bedroom, which was actually a suite, with separate dressing room and bathroom. The room was at the corner of the house, with windows on two sides, facing north and west, the slanting sun softened by the trees along the outside. The shadows danced in the breeze and sunlight. The room was large. Half was the actual bedroom; a sofa and a screen created another space, with a fancy antique desk and file cabinets. One wall was a huge bookcase. I glanced at some titles. Many were psychology; a couple were religion. This was the first time I saw the name Pierre Tielhard de Chardin. It was so mellifluous that I remembered this moment the next time I saw it. One title was *The Neurotic Personality in Our Time*, by Karen Horney.

Mrs. Wallis's checkbook was huge, six perforated checks to each page. She wrote a check for twenty-three dollars. Twenty was for the work, the three for transportation. "You can walk a block north. The red car stops at Chandler and Woodman. It'll take you all the way to the subway terminal."

"That's where I want to go."

"Can you drive a car better than a truck?" She was laughing.

I was blushing. "Oh, yeah, I mean . . . that was just—"

"It was my fault. I told you to turn. Tomorrow I want you to drive me on my errands. I've got arthritis in my hands." She held them up. Her joints had the telltale swelling. "Can you be here by ten?"

"I'll be here." Driving a rich woman around town was a different matter from laboring in the sun, and twenty dollars was twice what a worker got on the line at General Motors.

I walked out to the gate, where a button on the inside let me open it for myself. Trudging along Woodman the long two blocks to the Pacific Electric tracks on Chandler Boulevard, I saw a tract of California ranch-style houses being erected. Some were still skeletons of wood frame, others were covered with plaster skin, and from somewhere came the rhythmic banging of a hammer, the sound carrying in the afternoon breeze.

One of Pacific Electric's big red streetcars, actually two of them attached to each other, soon appeared and came to a stop. Running along a wide right-of-way in the middle of the divided road, it took me through North Hollywood and the edge of Glendale, past the temple built by Aimee Semple McPherson and Echo Park with its electric boats, into a mile-long tunnel at the end of Glendale Boulevard. The tracks ended far beneath the subway terminal building half a block north of Fifth Street on Hill.

I rented a furnished room near MacArthur Park. It cost seven dollars for the week. The bathroom was down the hall, but my room did have a sink. I felt good about it. There was a carpet on the floor, and it was comfortable. It was mine. I locked the door and took a nap. When I awoke it was time to go out into the Los Angeles night. The world knows that Southern California is warm in winter. It is less well known that night in the City of Angels is its best time. If the day was scorching, the moment the sun descends the world cools to the perfect comfort zone. I walked downtown, about two miles from the room, and went to see *Yellow Sky*, an excellent character-driven western, with Gregory Peck and Anne Baxter.

■ ■ ■

IN THE MORNING WE BEGAN the routine that would continue several days a week for the next few months. I would arrive after 9:00. Sometimes Mrs. Wallis was ready at 9:30, sometimes not until 11:00. While I waited, Minnie cooked me a great breakfast.

Sooner or later we left on Mrs. Wallis's "errands." We went in on Riverside if we were going to Paramount in Hollywood. She always got first-class treatment, for if her star days were long gone, "I'm still *Lady* Wallis," she would say, and wink like a conspirator. No doubt Hal Wallis was a movie mogul by anyone's criteria. I thought it strange that he was never at the studio when we visited. Was it something ulterior? Did she want me to kill him? Maybe that was why she seemed too interested in finding out about me and what I thought.

She loved to talk—and I have always been a listener. In bits and pieces I began to learn her story. She had been born poor, not impoverished but working-class poor. She had lived at Sixth and Kohler in the first decade after the turn of the century and had worked at the Bishop Candy Company, at Seventh and Central. She got fired (years later she confided that it was because she'd had an abortion) because she was too sick to work. She was looking for another job. A woman named Bertha Griffith, I believe that was her name, gave Louise a ride, found that she needed a job, and took her out to where Mack Sennett was making Keystone comedies. She got a job as an actress in Sennett's company because she could drive an automobile, a skill rare among women in the first decade of the twentieth century. Wearing trademark pigtails, she became a star of silent movies. "Not real big," she said, "but I had a long run." Indeed, she still worked occasionally after the arrival of sound, although by then she was the wife of Hal B. Wallis and had no financial need to act in a movie. When I once spotted an Oscar for Best Picture for *Casablanca*, Louise told me the tale. At one time Hal had run the Warner Brothers studio and the brothers Warner "loved him like a son," or so Mrs. Wallis said. A decade and some thereafter, the brothers Warner and Hal Wallis divorced with bile and acrimony. At the Academy Awards of 1942 or '43, when "Best Picture" was announced minions of Harry Warner blocked Hal from getting out of his seat to come onstage. They ran up and collected the Oscar. "They claimed it was the studio's . . . or something like that."

"So what happened?" I asked.

"Oh, you see where it is, don't you?"

"I don't even know why I asked."

"They hate him. Don't mention Hal Wallis at Warners. The last few years there, he'd been signing the talent to personal rather than studio contracts— actors, cinematographers, directors, several big ones. When he left and set up an independent production company at Paramount, Harry Warner nearly had a seizure. Cross my heart it's true." It was very entertaining to hear inside Hollywood gossip. It made me feel like an insider, too.

Often our route from her house was over the hills into Beverly Hills. She knew many famous people. Jack Dempsey was a friend from her heyday in the Roaring Twenties, when, she said, "I tried everything there is, and what I liked I did twice." Having heard that I had the idea of being a prizefighter, she took me to Dempsey's real estate office, I think it was on Santa Monica Boulevard. He had me throw a jab and held up a huge hand. The jab felt awfully weak, and I was slightly embarrassed. He was at least sixty and looked as if he could knock a mule down. Another time she took me to visit Ayn Rand, whom she knew because Hal had produced the movie of Rand's book *The Fountainhead,* which I had not then read. Ditto for Aldous Huxley, a tall, gaunt man. All I remember was that the house smelled of bread freshly baked by his wife.

The most memorable visit was on a trip over Benedict Canyon. It descended into Beverly Hills via many tight curves and switchbacks. Houses were few, and they were all flashes of red-tiled roofs behind walls draped in bougainvillea.

"Do you know who William Randolph Hearst is?" she asked.

I'd heard my father curse the Hearst newspapers as being "goddamned fascist propaganda." And somewhere I'd heard that the movie *Citizen Kane* was based on Hearst.

"Is he still alive?"

"Oh, yes . . . barely."

"The movie said he was dead."

"Oh no, W.R.'s still alive. He might be better off if he wasn't. He's had a couple of strokes. He hasn't been out of Marion's house for three years. That's where we're going." A little while later, she added, almost to herself, "God, how Marion hated that movie. Him, too, but she . . . she would have killed Welles . . . and Marion is really kind and gentle . . . and funny. Everyone thinks it was just W.R.'s money that made her a star, but she was a good light comedienne." Mrs. Wallis paused in reflection. "We had fun," she said. "It was almost shameful in the depression. W.R. would run a small private train from Glendale to San Luis Obispo; the Hollywood Train, they called it. Then everyone would pile into a string of limousines to *the ranch.* That's what W.R. called it. Imagine calling San Simeon *the ranch?* Everybody wanted an invitation. Chaplin went all the time. He was a good tennis player. Greta Garbo, John Gilbert. I can see them all now, swimming in the outdoor pool in the moonlight." She named other names that must have blazed across the firmament of fame once upon a time but failed to resonate in my memory. I did recognize Ken Murray, for my father had worked backstage at Ken Murray's *Blackouts,* a review that ran in Hollywood for years. Someday she'd show me San Simeon, she said.

As I recall, the Davies house was up Beverly Drive, north of Sunset Boulevard, where Beverly turns into Franklin Canyon, although someone told me that the house where they lived was in Whitley Heights above the older part of downtown Hollywood.

Marion Davies opened the door. She was in her fifties, although in the shadowed light of the entryway she looked younger. It was still easy to see why Hearst, then in his fifties, had been attracted to the twenty-two-year-old chorus girl. She embraced Louise and then turned to me. "Is this Brent? I haven't seen him since—" She extended her hand out about the height of her waist to indicate the size of a little boy.

"No, no, this is Eddie. He's my weekday son. Brent comes home on weekends."

Marion smiled warmly and extended a hand. "You've got a great weekday mother. She's been my buddy for a long, long time."

Marion Davies led us into a sitting room where they talked about Zasu Pitts, a mutual friend who had just undergone cancer surgery. Marion said that Zasu was okay. All her cancer had been removed.

While they were talking, I excused myself to use the bathroom. Marion led me to the hall and gave me further instructions. When I came out, they were gone. A French door was open onto a terrace, and I saw a flash of white and went that way onto the terrace. Its bricks were mottled with sunlight coming through a giant elm and stained with crushed red berries from a bush that had overgrown a masonry railing. A pair of squirrels were wild and noisy in a tree. There was lots of wild greenery on the slope beyond the wide terrace.

The flash of white had been a nurse's uniform. She was carrying a tray through another door in the house. Behind her, sitting in the single square of warming sunlight, was a man in a wheelchair. I moved closer, meaning to ask if he'd seen Marion and Louise, but when I got closer I decided against it. The face had familiarity. I must have seen it in newsreels or a *Life* magazine or somewhere—or maybe I imagined recognition. My knowledge was straight out of Orson Welles and my father's attitude, but for some reason I felt this man represented wealth and power beyond my conception of such things. What I saw was a big jaw and a huge, round skull with a few wisps of gray hair. He turned his torso to look at me with rheumy eyes. I'd felt awe because this was a man who had spoken to all of America whenever he desired. Presidents had consulted him and Churchill had visited him at Marion's beach house in Santa Monica, according to Louise Fazenda Wallis. But as he turned and screwed his mouth to speak, I saw the frailty of decrepit old age and disease. I think I viscerally understood for the first time that all men are mortal. He said something that sounded like, "Mom," with spittle on the corner of his mouth.

"What?" I asked, leaning forward.

"Marion," he said, or so it seemed.

"I'll find her," I said, turning forthwith. The nurse was coming toward me. "Do you know where Miss Davies and Mrs. Wallis are?"

"They were going into the kitchen."

I found them coming out of the kitchen. When I told Marion Davies about

Mr. Hearst, her face got red, but she made no comment. We were in the entry-way. Mrs. Wallis said we had to go and told Marion she would keep in touch. It was very friendly, but Miss Davies was manifestly distracted as she showed us out.

As I was driving back to the valley through the part of the Hollywood Hills called Beverly Hills Post Office, it was hard to keep the image of William Randolph Hearst out of my mind and to think of what I knew from *Citizen Kane*. I cannot separate what I knew then from what I've learned since, but I'd assumed without reflection that giants never got old and helpless. This was truly my introduction to the ultimate equality of human frailty and mortality. I never wanted to get so old that I was *that* helpless. But God, what a life he had lived until then.

Sometimes Mrs. Wallis's *errands* were really just that, trips to the market or flower nursery or to friends without particular wealth. Some she'd known since her movie days, such as the woman who did her hair and dyed it not quite platinum—and never got it exactly the same twice in a row. She was fun to be with. Once I accidentally ran a stop light on Riverside Drive. Mrs. Wallis said, "*Trucha . . . la jura!*" It was pure barrio slang for "cool it, the heat," and seemed very funny to me considering who she was. Another time she forgot the key that turned under the speakerphone and opened the gate. It was about 11:00 P.M. Instead of waking the servants, she took off her shoes, threw them over, and had me web my fingers together and boost her until she could stand on my shoulders and climb over the gate. It seemed so unaffected and unpretentious that it sent a wave of affection through me. By then I doubted that she wanted either a gigolo or a hit man; all she seemed to want was to help me, but I couldn't imagine why. Nor could Al and Emily Matthews when I asked them. "She just helps people," they said. "Don't look a gift horse in the mouth."

It was several years later that Mrs. Wallis told me the story of her philanthropy, which was always personal and individual rather than as part of an organization. She never appeared in the photos of the women's committee of this or that charity. She did her good works alone and quietly, although her obituary would be headed: "Angel of Hollywood."

Through the Roaring Twenties she did the Charleston and the Black Bottom and knew Al Capone and the "boys in Chicago. . . ." She once had a prizefighter boyfriend who left a suitcase with her. Soon thereafter the drug agents came for the suitcase full of morphine. She told the ribald tales with gusto, although she also became serious, and it was the serious demeanor she showed when she told me why she devoted herself to helping people.

"I wanted a baby and I couldn't get pregnant. The doctors speculated that the abortion had done something to me. Anyway, I went on a trip to France on the *Normandie*. I met some Hollywood people, and one day we went to Lourdes. You know about Lourdes?"

"I saw the movie with Jennifer Jones."

"Right. Naturally we'd been drinking since lunch and it was dark when we actually went to see. It was really moving, hundreds of people with candles in a line that snaked back and forth up the hillside to the grotto where she saw the Virgin. On impulse I got in line, and when I got to the grotto I promised that if I could have a baby I would spend the rest of my life helping people.

"Three months later I was pregnant."

In the eighteen years since then, she had fulfilled her vow. During World War II, she brought two children from the London Blitz to live in her home. She had helped several girls who had gotten pregnant. It was still a major stigma then to have a baby out of marriage, and abortions were illegal. After she took in one young girl, provided for her, paid for the delivery, and arranged for the baby to be adopted by a film director (she said "well-known" without giving a name), word got around the movie business and other girls were referred to her. Once she had arranged for a Tijuana abortion, "but I won't do that again," she said. One of her special works was the McKinley Home for Boys. It had occupied forty acres at Riverside Drive and Woodman since the time of William McKinley. It took in about a hundred boys from five to seventeen, mostly from broken homes, many with parental alcoholism. Some came from the Juvenile Court. She was McKinley's foremost benefactor. She paid to send one youth who had grown up there to the University of Chicago. He was destined to become the superintendent of McKinley.

She also helped Notre Dame High School. Over the years she tried to help Edward G Robinson Jr., a handsome but tormented youth with an affinity for trouble, who would die too young from too much wealth and insufficient responsibility. She told me, too, that thinking about someone else's troubles was a balm to her own. At the time I wondered what troubles she could possibly have. A week or so later, I read a newspaper feature story about "star maker" Hal Wallis and his latest protégée, the husky-voiced Lizabeth Scott, and recalled some hints and innuendos. Later on, I told Louise Wallis that I'd heard Lizabeth Scott was a lesbian. "I heard that, too," she said. "I don't know what that makes Hal."

As with virtually all reform school graduates, I had some haphazard India ink tattoos. I had a diamond in the loose strip of flesh between thumb and forefinger where most others wore a pachuco cross. It indicated my loyalty to La Diamond, the only interracial street gang of the era. I had wss and psi on my upper arm, the middle s serving for both—read one across and one up and down. Whittier State School, Preston School of Industry.

In my night world, after I left Mrs. Wallis for the mean streets, having been in reform school was no stigma. Indeed, it had a certain cachet. On one visit to Al Matthews's office, Emily called me aside and said that Mrs. Wallis wanted to pay to have my tattoos removed. That was fine with me—and thank God my defacement was so minor. Many of my comrades were highly illustrated men.

A week later, a Beverly Hills cosmetic surgeon removed the tattoos on my body. What was tattooed into my brain was a different matter.

My nights and weekends were spent in the underworld. I now had a furnished room in a residential hotel near MacArthur Park, half a mile west of downtown Los Angeles. Although just sixteen and not looking older than my years, I hung out in Robin's Club, on Eighth Street. It was literally a den of thieves, mostly artists of the "short con." The Match, the Strap, and laying the note (a form of short change) were standard games. The days of "long con" were over. In a short con, one simply takes what the sucker has on him. Long con is what the name implies, and a good example of a "long con" is the fake bookie parlor in *The Sting*. There were also till tappers and a few burglars. These were thieves who looked down on armed robbers and violence.

One night Sully, the bartender at Robin's who was also the patch (he took the payoff and gave it to the bunco squad), told the con men that Los Angeles was closed down. Con men couldn't work *the sheds*, the train and bus depot, where 90 percent of short con games originate. People who are going somewhere usually have a good amount of money on them. When they were on "juice," the bunco squad let them take off anyone who was traveling and wouldn't be around to make noise. Suddenly all the con men were closed down. They couldn't go into the sheds because the bunco squad detectives knew them by sight. Still, they had to make money. Most of them were junkies, the older ones on morphine, the younger on heroin.

Charley Baker and Piz the Whiz, whom I'd met in the county jail, asked me if I knew how to play the Match or the Strap. Although I'd had them explained to me and even performed for me, I had never played con, which is quite comparable to an actor memorizing a script and then performing. Indeed, the game is in the spiel, the script. I shook my head.

"Never mind. You don't need to play. All we want you to do is steer." They wanted me to go into the shed, find the suckers, and qualify them with a spiel. Charley and Piz would teach me from there. I was to bring the suckers out onto the downtown sidewalks where the con would go down. Usually the steer played the inside, but Charley and Piz would take over, one at a time, when I brought the sucker out. They would cut me in for a third. Was I interested?

I was very interested. I wanted to see these con games because it seemed awfully weak. I wanted to see someone go for it. Besides, it was a new adventure, and I was always prepared for new adventures.

I looked through the crowd for young men with short haircuts and ill-fitting clothes in the downtown Greyhound bus terminal. Anyone fitting this description had a high likelihood of being a serviceman on transfer from base to base, which meant he was carrying a few hundred dollars in cash, and a few hundred in 1950 was equal to a few thousand half a century later. "Hi, good buddy, where you stationed?" If the response was cold or hostile, I veered away like a shark looking for easier fish. If he said "Saint Louis" or "Oklahoma City" or wherever, I'd say, "You goin' on that bus?" Whatever bus he said, it was then,

"Me, too! That bus don't leave for an hour" (or until whatever time the bus schedule said). Next I'd tell him about some waitresses I had met. "They got bodies . . . mmmm, mmmm, mmm. C'mon; let's go check 'em out. I'll buy you a drink."

If he came along, out on the street we would go one way; then I would change my mind. "No, this way. C'mon." The idea was to ensure dominance and leadership. After half a block, Charley Baker would appear. "Hey, man," he would say to me. "I was lookin' for you. Those chicks are waitin'. C'mon." So three of us would be walking along the pedestrian-crowded sidewalk. On the next block, Piz the Whiz would cut into us, usually using either an Irish brogue or an Australian or country boy accent. He would claim to be lost. Then he would confide in us that he was in Los Angeles to settle his brother-in-law's estate for his sister: "Did pretty good for myself, too. Got an extra eight thousand she don't know about." He would give a long wink, and the inside man would whisper to the sucker, "That guy just beat his sister outta eight thousand dollars."

The conversation that ensued was essentially scripted dialogue between the inside and outside man, with an occasional nudge or whisper to the mooch by the inside man. The outside man would be loud and gross and often pretend to be half-drunk. He would want to gamble.

"We'll match coins. Odd man wins."

To the mooch, the inside man whispers, "Let's take this sonofabitch that stole from his sister. You take heads. I'll take tails. One of us gotta win. We'll split what we get."

As the coin match gets ready, the inside man says, "This is for three hundred dollars." They all flipped. "And I win!"

The outside man says, "Goddamn . . . you sure did." He would pull out a fat bankroll, usually a Philadelphia bankroll of one-dollar bills with a twenty on the outside and sometimes even paper. "Here you go." He would pay the inside man, who pulls out a wallet that has a zipper all the way around three sides. He unzips it and puts the money in. "C'mon; let's go," he tells the mooch. "We just made a hundred and a half apiece."

When they had gone about twenty yards, Piz the Whiz would hurry after. "Hey, wait a minute. How do I know I woulda got paid if I'd won? You got three hundred?"

"Hell yes. You know I got it."

"I don't know that he's got it."

"You've got it, don't you?"

The mooch nods.

"You say it, but I didn't see you pay off. Are you guys in cahoots against me? Maybe I better call a cop." And Piz starts looking around, as if for a police car.

"Show it to him," says Charley, playing the inside, whispering, "Jeez, we don't wanna see no cops."

As the mooch gets out his money, Piz demands that he pay off. If the mooch has it in a wallet, he can only open the wallet to the money compartment by using two hands. As he does that, the inside man plucks it out. "How much is here?"

If the mooch says an amount less than the amount of the wager, the inside man says, "I owe him the difference," and starts to hand it back.

Piz yells, "You guys are in cahoots! I want a cop!"

"No, no. We're not in cahoots."

"You're givin' him his money back."

"No, I'm not." He pulls out the zippered billfold, unzips it, and puts the money in. (He actually has two identical billfolds, one of which has a zipper that won't unzip.) "C'mon; let's go." He starts leaving with the mooch. "Boy, we almost got in trouble with the cops. Don't worry. I got your money. We still made a hundred and fifty apiece."

Piz chases them again, now loudly proclaiming that he knows they are going off to split his money. "Stop! I want a policeman!"

Charley, the inside man, stirs the pot of fear in the mooch: "Jesus, if he gets a cop, we're in trouble. Stop!" He turns on Piz. "Get away from us. We're not together."

"Then you go one way . . . and you go the other way."

This last move is the split out. Ideally, it happens at a corner. The inside man whispers to the mooch, "I'll see you at the bus depot." He goes one way, the mooch goes the other, and Piz stands at the corner looking both ways. If the mooch is going off, he gives the standard signal that things are all right: he rubs his stomach. In fact, throughout the con game there are hand signals for when to make the next move in the script. Sometimes at this last moment the mooch bucks; he won't let his money get out of sight. If he cannot be split out, Charley says, "Here, you take the money and meet me at the bus station." He then gives the billfold with the fixed zipper to the mooch, who won't be able to get it open. That, however, is a last resort. The con game unfolds in such a way that the victim never senses danger until the trap closes. Until then he has risked nothing and believes that he has made a hundred and a half dollars off a dirty son of a bitch who has stolen from his own sister.

The Strap is virtually the same con game, except the gimmick is not matched coins but rather an ability to stick a pencil in the center of a rolled-up belt. Laying the note is a short-change hustle where you buy something, hand over a bill, then decide to pay for it with another bill, and then the con is in the count. I know con men who try it with every cashier. It doesn't work with wizened cashiers, but young girls behind cash registers are raw steak to a lion for con men.

I'd been told about all these games in the county jail and at the honor farm. Also the various signals that con men, boosters, and card mechanics use. Actually, most who play one game can play the others, too. Patting your stomach means "okay, everything is cool." Tugging your ear means "get outta here." Tugging your sleeve means "get me outta here." Rubbing your nose means "come back in for the next step of the game." Sitting down in a card game, a closed fist on the table, indicates that "I am a card mechanic and want to work." A flat palm on the table in response tells the mechanic to go ahead; a closed fist means to freeze.

I absorbed everything indiscriminately. The lingo, too, the rhyming *lingua franca* passed down from seventeenth-century London. The rhyme was the key. A "bottle and stopper on the hammer and tack" means there's a copper on your back. "Oscar hocks" are socks. "Roses and reds" is the bed; "plates of meat" are the feet. Mix the rhyme with carney talk: "Beazottle steazopper ia-zon the heazammer," and the statement is plain as day in the thief underworld. Only those at home among thieves could handle it with any facility.

One night I was hanging out at the Traveler's Café on Temple Street between Figueroa and Beaudry. An archway went from the café to the adjacent pool hall. Most of the habitués of both were Chicano or Filipino, with lots of dyed blond whores coming and going. They told me they liked Filipino tricks because they weren't mules. They were quick and they liked head, which was the quickest and easiest for a whore. I liked watching the action, and I never knew what adventure would happen next.

Wedo, who would later be called Wedo Karate in prison, came in to the Traveler's that night wide-eyed. He was already a junkie and sometime dealer. He was looking frantically for someone. Spotting me, he came down the counter. I expected him to hit on me for enough to buy a fix, but he had other business in mind. Outside, around the corner, he had two "wetbacks" from Mexico who had two gunnysacks full of pot. "Damn near a hundred pounds," Wedo said. "They want a hundred dollars for both sacks. I only got thirty bucks, man. If you got the rest, we'll go in partners on it."

It was worth looking at, so I went outside and around the corner. Sure enough, waiting in Wedo's battered car (the left back door was held shut with wire) were two non-English-speaking Mexicans in straw hats. On the floor-boards at their feet were two big gunnysacks of jute that were stuffed like huge sausages. The smell was pot.

"Where can we go to check it out?" Wedo asked.

"Your place," I said.

"No, no. I got an old lady and a baby. She'll go ape shit. Let's go to your room."

That was where we went. We parked in the alley and went up the back stairs, the Mexicans lugging the big, fat sacks on their shoulders.

In my room, I stripped the sheets off my bed and spread them on the floor. The Mexicans dumped one of the sacks on the sheets. It was a big pile of marijuana. It wasn't the high-potency seedless buds of fancy Humboldt County horticulture. It was "weed" in the truest sense, full of stems and seeds, but it was the marijuana of the era, what everyone bought for a dollar a joint, three joints for two dollars, or ten dollars a can (a Prince Albert can at that), and there was a lot of it. It had been crushed into bricks, but they were shedding seeds and falling apart. Maybe it was a hundred pounds, maybe it was only sixty or seventy, but it was at least a couple hundred ten-dollar cans. I couldn't go wrong. Mrs. Wallis usually gave me twenty dollars a day, but on Friday she gave me sixty dollars for the weekend, and I had about ten more.

Wedo was half-Chicano and spoke Spanish. They wanted a hundred dollars U.S. He offered them eighty and promised them another twenty later. They took it. I was in the pot business. I drove Mrs. Wallis during weekdays and sold pot at night and on weekends. It was pretty good pot, too, at least for the time. In a few weeks I would be able to buy my fondest desire: a car. Wedo and I used to look at them in car lots with the yearning of the poor.

"I need to drive up the coast to San Francisco," Mrs. Wallis said one day. "I'm going to look at some locations for Hal. Want to come, or should I get someone from McKinley?"

"Oh no. I'll be glad to drive you. I've never seen San Francisco."

"We'll have a nice trip. We do have a good time together, don't we?"

It was true. I enjoyed her company as much as if not more than that of any nubile sixteen-year-old female I knew. Some of them were high-breasted and had round asses; they could arouse desire almost blinding in its ferocity, but they were invariably ignorant of anything beyond their truncated world of the street. I cannot recall any who had ever read a book. They blossomed in the cracks of the mean streets, full-bosomed and empty-headed, and of course they simply reflected the world where they had grown up. I had never met the daughters of doctors and lawyers. Louise Fazenda Wallis had wit and wisdom and many interests. She had great stories to tell, of Capone sending emissaries to the train when she arrived in Chicago, of Hollywood in the heyday of silent films. Mabel Normand, Desmond Taylor, and Louise Brooks had been her close friends. She introduced me to a world I'd never imagined seeing firsthand. My image of success was to own a cocktail lounge, wear Hickey-Freeman suits, drive a Cadillac, and sport a blonde in a mink stole. Mrs. Wallis planted the seed in me of greater dreams.

There was no freeway to San Francisco back then. Ventura Boulevard was U.S. 101. Beyond Sepulveda Boulevard it was mostly desert with some citrus groves. The towns of Encino, Woodland Hills, and Tarzana were tiny hamlets. We passed children riding bareback and barefoot on the shoulder of the highway, which was just two lanes along the base of the Santa Monica Mountains. Somewhere between Tarzana (so-named because Tarzan's creator lived there) and Thousand Oaks we stopped at a wild animal compound in a stand of eucalyptus. Here were lions and tigers and elephants rented out to the movies. She knew someone in Tarzana from the "old days."

The big, heavy station wagon we drove ate up the road. When we came down from a pass through the half-mountains into a broad valley and Ventura County, the landscape was all lush farmland. The sun was hot and the fields were full of pickers bent low.

"Strawberries," Mrs. Wallis said.

As if confirming her words, a truck stand beside the road had a sign: FRESH STRAWBERRIES. Farther on were vast alfalfa fields growing lush under the whirling sprinklers that threw glittering water through the air. Then there were ranks of trees I did not recognize. "What are those?"

"Walnuts."

"Everything grows in California."

"Yes, it does."

Beyond the town of Ventura the highway followed the shoreline. The big station wagon seemed to race the rolling surf for miles. Traffic was light and I was going fast when I saw my first sports car, an XK 120 Jaguar roadster. It was silver and fast and it first appeared in the rearview mirror, then blew by me. "Buy me one of those," I said.

It made her laugh. "You like that, huh?"

"Oh, yeah." At the time I had no idea what kind of car it was, only what it looked like and how fast it was.

"I don't know about buying it for you . . . but you could have that. . . . You could have anything you want if you want it bad enough." She laughed. "I'm a believer in perseverance. It is the number-one ingredient to success."

Following lunch in Santa Barbara, we drove to Pismo Beach, where Mrs. Wallis was met by a town official. He had been told what she sought and had a list of possibilities. Mrs. Wallis produced a camera and took pictures. It was midafternoon when we finished in Pismo Beach.

"We won't make Monterey today," she said when we were under way again. "Stop and let me make a phone call."

At the Madonna Inn just south of tiny San Luis Obispo, I waited while she went inside to use the telephone. She was grinning when she came out. "I called Marion and we're spending the night at San Simeon." She was excited, but I had no frame of reference, so I didn't react. She added, "In *Citizen Kane*, remember Xanadu . . . 'the stately pleasure palace,' or something like that."

I did remember, vaguely about Xanadu, but I rejected that film fantasy as exaggeration. Nothing could be like that. I was wrong, of course.

Above San Luis Obispo we turned from U.S. 101 in California Highway 1. From Morro Bay north, the narrow highway hugged the cliffs, below which the Pacific slammed into jagged rocks. The trees were twisted by perpetual wind; their roots seemed to penetrate the rocks themselves. Seagulls soared and screeched. There was almost no traffic. On the rocks below, seals basked.

"The first time I came here," she said, "most of this road wasn't paved yet. Let's see; Hal and I were in a car with Marie Dressler. Do you remember her?"

I shook my head.

"Ah, how transitory is fame," Louise said. "She was a big star in the thirties."

"I've probably seen her. I just don't remember the name."

"Everybody calls San Simeon the Hearst castle. He called it the ranch. Believe me, it's more castle than ranch . . . although it's two or three hundred thousand acres."

". . . *hundred thousand?*"

"Something like that. I guess most of it is pretty worthless. The big thing used to be long horseback rides on Saturday. He had giraffes and herds of zebras running wild. We'd be out in the middle of nowhere, come lunchtime, lo and behold, there were the servants with linen-covered tables under wild oaks with some wildebeests or something looking on. You'd think you were on the Serengeti." She brayed her big laugh that always made people smile. She manifestly took great pleasure in telling me about W.R. bringing the ceilings from a tenth-century abbey and making a guest house fit under it. "There's two swimming pools. The indoor pool cost two million dollars, and nobody ever used it except the servants. Imagine that."

It was hard to imagine. Two million dollars for a swimming pool!

When we passed through the tiny hamlet of Cambria, she was excitedly telling me one anecdote after another. As we got close, proximity refreshed her memory. "I'll never forget the girl Chaplin brought one time. She was . . . maybe sixteen . . . and that's giving him the benefit of the doubt. Boy, he did like them young. She didn't know if she was a temptress or entrapped by a child molester.

"The servants used to go through your luggage when you arrived and when you left."

"You mean they searched your suitcases?"

"They didn't do it in front of you. They did it when they took your bags to one of the guest houses . . . or to the cars on the way out."

"Why would they search when you came in?"

"Booze. W.R. allowed one drink before dinner. It was a boozy time, and lots of Marion's friends had hollow legs . . . except for a few who did dope. One time we were getting ready for dinner, waiting for W.R. and Marion to come down. Mabel Normand came in the door, mad as hell, and yelled, 'Some sonofabitch stole my morphine!' I think Marion got it back, but I don't think Mabel ever visited again.

"Did I tell you that the way I set my table, with mustard and ketchup and all the condiments in their jars in the center of the table, is a copy of San Simeon's table?"

A minute or so later she said, "Look, look, over there to the right . . . up . . . up . . ."

Miles away, crowning the hills several miles from the shore, was a flash of white towers. The view was suddenly blocked by a line of eucalyptus along the roadside.

"Watch for the entrance on the right." She paused. "The last time I was here was in thirty-six. Good God, how time flies. I remember the big concern that weekend was the Spanish Civil War. W.R. was getting dispatches upstairs. We were asking each other where W.R. stood. All of us movie people were for the Republican side, but we didn't want to make any gaffes if W.R. was for Franco."

"How did he stand?"

"You know . . . I can't remember."

THE CASTLE WAS SEVERAL MILES from the highway. The private road zigzagged through the hills. The castle appeared and disappeared, growing larger each time we saw it. The twin spires reminded me of an old Mexican cathedral I'd seen in *National Geographic*. To me it looked more like a palace than a castle.

Down on the highway, the ocean had kept the air cool, but a mile or two away from the sea breeze, the air was heated from the sun pounding down on desert mountains. We finally reached some green landscaping. The main buildings were still some distance away.

"Keep going," Louise said when we reached Casa Grande, as it was called. She had me go around it to some steps. They were few, but very wide. Looming above us, seeming bigger because it sat atop the Enchanted Hill, as Hearst called it, was Casa Grande. I looked up at the top, which caused me to crane my neck.

"Close your mouth," she said. "You'll catch a fly."

It was true. I was standing with my mouth agape.

A housekeeper was descending the steps. Behind her were servants. I had already seen and experienced many things in my sixteen years, but not until Louise Wallis had I had a servant to do my bidding. I unlocked the rear of the station wagon, intending to pull out our two bags. Mrs. Wallis was talking to the housekeeper, but when she saw what I was doing she gestured for me to stop. "Leave those. They'll take care of it."

The housekeeper led us up the steps. I was looking around in awe, so I failed to notice Mrs. Wallis's dissatisfaction until I heard her mutter, "Shit." It was her favorite bad word, she once told me.

"What's wrong?" I asked.

"We can't stay in the main house. Some of the family are here."

I scanned the immense building; it seemed as large as Notre Dame. "They need the *whole* house?"

Mrs. Wallis laughed. "No . . . but we are here because of Marion . . . and the Hearsts hate Marion Davies. Mr. Hearst's wife is still alive, you know."

"No, I didn't know. I didn't know he was married."

Instead of leading us into Casa Grande, the housekeeper led us along an immense veranda or terrace around the house. Flowers were everywhere, and amid them was a lass of alabaster marble crouched beside a goat. It was all like the fantasy set of a silent movie. Ornate. Fluted columns topped with round white spheres—lights for the nights.

The housekeeper led us toward an intricately carved door that may have graced a Venetian palace in the fifteenth century. She opened it and ushered us in.

A guest house? Bullshit! It was a museum of some kind. In time I would come to appreciate the art and artifacts collected around the world that graced this room, but back then it all merely seemed old to me. Wealth to me was glittery black-and-white art deco back then. Or maybe my reaction was governed by the stuffy heat of the room. The sun slanted on a low angle through a huge window overlooking the sea far below. The guest house had no air-conditioning. Indeed, that was what had miffed Mrs. Wallis, for the big house did have air-conditioning. Her dark attitude was temporary. Within a few minutes her humor was back. She appreciated all of life. She showed me around the guest house. The bedrooms were abundant, but there was no kitchen. "The kitchen's in the big house. Come on; flop down on Cardinal Richelieu's bed."

"The guy in *The Three Musketeers*."

"I think so."

"I'm ready for a little nap in Richelieu's bed."

"Go ahead. I've got some letters to write."

The bed had a huge dark headboard and was so high off the floor that I had to stand on a chair to reach it. Mrs. Wallis said that beds were so high off the floor to keep away from the rats that ran across even palaces' floors. The bed was soft but lumpy. Being accustomed to jail bunks and concrete floors, I did manage to sleep for an hour. The sun was orange and just beginning to dip into the Pacific when I woke up. I was hungry.

Mrs. Wallis was reading a book when I came in. "Feel better?"

"I feel great. When do we eat?"

"I've been thinking about that. I don't know which of the family is in residence . . . and I really don't want to run into them in the dining room. But I want to show it to you. If it was round, you'd expect King Arthur and his knights to be there. Here's what we'll do. You take a swim while I go to the kitchen and see what's up. Use the Neptune Pool, the one outdoors."

She saw my hesitancy. "It's okay," she said. "Nobody'll say anything and it's something you'll never forget."

"I didn't bring any trunks."

"You've got an extra pair of Levi's, don't you?"

"Uh-huh."

"Use those."

"Where is it?"

"Right around the stairs. You can't miss it."

Barefoot and shirtless and carrying a towel, I went outside. It was magic hour, that time when dusk smooths all the world's wrinkles and blemishes. Everything seemed hushed and there was a feeling of enchantment. Gone were the weighted heat and the squinting glare. The softer light brought forth the luster of the marble. There was an evening breeze just beginning; roses, red and yellow, danced in it. Jasmine was already making perfume in the air. Ever since that day the scent of jasmine has called up my memory of San Simeon.

The steps to the Neptune Pool were two strides wide, so I descended slowly. Fountains of intricate beauty fell in stages to the pool. Decades later, in Rome, I remembered the fountains of San Simeon when I saw those of Bernini. All were marble, as was the pool itself.

I stopped in unabashed awe. It was truly an enchanted moment in an enchanted place. Across from the fountains where I descended were pillars holding up an arch with a statue of Neptune. The hillside beyond fell away to the distant sea, into which the giant orange-red sun was inexorably sliding. Its rays came through the pillars and bathed the world in a golden hue. It was so wondrous that I ached with inchoate longing as I looked at it. I turned to face Casa Grande above and behind me. The twin spires were superimposed against faintly pink clouds moving slowly across the sky. The rich reliefs and detailing blended into the towers.

The breeze moved the water, and the geometric designs at the bottom shimmered ever so slightly. I paused on the pool edge. Into memory came my moment with William Randolph Hearst, old and gaunt, sick near death. If he had done nothing else, this alone was a monument that would last as far into the future as I could imagine.

I plunged into the water. The cold shock changed my thoughts. I swam hard to warm up, finally floating on my back, which gave me a better view of Casa Grande. What Mrs. Wallis had once told me was true: this had been Mount Olympus for the twentieth century versions of gods and goddesses, the stars of the movie screen. She told me that Chaplin had loved this pool and that Greta Garbo and John Gilbert had made love in it. George Bernard Shaw had done a lap or two; Winston Churchill had floated here.

Through Neptune's fluted pillars came orange twilight glare. I swam through molten gold toward the sunset fire. I was certainly in a world removed from the swarm. I remembered the Griffith Park public swimming pool where the children of the city were packed like a school of tuna. I much preferred this.

I heard Louise calling me: "Eddie! Eddie!" She was coming down the wide steps to the poolside. I swam across and grabbed the edge. Her face was somber. "Marion just called. Mr. Hearst died an hour after I talked to her. I think we'd better leave."

I hoisted myself from the water, and we walked up to the esplanade. "She said the family took his body away that quick." Louise snapped her fingers to illustrate. "They hate Marion, and without W.R. she doesn't have any authority here. Maybe they wouldn't say anything, but maybe they would. I don't want to be embarrassed."

I could understand, but it seemed weird, too. I thought she was too rich and powerful for such things.

Going down the long, winding road, I looked back. The canyons were deep purple and black, but atop the Enchanted Hill, Casa Grande gleamed in the last rays of the sun. The spires sparkled and flashed. The old man in the wheelchair had certainly left a great monument. What would I leave? Was there purpose? Could I make a purpose?

When we reached the highway, Louise said, "We were the last guests of the great lord and lady."

We stopped in Big Sur for dinner. She called Hal, who was on location in Missouri. He called the Fairmont Hotel in San Francisco for us and made reservations. When we arrived, they put us in the Presidential Suite. It had two bedrooms. The next morning, every newspaper had William Randolph Hearst's image on the front page. The last mogul of the Age of Moguls had died.

5

NIGHT TRAIN
TO SAN
QUENTIN

I TRADED TWO CANS OF GRASS for a '36 Plymouth four-door sedan with a ship emblem on the hood. The guy who traded me the car was the older brother of a reform school associate. It had license plates from Fulton County, Kentucky. He told me a story about the papers having been sent to Sacramento to register it in California. I believed him.

I drove the car for about a month without registration and without a driver's license. It scares me now; back then I didn't worry about it. When I went to Mrs. Wallis's, I parked a couple of blocks away and didn't tell her I had a car. Our relationship had reached the point where she had paid to have my few tattoos removed and she and Al Matthews were discussing my going to college and then to law school. All that was great, but far away. If anything is true in a young criminal's mind, it is the need for immediate satisfaction. Truly the place is here and the time is now. Delayed gratification is contrary to his nature. So though law school was great on the far horizon, for now I continued selling the gunnysacks of grass. It was going faster and faster as I got new customers—joints and cans. It was a time when pot was considered true "devil weed." A girl in Pasadena who blew marijuana smoke into a bag she put over her cat's head made the front page and *Time* magazine. She was regarded as some kind of cruel monster. Under the laws of California, marijuana was the same as heroin or cocaine; possession or sale of any amount carried an indeterminate sentence of six months to six years. A young man went to San Quentin for three seeds vacuumed from the floor mats of his automobile.

Somebody the police arrested offered as a conciliation to set up someone who was selling loose joints and called me wanting a "lid," a one-ounce Prince Albert can. Ten dollars was the standard price. I put a lid in my pocket and went out to the Plymouth.

As I pulled up to Beverly Boulevard and St. Andrew's Place for the red traffic light, a car pulled up to my left. Inside it were Hill and O'Grady, a famous team of Hollywood narcotics officers of the era. "Pull over to the curb," one of them said to me.

A car was turning right on my right. The light was red, but there was no traffic. I hit the gas, shot into the intersection, and turned left onto Beverly directly in front of the detectives. They slammed on their brakes, and I kept going. The chase was on. The detective car had no siren, so it gave me a chance.

As Beverly Boulevard neared Rossmore, the traffic light was red. Cars were lined up in all the lanes going my way. I swerved left into oncoming lanes, which were stopped across the intersection because of the light. Without hesitation, I put the accelerator down. If I could get across I figured I would get away.

An old coupe came from left to right, almost as if I were in an arcade game and it came into my sights. I hit the brakes and for a moment thought I might miss the coupe. Alas, my right front fender hit the back end of the other car, spinning it and sending me careening off to the left.

A heavy U.S. Mail truck was first in line at the red light. I hit it on an angle at the left front wheel. The collision knocked the mail truck's axle out the other side and slammed me into the steering wheel hard enough to drive my teeth through my lip. I tried to open the door, but it was jammed shut. I tried to get out the window, but the moment I moved, my knee started throbbing with an awful pain.

When I got my head and shoulders out, I was looking into the muzzle of a .38 Police Special.

I never knew how it was done, but between Mrs. Wallis and Al Matthews the district attorney was convinced not to file charges. Instead I was taken before Judge Ambrose on a probation violation. He gave me one year in the county jail and continued the probation. He thought I was still too young for San Quentin.

The sheriff's department once more sent me to the Wayside Honor Rancho. Several months later, a deputy smelled a joint I was smoking behind the barracks. He didn't get the joint, but he took me to the administration building. It was at night. The watch commander sent me to Siberia in the new maximum unit. The next day, the deputy in charge of investigations called me out. I told him that I would find out who was bringing in drugs if he let me go. He sent me back to the barracks. As soon as darkness fell again, I went over the fence. I hiked west for ten miles and hitchhiked to the Coast Highway and then back to Los Angeles.

Months later when they caught me before dawn in a car on Eleventh and Union in Pico-Union, outside where Wedo lived with his mother, the police kicked the apartment door in and found a pound or so of the marijuana left from the gunnysacks, plus several hundred dollars. They pocketed that to let me say the marijuana was mine. It got Wedo released, and I was going to San Quentin anyway. It was an obvious destiny if ever one existed.

SURE ENOUGH, JUDGE AMBROSE VACATED the probation and sentenced me to the Department of Corrections for the term prescribed by law for violation of Section 245 of the Penal Code, Assault with a Deadly Weapon (ADW) with intent to do great bodily harm. It was an indeterminate sentence of six months to ten years, although the many ex-cons in the tank, considering the cases they knew, said I would do two and a half to three years. One ex-con thought it would be less, maybe eighteen months, but wiser men said it would be more—the adult authorities were hard on ADW. Al Matthews had given up, but Mrs. Wallis wanted me to put her on my mail and visiting list. I was so blasé when the judge passed sentence that I was cleaning my fingernails and winking at the buxom Italian sisters Wedo had brought to court. He eventually married one of them and had two children; then he, too, came to San Quentin. By that time I was on parole.

Because there had been some marijuana on the arrest report, the booking deputy put me in the white drug tank, designated 11-B-1. The eleventh floor was an outside tank facing Chinatown, with the unfinished Hollywood Freeway stretching out to the left. I could see the city at night by standing on the first crossbar and peering through the small opening of the outer bars. In those days all known drug users, including potheads, were in special tanks. There was one thirteen-cell tank, 11-B-1, for white dope fiends and one twenty-two-cell tank for black dopers and two tanks, one of twenty-two cells and another smaller, for Chicanos. There was a camaraderie among the white junkies, many of whom knew each other from the streets. It was said that they were the best con men and thieves because they needed to succeed. "That Mexican selling caps don't give no credit."

Each of the thirteen cells had two bunks chained to the steel wall. Under the bottom bunk were three more mattresses, except for the first three cells. Those belonged to the tank trusties. Cell #1 had two bunks and two occupants—unless they invited a friend to move in. Cells #2 and #3 had three occupants, one of whom slept on the floor inside the cell. The men in those cells ran the tank. They distributed the food, they assigned the cells and the bunks in the cells, keeping a list of who had seniority in each cell, and they made sure that everyone lined up in ranks of three for the deputies to count as they walked along outside the bars. In the event of trouble, if someone took umbrage at what was dipped from the pot to the plate, all eight acted in unison. Not even King Kong could hope to prevail alone, and if someone started to seek allies for rebellion, word easily got to the trusties. How could it miss in a world of thirteen cells and the width of a sidewalk? The trusties would appear at the rebel's gate, with lookouts at each end of the tank and their friends ready to yell and bang the cups to hide the noisy counterrevolution stomping the crap out of an erstwhile rebel.

THE "CHAIN" TO SAN QUENTIN left on Friday afternoon. Everyone sentenced to the Department of Corrections left on the first Friday ten days after judgment. The ten-day wait was because by statute every defendant had ten days to file Notice of Appeal. I played poker while waiting for the train.

The poker game ran as long as the cell gates were open, which was all the time except before chow. The cells were closed while things were set up. They were also closed after chow while the tank was being swept and mopped. The game broke up for the night at lights out.

The money man came on Wednesday. Prisoners with money in their accounts could draw ten dollars each Wednesday. That and the three dollars a prisoner could get twice a week from a visitor was all anyone was allowed. A few dollars went far in '51, when a pack of Camels cost twenty cents, a stamped envelope cost a nickel, a small tube of Colgate cost fifteen cents, and a paperback book cost a quarter. We could buy candy bars (five cents), quarts of milk (sixteen cents), and small pies (twenty cents). The sheriff's brother-in-law owned the concession.

I was a good jailhouse poker player by then, and jailhouse poker is as tough as poker anywhere and for any amount. There was an overabundance of players on Money Day, but by the weekend the best four or five were all that remained. I was among them. I also ran a store. On Friday, I stocked up on cigarettes, candy bars, milk, and pies. The vendors didn't come on weekends— but new prisoners poured in. Their cigarettes were confiscated in the booking process downstairs. By Sunday noon I had always sold out my stock and doubled my investment. Nobody visited me or put money on my books. I had to survive by my wits if I wanted any of the amenities allowed in the Hall of Justice jail in November and December of '51. I was also trying to accumulate $100 or so to take to San Quentin.

I remember the sweaty, slightly bent Bee playing cards sliding across the gray blanket on the runway floor one particular evening. At distant tanks the "roll ups" were being called. Several names were announced, followed by: "Roll 'em up!"

My cards that evening were an ace, deuce, trey, and five—with a face card. Four cards to a wheel. If I could draw a four, I would have the best hand in lowball. A six would make it the third-best hand. A seven would make a powerhouse, and even an eight would give me a good hand.

I was hot and the cards were running my way. I raised whenever I had a good one-card draw. If I only raised when I had a pat hand, everyone would know I was pat when I raised and throw in their cards rather than risk a two-card draw.

From the tenth floor, up an open steel stairwell, came the voice: "Jones, Black, Lincoln . . . roll 'em up!" It was a tank of black prisoners. Next was the eleventh floor, A and B decks.

"Bet's on you, Bunk," someone said.

"Yeah, I was distracted by the rolls ups. I raise." I dumped the money from my shirt pocket to the blanket. I'd been catching good hands since morning.

One player behind me called the bet. He deserved watching. He had come in cold after a raise. One who was already in for his original bet also called the raise. A third player threw his hand away. "You're too hot today," he said.

"Cards to the players," said the dealer.

The player ahead of me held up two fingers.

The dealer burned off the top card and dealt two across the blanket. The player threw away his discards and gathered the new two.

I discarded the face card. "Gimme one. No more kings."

The card came across the blanket.

"I'll play these," said the man behind me.

I turned to look him over. Alarm bells were ringing. He had come in cold behind my raise, called the bet without raising, and now played pat. Was he a fool? Had he shown weakness by not raising my raise, or did he have such a powerhouse that he wanted everyone in? He had no idea that one of them would pass because I raised. Had he reraised, he would have lost anyone drawing two cards. That was how to play it if he had a pat eight or a nine. He didn't want too many drawing cards.

A big steel key banged on the front gate. "Eleven-B-One . . . roll ups. Bunker, Ebersold, Mahi, roll 'em up for the night train north!"

"That's you, Bunk," said the dealer.

"They won't go without me." I squeezed out my cards, saw the faintest hint of a curve, and knew I had a six. "On you," I said to the player ahead of me.

"Check."

It was ambush time. "Check," I said, and even made the slightest motion of throwing my hand away without further ado.

The player with the pat hand saw it, sensed weakness, and fell into the trap. "Ten dollars," he said.

The first player threw his hand away.

"Where are my roll ups?" yelled the deputy through the front gate. He was looking down the runway in front of the cells. He saw the poker game, and he knew my name. "Bunker, roll 'em up, goddamn it!"

Ignoring the deputy, I dropped three ten-dollar bills in the pot. "I raise."

The man with the pat hand turned beet red as he felt the trap close. As a poker player, I usually prefer to bet my own hand rather than play check and raise. Now and then it is good to do because it warns other players that a "check" is not tantamount to surrender.

He looked at his cards. He couldn't decide what to do.

"Bunker! *Roll it up!*" the deputy yelled.

I raised my hand and waved. "Pass or call or raise," I said, getting up on my haunches. I had to go, no matter what.

"Don't rush me, man," he said.

The tank trusty came out of the first cell and headed down the run. "Hey, Bunk, you better go. That bull is an asshole."

"I'm comin' as soon as this guy decides whether to shit or get off the pot."

Dell Ebersold and Sam Mahi were already on the tier with their personal property in hand.

My opponent wanted to exploit the situation. He squeezed his cards, as if to look at them.

"Bunker!" the deputy yelled down the tier. "You better move your ass or there won't be a card game in Eleven-B-One."

I stood up and leaned over the other cardplayer. "You either throw your cards in or call the bet . . . right now . . . or I'm . . . going to kick you in your motherfuckin' head in about two seconds. Don't try to get up."

He threw his cards away. I gobbled up the money in the pot and hurried into the cell. My cell partners had gathered the meager gear I was taking with me. I rolled the money tight, coated it in Vaseline, and stuck it up my ass. Cash money is useful in San Quentin.

Ebersold and Sam Mahi were waiting at the tank gate. I knew Ebie's younger brother from reform school, but I had met Ebie and Sam Mahi here in the county jail. I would know them both for decades to come.

The deputy unlocked the gate. "The adventure begins," Ebie said. He and his brothers were already legends in the San Fernando Valley. Although Ebie was virtually illiterate, he was one of the world's great raconteurs. His speech rhythms were fascinating. He gave me a wink and a thumbs-up. We would be friends for many years without a single disagreement. Sam Mahi also would be a friend for twenty years, but because he was a friend to everyone who had any status, the depth and strength of his loyalty were always suspect. He had no enemies, and a man without any enemies usually doesn't have any real friends either.

We three joined the stream of prisoners from all over the Hall of Justice, about two dozen riding the prison train, the weekly catch of fish en route to California's three prisons. Everyone was in the bathroom, changing into whatever civilian clothes they'd worn when arrested, had slept in for several days at the precinct, and had worn to court appearances. Most were scruffy by the time they reached the county jail. Their civilian clothes had been stored on hangers, crushed together, so they had no air. Now they also had a musty smell. Just one man looked sharp; he wore a double-breasted gray sharkskin suit. A tall and handsome light-skinned black man named Walter "Dog" Collins, he was a junkie con man to whom Ebie introduced me. I would get to know Collins better in the penitentiary. He was clean because he'd been on bail until he was sentenced.

When we were dressed, deputies checked our names off the list and chained us up in batches of six. In two groups, we were loaded onto the huge freight elevator and taken to the basement tunnel, where signs pointed to CORONER'S OFFICE and COUNTY MORGUE. A sheriff's department bus took us a short mile to Union Station, where a section of booths in the Harvey House was roped off. Hamburgers and fries had been preordered. We could choose between coffee and Coca-Cola, served by a whey-faced young lass who was nervous indeed. Nobody said a word, but eyes burned through her clothes, noses flared, and fantasies were rampant. It would be years before any of these men scented another woman.

The prison train was actually a single coach with sheer metal welded over the windows and a wire-mesh gun cage at one end. It was December and dark early. A misty rain fell when we boarded. As we did so, a deputy put leg irons on most, then released them from the six-man chain. That way they could at least make their way alone to the toilet across the aisle from the gun cage. Nobody was ever out of sight. Three, including me, had both leg irons and handcuffs. Some authority had designated us for tighter security. It made the other prisoners look at us with wary respect.

The rolling crash of steel couplings heralded a jerk—and we were under way through the night. Within seconds the coach filled with clouds of cigarette smoke as nearly everyone lit up—but after that it was more moderate.

Throughout the night the train stopped for other men sentenced to San Quentin. In Santa Barbara we added two; in San Luis Obispo it was four. I was made to sit in front of the guard in the gun cage so they could keep an eye on me. Beside me was a man named Ramsey who had been to the joint before. He seemed happy to be going back. He liked to talk about how things were there and what he would do when he got there. I pumped him for a while but quickly decided he was a phony and cut him off.

The sheet of metal outside the window had a three-inch space. When I pressed my face to the inside glass, I could see a narrow slice of landscape. It was Stygian blackness most of the time, broken without warning by a few seconds of light as we flashed through a hamlet, whistle blowing warning. *Clickety clack, clickety clack, clickety clickety clickety clack,* the steel wheels had an endless chant. For a while the tracks ran beside a highway. I realized that this was the same route I'd taken riding the freight train when I was seven years old.

The gun cage was close behind me. I could lean my head back against the mesh screen. Across from the gun cage, over my left shoulder, was the toilet. It had a partition toward the seats, but it was open on the side so the gun guard could maintain surveillance through Plexiglas. Maybe they worried that someone would flush himself onto the highway. What an escape that would be.

One thing that wasn't escaping was the stench. "Goddamn!" said a loud voice several rows away. "Somebody's dead and rotting away. Good God!"

The way it was said brought a titter of laughter. Amid the ozone of fear of the unknown ahead there was a convivial leavening.

Darkness still reigned over the Bay Area when the prison coach was unhooked from the train and put on the ferry that crossed the narrows from Richmond to San Rafael. On the other side we moved onto a bus for the last mile to the prison. It had stopped raining, although the clouds promised more and the ground was wet when we pulled up at the outer gate. Half a mile ahead was the actual prison. A giant cell house stretched off to the left along one shoreline of the peninsula. The silhouette of a huge tower offshore reminded me of something from the Middle Ages. It was #1 Gun Tower, the prison arsenal.

Outside the bus, an old black convict, in a yellow rubber raincoat and rain hat, stood beside the first gate, made of chain link on rollers. The guard in a little booth called ahead, then signaled for the black con to roll it open. As we drove by, he grinned and shook his head in mock commiseration. A good look at his face told me that he was at least seventy.

The next gate was also made of chain-link fencing, but it was topped with rolled concertina wire brown with rust. The #1 Gun Tower looked down on the bus as it made a half-circle and stopped a few feet from an older building. Several guards were waiting. The step from the bus to the ground was too far for the leg irons, so as each fish stepped into the doorway a deputy unlocked the leg irons and let them clatter to the ground. The fish walked between the prison guards into the sally port. My leg irons were removed; my handcuffs remained.

As I stepped inside, a guard was telling each man, "Watch your step." We were going through a pedestrian gate set into a vehicle-sized gate. The smaller gate had a ridge several inches high. Despite the warning, the man ahead of me tripped and nearly fell. That warned me.

Beyond the gate was a tunnel of about twenty yards' length. At the other end was a big steel door framing a smaller steel door, which had a tiny observation window. A guard sat there, looking through the small window and opening the door for authorized persons. Both gates were never opened simultaneously.

A bench was bolted along both side walls. Near the other end was an open door on the left. A sign read: RECEIVING AND RELEASE. The new arrivals were being directed through it. Inside were three rows of benches, already full except for one space. Behind me the sergeant stopped the newcomers: "We'll do it in two groups. Sit the rest out there.

"Strip down until you're butt-ass naked. If you want to send your clothes home, you have to pay for them. If you want to donate them to the Salvation Army, throw them in that laundry hamper over yonder."

Nearly everyone, including me, threw their clothes in the donation hamper. We went back to the benches, all of us buck naked, some fish white, some nut brown, some fat, some skinny, some soft, some muscular as panthers.

The sergeant took a position in front of us. "Shaddup and listen up!" he commanded. Most fell silent, but someone in the rear continued to whisper to his companion. "Shaddup back there. You might learn something if you listen."

"Hey, Sarge, I heard you give this speech five years ago."

"Hear it again." He waited until the room was silent and began: "Everybody here has already thought about escaping. As soon as you drove up, you wondered if you could find a way out.

"You might escape. Every few years we lose somebody from inside the walls. I've been here sixteen years and we've had three from inside the walls. Outside the walls, that's easy.

"Whatever way they go, we get all of them back. We only have one who's still gone. He was from Ecuador. He got away about eleven years ago.

"But let me tell you one thing: nobody gets out with a hostage. You can take me; you can take the warden. Shit, you can take the warden's daughter—"

"He ain' got no daughter," said a voice.

"*If* he had a daughter . . . *if* you take his wife . . . nobody is going to unlock the gate. No matter what, *nobody* gets out with a hostage. It's against the law to open the gate in a hostage situation. If the governor *orders* a gate open, nobody's going to open it."

At the rear of the room, a steel door opened. The speech stopped and heads turned. A skinny lieutenant with deep acne scars came in, accompanied by two correctional officers. The guards waited while the lieutenant went up front to consult with the sergeant.

"Is Bunker with this group?" asked the lieutenant.

I put up my hand. "Yessir." I had learned to say "sir" a long time since. "Come here."

Naked, embarrassed, I sidled along the aisle of other naked bodies and went up front.

The lieutenant was disconcerted. "You're Bunker?" he asked, a note of incredulity in his voice.

"Yessir."

"You know Cap'n Nelson?"

"Oh, yeah. From Lancaster."

"Well, he's captain here now." The lieutenant looked me up and down. I was a skinny seventeen-year-old with freckles, five-eleven, and weighed about 145 pounds. "You don't look tough," he said, almost as if thinking aloud.

"I'm not tough. Tough guys are in the grave." It was a convict observation I'd heard in the county jail—and would hear often in prison as the years went by.

"You're not going to be a troublemaker, are you?"

"No, sir."

"This ain't a kiddie school. This is San Quentin."

"I know, sir." My military school training was occasionally useful.

"Go sit down. Stay out of trouble."

As I walked back, my peach-fuzzed cheeks were red. I tried to look hard. I made my eyes appear mean to the naked men watching me but avoiding my gaze. Had anyone looked me in the eye, I would have forthwith asked him what he was looking at. If the reply struck me wrong, I would ask if he wanted trouble. If I disliked the ensuing answer, I would Sunday-punch him. Maybe he'd go down, maybe not, but either way my arrival in the penitentiary would be noted. I'd been taking courses in prison survival since my first trip to juvenile hall at ten. Although men in prison might respect wit and intelligence, the violent had the power. If seeking help from the authorities was a mortal sin no matter what, it followed that each man—often with the help of friends—had to protect himself and make his own space in the Hobbesian world behind the walls. Stripped away were facades of class, family, money, clothes. There was no legal redress for injury or insult.

When the lieutenant was gone, a convict dragged a laundry hamper into the middle of the floor. It was filled with rolled-up white jumpsuits, one size fits all, pockets sewn so nothing could go in them—plus pairs of socks and cloth slippers.

While we were still getting dressed, inmate clerks began taking our fingerprints, rolling each digit across a card, then the thumb flat and four fingers flat. Each new inmate had four cards: FBI, Sacramento, Department of Corrections, and the prison itself. It took a long time. As the fingerprints were finished, we were photographed front and profile, with a sign. CALIF. DEPT. OF CORRECTIONS, with the date and name and number. Mine was forevermore A20284. The man ahead of me was A20283 and the one behind me A20285. It was a brand as a matter of chance. Every memo in my prison life would be labeled "A20284 Bunker." Eventually it would be on a *Harper's* cover, but that was decades away from the rainy morning when A20284 became my primary name.

I'd just finished with the mug photo when the same lieutenant with the same two guards appeared. He carried a sheet of white paper, a form of some kind. Later I would recognize it as a lockup order. I sensed his purpose now, so I wasn't surprised when he spotted me and said something to the guards and all three headed toward me.

On the way out, the lieutenant was almost apologetic: "I wasn't going to lock you up. This came from the captain himself. He's locking you up until he can talk to you."

They walked me from Receiving and Release through the tunnel and out the inner door to the world of San Quentin. My first vision stopped me cold. At my feet was a formal garden about an acre square. It was crisscrossed with walking paths. Even in bleak December it was impressive. If some of it was winter barren, other places had bright red chrysanthemums and a carpet of yellow and black pansies. I remembered being told about it: *the Garden Beautiful,* they called it.

Facing the garden on the right was a huge Victorian mansion. Once it must have housed the warden, now it was the Custody Office. A porch ran along its front with two doors and a teller's window where passes were issued.

We didn't cross the garden. We went left along the base of the building we'd just exited. It served as a wall with a catwalk running along its face. A guard with a carbine walked along above us, looking down to give cover if necessary. The catwalk led to others throughout the prison. It was designed so men with rifles could disperse to almost anywhere inside the walls without coming down to the ground.

Across the garden from the mansion was a hundred-year-old cell house. The roof was of corrugated sheet metal. The second and third floors had wooden slat walkways, a tiny space between each. The heavy solid-steel doors had observation slits at eye-level. The cell doors fastened with huge steel straps on hinges and swung over hasps so a huge padlock that hung on a chain could be snapped shut.

Reaching the walkways necessitated going around the vintage building. It was called the Old Spanish Block. There was a fence topped with barbed wire. A grizzled sergeant opened the gate and took the paper from the lieutenant. "He's been searched?"

"Yeah. He just got off the train."

"You're startin' quick, boy," the sergeant said, peering at me down a cigar clenched in his teeth. "C'mon."

He unlocked a gate to some stairs leading to the walkways around the building. He led the way, I came next, and the lieutenant followed. The two guards waited below. On the second tier the sergeant walked around to the side facing the garden and the mansion beyond. The solid-steel doors had observation slits at eye-level. Someone inside could stick out four fingers, nothing more. Eyes peered from one or two. As we passed one, a voice called, "Hey, Sarge, lemme see you for a minute!"

"On the way back," the sergeant said.

At the last cell the sergeant produced a big key that fit a big padlock. He removed the padlock and peeled off the steel strap. Using another key, he opened the steel door.

The entrance was a round arch about three feet thick and made of brick. Later I would learn that the brick and mortar were both rotting. A diligent convict with a spoon could dig himself out, or at least into the next cell, which is what two lovers would do.

"Step in," the sergeant said.

I entered and the steel door slammed into the steel frame, cutting off all light except the sliver that came through the observation slot. The lieutenant's eyes blotted out that as he looked in. "You've got two buckets in there," he said. "One's got drinking water; the other is to shit and piss in. I don't think you'll mix them up. They'll bring you some bedding after count. Take it easy."

Their footsteps sounded as they moved away. I stood at the door, my eyes adjusting to the near-total darkness. I could see the shape of the sagging U.S. Army cot, circa 1917, with a thin mattress that sagged with it. The cell block was built before the advent of electricity, so the meager wiring came through a conduit along the ceiling. Wires dangled and held a bare forty-watt lightbulb.

It went on when I screwed it tighter. Its glow was meager; then again, there was little to see. The old cot had missing springs along the side, so when I stretched out that side gave way. I dragged the mattress onto the floor. They would see me easily enough when they looked through the slot. Sleeping on the bunk was out of the question.

Against the back wall was a bucket with a folded newspaper on top. I lifted the newspaper and immediately put it back on the bucket. The *other* can was the drinking water. It was a gallon can, on top of which was a book with the cover torn off. The can held a couple pints of water, the book was Ayn Rand's *The Fountainhead*. Otherwise the cell was empty. Hearing something outside, I went to the slot and peered out. The batch of fish with whom I'd arrived was moving in a cluster through the garden. They disappeared from view. Across the way, I could see blue-clad convicts going onto the porch of the mansion and up to the window that reminded me of a bank teller's. It was, I would learn, the Pass Window. If someone had a visit, he got his pass at that window. If he had a medical lay-in, it was issued by the Pass Window. They circled the garden to get there. Only free personnel and convicts under escort used the pathways through the garden. Some went from the window to the sally port gate, while others came back and moved out of sight. Some wore bright yellow rubber raincoats; others had on long-billed convict hats and turned up their collars. Some passed nearby and yelled up to someone in a cell near mine. If they tried to loiter, the gun guard over the sally port gate chased them away.

A steam whistle blasted. It was a signal that made both convicts and guards quicken their pace. The steam whistle signaled the main count lockup. Within a couple of minutes, no convicts were visible. It was time to lie down and read. Thank God someone had left a book, one I'd heard mentioned in the county jail. The first page was gone, but that was a minor obstacle. Within a minute I was enmeshed in the tale of Howard Roark, architect of genius and integrity who stood unbending and alone with the pack of mediocrities nipping at his heels, hating him because he would not compromise his ideals. Even more than Howard Roark, I was enchanted by the newspaper publisher who had fought his way to wealth and power and had a penthouse with glass roof and walls, so when he opened the drapes he could make love under the stars and above the metropolis. I quickly realized that this was different from any other book I'd read, and it had me mesmerized and turning pages. I realized on my own, without ever having heard of literary criticism, that the characters weren't supposed to be real people. They all represented ideas of some kind: the individual idealist, the altruist who wished to destroy the individual who dared to stand alone without obeisance to the swarm.

A key in the lock made me slip the book under the mattress. Maybe reading was forbidden in here, I thought. A guard held the door open, and a convict appeared carrying a stainless-steel tray. He stopped in the doorway, and I took it from him, standard institution fare consisting of watery spaghetti, overcooked string beans, three pieces of bread with white margarine (the law forbid margarine makers from yellowing it to resemble butter), a dessert of tapioca de San Quentin, and a stainless-steel cup of weak coffee—made weaker by the inmate cooks who stole and sold it. It was edible but far from appetizing. "Oh well," as some ex-con said, "they treated me better than I would have treated them." I ate everything but the string beans. They were canned string beans boiled to death.

Outside on the tier, a heavy key banged on a pipe and a voice bellowed, "Count time on Two!"

Time to stand up where I'd be easy to see. A shadow appeared. "Let's see a hand," said a voice. I put my fingers to the wrist through the slot. Two guards went by, each counting to himself. At the end they compared figures. If both were the same, the count was phoned to Control. The calls came from cell houses, condemned row, the hospital, and the ranch. When each unit was right and the total was right, a steam whistle blew the all clear.

I happened to be peering out of the slot. Within a minute of the all clear, a torrent of guards began streaming through the Garden Beautiful toward the pedestrian sally port. It was the day shift going off duty.

I went back to *The Fountainhead,* the heroic architect, the cynical publisher, the woman columnist who had married the publisher and loved the architect. Much of my childhood and youth had been spent like this, locked in a cell with a book. Far more than most, what I thought about the world was the imprint of what I read, filling the void usually reserved for family and community.

A key turned in the lock. Two guards passed in two gray blankets and a pillowcase carrying a fish kit. It had several items: a toothbrush, a tiny brown paper bag with tooth powder, a three-piece safety razor, and two Gillette *thin* blades. There was a sharpened pencil stub (actually a pencil cut in half), two sheets of lined paper, and two stamped envelopes. There was a booklet: *Dept. of Corrections, Rules and Regulations.* There was a form: *"Application for Mail & Visiting."* We were allowed ten names, excluding attorneys of record.

Whom should I put on the list? Mrs. Hal Wallis for sure. Not Al Matthews. He had given up. Yes for Dr. Frym. He knew San Quentin's chief psychiatrist—and wherever I went they wanted psychiatric reports. My Aunt Eva, yes. My only contact with my father, she would tell me how he was getting along. Thinking about my father in the dreary rest home stung my eyes. At least he wouldn't know where I was. What about my mother? Should I put her on my list? She might send a few dollars and that could make life easier in San Quentin, but the sad, simple truth was that I had no affection for her. The State of California had raised me. She had another husband and another child, she had a decent, if dull, life. I was a leftover from her youth. The bottom line was being unable to forgive her for telling a Juvenile Court judge that she could not control me. That ended the last vestige of affection. I scarcely knew her, and this was the time to end the charade of mother and son. She would be better off, too. I left her name off the application. Some months later the Protestant chaplain called me in and said she had written the warden, who had referred the matter to him. I told him that I didn't want anything to do with her. When he tried to convince me otherwise, I told him to mind his own business.

Was there anyone else? No. Voices summoned me to the slot. Down below, the misty raindrops were caught in powerful floodlights. Convicts with collars turned up and books under their arms trudged in lines with their heads down against the wind, no doubt coming from night school. The last time I'd gone to school, I was ten years old. In reform school we were supposed to go to school for half a day, but I was always in lockup for one thing or another, fighting another kid or the Man. I couldn't do that here. The walls had eaten tougher men than me. Nobody was going to send me to Broadway because I was too much trouble. *Nobody* was that tough. Without anyone telling me, I knew that anyone too tough to handle would simply be killed, one way or another. This was no kiddie playpen like the other places I'd been. This was San Quentin. The question was: how different could I be? We don't really choose what we are except within a certain range. Yet looking through the narrow slot at the rain falling through the floodlights onto the prison, I did make one vow: I would feed my hunger for knowledge. I would make this time serve me while I served it.

I was still reading when I heard the lament of a trumpet blowing "Taps" somewhere nearby. For a moment I thought it was a dream or delusion, but it was real, the long, sad notes blowing across San Quentin prison. A minute later the cell light was turned off from somewhere else.

Later, a flashlight beam in my eyes awakened me. A guard was taking count. When he was gone, I was still lying on the floor, looking up through the narrow slot. I could see an inch of night sky and a single glittering star. It was hypnotic. I remembered a book from reform school: *The Star Rover*, by Jack London, the tale of a man in a San Quentin cell like this, perhaps the very same cell that I occupied. He was put in a straitjacket, this man of awesome, unyielding willpower. He would fix his mind on a star and somehow project himself through space and time and live other lives. Was it real or only in his mind? I couldn't remember which, or if which had been clarified. It didn't seem to matter for the theme of the tale, which was that he could escape his torment through the use of his mind.

Thinking of *The Star Rover* excited me. Knowing history let anyone see more of life. How could we know where we were if we didn't know where we'd been before? Now I was in the Big House, as they called it in the movies. How long would I be here? Up to ten years was what the statute said, six months to ten years, a truly indeterminate sentence. The idea of the maximum was un-thinkable, but the difference between three, four, five, and even six years was a lot of indeterminate time. Convicts knew the average usually served before parole, but I was never average in the judgement of the authorities. Then, too, would I survive? Men died in prison, especially those who were magnets for trouble. If past is prologue, I belonged in the magnet category. Fear was in my belly and resolve in my heart when I finally fell asleep that rainy first night in San Quentin, A20284 BUNKER, E. H.

THE HEAVY THUNK OF THE TURNING KEY brought me simultaneously awake and on my feet. One inmate filled the door. "The tray," he said, extending a hand.

I grabbed the preceding evening's tray and handed it to him. He backed out and another inmate handed me another tray. Breakfast was cold grits and a cold fried egg. Actually, it was burned crisp brown on the bottom while raw on the top, so saying it was cooked might be in error. I mixed the runny part with the grits and folded the burned part in a piece of bread and washed the whole mess down with weak lukewarm coffee.

It was still too early for much activity around the Garden Beautiful and the Captain's Porch in the old mansion across the way. I went back to Ayn Rand. Howard Roark had blown up his own buildings because his plans had been changed. Although I was in his corner, I thought he overreacted just a little.

Steel doors were being opened down the tier, the sound growing louder as they worked closer. Mine finally opened. A guard stood there. "Wanna empty that shit bucket and get some water?"

"Sure do, boss." Experts had taught me how to "buck dance" for the Man.

Grabbing the water can in one hand and the shit bucket in the other, turning my head away from the latter, I stepped out of the cell onto the walkway. The post-rain morning was sunlight bright; it made me turn my eyes aside. Below me and off to the left I could see several convicts loitering while trying not to attract attention. They strolled in one direction for fifteen or twenty feet, then turned and went the other way, trying to blend into the stream of convicts going and coming. Standing still would more swiftly attract the eye of the gun guard on the catwalk over the pedestrian sally port. The cons were trying to surreptitiously talk to someone off to my right.

A figure was coming from each cell, and each carried the water can and the shit bucket. I had to pause while a convict swept the trash from his cell onto the walkway, where most of it fell through the slats to the ground below. His shirt was off and his muscular body was marked with blue tattoos. When he turned his head, I saw plucked eyebrows, eye shadow, and red lips. His jeans were absurdly tight. He was a screaming faggot who looked like a linebacker. He stepped into his cell to let me go by. That was when I smiled to myself.

From another cell stepped a petite Chicano, doe-eyed pretty and swishy as a model. Then I saw two more female parodies, shirttails tied at the waist.

I was momentarily weak, as if punched in the stomach. Capt. L. S. (Red) Nelson had taken revenge for my pulling off his gas mask and belting him in the chops. He'd put me on Queens' Row.

The weakness was inundated by blinding rage. "Bullshit!" I screamed, swinging the shit bucket in a wide arc. It slammed into the wall and splattered several sissies with shit and piss. They screamed and bolted down the tier toward the rear. One or two jumped into their cells and closed the door. The loitering convicts below stopped pacing and simply stared.

"I ain't no punk!" I yelled. To be so labeled was to forfeit all standing. It was to be an object without manhood. Only child molesters and stool pigeons had less standing in the prison hierarchy. It was terrible! It was untrue!

I heard the *click-clack* sound of a cartridge being levered into a rifle's firing chamber. The gun rail guard had moved along the walkway. It was about fifty yards. On the ground next to the garden, a crowd of convicts was quickly growing. Except for me, the tier was empty, although one sissy down the way was peeking around the corner of his doorway.

A guard appeared at the end of the tier. He stopped a safe distance away. "What's going on?"

"Hey, I'm not no fuckin' punk, man!"

"Who said you're a punk?"

A second guard appeared on the gun rail.

"Shoot! Goddamn it! Go ahead and shoot! I ain't staying here."

A sergeant came around the end of the tier. He had a big white mustache and the face of experience. He moved toward me, slowly, carefully maintaining enough distance to avoid a swing of the bucket. Before I could move into range, the two gun rail guards would add some lead to my body weight.

"Take it easy, kid. Nobody says you're a punk."

"I'm here . . . with the punks. I'm not stayin' here. You gotta kill me first."

"We can do that," said another voice. A lieutenant in a creased uniform had come around the other way. He was closer, but he was at an open door, ready to duck inside if I swung. He had a gas billy in hand. "Now put that bucket down and get in your cell."

"So all of you can dance on me."

"Nobody's gonna do that."

From below the voices yelled: "Don't do it!"; "Don't believe 'em!"; and so forth.

"I'm no fruiter . . . no faggot . . . no punk . . . and I'm not fuckin' stayin' here. I don't give a fuck what you do."

"Ho-hold it. You've got it wrong. Those first two cells, they're not Queens' Row. They're holding cells."

The sergeant, too, had moved closer from the other direction but still maintained a safe distance. "You're on holding cell status until you see the cap'n."

As I looked at the sergeant, the lieutenant came on fast tiptoe. "Look out!" yelled the convicts below.

I turned to face the lieutenant just as he extended his arm and fired the tear gas directly into my face. The explosive charge was a shotgun cartridge, but instead of shot there was tear gas. It instantly blinded me. The force drove my head into the wall.

They were on me instantly, a fist in the gut, a towel around the neck. The towel was twisted. It cut off the blood to my brain, and within a few seconds I sank into black unconsciousness. Such choke holds can kill very quickly if the pressure is maintained, but if it is released, the blood flows back and consciousness returns.

The cell door was closing behind me as I revived. I wanted to cry, but my eyes were already on fire. I'd eaten tear gas before, but that didn't make it any easier. At least it had happened outside the cell. If it had been inside, for days afterward the particles of gas would stir up whenever I moved. I knew from experience that it was best to lie down and let it settle, which is exactly what I did.

It still burned but was bearable an hour later when a key banged on the door and eyes appeared at the slot. "Cap'n wants to see you. Don't give us trouble when we open the door."

The key turned, the door opened, and I got up, my eyes burning more as my movements stirred up the particles.

In a tight group, three guards and me, we went down the rear stairs, through the gate, and across the garden to the porch. One door was marked: CAPTAIN'S OFFICE, and one next to it said: ASSOCIATE WARDEN, CUSTODY.

The lieutenant motioned me to wait as he went inside. His name, I would learn, was Carl Hocker. He was called the Hawk and was already a legend in San Quentin. As the yard lieutenant he had more power than other lieutenants. He would eventually become the warden of the Nevada State Prison at Carson City, the only American prison with sanctioned gambling.

One of the guards watching me told the other, "Here comes the warden."

True enough, along the walkway to the porch came a man in a business suit. The gun rail guard trailed along above him. He nodded at the guards, and they said, "Good morning, Warden." He glanced at me and went through the door into the Captain's Office.

"This is the first time I've seen him inside the walls," one guard said.

"He was inside a month ago."

"Yeah . . . when the governor was making a tour."

It was true, as I would learn, that wardens almost never enter the walls of the prison they supervise. Associate wardens, the captain, and his lieutenants run the world within the walls. The San Quentin warden deals with Sacramento and the Department of Corrections bureaucracy.

A minute later Lieutenant Hocker opened the door and beckoned me.

Captain Nelson was behind the desk. Warden Harley O. Teets was seated to the side, while Lieutenant Hocker stayed a little behind me to the side, where he could jump me if I tried anything.

"Here he is," Red Nelson said to Warden Teets. "One day . . . not even one day . . . and he's causing trouble."

"Wh-wh-why'd you put me with the queens? I thought you were trying to put a fag jacket on me."

Nelson "tsk-tsked" and shook his head. "You blew your top before you knew anything. I put you there until I could talk to you."

"You didn't tell me that."

"I don't have to tell you a goddamned thing . . . convict!"

"That's right. You don't have to. But if you don't, how do I know what you're doing? How would you feel?"

Behind me, Hocker laughed, and even Warden Teets put a hand over his mouth to hide a grin.

Red Nelson was always conscious of his image. He wanted everyone to know that he was a hard man—but a fair man, too. "Don't run your mouth," he said. "Just listen for a minute."

I nodded.

"I'd be justified in locking you up in segregation for a year or two for this incident. We should send reports to Sacramento over the tear gas. It was almost a serious incident. With your background, nobody would question it. I'm not going to . . . not this time. Warden Teets and I have talked it over. We're going to give you this one break. I'm going to put you in the yard with a clean slate. The first time you cause trouble, you'll rot in the hole. Got it?"

I nodded. "I got it." I felt good. I was going to general population. I also felt fear, for San Quentin's general population—*on the yard,* it was called—was an unknown terrain fraught with dangerous men.

Red Nelson looked to Warden Teets. "Let's classify him maximum custody right now."

"Sounds good," the warden said; then he looked at me. "You're just a kid. You can straighten up your life if you want. If you don't, if you give us trouble, we can handle you; I guarantee it. Nobody is too tough for San Quentin—"

"Nobody we've met," Lieutenant Hocker added.

Red Nelson wrote something on a form and signed it. He held it out and Lieutenant Hocker took it. "I'll let him out after work call."

"Good enough," Red Nelson said.

Lieutenant Hocker crooked a finger. "Let's go."

I followed him out onto the porch overlooking the Garden Beautiful. In an hour I would be on the Big Yard. Thus did I enter San Quentin, the youngest convict there at the time.

I SURVIVED MY LATE TEENAGE YEARS in San Quentin. Joseph
Welch squelched Joe McCarthy (such matters were unnoticed in the prison
universe) and Willie Mays made the miracle catch on Vic Wertz's towering
drive to the deepest part of the Polo Grounds (that did get attention, for betting
on baseball was a big thing at the time), and when I crossed the Big Yard many
convicts said hello or nodded or otherwise gave recognition.

I lived two lives, one in the cell from 4:30 P.M. to 8:00 A.M., the other in the
Big Yard and elsewhere behind the walls. In those days convicts had the run of
the inside of the prison. Each morning when the cell gate opened, I sallied
forth to find adventure. Just before I arrived, the jute mill had burned to the
ground, leaving the prison short of jobs. I was one of three hundred who were
unassigned. Being without a job was virtually a waiver of parole consideration,
but I'd been in too much trouble to get a parole even if I worked seven days a
week in three jobs. The parole board had a written policy of not even considering parole if the inmate had had any disciplinary infraction within six
months. In '54, I had just gotten out of segregation for a brawl in which my jaw
was sliced from temple to lip (goddamn it bled copiously), so I had no imminent chance for parole.

I gambled on all sporting events, except the horses. The tote board is too
hard to beat, and who knows what a horse will do or what the trainer will want
him to do in a particular race? No, no, not the horses. I bet boxing matches (the
easiest except when two black heavyweights were involved), college and professional football, and major-league baseball (the hardest), and sometimes a
Pacific Coast League game if it was being broadcast and I needed something
to listen to on the earphones in the cell. By '54 I had gone through being
a bully and a tough guy. Bullies and tough guys have high mortality rates:

sometimes they can scare the wrong person. My friends were numerous, in a variety of *tips*, as they were then called. Now they would be called *sets*. Most of the troublemakers and tough guys were friends of mine, but by '54 I was drifting away from them toward the real professional thieves and confidence men. They got respect but avoided trouble mostly by staying within their group. They had the good prison jobs with various fringe benefits. Paul Allen, for example, was assigned to the kitchen—but he was the death row cook. The condemned, who were far fewer and more quickly executed back then, were fed far better than the mainline convicts, or at least far greater care was taken with the preparation. The death row cook, as a fringe benefit, was allowed to make steak and egg sandwiches for friends or for sale. Another buddy worked in the laundry, so he provided *bonaroo* clothes, jeans and shirts starched and pressed. Best of all was the Dental Office. Back then, convicts did the teeth cleaning and simple fillings. Extractions were by the dentist. Jimmy Posten, a baby-faced safecracker, was the chief dentist's assistant. Jimmy ran his own dental practice during the lunch hour. Using the gold salvaged from extractions, he took impressions for bridgework and crowns, treatments not provided by the institution. He accumulated hundreds of cartons of cigarettes and a considerable cache of U.S. currency, which was contraband. I would visit him at work a couple times a week. Once I arrived as he was splitting up a pound of marijuana. By the late sixties nearly all prisons were flooded with all varieties of drugs and it was even possible to maintain a "habit" while doing time, but back in the early fifties real drugs were rare. Getting high was limited to home brew, nutmeg (it will get you high about three hours after you take a spoonful), and Wyamine inhalers, which had some kind of amphetamine mixture, items a guard could purchase and carry in his lunch box. A Wyamine inhaler cost fifty-nine cents at Thrifty and sold for five dollars on the yard. It was a rare coup to get a pound of weed. I felt a member of the elite when Jimmy put a bag aside for me.

By '54 I had retired from my brief boxing career, three wins and three losses in six bouts through late '52 and '53. I maintained a locker box with hand wraps, mouthpiece, and boxing shoes, and I frequently went to the gym during the day to work out or visit friends assigned to the gym, which covered the long top floor of the Old Industrial Building and was divided into sections: boxing, weight lifting, wrestling, plus a handball court and a room with a couple of Ping-Pong tables and TV sets. Each section had a private office, a spot, as it was called, for the two or three convicts assigned to it.

The boxing room had the look and smell of all boxing gyms—a mix of blood, sweat, and leather. Posters of Bay Area fights and tall mirrors for shadowboxing were on the walls. Activity was regulated by the boxing cycle of three minutes work, one minute rest. A timer automatically rang a bell on that sequence. When it started, speed bags rattled like machine guns and the heavy punching bags thudded loudly and jumped on their chains. Fighters grunted and exhaled as they threw a punch. It automatically tightened stomach muscles at the moment of their greatest vulnerability: when their arm was extended away from their body.

There were two boxing rings, one for shadowboxing and teaching, the other for actual boxing or sparring with another fighter. When the bell rang again, everything stopped. The fighters replenished their wind, and the trainers admonished and instructed.

A convict ran the boxing department, issuing the training gear and deciding who would fight on the various boxing cards held several times a year. The convict with that job had to be both diplomatic and tough.

If the gym was boring, I might visit the barbershop, which was then in Shiv Alley. It had about twenty-five barber chairs, five for blacks. Two friends of mine, Don "Saso" Anderson and "Ma" Barker, had a chair in the corner. When they got out, they robbed a bank in Reno and Saso accidentally shot Ma in the chest. For hours they drove through the woods. Ma refused to see a doctor and died.

At 4:00 P.M., the Big Yard filled as convicts trudged up the worn concrete stairs from industries, the furniture factory, and Navy Cleaning Plant. When four thousand voices were caught in the canyon formed by the immense cell houses, they made a roar like the sea.

When the whistles blew, lines were formed outside each cell house. To indicate that someone was or had been a close friend, the common phrase was: "I lined up with him." Blacks were segregated in the lineup and mess halls. I had many friendships and was welcomed in several tips, including that of Joe Morgan, who had been transferred from Folsom while awaiting release on parole. Two decades later he would be the *caudillo* of the Mexican Mafia, but even in '54 he was a legend. It added to my status that his entourage saved a place in line for me. Of all the men I would meet in the next two decades, Joe Morgan was the toughest by far. When I say "the toughest," I do not necessarily mean he could beat up anyone in a fight. Joe only had one leg below the knee. The other had been shot off by the LAPD in East Los Angeles when he was eighteen. He was still pretty good with his fists, but his true toughness was inside his heart and brain. No matter what happened, Joe took it without a whimper and frequently managed to laugh. I will talk of him more later.

When all the lines had filed inside, the Big Yard was empty, and the cell house tiers were packed, the lockup bell sounded. The security bars were raised, and everyone pulled a cell gate open, stepped inside, and closed it. In an instant the tiers were cleared of convicts and the security bars dropped down.

Along each tier walked two guards, each using a hand counter—*click click, click click, click, click click*—and at the end they compared their count and called out to a sergeant on the cell house phone: "D Section, first tier, forty-six; second tier, forty-nine; third tier, fifty-one . . ."

The sergeant called the count to the control room sergeant, who had a wall-sized board with tags in slots for every cell, every hospital bed, and even the morgue, for if someone died, the body was counted until taken away. The count was phoned to Sacramento, the final tally keeper of how many men were in San Quentin. Unless there was a problem, the whole process, from lockup to all clear, took twelve to fifteen minutes. The most common problem was for one cell house to be missing a body while another cell house had an extra. The all clear bell didn't ring until that was straightened out. If someone was really missing, it was a couple of hours before the chow unlock started. This was infrequent, although over time I saw several escapes and near-escapes from inside the walls. More common than an actual escape attempt was someone hiding out because he was afraid of someone or in debt. They were always found and put in the hole; it was a way of getting locked up without going to the Man and asking for protection, which carried permanent stigma on one's manhood.

Following the evening meal, usually a few minutes after 6:00 P.M., those on night unlocks were checked off lists: night gym, school, choir practice. The rest were locked up for the night.

I preferred the cell. If I lacked the mental powers of Jack London's *Star Rover*, I had the printed page to guide me through myriad eras and countless lives. I conquered Eastern Europe with Genghis Khan and stood with Spartans against Persians at a place called Thermopylae and, thanks to Emil Ludwig, watched Napoléon's hubris destroy the Grand Army in the snows of Russia. Bruce Catton escorted me through the American Civil War. Although I'd been a voracious reader since the age of seven, I had no discretion or sense of literary value. A book was a book until Louise Wallis ordered me a subscription of the Sunday *New York Times*. It arrived the following Thursday, so fat it barely went through the bars. It took two evenings to read, even though I skimmed most of it. The book reviews got most of my attention, and although the new books being reviewed were unavailable, reviews and columns talked about other writers and other books: Thomas Wolfe, John Dos Passos, F. Scott Fitzgerald, Faulkner, Hemingway. The library shelves did have Theodore Dreiser's *The Titan, The Genius,* and *An American Tragedy*. Of Thomas Wolfe, I first read *You Can't Go Home Again,* and the words were a prose symphony unlike anything I'd read before. Wolfe's descriptions of America, of the old Penn Station that "captured time," and the prose poem where he describes the nation from a perch on the continental divide moved me to an ache near tears.

My library day was Saturday. We were allowed to have five books checked out at one time. I tried to read all five in seven nights, so I could get five more. I was no speed-reader, but I had six hours every night and half an hour in the morning. Sometimes if I was entranced, as with *The Sea Wolf,* I came back to the cell after breakfast.

I read fiction and nonfiction. Psychology books were in great demand. It was an era when a criminal act was *prima facie* evidence of psychological abnormality. Group therapy was gathering momentum. Advanced penologists saw the ideal prison as really a hospital and wanted all terms to be from one day to life, depending on when the individual was "cured." In some cases, and I was among them, the parole board specified psychotherapy. The idea that poverty was a breeding ground for crime was never discussed. I assumed that something was wrong. Imagine turning twenty in a gray rock prison after a childhood in schools for crime. Only a true cretin would not wonder why. Was I simply bad? I'd certainly done bad things, and a few that made me feel terrible to recall, and God knows that terrible things had been done to me—in the name of society or somebody. I'd suffered beatings and torture in a state hospital. I'd had a fire hose turned on me through bars when I was thirteen and spent the night on the wet concrete, so I caught pneumonia. How many punches and kicks I'd gotten from authority figures over my brief life was beyond estimation. Had I declared the war on society, or had society declared war on me? The authorities wondered if I was crazy, and so did I. Not in the normal sense; I had no delusions or hallucinations. I satisfied the classic criterion for what was then called the criminal psychopath (now called sociopath): a person who talked sanely but behaved insanely. It was insane to take on the whole world even if the world started it. In the argot of shrinks, I had an id-permeated ego and a stunted superego, which is something like conscience, or a governor on a car that keeps it from going too fast. The literature said there was no treatment, although it was common for burnout to occur around age forty. My hope was to use intelligence to govern my impulses. I knew that some sociopaths are very successful, and I knew that smart people don't commit street crimes. Nobody had a Beverly Hills mansion from cracking safes. I vowed that I would be as smart as I could be whenever I walked out of San Quentin's walls. I would suck up all available knowledge. I planned to never commit another felony, but when Goose Goslow told me how to peel a safe open or make a device that would allow me to drill a floor safe, which is a tough safe to crack, I also sucked up that knowledge, just as I wrote down words I didn't know and later looked them up in a *Webster's Collegiate Dictionary* that Louise Wallis sent me.

She wrote me, not every week or even every month, and when she wrote it was liable to be several partial letters she had started but not finished. She jammed them in an envelope and sent them together. She wrote well, and her wisdom affected me. We could lose our misery by concern for someone else. She wrote me from on board the *Queen Mary* and from Saint-Tropez, describing the unique blue of the Mediterranean. By now I was starting my letters to her: "Dear Mom," and felt a strong filial bond. She told me that I was destined for a wonderful life and she would do everything she could to help me help myself. I had no idea what I wanted except I had both a rage to experience life and a pervasive craving for knowledge. Faust's deal would have tempted me: give me knowledge and take the soul, for knowledge was God anyway. On one occasion I avoided stabbing someone who deserved it because I had dreams for the outside that Louise Wallis had given me.

One night in '53, the spring broke the same way it had in the holding cell. Again I put the mattress on the floor. As San Quentin's cells were only four and one-half feet wide and eleven feet long, lying on the mattress up against the cell gate certainly left me visible to passing guards. In fact, my pillow was resting against the bars. I wore my earphones, listening to a soft music program sponsored by American Airlines. It blotted out the coughs and curses and flushing toilets, the rude noise of a dark cell house.

The next thing I knew, a bull, as all guards were called, was shaking me through the bars. Flashlights were playing on me. Two guards were on the tier, one with a clipboard, which meant they were checking cell by cell, that they had counted and recounted and were now looking for where the body was missing.

They were angry, accusing me of obstructing the count. I tried to show them the broken bed. It made no impression. I finally told them I didn't want to hear "Socratic dialogues or the orations of Cicero."

They departed and I went back to sleep.

In the morning, fastened within the clothespin attached to the bars for such things, was a pass typed in red: "Disciplinary Court, 8:00 A.M." After breakfast, I reported to the Custody Office, where a few others were awaiting disciplinary court. Usually it was the captain or the associate warden, but this morning it was the second watch lieutenant, A. J. Campbell. He had the blotchy red face and blue nose of an alcoholic and was known for both his vitriolic temper and his fear of convicts. He had never been seen on the yard. Campbell was in a really bad mood this morning. I was charged with messing up the count and using profanity to the officer who had tried to counsel me. I pleaded not guilty, explained about the bedspring, and repeated my statement about Socrates and Cicero. I was surprised that I'd been written up. At the very worst, I thought I might get thirty days' loss of privileges. Instead, Campbell said he was referring the matter to the full disciplinary committee and putting me in isolation.

Isolation! The shelf. Indignation welled up, and when he looked up and sneered and said something about Cicero, my indignation overwhelmed my good sense. I grabbed the edge of the desk and lifted. It began to tilt; drawers ran out onto the floor. He began to yell for help. One more heave and over it went. He managed to slide back and jump up, but he was screaming in fear. *"Help! Help!"*

The escort guard leaped on my back with a choke hold. Other guards came from everywhere. Oh God! What had I done?

The journey to isolation was across the Big Yard, through steel doors across the North Cell House rotunda, through another gate of heavy mesh and a steel door into another rotunda. To the right was the green steel door to the overnight condemned cells, where those being executed in the morning were taken the night before. To the left was the elevator to isolation and death row.

I expected the elevator to stop between floors for an ass kicking. It was standard procedure following an assault on a guard. None was forthcoming. The three guards with me thought what I'd done was funny.

When the elevator stopped, we stepped onto a landing outside another mesh gate and a steel door. The mesh gate could only be unlocked from the outside, the steel door from the inside. A face appeared at an observation window, followed by the door opening. "Ah, Bunker, you haven't been here in a few months," said Officer Zeke Zekonis, nicknamed Dipper Shaker from the way he leveled the ladle when passing out food.

The escort guards waited while I danced through the routine of stripping naked for a search. We were in the front service area. Through a set of bars covered with wire I could look down death row. Some of the doomed men, fat from too much food, pale from too little sun, were outside their cells. I recognized two of them, Caryl Chessman and Bob Wells. Neither had been sentenced to die for murder, although Bob Wells had killed a man in a prison knife fight. He was a prison legend long before I went to juvenile hall. *The San Francisco Chronicle* had run a feature article saying he was the toughest man in San Quentin. He was sentenced to die for slugging a guard with a spittoon and knocking out his eye. Wells was sentenced under Section 4500 of the California Penal Code. The jury had no idea that once they found him guilty of the assault, the death sentence was mandatory. Bob had been on death row for several years. Walter Winchell had come to his aid "coast to coast and all the ships at sea . . ."

Chessman I knew vaguely from my previous sojourn in isolation.

They were pacing the range outside the cells. As they got close to the front, Chessman recognized me and stopped. "Hey, Bunker, they got you again."

"Looks like it."

"Yeah," Zekonis chimed. "He turned Campbell's desk over on him."

Bob Wells: "Say what? A. J. Campbell!" He burst into laughter and showed a gap where several teeth were missing, broken off at the gums with a club.

Chessman: "That was a *baadd* idea."

"I wasn't thinking very clearly."

"I guess not."

"Knock it off, Bunker," admonished an escort. He said nothing to the men behind the mesh screen and bars. What could he say to men awaiting a trip to the gas chamber?

Wearing white undershorts, I was escorted down the other tier, passing cells where men looked out, a couple of them nodding at me as I went by. Lined up on the floor next to the outer wall of bars were the folded mattresses. They were taken away at 8:00 A.M. and returned at 8:00 P.M. A year or two before I arrived, Warden Clinton Duffy had stopped the practice of making prisoners in isolation stand on *the spot,* an eighteen-inch circle painted red, from 8:00 in the morning to the afternoon count. Talk was forbidden then and still was now.

Zekonis stopped at an empty cell and turned the key, then signaled the bull up front to pull the security bar. After I dragged the mattress onto the tier, the gate closed and the security bar dropped. Here I was again. Damn!

I expected the disciplinary committee, usually chaired by the captain or associate warden, to give me twenty-nine days in isolation (all that was allowed) and assign me to segregation for six months or so. Captain Nelson and Associate Warden Walter Dunbar were in Sacramento for the day, so the business manager chaired the committee. They gave me ten days, which would put me back on the yard the following Monday. I anticipated that release very much as I would anticipate a release to society, except I had no idea when that would be.

All we were allowed in isolation was a comb, toothbrush, and a Gideon Bible, which I studied whenever I was in the hole, not in search of God but for the secular wisdom within its pages, such as: "Speaketh not to fools, for they despise knowledge." And, "It is better to live in one small corner of the attic than in a wide house with a brawling woman."

Thursday morning, Captain Nelson and Associate Warden Dunbar came along the tier. They were commuting isolation sentences. That afternoon, everyone was released except a black convict who'd been caught with a shiv—and me. I asked Zekonis what was going on. He explained: "Santo, Perkins and Barbara Graham are going to be executed tomorrow. They want Barbara downstairs in one of the overnight cells. Santo and Perkins are coming over here . . . up front."

California law required that those about to die by cyanide gas had to be moved away from the other condemned prisoners the night before the execution. Downstairs were two overnight condemned cells, side by side. The so-called last mile was more like five steps. Next to the first cell was a steel door painted San Quentin's ubiquitous green. Three feet beyond was the door into the octagonal gas chamber, also green. Barbara Graham, the junkie whore sentenced with Jack Santo and Emmett Perkins, had been transferred from California's only women's prison eight or nine months earlier. She'd been held in the prison hospital those nine months, teasing convicts through a window strip. At count time, when the prison was locked down, she was moved to one of the cells downstairs.

From up front I could hear Santo and Perkins being moved into the first two cells, the security bar going up, the resonance of steel on steel as the tier gate opened and shut, the loud *click-CLACK* as the big key turned the cell lock. Voices, a scattered word or phrase: ". . . open telephone," "all night," "attorney," "governor . . ."

The security bar dropped, the outer gate clanged shut, and the voices were more distant. I could hear the elevator faintly, and I was pretty sure no guards would hear me.

"Hey, Santo! Jack Santo!" I called. "Emmett Perkins!"

"Yeah. Who's that?"

"A convict who thinks you motherfuckers are dog shit!"

"Fuck you, asshole!" one yelled, and the other added, "Fuckin' punk."

"Tell me that tomorrow afternoon . . . ha, ha, ha. . . ." I really despised them. In addition to the murder of an old woman in Burbank, who supposedly had a stash of cash from a bookmaker son, for which all three were sentenced to die, Santo and Perkins had murdered a small-town grocer and his five children, stuffing the bodies in the trunk. The grocer had been carrying his money from Nevada City to Stockton or Sacramento. The slaughter of innocent children made me sick. I knew armed robbers who killed when someone reached for a gun or tried to jump them, and although society would judge them, I would not. That was life's first law, to survive. They paid their money and took their chances. This was a slaughter of the innocent, five children and a grocer—for perhaps two thousand dollars. Jesus. *You motherfuckers deserve to die!*" I yelled, and within seconds heard keys jangling and the squeak of crepe soles on the polished concrete. I was supine on the floor with the Gideon Bible when the guard on the gun walk looked in and kept going. He must have thought the bellow came from Santo or Perkins up front. They had more to scream about than I did. The other guy, he with the stabbing, was in one of the last three cells; they had soundproof doors about three feet in front of the cell bars. For some reason they had left me about ten or twelve cells from the front.

The gun bull came back and went around the rear. He also covered condemned row.

"Hey, convict!" Jack Santo called in a softer voice.

It had to be for me. "Yeah," I said. "Whaddya want?"

"You're a convict, huh."

"I'm not an inmate, that's for goddamn sure."

"Then why don't you do your own time?"

I looked out and saw the gun bull in front of my cell. I dared not answer. Talking would get me another five days. As if to emphasize my danger, the gun bull nodded knowingly and shook an admonishing finger. Fuck Jack Santo. Telling him what I thought wasn't worth five more days in isolation. I did, however, *think* about his admonishment to do my own time. It was the number-one rule for a convict doing time. It meant what it said: Mind your own business; worry about your own crime, your own time, your own punishment. See nothing; hear nothing, and, above all, say nothing. If Christ could not find one in a crowd of average citizens to throw a stone at a sinner, where in a universe of criminals could one be found? Let these three die by themselves. Still, they gave thieves a bad name.

A dinging bell announced the elevator, and a moment later there was the rattle of the food cart. Even with just two of us, Zekonis shook the dipper level and laughed when I shook my head. Other guards scooped up all the dipper would hold and dumped it on the paper plate. What the hell did they care how much spaghetti a convict got? I knew better than to complain.

When Zekonis handed me the plate, he said, "Chessman says hello."

"Thanks, Zeke." I'd learned that it was better to have even a mangy old dog for a friend than an enemy, a piece of convict proverb with efficacy.

I saved a cup of spaghetti and a slice of bread. It tasted better cold and late at night. On the yard, I ate meagerly, but up here with nothing else to do and meals the mark of passing time, I was hungry most of the time.

Isolation was always silent and gloomy, the light dim outside the cells, the shadows angled and sliced by vertical bars, horizontal crossbars, and grids from the wire mesh. As it got dark, by pressing my left cheek to the bars I could peer at an angle to the front of the tier. A Death Watch guard was visible, seated at a card table up against the gun walk bars. He had a telephone and a radio, coffee, and Camels. It was said that just before it was time to go, the prison doctor gave you a choice of a shot of morphine or a double shot of bourbon. I had no idea if that was true, but once when I'd seen the pharmacological safe open in the hospital there had been a sealed fifth of *I. W. Harper's.*

After the elevator arrived again, the outer gate opened and a cart wheeled in. It had the meals of two doomed men. I could hear rattling pans, and soon came the powerful odors of steak, onions, and good, strong coffee. Its rarity made it more intense. Goddamn what I'd give for steak and onions and fresh ground coffee. On the other hand, I wouldn't want to eat their meal. They might eat it, but they wouldn't get to digest and shit it before they were dead meat themselves.

How did it feel to be strapped into a chair and put to death? Nobody could answer *that,* but I did know two youths who escaped from a juvenile camp and were caught up north, perhaps in Portland, and when two rural county deputies were bringing them back, the youths somehow overpowered and killed them. Sentenced to die, they had been on the row for nearly two years before the California Supreme Court affirmed the conviction but overturned the death sentence. Rather than retry the whole case, the district attorney of the small county let the judge sentence them to life. When they were on the yard I asked one of them how it felt and what he thought. This was a time when executions happened regularly. Bobby told me, "Any time they take a guy downstairs and *top* him, you die right with him, and every night thereafter. I reached the point when I was so accepting that I wanted them to kill me rather than play more games." I could viscerally feel what he was saying.

Now I was sitting the night out with men awaiting execution. The elevator came and went; the outer doors on the tier clanged open and shut. Words were exchanged. The priest came and was chased away. The sweep hand turned slowly but inexorably, and the other hands moved with the same relentlessness. Midnight came and went.

Barbara Graham was downstairs. Al Matthews had taken her case a few weeks ago. Would he save her? Maybe. Very few women were put to death, none so far in my sojourn, although they took a man every Friday at 10:00 A.M., or at least it seemed every week. As for the deterrence of it, convicts on the yard seldom knew who was being executed or what they had done unless it was a headline case. They did know about Jack Santo, Emmett Perkins, and Barbara Graham. Ex-cons with multiple killings and a sexy broad, that got their attention. The fool who went before them had been executed for punching a child molester they put in his cell in the Fresno County Jail. The victim's head had hit the edge of the bunk. His family screamed like banshees, and poor Red didn't have a penny. The lawyer they appointed him was nicknamed Death Row Slim, so we know what his clients thought of him.

Even when the convicts didn't know who was being executed or what the person had done, they did know that someone was going. It was always at 10:00 A.M. on Friday. Gas chamber day. The red light was turned on atop the North Cell House. When everything was normal, the green light was bright against the sky.

They were late returning our mattresses. It was almost 10:00 P.M. when two guards and a sergeant pulled the security bar and unlocked the isolation cells, one at a time, so we could step out and carry our mattresses back in. As I passed the sergeant, I told him I needed some toilet paper.

"We'll bring you some at count."

Count was an hour away. I could wait that long.

The mattress was comfort manifest after fourteen hours on the concrete. I tried to read the Bible, but the archaic English of the King James era took more concentration than I could muster that night. I was left with listening to the faint sounds of the radio outside the cells of the doomed killers and to the comings and goings of officials. Once again I was alone with my thoughts, a situation I found myself in far more than the average person did. I'd seemingly spent an inordinate amount of my life meditating in a dungeon. Nearly everyone I knew had done some time or was doing it, whereas the average person had not merely never been arrested but also didn't even *know* anyone who had been in jail, much less state prison. Driving Mrs. Hal Wallis around Beverly Hills to visit her friends and take care of her business had let me peek into a world I had never previously imagined. She had come from Sixth Street and Central Avenue, as scruffy as anywhere in Los Angeles. I had personally experienced the difference between rich and poor. I conjured memory of San Simeon's Neptune Pool in burning twilight. By now I'd read *The Age of Moguls* and *Citizen Hearst* and knew that *Citizen Kane* had failed to capture the scintillating truth of William Randolph Hearst. Good God, why wasn't I dealt that hand? Still, if I looked from the view that all things are relative, which they are, my cards were better than those of most of the world. If I lacked the advantage of family wealth, at least I had the advantage of being white. I was an American, not from some impoverished banana republic. Where would it end? I had no idea. Maybe it would be awaiting the executioner's summons. If someone scared me and I believed him dangerous, I would try to strike first. I might lose my temper and ice somebody in a half-accident, like what had happened with Red. What if a crime partner went crazy and killed someone on a caper? All that shit could happen. . . .

Into the silence came the sound of the elevator. It seemed louder because there was less background noise. The outer door opened. Voices. Words indecipherable. The clank of the gate onto the tier. I looked up. Sure enough, the security bar was raised, followed in a second by a key turning a cell lock up front. One of the doomed duo was going somewhere. That would take authorization from the warden. There was the same crash and bang and whir in reverse sequence. Which one was leaving? Where to? *"I don't think he's going to get a vaccination,"* I half-muttered, then laughed loudly at my sick humor. I had a laugh that sounded like a braying jackass or a maniac. I would hear just one like it over the years: the laugh of Joe Morgan.

The gun bull came by, a shadow behind two sets of bars and the mesh wire. "What's so funny, Bunker?"

"Life. . . . Hey, who'd they take out?"

"Santo. To see his lawyer."

"I hope it's bad news."

"You're not rooting for your team?"

"Shit, he ain't on my fuckin' team. I'd throw the switch on them two."

"What about Barbara?"

"I dunno about that. She's pretty fine."

"You *have* been locked up a long time."

"Not all that long. Just over two years."

"I'd go crazy if I went two years without pussy. You mess with those toy boys?"

I shook my head. "Hell no!" It was true, but it was also a lie. One or two of the effeminate young queens really looked like pretty girls with fine asses in tight jeans. They were "she" to everyone. For all I knew, they really were women. But the one or two who might have stirred me were the property of terrible killers. Until race became the main issue for prison murder, the easiest way to get killed in San Quentin was to mess with someone's *sissy*.

Within the hour, Santo returned. As the tier gate opened and the security bar went up, I heard Emmett Perkins: "What happened?"

The reply was delayed by the sound of the cell being slammed and locked. The security bar dropped. Then I heard what I doubted for a moment: wheezing, sobbing tears. Then Emmett's voice came again, ice-cold steel: "You weak motherfucker! You better die like a man or I'm gonna spit in your face from the chair next to you."

Wow!

Then I heard a third voice, but the words were too soft to decipher. It was the Death Watch bull.

The elevator came again, and the doors and gates opened. Hearing voices down by the first cells, I pressed against the cell bars and peered down the tier as best I could. I could see shadows from figures cutting through the bright floodlight glaring into the two cages. I had given that up and was taking a leak when I heard someone behind me. I turned my head. It was Warden Teets. Damn.

"How are you getting along?" he asked. Behind him was one of his retinue. Wardens always have retinues. Nobody ever sees one alone.

". . . Bunker," one of them said, telling him who I was. He came up to the bars. By now I had given it a good shake and buttoned up my pants.

"I had a letter from Mrs. Wallis," he said. "She's going to be in San Francisco next month. She wants to visit you, but she's going to be busy during visiting hours."

I must have shrugged a certain way or grunted in a sound of defeat. If she was busy during visiting hours, the case was closed.

The warden said, "Don't give up. Maybe we can work something out."

"That sure would be great."

"Take it easy."

He went to the silent cell at the rear, and a guard opened the outer door. It was the same question. "How are you getting along?"

The answer I could not hear. Warden Teets said, "Take it easy."

A moment later they passed my cell. Teets gave a little wave. I didn't hear them go out the gate. Now I had suspicious thoughts. What did he mean about maybe we could work it out? Could he possibly mean that he and I could work it out? Was it a solicitation to be a stool pigeon?

It seemed unlikely. Obviously he meant "work it out" with *the* Mrs. Hal B. Wallis. Hollywood's star maker, they called Hal Wallis. He sure liked making those ice blond American Beauty roses. If it took putting them in a movie with Burt or Kirk, he'd do that, too.

I was so excited about the possibility of a visit, I paced back and forth and forgot the two men in the first and third cells, although on the periphery of attention I was aware that they were talking. My focus shifted when I heard the music on the radio in front of their cells. It was the slightly saccharine sound sponsored by American Airlines. It was on the earphones in the cell house because it was good to sleep by. I listened to it for its soothing qualities. But why in hell were they listening? If they liked anything, it would be Patsy Cline or Hank Williams. Both of them were country to the core. This was a puzzle I never pieced together, for I fell asleep. Thinking about it later, I decided that they were waiting for the half-hourly news bulletins. A petition for *habeas corpus* had been filed in a U.S. District Court. With the petition was a motion for a stay of execution while the court decided if the petition had merit on its face. Because the world was waiting for them to die, what the judge did would come by radio faster than the warden could walk over from his office.

I was rudely awakened by a screaming Jack Santo. "Lemme talk to the governor! I'll tell 'em about some unsolved murders—murders we didn't do. I know who iced the two Tonys! And Bugsy! I have a lot of things I want to tell somebody. I know who killed two kids in Urbana back in forty-six."

Beneath the cries, in counterpoint, were Emmett's vile curses hurled with contempt at his crime partner. Thieves fall out. This time it was surely true.

A giddiness overcame me. I felt the fool in a wild carnival. *"Toilet paper!"* I yelled at the very top of my lungs. *"Toilet paper! I gotta wipe my ass! Help! Toilet paper!"*

The first watch sergeant appeared outside my cell. "Bunker, what are you screaming about?"

I felt guilty. It was Sergeant Blair, one of the kindest human beings I ever met in my life. He had worked in San Quentin for over twenty years then and would stay nearly another twenty and write just one disciplinary report in all that time. He was not unctuous; he was no religious fanatic. He was simply a nice guy when he was young and would stay nice when he got old. "Sorry, Sarge . . . but I do need some toilet paper. Whaddya want, I should tear off my shirttail and wipe my ass with that?"

"No. I'll get some. Hold it down, would you?"

"Sure, Sarge. I'll do that." How could I do anything else? I was the only prisoner on the tier. Any disturbance had to come from me, and most guards would be less forbearing than Sergeant Blair.

During the long night of waiting, I sat leaning against the cell bars. I dozed off once or twice, only to be snapped alert by some sound down the way, a key rammed in a lock and the voice of the chaplain, which I recognized although I couldn't hear what he said. I did hear Perkins tell him, "Get the fuck outta here, you psalm-singing sonofabitch!" Although I would have gladly thrown the switch on both Santo and Perkins, I had a grudging respect for Perkins, who was facing his mortality with courage (far more than I would have shown), whereas Santos was a despicable, sniveling cur. I could hear his sobs from time to time.

Soon enough the high window outside the walkway slowly turned gray and the rising sun made the bars cast shadows across the polished concrete floor. The elevator came often as officials brought word of final denials from the courts. The morning was bright when the elevator came for the last time. I could hear many guards down the tier. The condemned men would be cuffed and put in restraints. The guards would press tight around each of them, so they could do nothing but go along. Down the elevator, through the green steel of the rotunda, through another steel door, they would walk past Barbara Graham. She was in the overnight condemned cell. On this morning it would not be a courteous "ladies first."

Good-bye, fellas, you lousy child-killing . . . Killing a threat, an enemy, for vengeance and for gain, that could at least be understood. But killing five children for no reason but for viciousness . . . good-bye and go to hell, and even Lucifer, the Great Satan, might not want you.

The beam of sunlight on the floor had moved almost to the mesh. The gun guard walking behind the mesh threw his shadow through the screen onto the concrete outside my cell. I looked up from the rich poetry in *Song of Solomon*. "They went. She got a stay," he said.

"What kind of stay?"

"I dunno. A stay of execution." He turned back and disappeared. Normally he would have continued on crepe soles all the way to the front, but this morning I was the only convict in isolation. Ah well, what the hell . . . back to *Ecclesiastes*. There is timeless wisdom. *"The words of a wise man's mouth are gracious, but the lips of a fool shall swallow him up . . ."* If you don't learn to follow that wisdom, you are fool indeed.

A COUPLE OF DAYS LATER, when I was partaking of my daily hour walking up and down, a key banged on the gate up front. I thought it was a signal to return to my cell until I saw the front gate open and the bull, big Zeke Zekonis, his hat cocked wildly to the side, standing there beckoning me. I pointed to myself, disbelieving. He nodded. I went, albeit warily. Maybe they were around the corner, wanting to stomp me good for turning the desk over on a lieutenant.

As I neared the gate, Zekonis extended a folded magazine. I wondered why. My first thought was not that he was handing it to me. Except for the good old Gideon, reading was *verboten* in the hole.

"Here," he said, erasing doubt. "Chess sent it over."

He meant Caryl Chessman. I sputtered my surprised thanks. Zeke was not known for doing favors for convicts, but he had done this one. It wasn't smuggling a gun or even drugs, but it was against the rules and could get him a suspension.

I waited until the evening meal trays were collected and the mattresses returned; then I took out the *Argosy* magazine. A men's magazine, it had several million readers. It was on the cover, the lead piece. Caryl Chessman, Los Angeles's notorious Red Light Bandit, had written a book: *Cell 2455, Death Row,* that was scheduled for publication in a few months. *Argosy* had excerpted the first chapter. I turned to it forthwith.

Although the complete book, which I would soon read, was about Chessman's life, the first chapter recounted how a convict named Red was put to death in the gas chamber. It began with the evening count the night before. The entire prison was locked down; that was when the doomed man was moved to the overnight condemned cell. First he was given all new clothes, including underwear. He was cuffed through the bars before the gate was open. Surrounded tightly by four or five guards and a lieutenant, Red was allowed to start at the rear of death row and walk to the front, saying his good-byes to the others waiting to die. His personal possessions had already been given away or packed for shipment home. They took him down the elevator and through the green door to where he spent the night.

Chessman's written words took me step-by-step to Red's death at 10:00 A.M. Red had a photograph of President Eisenhower. As he stepped into the gas chamber, he handed it to a guard and said, "He doesn't belong in here." The cyanide pellets were dipped into the sulfuric acid, and deadly cyanide gas rose around him.

I couldn't judge the writing, but it was so real to me that my heartbeat increased. Of course I had the advantage as a reader of being where I was, not far from the reality. I read I again, and although I had no training for critical judgment, it was impossible to be more astounded. A convict had written it, a convict I knew, and had it published in a huge national magazine, not the *San Quentin News*. A book was coming out soon. Writing a book took a magician, or even a wizard, or an alchemist who took experience, real or imagined, and used words to bring it to life on a printed page. I have many flaws, but envy is not among them. Yet I was afire with envy that late afternoon in the hole of San Quentin.

Dusk became darkness. The lights gained power. Zekonis came for the magazine before going off duty. If I were farther down the tier, I could talk to Chessman through the ventilator, but he was at one end on one side, and I was at the other end on the other side. I could hear him, or at least his typewriter. It rattled through the night. The only time it hadn't was when Santo and Perkins were on Death Watch.

Sounds from below marked the evening's passage; footsteps and voices echoed against the building-formed canyons. Convicts were filing back to the cell houses for the night. Soon the sound of "Taps" would waft through the prison. The shadow of the gun bull passed outside the mesh wire and steel bars. Chessman's typewriter stopped. Why was it he who had written a book? He was on death row. The book wouldn't change that. If it were me, it could change my life.

Suddenly, with the force of revelation, I said aloud, "Why *not* me?"

The idea was so sudden and intense that I jumped up from the mattress and immediately got dizzy and grabbed the bars for support.

As quickly as the thought had come, I sneered at my own hubris. How could I write anything worth publication? I was in the seventh grade the last time I attended school. Voracious reading was a different game from writing. Writers went to Harvard or Yale or Princeton.

But Chessman hadn't gone to Harvard. He'd been in Preston School of Industry, the same as me. If he could write a book, why couldn't I do it? I'd had detectives say I was like Chessman. At least I didn't have the pressure of a death sentence. I had time on my side—and desire. I would rather be a writer than movie star, president, or justice of the Supreme Court, all of which were closed to me anyway. I went to sleep thinking about it.

I woke up and it was the first thing on my mind.

▪ ▪ ▪

WHEN I GOT OFF THE SHELF, I wrote Louise. By now not only was I opening with *"Dear Mom,"* but she signed with the same word. I told her I wanted to become a writer. Would she send me a portable typewriter?

Of course she would. It was a secondhand Royal Aristocrat. The case was covered with a heavy waterproofing, and it had a key face unlike any I'd seen. It was seemingly brand-new.

A convict clerk in Education brought me a *20th Century* typing book. The lessons were page by page. At first I put a small sheet of wood on the cell toilet and sat the typewriter on a stool. I learned the keyboard. Once I had that, I threw the book away. Practice was all I needed. When the toilet bowl and stool setup became too painful for my back, a convict in the carpenter shop fabricated a table just wide enough to hold the typewriter. The passage between the side of the bunk and the other wall was less than two feet, considering that the cell's entire width was four and a half feet. Still it was better sitting on the edge of the bunk to type than bent over the toilet bowl.

Instead of simply starting with *"once upon a time,"* I sold blood to pay for a correspondence course from the University of California. This was in the brief era when society thought education was a path to rehabilitation. The first lessons were about grammar and diagramming sentences, which I never came to understand, and it showed in my grades. But when the lessons became actual writing, grades were all A's and the instructor, probably a postgraduate student, deluged me with laudatory comments. When the course was over, I set sail alone on the sea of the written word: "Once upon a time two teenage boys went to rob a liquor store . . ."

I had no creative writing course, no mentor. The only writer I'd ever met, except for Chessman, was an alcoholic newspaperman in Camarillo State Hospital. He was writing a book in the linen room where he worked. To get some sense of what I was doing, I subscribed to the *Writer's Digest*. Maybe I learned something from its many articles of "how to . . ." I bought several of the books it advertised. The most useful was by Jack Woodruff (I think that was his name), as he advised to picture the scene in your mind and simply describe what you saw.

In the library I found anthologies and books of literary criticism, from which I learned bits and pieces. W. Somerset Maugham's *A Writer's Notebook* provided me some advice. At least I remember it. If I mined one bit of advice that I could use, a book was worthwhile. At first I tried short stories, but the censor was the librarian, and the Department of Corrections had rules against writing about crimes, your own or others'. I could not offend any race or religion or criticize prison officials or police or use vulgarity—and other things. Besides, I had to sell pints of blood to obtain the postage. I had plenty of prison money (cigarettes) and even cash, but it had to be in my account. I decided to learn my craft writing novels. I would only have to deal with the censor every year or so, and I would decide what to do when I finished.

It took about eighteen months to finish the book. I felt as if I'd climbed Everest when I wrote: *"The End."* Instead of going through the censor, who would reject it and might confiscate the manuscript, a friend of mine had his boss, the dentist, carry it out. Smuggling a manuscript from prison isn't immoral. The dentist mailed it to Louise Wallis. She gave it to knowledgeable friends to read. All said I had talent. Despite moments of unreasonable hope, I knew it would never be published. I wrote it to learn my craft. I still have the manuscript. My wife says that if she had read it, she would have advised me to give it up. But it is well known that fools rush in, and so I started my second novel. I never imagined it would take seventeen years and six unpublished novels before the seventh was published. I persevered because I recognized that writing was my sole chance of creating something, of climbing from the dark pit, fulfilling the dream, and resting in the sun. And by reading this far you must have realized that perseverance is fundamental to my nature. I get up from every knockdown as long as my body will follow my will. I've won many fights because I wouldn't quit, and I have also taken some awesome beatings for not knowing when to quit.

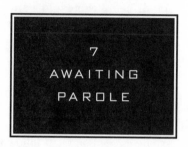

WHEN I HAD SERVED FOUR YEARS in San Quentin, Louise Wallis hired an attorney recommended by Jesse Unruh, known as "Big Daddy" in California politics. The attorney talked to people in Sacramento about getting me a parole. In four years I had been to the hole half a dozen times and I had two score disciplinary reports. It was a far worse record than most convicts', but far better than one would have expected from my history. I'd been in several altercations, but only a couple had come to the attention of the officials. Besides being sliced from temple to lip by a cell partner I'd been bullying, I was stabbed in the left lung by a queen protecting his joker. I never saw him coming. On another occasion I was suspected of having stabbed another convict. The victim refused to identify me, so the captain let me out of the hole. He warned that he was watching and one slip would get me a year in the hole followed by a transfer to Folsom.

Nothing I'd done was really serious, considering how impulsive and explosive I had been at eighteen when I started walking the Big Yard. Had I not had Louise Wallis writing me from the *Queen Mary* and Saint-Tropez, describing the unusual blue of the sea, telling me what a good life I could have, I might well have escalated my war against authority—the war the world declared on me when I was four years old. Every place I went authority told me, "We will break you here." They said it in juvenile hall, in various reform schools, and in the reformatory at Lancaster. I cannot recount how many beating I'd had—at least a score, three of which were really savage. Tear gas was shot in my eyes through the bars; fire hoses had skidded me across the floors and slammed me into walls. I'd spent a week naked in utter blackness on bread and water when I was fifteen. When I was in Pacific Colony, at thirteen, I was fastened by a long canvas harness to a hundred-pound concrete block wrapped in blanket. I dragged it up and down a corridor covered with paraffin wax for twelve hours a day. I fought back and they punched and stomped me until my face looked like hamburger—and a doctor with an accent did nothing. The hospital did say I wasn't crazy and returned me to reform school. They could make me scream and cry out for mercy, but as soon as I recuperated, I always rebelled again. They expelled me from reform school; I was too disruptive.

In San Quentin, however, they said they would kill me if I stabbed a guard and would kick my brains in if I even took a punch at one. I also knew that I would not be expelled from here. Without Louise Wallis and the hopes and dreams she represented, I might have ignored their threats and escalated my rebellion. I hadn't cared. Now I did care. I wanted out. I had more going for me than anyone I knew. I even managed to have six months' clean conduct when I went to the parole board. Although I didn't know it for years, the prison psychiatrist recommended against my parole. But Mrs. Hal Wallis had more influence. In February, the adult authorities fixed my term at seven years, with twenty-seven months on parole. That meant I had six months to go, assuming I could stay out of trouble.

MEMORIAL DAY. LIKE ALL DAYS, it was announced long before dawn by the raucous clutch of birds, pigeons, and sparrows in the outside eaves of the cell house. No rooster ever crowed earlier or louder, although convicts slept through it. Then came the early unlock, guards letting out men who went to work before the main line. On weekdays I was on early unlock. During my last year and a half I worked on the early laundry crew, but not today. This was a holiday.

I woke up when the convict key men began unlocking the cells. Using huge spike keys, they could hit each lock while walking fast—*clack, clack, clack,* the sound grew louder as the key man came closer on another tier, then receded as he passed, and grew loud again as one came down the next tier.

The convict tier tender then was pouring hot water through the cell bars into gallon cans placed next to the gate. The cells had only cold water, and the toilets used water from the bay.

From my cell I could see through the outer bars. It was sunny and bright out, but nevertheless, I took a jacket. It was always wise to take a jacket when leaving the cell in San Quentin. San Francisco might be sunny and bright while the Big Yard was windy and cold.

A bell sounded, followed like punctuation by the ragged volley of the fifth-tier convicts exiting their cells and slamming their gates shut. A torrent of trash poured past as men kicked it off the tiers above. Every so often, the falling newspapers and other effluvia had an instant coffee or peanut butter jar wrapped in them that exploded as it hit the concrete, sending splinters of glass flying. A voice called out, "If I knew who did that, I'd fuck you up . . . punk!" Nobody responded. It would be another fifteen minutes before the unlock worked its way down to the second tier. That was when I got up and got dressed. I crossed off another day on the calendar. I had sixty-some remaining; I cannot now recall exactly how many.

As it was Memorial Day, there would be a boxing card on the lower yard in the afternoon. I hadn't boxed in two years, but my former trainer, Frank Little-john, had asked me to substitute for someone he trained because he was afraid the man would take too bad a beating. Why not? It was only three rounds. I pulled a box from beneath the bed and extracted sweat- and bloodstained Ace bandages that I used for hand wraps, plus my mouthpiece and boxing shoes. It was a wonder they didn't have spiders in them considering how long they had been in the shoe box.

As soon as the tramp of feet receded above, another security bar was raised and another tier of convicts came out with another deluge of trash. I gathered what I was taking to the Big Yard. In addition to the boxing equip-ment, I put a loose carton of cigarettes inside my shirt to pay a gambling debt. The goddamned Yankees had lost the night before. What was the adage of my childhood, never bet against Joe Louis, Notre Dame, or the New York Yan-kees? Bullshit! I picked up a book I was returning to my friend Leon Gaultney: *Science and Sanity,* by Alfred Korzybski, the fountainhead of general seman-tics. Frankly, it had too many examples in mathematical equations, which turned off my brain as if by a light switch. I thought semantics was an impor-tant discipline in understanding reality, but I preferred the books of S. I. Hayakawa and Wendell Johnson.

I debated carrying out the pages of the new book to show Jimmy and Paul and Leon—but decided that I was packing too much already. I would have to carry what I took all day.

I was waiting when the second tier was released. I stepped out, closed my cell gate, and waited until the bar went down. Some cell thieves lately had been running in and out of cells to grab things if the occupant walked away be-fore the security bar went down.

The nearly two thousand convicts in the four sections of the South Cell House walked to the center stairway that led down to the rotunda and the steel doors into the mess hall. As usual, the food was barely edible. The menu proved that between the word and the reality lies the chasm. I could eat this one breakfast, oatmeal and a hard cinnamon roll with peanut butter. The roll softened in the tepid coffee. I got the food down and went out into the yard.

The Big Yard was already full. The South Cell House ate last. Exiting the mess hall door, I plunged through a wall of sound made by four thousand num-bered men, all convicted felons imprisoned for murder, robbery, rape, arson, burglary, selling drugs, buying drugs, buying and selling stolen merchandise, all the crimes set forth in the California Penal Code. The crowd was thickest near the mess hall door, for although a guard told everyone exiting to move out, they tended to go ten feet and stop to light up cigarettes and greet friend. As I squeezed through I was sure to say, "Excuse me . . . excuse me," if I brushed against or bumped someone. Convicts may have the foulest mouths in the world, but unlike the images set forth in movies and television, they are better than New Yorkers about certain amenities. Among the numbered men there were always a few with paranoid streaks. One young black bully straight from the 'hood not only failed to excuse himself but also said, "Get outta the way, fool," to a very skinny white guy who was being held in California for Utah, where he had already killed another convict. The "fool" brooded for nearly a month and then walked up behind the bully as he sat eating in the mess hall. The knife paralyzed the bully from the neck down. He was a bully no more. The prison adages include: Everybody bleeds; anybody can kill you. Where anyone can get a big knife, good manners are the rule of the day—even if they are accompanied by vulgarity. Think about it.

Beyond the packed crowd there was more room. I circled the yard counterclockwise, looking for my friends. First I headed for the inmate canteen. Only convicts actually in the canteen line, a row of windows reminiscent of those at the racetrack, could cross the red "deadline" thirty feet away. Above was a gun rail with a rifleman, looking down on the crowd. I saw many men I knew, but none of those I was seeking at the moment. I was both confident and watchful, for while I had many friends, I also had my share of enemies. I didn't want to come upon them unexpectedly; they might think I was trying to make a sneak attack.

Outside the gates to the East Cell House I saw San Quentin's two pairs of bookmakers. Sullivan and O'Rourke were the Irish book; Globe and Joe Cocko were the Chicano book. Each pair had a green sport page from the *Chronicle*, checking race results from the Eastern tracks. Waiting nearby were the horseplayers. Most of them were compulsive horseplayers, and some were quite good. They had lots of time to study the charts.

I walked between the East Cell House wall and the domino tables. The games were hot and heavy, the sound of plastic dominoes loud as they were slammed to the tables. Double six went down first.

The next player had six three. He slammed it down. "That's fifteen."

"Goin' behind the house for the change," said the next man, playing six two on the six.

Each game was owned by a convict who took a cut, collecting from the losers and paying the winners. I knew how to play, but not well enough to gamble. It had been too expensive becoming a first-class poker player to now get involved in dominoes. These were some of the best domino players in the world. They played from breakfast unlock to afternoon lockup. They even played in the rain, holding newspapers over their heads if they lacked rain gear.

The East Cell House wall intersected with the North Cell House rotunda door. The yard outside the North Cell House was first to catch the warming rays of morning sun. The Big Yard was usually cold in the morning. The concrete seemed to hold the night's chill until the sun was high. Most blacks congregated in that area. Although each race tended to congregate with their own, there was little overt racial tension or hostility. That would change in the decade ahead.

I wasn't looking for him, but I spotted Leon Gaultney standing with two other blacks, one being Rudy Thomas, the prison's lightweight champion. Rudy had the skills to be a world champion. Alas, he was a junkie. Also standing there was the heavyweight champion, Frank, who was doing time for killing a man with a single punch. He and I were civil to each other. He had once threatened to break my jaw, and I had said that I would stab him in the back. I was bluffing, confident he would back off, which he did.

Rudy Thomas and I were friends, but I think he suspected all whites of being racists at some level. True enough, if it came to a race war, I was white and I would fight, but I didn't think anyone was better or worse than anyone else because of race.

Then there was Leon. Leon Gaultney. Over my life I've had an unusual number of close friends. American men seldom have really close male friends, the kind that can be called brother. I've had at least a dozen, or twice that, and scores who were partners. Leon was among the top half-dozen, and for a while he was my very best friend. I don't recall how we met. During my first year or so I would have been too self-conscious to have a black man as a running partner. I had several black friends, guys I'd known from juvenile hall through reform school and now, in San Quentin—but they were not running partners. I did not walk the yard with them. Now, however, I had enough recognition and status, despite being just twenty-one, that nobody would think anything, and even if they did, they wouldn't say anything. Moreover, through me, Leon developed friendship and respect from many white convicts of high status. Jimmy Posten had gotten Leon a job in the dental clinic. The chief dentist would not sign a job change for anyone without Jimmy's giving a nod. Leon was the only black to work there. It wasn't because of racism; it was because you get your friends the good jobs.

Leon was precisely six feet tall and weighed 175 pounds. He was average-looking and never wore starched and pressed *bonaroo* clothes. It was when he talked that one saw how unique he was. All traces of the common black accent had been effaced in favor of precise enunciation. He told me that he had studied Clifton Webb and Sydney Poitier for their speech and practiced by reading James Baldwin and others aloud. In the three years Leon had already served, he had taught himself Spanish well enough to translate Shakespeare back and forth. He had also become fairly fluent in French and Italian and was currently studying Arabic. The only decoration in his monkish cell was a pencil sketch of Albert Einstein. Leon was the most intelligent man I'd met in prison. Few of those I'd known in reform school could be called intelligent. It wasn't the breadth or the depth of his knowledge that was so impressive. I'm sure I was more widely read. He seldom read fiction, whereas I believe that nothing explores the depths and darkness of the human mind better than great novels and even an average novel can throw a beam of light into an unknown crevice. Dostoyevski makes you understand the thoughts of gamblers, murders, and others better than any psychologist who ever lived, Freud included.

As I walked up, I nodded to Frank and Rudy and patted Leon on the back. "What's up?" I asked.

"I saw your name on the boxing card," Rudy said.

I nodded. "Yeah. Frank talked me into it. He said Tino Prieto would hurt Rooster."

"When's the last time you had the gloves on?"

"I dunno. I guess about a year ago."

Rudy shook his head and looked to the sky. "He might hurt you, too. He's old and he's got a little gut, but he had about thirty, thirty-five professional fights. Look at his face."

"I know . . . but fuck it, you know what I mean. I've got about ten or fifteen pounds on him. He's really a lightweight."

"He's in good shape and you damn sure ain't in good shape."

"Too late now."

Leon interrupted. "Let's go. Littlejohn wants to see you in the gym."

It was just after 9:00 A.M. The yard gate had just been opened so convicts could go down the concrete stairs to the lower yard. The first fight wouldn't be until 1:00. Mine was the third bout. I wouldn't answer the bell until at least 1:30.

I nodded, then said to Rudy, "Are they gonna bring that lightweight in from Sacramento?" Frankie Goldstein, a fight manager who often came to San Quentin for fight cards, to referee and simultaneously see if there was any talent in the prison, was supposed to bring a lightweight contender to box an exhibition with Rudy, who had gone through everyone who would get in the ring with him. I had sparred with him in the gym when I had secret ambitions to be a great white hope. I had never landed a clean punch. And when he hit me, I seldom saw it coming.

"Supposed to bring him in. We'll see."

I gestured good-bye to big Frank; he nodded impassively in response.

Leon and I walked away. "When you get done this afternoon," he said, "I've got something to get high on."

"Let's do it now. What is it?"

"Hey, I'm not gonna get you loaded and then send you into the ring. You'd get beat to death and wouldn't even know it."

"So it's better that way."

"Not if you get your brain scrambled. Sometimes one terrible ass kicking will do it."

"I see you've got a lot of confidence in me."

"I think Jimmy Barry set you up . . . over that thing last year."

"That thing last year" was a fight between Leon and Jimmy. It happened after I'd gotten to know Leon but before we were partners. I'd been working out, shadowboxing in front of a full-length mirror, when someone said a real fight was in progress. I had to be a spectator. It was happening in the handball court at the other end of the gym. When I got there, Leon and Jimmy were fighting. Jimmy was twenty years older and twenty pounds lighter than Leon; plus Leon was a good amateur light heavyweight. Jimmy, however, had been a top-ranked welterweight. He was the matchmaker; he ran the boxing department. He also had a bad name and a rat jacket. Good convicts shunned him as much as possible, but it was hard to do so completely because of his position. He controlled the boxing department. He distributed all equipment. Nobody was assigned a locker or issued boxing shoes and mouthpiece except through him. He made the matches, deciding who was to fight whom.

About a dozen convicts had been standing outside the handball court watching the fight. Leon was forcing the action, trying to come in behind a jab and hook to the body—but Jimmy was slipping the jab and blocking the hook. Neither was doing any damage until Leon barreled in with his shoulder and rammed Jimmy back against the wall. That brought a gasp as he fought to retrieve expelled air. Without warning, from the sidelines, Jimmy's "kid" sprang upon Leon's back and tried to stab him in the face or eye with a ballpoint pen.

"Get him off me!" Leon yelled.

To my great shame, I hesitated. Leon and I were not as close as we would become, but we were friendly. Moreover, he was a solid convict and Jimmy Barry was a reputed stool pigeon. Yet he was white and Leon was black. Race made me pause for ten seconds. Then I moved toward the door into the handball court, yelling, "Get off him!" Jimmy Barry was looking at me over Leon's shoulder. Before I could get through the door, someone else pulled them apart, and some other convict called out, "The Man's coming!" Everything broke up before the patrolling guard arrived. He could feel the electricity or ozone but had no idea what had happened. Everyone broke around him as if he were a rock in a river. Befuddlement was written on his face. En route to the yard, I found myself walking with Leon. "Thanks," he said. He was holding a handkerchief to his cheek. It was bleeding slightly from the puncture wound by the ballpoint. Was there a note of sarcasm? Maybe he hadn't known that I was among the spectators. That was immaterial. What mattered to me was that I had failed to behave as my own values dictated.

The fight in the handball court had occurred more than a year earlier. It was since then that Leon and I had become close friends. He was respected by white convicts. Whites were still about 70 percent of the prison population. There was little racial tension. If there was an altercation between convicts of different races, it only involved them and, perhaps, their close friends. Leon also had status with many young blacks, especially those from Oakland and San Francisco.

The months passed. I went to the parole board and got a parole date. A few weeks after that, I got in an altercation with two of San Quentin's toughest black convicts: Spotlight Johnson and Dollomite Lawson. Either one could have whipped me without much difficulty. Both were squat, powerful men— and ugly as sin. In the LA County Jail, the deputies would put Dollomite in a tank to "straighten things up." He had rammed one man's head into the bars and killed him. Spotlight lived in the East Cell House, but I did not know what tier. Dollomite lived on the fourth tier of the South Call House. He would not expect me to be out of the cell first. He would go out to the yard so he and his partner could brace me together. Instead I would stick Dollomite the moment he stepped out of the cell. He would never think about the early unlock. He was a stupid, illiterate brute. Alas, he was a very tough stupid, illiterate brute. In a primal milieu to which he was perfectly adapted. But I knew my way, too.

Through the evening I dwelled on the problem, sometimes enraged, some- times aching inside because it would be a Pyrrhic victory at best. It would cost me at least six or seven more years even if I didn't kill him. He wasn't worth it.

At 10:15, convicts started returning from night activities. As their feet sounded on the steel stairs, some went past my cell.

Leon appeared and stopped. "Somebody said you had words with big head and his pal. Is it over?"

I hesitated. I wanted to tell him everything and seek his help, yet my own code, personal and perverted as it may have been, said that I would take care of my own trouble. I said, "It's not quite over." And as soon as the words were in the air, I felt guilty.

A guard at the end of the tier raised the security bar. Convicts who were waiting stepped into their cells. Leon was alone on the tier.

"Where are you supposed to be?"

"I'm going there, boss," Leon said. "See you in the morning," he said to me.

Soon began, the *clack-clack-clack* of each cell being locked, and the softer *click-click-click* of the guards pressing the counters they carried.

It seemed that I was awake the entire night, but I must have slept a little, for when the guard tapped the bars and shone his flashlight on my face, it awakened me. "Bunker . . . early unlock."

"I got it."

Ten minutes later the security bar went up and the guard unlocked my gate. As I stepped out, a couple of other figures were on the tier.

It was summer and already daylight when the laundry foreman took his washing machine crew across the Big Yard, empty save for a few seagulls and pigeons. The washing machine crew was all white, the tumbler (huge machines that wrung out excess water by spinning at high speed) crew was all black, and the drying machine crew was Chicano. Each had to cooperate with the others to get their *bonaroos* done. The steam presses were divided evenly. The con boss was black.

As soon as we entered the building, I went to my stash and got my knife. It was sixteen inches overall, its handle wrapped in electrician's tape. It had the Arkansas toothpick shape, a sharp point that widened a lot. I carried it over behind a huge washing machine where my rubber boots waited beneath a bench. The shiv went down the side of my big rubber boot.

All morning, I watched the clock. At 7:44, I told the foreman that I was going up to sick call.

It was a bright morning and a very long walk across the lower yard, up the stairs into the Big Yard. The first convicts from the West and North Cell Houses were beginning to exit the mess halls. As I went into the South Cell House and up the stairway, the fifth tier was coming down. Good. Dollomite was still in his cell. On the third tier, I turned to walk in front of the cells. Ahead of me was Leon, standing in front of Dollomite's cell. Leon saw me and gestured with his hand down beside his leg: go back.

I stopped and stepped back. A minute later Leon came toward me. "C'mon," he said, leading me down the stairs.

"What's up?" I asked. I was mentally ready and, being ready, resented being called off.

"It's settled," Leon said. "They really don't want trouble. They're running a game on Fingers, too. And they think you're crazy . . . and being known as slightly crazy is an advantage around here."

Leon had saved my parole date and probably saved me from an additional sentence for assault or even murder. It was a great debt made even greater by my earlier hesitance in helping him. He was really my friend. (I must insert parenthetically, especially to convicts who read this, that such a friendship would never had started in San Quentin after the early part of the 1960s, when the race wars began.)

BUT TODAY WAS MEMORIAL DAY and I was being paroled in the first week of August. As Leon and I walked toward the gym, the 'Frisco Flash, a skinny little character, arrived and beckoned Leon to the side. The conversation was brief.

Leon came back shaking his head. "I fucked up. I shouldn't have given it to him."

"Given him what?"

"Some pot and pills. He was selling them for me. You know Walt and Country and Duane, don't you?"

"Yeah . . . all my life."

"They got some reds from him and claimed they were bogus. They burned him."

"Let me talk to 'em."

"I don't want any profit, but I would like my investment back."

"No problem. I'll take care of it." I thought it would be no problem. All three were friends with some obligation to me. I changed the subject: "Littlejohn will need somebody to work my corner with him. Are you up to it?"

"Sure. I'll stop the blood."

"I love your confidence. Keep the towel ready in case I'm getting killed."

We went up the stairway to the top floor of the Old Industrial Building. It was where the gallows had been when they hanged the condemned in California. The first floor was divided into maintenance shops, and part of the second floor was the Catholic chapel. Two other floors were empty space, with the gym on top. It was built at the bottom of a hill at the edge of the lower yard. Until recently, to reach it one had to walk down the alley past the doorways into the maintenance shops and then trudge up five flights of stairs affixed to the outside of the building. After Popeye Jackson (later killed on the streets of San Francisco) hit somebody with a hatchet and an older guard had a heart attack running up the stairs, a bridge-ramp was built from the top of the hill to a gym door. This made it easier to control pedestrian traffic in and out of the gym; plus the guards could get there faster.

Paapke, the three-hundred-pound Hawaiian guard, was at the ramp entrance, checking ID cards against a list. Knowing me, he waved me through without checking.

The boxing department was quiet. The bell that ran in a three-minute, one-minute sequence had been turned off. The constant staccato sound of speed bags was missing, as well as the splat of hard punches landing on the heavy bag. Conversations were unusually soft as the gladiators got ready for battle and the trainers hovered about with help and advice. The payoff for fighting was two photos taken during each bout. Frank Littlejohn was supposed to be there with his two champions, Rudy Thomas and Frank.

"Hey, we meet again," Leon said to Rudy and Frank. Then to me: "I'm gone. I'll see you when you get down there."

I nodded and asked Rudy, "Where's Littlejohn?"

Rudy indicated the doorway to the matchmaker's office at one corner of the boxing section. It was an indoor shack with a glass-windowed office and a back room with a window where gear was passed in and out. It was also a private space where nobody could see what was going on. As I headed in that direction, I saw Country Fitzgerald and Duane Patillo come through the door. Country was a known con man who would chastise a sucker unmercifully. He had gotten the drugs from the 'Frisco Flash. Duane was the muscle if muscle was needed, a real tough white boy out of Compton, and Walt was an all-around co-conspirator with them.

I veered to intercept them. They stopped, faces affable. We were friends. "Hey, that stuff you got from the 'Frisco Flash. That belonged to my friend Leon. He doesn't want whatever you said you'd pay, but just what he had invested. And you don't have to pay right now if you haven't got it. Put a day on yourselves."

"Oh, man, it didn't belong to the Flash?"

I assured them that it did not.

"We don't have it right now."

"When can you get it?"

"Probably next week."

That seemed reasonable to me, and I was sure Leon would agree. It was more a question of saving face than the value involved. "I'll tell him," I said.

AS IS COMMON IN THE BAY AREA at the beginning of summer, the morning fog burned away and the afternoon was bright and warm. Forty-two hundred convicts were in the lower yard. Boxing was a big thing in San Quentin. Several contenders had come from behind the walls. Whenever champions were in the Bay area, they visited San Quentin. The walls of the boxing department had their signed photos: Archie Moore, Bobo Olson, Rocky Marciano. Most of the forty-two hundred stood in the outfield and around the ring, but free-world visitors and a score of important convicts sat in ringside folding chairs.

Today there were to be eight bouts, three preliminaries and five for prison championship in the various weight divisions. I was in the third preliminary, supposedly welterweight. Actually, I weighed a few pounds more, around 150 pounds, and my opponent was actually a lightweight, weighing in at 137.

The first bout was a pair of featherweights having their first fight in the ring. True, they had boxed many rounds in the gym; trainers had drummed into them what to do—but as they caught the electricity generated by the crowd, they forgot what they should do. They circled cautiously, hands high, sort of dancing. One extended a tentative jab; the other swung a right hand that landed. Both began swinging like windmills, heads down, arms flailing, very little landing with much effect. The convicts loved it. They yelled and clapped and bent over with laugher. The decision was a draw.

I paid little heed to the second bout. I was getting loose, warming up, moving around. A sudden mass bellow went forth ringside. I turned to look. One of the fighters was sitting on the ring floor, one hand holding a bottom rope. He was trying to use it to get to his feet.

The referee stepped forward, waving both arms over his head. The bout was over. "In one minute and nine seconds of the first round . . ."

Littlejohn was lacing on my gloves, pulling them up tight. God, they gave a headache. If I have to be punched, I much prefer a bare fist to a boxing glove.

The knockout victim came past me, his legs still wobbly, his eyes glazed, his manager in his ear: "Goddammit! I told you to watch out for that overhead right."

Leon went up the stairs to the ring apron and held the ropes apart so I could slip between them. I went to the resin box and did a little dance so the soles of my shoes scraped the resin. It kept my feet from slipping on the canvas. When I turned away, my opponent was waiting to use the resin box. I was bigger and younger, but on his face were etched forty-two professional fights, mostly around Tijuana. I was already uptight. Now my stomach churned, too.

Back in the corner, Littlejohn told me, "Stay away; move on him. Use the jab. You've got a good jab."

Frankie Carter, the referee, motioned us to the center of the ring. "You know the rules. Break when I tell you. Protect yourself at all times. . . ." While the referee gave the standard instructions, I looked at my opponent, not with the intimidating glare now popular in many sports. Rather, I was looking him over. He was shorter than me, stockier, with thinning black hair. His arms were short, the biceps strong but not remarkable. His forearms reminded me of Popeye. He was covered with blue India ink tattoos, ugly and forever. They were a brand.

While standing there I was conscious of the sun's heat on my bare shoulders.

We went back to our corners. The bell rang and the fight was on, three rounds, each round of three minutes' duration. Because I was in such poor condition I planned to take it easy in the first round, jab and keep away. If he pressed me, I would hold and conserve wind and energy. That was my plan.

I circled, stuck out a jab—and got hit flush in the left eye with a hard overhand right. It made lights explode in my brain. Oh shit! I reached to grab and he hit me with an uppercut body punch that almost lifted my feet from the canvas. *Ooof!* I realized I was in serious trouble. I managed to clinch and pin his arms. When the referee said, "Break," I ignored the order. He had to pry me loose.

Somehow I got through round one. I was happy when the bell rang. When I flopped on the stool, panting, I looked across the ring. My opponent was standing as he talked to his trainer. Was he grinning?

"Jab him!" Littlejohn kept saying. "Use your reach to keep him away. Box his ass. Move and stick . . . move and stick . . . How's your gas?"

"Okay . . . so far."

The referee came over. "Seconds out."

Leon wet my mouthpiece and stuck it back in my mouth.

The bell rang. The second round was better than the first. My legs felt better and I was able to move, move, move—and when my opponent got overanxious, I stopped and stuck a jab in his face. I stuck out a jab, came in behind it, and hooked him hard in the stomach. His "ooof" said I'd hurt him. I was dancing like Fred Astaire.

I was winning the round until the last thirty seconds. All of a sudden, like air going from a balloon, I ran out of gas. My legs became lead. He came at me and I meant to slip the punch and move away. My legs refused the command. They got crossed up and I tripped myself, stumbling and almost going down. He hit me in the rib cage under the heart. It hurt. Next came two punches in the face, both of which sent coruscating lights to my brain. Instinctively I grabbed for him. My extended arms let him punch over the top. Another flashing light. Damn!

The bell rang. Thank God. Where's the corner?

". . . doin' good," Leon said, taking my mouthpiece.

Littlejohn rubbed my legs. "Do what you were doin'. Jab and grab. Jab and grab." Even as he spoke, I remembered that jab and grab was how Joey Maxim beat Sugar Ray Robinson on a sweltering New York night in Yankee Stadium. Robinson won every round until the thirteenth, then he quit in the corner from exhaustion and dehydration. He'd lost over twenty pounds in the thirteen rounds. Why did I think of that? Who knows.

The bell rang.

I remember little of the third round, except that it took three hours. The referee would have stopped it except that I kept coming forward—and Tino Prieto kept hitting me until he got arm-weary. One time when I stood in the middle of the ring, half bent over, somewhat like a bull awaiting the final thrust, I heard Littlejohn yelling, "The jab! Use your jab!"

I stepped back, looked over my shoulder, and said quite loudly, "Hey, Frank, I would if I could. I can't!"

Littlejohn closed his eyes and shook his head in disbelief. Leon grinned.

The convicts at ringside laughed once more. I tucked my chin against my shoulder and kept my right hand high, my elbow in tight, and walked into Prieto's punches, moving my head from side to side. Every so often I'd throw a haymaker left hook that landed just once, and even that was up high where it mussed his hair and nothing more. Anyone who hasn't been there can imagine how long it takes for a three-minute round.

When the final bell sounded, four thousand convicts were jumping up and down and screaming. I barely made my stool.

"Get up. Wave!" Littlejohn said.

"Are you crazy? You might have to carry me outta this fuckin' ring. If I *ever* put on another pair of boxing gloves—"

"We have a split verdict," said the announcer. "Referee Frankie Carter scores it twenty-nine to twenty-eight for the blue corner. The two judges, Willy Hermosillo and Frank Washington, score it twenty-nine to twenty-nine. The fight is a draw by majority vote."

A draw! A draw! Unbelievable. I was so surprised and excited that I overcame my exhaustion and stood up. I managed to wave to the crowd and embrace Tino Prieto. He looked bewildered and returned my hug without enthusiasm. Later, I looked at the scorecards. Two judges had scored the first round even, ten points to ten points; they gave me the second round by ten points to nine points and Prieto the third round by the same ten to nine.

When I came down the steps from the ring, Rudy Thomas was grinning. "I didn't know you could box that good," he said.

"Desperation," I said. "And I'll never put on another set of boxing gloves, believe me."

Later, in the gym, my opponent came out of the shower. I was combing my hair at a sink, and he had to pass behind me. Our eyes caught in the reflection. "Good fight," he said.

"You, too, man."

"I'm kinda glad I didn't win."

"What're you talkin' about?"

"Now I don't have to worry if you're going to stab me."

"Oh, man, I wouldn't do that."

"I know it." He grinned, one tooth missing, and went his way.

I finished combing my hair, aching all over and thinking about what he'd said. Was it paranoid? Sure it was, yet it was also an admonition to me. I'd deliberately established a reputation for being a little crazy. The purpose was to warn others away, as the skunk's white stripe does. But if someone thought I might stab him over a boxing match it might defeat its purpose. If someone thought me that crazy and we had words, he might stab me in a preemptive move. All I hoped was that it didn't happen in the next two months. After that I would be back on the streets of Los Angeles.

Later, during the main count lockup, I bent over to straighten my bunk and a bolt of pain shot out from my ribs. When I came out on unlock for the evening meal, I asked the cell house sergeant to call me through to the hospital. The convict nurse on duty poked the rib and I winced. He thought it was cracked, but that wasn't enough to call for the medical officer of the day to come inside the walls. However, an older convict was experiencing a heavy chest pain and streaks of pain down his left arm. A possible heart attack was enough to bring the medical officer of the day. It took an hour before he arrived in shorts and sweatshirt. Thank God the convict with chest pains wasn't having a heart attack. When the doctor got to me and found that I'd gotten the injuries in the boxing ring, he muttered something about ignorance—but he ordered an X ray and found a hairline crack. It hadn't separated. As long as it was immobilized, it would heal. This was accomplished by a sheet of white adhesive covered by Ace bandage around my torso. When a guard escorted me back to the cell house it was about ten-thirty. I had to wait at the Sergeant's Office to be checked in, while around me convicts streamed in from night unlocks. They climbed the stairs and stood in front of their cells for lockup.

Walt came in, saw me, and came over. "Damn, man, your eye . . ."

"I've had worse. It'll be all healed when I walk out the gate."

"How much you got left?"

"Sixty-two days and a getup. You get that business straight with Leon?"

"Yeah, it's straight."

There was something in his voice that contradicted his words. "Hey," I said. "All he wants is what he invested."

"Yeah, well, uhhh, we talked it over. We're gonna give that *nigger* what we think he's got comin'. If he don't like it, fuck him in the ass."

The words were slaps across my face. Each one pumped more red into my brain. I nearly choked and had to clear my throat. Meanwhile the lockup bell rang and convicts still far from their cells began to scurry. I managed to choke out: "I don't know what he wants . . . but lemme say this: if it ain't right and there's some trouble, I'm backin' that *nigger* . . . all the way to the gas chamber if necessary. You think about it; I'll see you tomorrow."

A guard appeared at the section door and put his flashlight beam on us. "Lockup. Move it."

"I'm waiting to check in," I said.

Walt disappeared up the stairway to his tier.

They counted me at the Sergeant's Office. When the count cleared, a guard escorted me to my cell.

It was a bad, sleepless night. I can't imagine that many readers will have spent a night thinking they may have to kill someone with a knife—or be killed the same way—when the sun comes up. It is not conducive to peaceful sleep or any sleep, although I might have dozed for a moment or two during the night. My cracked rib throbbed; plus my swollen eye was nearly closed. I counted my remaining days in San Quentin. Sixty-one. Was I crazy, letting my mouth get me into another shitstorm? I could have been more diplomatic. I didn't have to throw down a threat the first thing. Still, he'd been an asshole, referring to Leon as a *nigger*. There were plenty of niggers around, loud, gross, ignorant—and plenty of white niggers, too. Come to think of it, Walt was illiterate and ignorant. A convict comic had handed Walt a book of matches, offering a carton of Camels if he could read the ad on its face. Walt looked, threw the matchbook down, and said, "Fuck you!" He probably hated Leon doubly because Leon was so well educated.

No matter. They'd made their declaration; so had I, although I was now tormented with misgivings. I wanted to go home. I hadn't realized what I had going for me when I first met Mrs. Hal Wallis. Now she signed her letters "Mom," and I felt that she *was* Mom. She wanted to open doors for me; she wanted me to help myself. She'd arranged a job at the McKinley Home for Boys. It was on Riverside Drive and Woodman. It would become a giant shopping mall, anchored by two department stores, but that was two decades away. Now it was a still-rustic home for boys. Louise Wallis was their foremost benefactor—and mine. Because of her I had a chance to fulfill my dreams—or at least I had a chance until morning. This seemed like a repeat of a few weeks earlier when Leon had interceded for me. He'd saved my ass, one way or another, from getting my brains kicked in or being charged with a felony for sticking one or both of my enemies. How could I have gotten into almost the same situation? It was because I had originally spoken to them and told Leon it was okay. I'd put myself in the middle, and I was responsible. I still felt guilt for not instantly pulling Jimmy Barry's punk off Leon, and I felt a debt because he had saved my parole by getting between me and the dynamic duo of Spotlight and Dollomite. God, they were ugly.

This time I wouldn't let Leon down, no doubt of that—but goddamn I wanted to get out. I'd been too quick with my retort. Why did I have to declare myself when Walt told me how they intended to pay—or not pay? I could have played it off and gone off to plan something instead of this gunfight at the O.K. Corral kind of confrontation. I should have at least gone to see Leon before threatening to kill people. For a smart guy I was sure dumb sometimes. Still there was no way back without putting my tail between my legs.

At least I had behaved so I could look in the mirror. Mine was a *macho* world, with some rules that belonged in the Code of Chivalry. Fuck it. Whatever happened, happened. The first birds were beginning to chirp. Soon enough the early-morning unlocks would start.

I was waiting fully dressed when the flashlight beam probed the cell and the silhouette called softly, "Bunker."

"Got it, boss."

Ten minutes later, I stepped onto the tier and closed the cell gate. Down the tier another figure was dressing. I headed for the stairway to the South Dining Room. As I entered, instead of grabbing a tray and getting in line, I walked up the center aisle, circled behind the steam tables, and entered the main kitchen. Other convicts assigned to food service were coming to work, going through the kitchen to a locker room where they changed into white kitchen clothes or at least a white jumper. Instead of entering the locker room, I went down a corridor through double doors into the vegetable room. The vegetable crew, eight Chicanos, was peeling potatoes that they threw into huge pans of water. They looked up without expression as I passed through and opened the rear door onto the loading dock behind the kitchen. The kitchen had its own yard with weights. It had a wall on one side. The wall overlooked the lower yard on its other side. The gun bull with the carbine watched both. He had a route he patrolled that took him away from the kitchen yard. The other side of the kitchen yard had a fence, beyond which was a yard for the West Honor Unit, where convicts could come and go from their cells from 6:00 A.M. to 11:00 P.M. Leon's cell was on the fifth tier at the rear. He'd moved to the honor unit a couple of weeks earlier. I'd helped him carry his gear.

A couple of convicts wearing high boots, heavy rubber aprons, and thick gloves were using steam hoses to clean garbage cans. I feigned interest in that until the gun bull turned his back to walk the other way. Then I scrambled over the fence. It rattled loudly, but the gun bull never heard it.

Across the honor unit yard to the big steel doors into the building rotunda. I pulled one door enough to make sure it was unlocked. I hesitated to pull it open. Across the rotunda, just within the cell house itself, was the small

Sergeant's Office. During the day convicts came and went freely, but maybe he would notice someone entering at this time of morning. The sun was up because it was summer, but the main line had not yet begun the breakfast unlock.

As I debated what to do, the rotunda door was pushed open from the other side. Three convicts came out. "Where's the bull?" I asked.

"He's up on the tiers," one replied.

I slipped inside, crossed the rotunda, and walked the length of the cell house under the second tier overhang. At the rear stairs I went up two at a time. When I reached the top, I swung around the corner. Leon lived half a dozen cells down the tier. The gate was open and Country was leaning against the door frame. What was going on? I was only three or four steps away, the cells being four and a half feet wide. Seeing Country surprised me. I stopped. My face must have taken on a weird expression that the human animal assumes in such situations. My mind had been locked into stabbing this man, but I had no knife. I'd planned to get it after I talked to Leon.

Country started with surprise. "Bunk! You live here now?"

"Naw. I'm still in the garbage can."

Leon came to the doorway. "What's up?" He was wearing white shorts and T-shirt; his hair stood up like watch springs, which would have made me laugh at another time.

"I wanted to see you," I said.

"Wait a minute until I roll this joint." He had an open magazine on the top bunk. On top of the magazine was an aluminum foil bag of Topper, a rough tobacco that was once issued to California convicts. The situation looked more convivial than confrontational. Leon finished rolling the joint and handed it to Country.

"I gotta go," Country said. "See you."

"Yeah. Right."

Country walked away.

"What brings you here this time of day?" Leon asked.

I quickly told Leon what had happened, what Walt had said and what I had said, and that it was at the last lockup last night.

"Country showed up when they opened up this morning. He asked me what I'd lost and kicked it out. No hassle." Leon held up some U.S. currency. "What do you think?"

"Who knows? Walt couldn't have sent word since I talked to him. He's still in his cell right now."

Leon looked puzzled. "I'll bet Walt was just talking for himself, y'know what I mean? And I don't think he expected your reaction. He was just fat-mouthing." Leon grinned. "He didn't know you were deadly serious."

"I guess. You got enough to give me a joint?"

"Of course."

As I waited, I decided that Leon was right. Country had intended to pay all along. I had spent an unnecessarily sleepless night working myself up to murderous violence. I felt as if a ton of weight had been lifted from my shoulders. I wouldn't lose my parole and spend a couple of years in segregation.

I never talked to Walt again. Years later when he was dead (in a wreck after a highway patrol chase), I learned that he had managed to send word to Country by a convict nurse who came up on the tier to deliver medication to another convict. The nurse got off duty at midnight and lived in the West Honor Unit in a cell next to Country's. They had planned to stiff Leon. They never thought I would get involved, because they were white and friends of mine. Besides that, all three were pretty tough. Duane, by himself, could punch me out very quickly in a fistfight. But they also thought I was crazy—and having trouble with a knife-wielding maniac wasn't what they planned. What I did for a black friend in the mid-fifties is something I would never have even considered a decade later. Back when I did it a few would mutter, "Nigger lover," but not loud enough for me to hear. That would end it. But when the race wars were in full swing, it would have been like a Tutsi having a Hutu friend, or vice versa. By the time Martin Luther King, Jr., was assassinated, racial estrangement was absolute in San Quentin. And it remains almost the same three decades later.

IN THE SUMMER OF '56, I was paroled from San Quentin. Louise Wallis arranged for me to pick up a ticket at the United Airlines office on Union Square in San Francisco. It was still the age of low-flying prop airliners, so as I hurtled through the afternoon light above the Salinas Valley, I could see the plane's shadow racing across the geometric patterns of green and brown fields below me. There were white farmhouses, each one encircled by a stand of trees. Everything looked so neat and so empty of people. I thought of Steinbeck's tales mined from this relatively empty land. If he could find *The Grapes of Wrath, East of Eden,* and *Of Mice and Men* down there, my meager writing skills should have been able to find stories in the places I had been and from the people I had known. Reading taught me that prison had been the crucible that had formed several great writers. Cervantes wrote much of *Don Quixote* in a prison cell, and Dostoyevski was a mediocre writer until he was sentenced to death, commuted within a few hours of execution, and then sent to prison in Siberia. It was after these experiences that he became a great writer. There are two worlds where men are stripped of all facades so you can see their core. One is the battlefield; the other is prison. Beyond any doubt I had plenty of raw material; the question was my talent. Louise reported that friends of hers had read my manuscript and said it wasn't publishable but showed promise. I'd felt great simply finishing it, but when I read it a year later it seemed pathetic, although I saw improvement between the first and the last chapter. I'd learned something in three hundred pages. Now I was almost a hundred pages into my second novel and hoped it would be a quantum improvement. I really wanted to be a writer, although I didn't yet have all my hopes and dreams invested therein. Who knew what I would find in the world outside? Maybe I would feel different about everything. Erich Fromm had made me aware of one aspect of my nature: I had the hunger to transcend.

As I was sipping a bourbon and 7 UP and looking down at the plane's shadow rushing over the terrain, many things went through my mind. I was free. I had gone into San Quentin at seventeen and now was out at twenty-two. I had grown to manhood behind high prison walls. As I mentally weighed my assets and liabilities it was obvious to me that I had more going for me than almost anyone else I knew. Mrs. Hal Willis signed her letters: "Love, Mom." She would help me to help myself. What else did I need? I'd never heard of anyone being released without being issued a package of work clothes—except me. The field parole agent sent word that she would take care of my wardrobe. She had an apartment for me, too, although she hadn't divulged the address because she didn't want me to hand it out to my convict pals. That was okay, for although I had many friends, I would only keep in touch with one or two, and I could send them the address after I was free.

Even without Mrs. Hal Wallis, or anything else, I was confident of my abilities. In a test that compared anyone taking it to a graduating class of Harvard liberal arts majors, I was equal to the top 5 percent; plus I had skills they never dreamed about. I had knowledge about life that many people never learn and never have need to learn. But I knew I had gaping flaws, too, emotions and impulses without the internal controls that we learn from parents and society. Most people obey the law not from fear of the consequences but because they have accepted the beliefs as their own. My beliefs were based on what I had learned from the underworld and jail. I would never have followed Raskolnikov's example and made a spontaneous confession to murder because of conscience. For years after reading *Crime and Punishment* I thought Dostoyevski was wrong in that regard—until I saw two men I knew quite well, men I had thought were hard-core convicts, turn themselves in on murders for which there was no evidence against them. That would never happen to me. For one thing, I wasn't a killer, although there had been times in prison when I would have killed in self-defense. I wasn't going to run. I wasn't vengeful, nor did I feel remorse for most things I had done. I believed that yesterday could be learned from but never erased. If I had dwelled on my past there is a good chance I would have gone insane. I had done too much already, and too much had been done to me.

Still, all this was simply squirrel-caging, running around in a circle. Leon gave me the only advice that mattered. "You're not normal, but you're not crazy. It's up to you if you commit another crime. Whether you do or not is all that matters."

It was true. I was different. How could I be anything else after going to juvenile hall at ten, reform school at thirteen, and San Quentin at seventeen? I would never view the world or behave as a member of the bourgeoisie, nor did I so desire. I craved experience and wisdom, not the average life of quiet desperation. The best I could hope for was a marginal adjustment, but that was all I needed. It was up to me not to risk another prison term by committing another felony. As long as I didn't do that, nothing else really mattered. I had brains, I had Louise—and as the plane came over the mountains and the LA basin was below, I had great expectations.

It was twilight when we landed. Instead of the raised tunnels that fit against the plane, in those days we still descended onto the tarmac and crossed the field toward a chain-link fence, behind which stood the people awaiting arrivals. I saw Louise from some distance—her white clothes and blond hair made her stand out; plus she was enthusiastically jumping up and down and waving. It made me grin and surge with affection. I was a lucky ex-convict; there was no way else to put it.

She met me at the gate and hugged me enthusiastically, then pushed me back and looked me up and down. "We'll get rid of those clothes," she said. "Tomorrow."

"I have to see the parole officer tomorrow."

"No, no. I took care of that. He'll come by to see you in a few days. Let's go."

As we turned to push through the crowd, I noticed that she was accompanied by a youth of sixteen or so. She introduced us as we headed toward the parking lot. His name was Mickey, and he was her driver from the McKinley Home for Boys, which was giving me a job. "You'll have a room at McKinley and the apartment where we're going now. Here." She gave me a key on a key ring with a religious medal of Saint Francis. "Blessed by the pope," she said. "When we go to Europe, I'll take you to meet him."

The apartment was over a four-car garage behind a two-story Victorian-style house on the edge of Hancock Park. She had built the house before she met Hal. Her parents had lived in the apartment over the garage. It was different from most apartments, for the house was on a corner, the driveway entered from the street where the house faced, a wall ran alongside the house, the apartment's door was up a stairway around the corner from the driveway, and it was difficult to see that it was a garage apartment.

Louise and Hal had just purchased the estate of Joan Bennett and Walter Wanger on Mapleton Drive in Holmby Hills. Walter Wanger was in deep financial trouble at the time. Ingrid Bergman's *Joan of Arc* had collapsed at the box office, and Walter Wanger had spent a few months in the LA County Jail for shooting Jennings Lang (who would later become the head of Universal Studios) in the parking lot. It was all over Joan Bennett. The end result was the need to sell the house as quickly as possible. Louise said she got it for the value of the lot, $90,000. The house's value back then was about $250,000. Thirty years later, when Hal Wallis died, the same house sold for $6,500,000.

At the time of my release, Louise was still residing at her Van Nuys estate. It had been condemned under *eminent domain* and was to be used for a school. She had gotten what was a fortune in '54, but for a twenty-acre estate she got the price of an average house south of Ventura Boulevard today. She had written to me about it. She had a long time to move, a year or two at least.

She was excited when we went up the stairs and opened the apartment door. It was a one-bedroom apartment, perhaps eight hundred square feet, neatly designed. It was narrow, of course, for it was above four garages. The doorway at the top of the stairs opened into the living room. It had windows overlooking sycamores on the street and the front house on one side. The other view was the blank wall of a new apartment building. It provided absolute privacy. The living room was very comfortable and also tasteful. The sofa and overstuffed chair were in gray slipcovers; the walls were burnt orange or some color like that which I cannot name. On one wall were two small watercolors in ornate frames. I would learn that the artists were well known. What dominated the room from a corner was a huge ornate antique secretary. Its burled wood gleamed in deep, dark colors. "I had it and I didn't know what to do with it," she said. "So here it is." She leaned closer, confidingly: "It's worth forty thousand dollars." She winked. I didn't know why she winked but simply smiled as if I did. She showed me the rest.

The bathroom and the kitchen faced each other across a narrow hallway. It was a smart use of space. Beyond the bathroom, the hall opened onto the bedroom. It was adequate—much larger than any cell I'd lived in but perhaps smaller than a bullpen. It had classy windows, the kind with wooden frames and small panes and a latch that turned, along one side and the rear. The bedroom furniture was simple and expensive, she told me. It had come from the Wanger residence. The closet was a full-sized walk-in. "We'll put some things in it tomorrow," she said. "Get rid of those things." she added, pointing at my clothes.

I started to protest. The gray flannel slacks and the navy blazer went everywhere then and now. They were good quality. The label read: HART, SHAEFFNER & MARX. It wasn't Hickey-Freeman, but it was excellent. "They look good, don't they?"

"Yes, but they came from prison."

"So did I."

"I know. I know. But for me, get rid of them."

"Sure."

She opened a French door into a breakfast nook at the end of the kitchen next to the rear stairs.

"Well, whaddya think?" she asked.

As her question was uttered, I spotted a new Royal portable typewriter on a bedroom writing desk next to a window overlooking the swimming pool. I was literally choked speechless, a response unheard of for me. Tears welled into my eyes. How could I fail? How could I let her down? She had made the dream real for me. She wasn't going to give me the world on a platter, but she would help me to help myself. She would open doors, although I had no idea what those doors were.

"You'd better do some writing on *that*," she said.

"I will," I said with all sincerity, although future months would expose the sincerity as hollow. I meant it, but the lure of bright lights, fast cars, and sweet-smelling young women with long legs was too much for me. It would be decades before I spent one night at home when not incarcerated. I would sleep when I was tired and eat when I was hungry—and every day outside prison was swollen to bursting with possibilities for adventure after the first few months of acclimating myself.

Late the following morning, she arrived with Bertha Griffith, whom I'd met before going to prison. Even then her husband was a wraithlike figure ravaged by paresis, twisted facial muscles, and distorted movements. He was a former silent film director who had caught syphilis from a young actress fifteen years before antibiotics could cure it. I wanted to ask her how he was but sensed it would be an impropriety and kept silent.

Using Louise's long white Chrysler station wagon, we drove a few blocks down to the Miracle Mile. The facades of fancy shops and department stores faced Wilshire. The shopping area was planned with the automobile in mind, for it had large parking lots behind the stores. It was considerably more taste-ful than the giant shopping malls of the future. At the time, this stretch of Wilshire was considered the most expensive real estate in Southern California.

Starting at the art-deco masterpiece of Bullocks-Wilshire, we worked west, shopping for my wardrobe as we went. She bought me everything. The rear of the station wagon was piled high with boxes from Bullocks and Desmond's and Silverwood's. In one department store, a dazzled salesclerk followed Louise with a chair. When she stopped and sat, he shoved the chair under her. She whispered to me, "I'm Lady Wallis, remember?" In her pristine white gabardine pants suit, it was impossible to forget. Playing Lady Wallis was one of her greater enjoyments in life. It was a scene out of many movies made real. I was awed and grateful. It was so munificent that I felt a guilty discomfort. Still and yet, beyond doubt I would take it all—and thank you.

In Beverly Hills, we went to Oviatt's, the most elegant classic tailor in Southern California back then. Hal's suits were made here. She had me fitted for two suits, one a worsted navy ("If you have nothing else, you have that," she instructed), the other a lightweight white flannel. It was soft and smooth between my fingers. "They'll think you're Gatsby," she said.

Gatsby was great, but most unlikely. Gatsby was too unreal. Although I thought Fitzgerald wrote as well as any American novelist in the twentieth century, Gatsby was as far from truth as Fu Manchu. He was too soft to be what he was storied to be. Gatsby might be a cat burglar, but Gatsby was definitely not a gangster. He lacked the force of will to compel tough men to his bidding simply by force of will. He failed another test; he was too weak for a broad.

"I was in several movies from his stories and books," she said.

This was something I have never verified. And today I simply repeat what she said, which is how an honest memoir should be. At the time, I wondered how they could catch Fitzgerald's character nuances in silent movies, or any other for that matter.

From the Beverly Hills of two-story buildings, courtyards and fountains, and many red-tile roofs, circa '56, we crossed Beverly Glen into the San Fernando Valley. About a mile from the Wallis estate was the McKinley School for Boys. It had about a hundred and twenty boys, from age five through high school, and several boys who had grown past eighteen but were still not ready to leave who stayed on as employees. They had a building of their own. In '56 the boys of McKinley were predominantly white, but there was a liberal collection of colored kids and Mexicans, the operative and acceptable terms then. Most came from homes of drunken abusers, some were sent by social agencies, and a few came from the Juvenile Court. Once upon a time they had tried to put me here. In the parking lot I had thrown a tantrum of such maniacal ferocity that whoever was looking out an administration building window decided not to accept me. I felt wonderful then. I would get to stay with my father in his furnished room, sleeping on the army cot in the corner, for at least a couple more weeks. My father's face was scarlet; veins stood out in hard ridges. He was stifling rage. I had perfected getting thrown out of these homes and schools that I hated; now they wouldn't even take me.

Not long thereafter, I went from being the concern of social service agencies to that of the juvenile justice system.

Louise turned off Riverside and passed through the tunnel of trees to a parking lot. It was full of cars, but the only person visible was an eight-year-old in a bathing suit starting along a sidewalk in front of the parking lot. As soon as his bare feet hit the hot cement, he danced and jumped off onto the lawn. He disappeared around a two-story masonry building. We went that way. Before we came around the building we heard splashing and excited voices cheering, "Go! Go! Go!"

When we came around the corner, we saw the Olympic-size swimming pool and a swimming meet was in progress. A white-haired man of sixty separated himself from a group of adults near the pool and came to greet us. He was Mr. Swartzcoff, the superintendent. It was he who had offered me a job to satisfy the requirements of release on parole. Although it was much easier for an excon back then, jobs in general being more plentiful, there was still a stigma, so I was trying to read Mr. S., as he was called by the boys and the staff alike, for I wanted to know if the offer had been made willingly or because Mrs. Hal Wallis was the McKinley Home's foremost benefactor. Hiring me actually cost them nothing. Mrs. Wallis wrote them a check for the amount of my salary, and immediately deducted it from her taxes as a charitable contribution. Had she paid it after taxes it would have cost her several times the amount, for after-tax income was about 15% of before-tax income.

Mr. S. was affable enough, but it was the effusive Mrs. S, his wife, that made me feel comfortable and showed me around the home. I wasn't starting work until the next Monday. Although there was no real slot for me to fill, with

120 boys there was plenty to do. Sometimes I would watch the pool, although every boy at McKinley could swim like a fish after the first month of summer. I would drive boys to appointments with doctors, dentists, and social workers.

My room was above the kitchen. It was quite large and had a balcony overlooking the driveway and the walkway to the mess hall. I could stay here during the week and at my apartment on the weekend.

We unloaded the many packages and shopping bags marked DESMOND'S, BULLOCKS, and SILVERWOOD'S and piled them on the floor next to the bed, not hiding them, but making them inconspicuous as a matter of course. I was given the key, and I laughed as I inserted it and turned. It was the first door I could remember locking. It seemed funny—but many things have seemed funny to me and un-funny to most others.

It was time for a late lunch, and the gate to Wallis Farms was around the corner and down Woodman about half a mile. I asked her why it was called a farm, and she told me so they could pay the cook, maid, chauffeur, and gardener as farm employees, not servants.

We turned off Woodman and curtsied for the solid green gate that was already swinging open. It was familiar, yet entirely new. It was certainly more vivid after five years of San Quentin polishing my lenses of perception. The roses were a riot of color, and as we walked from the car to the front door a wisp of breeze blew the sweet scent to me. God, it was good to be free.

During lunch, Louise told me about Mr. and Mrs. S. and how fond she was of them and what good work they did at McKinley.

After lunch, Bertha departed. Louise snapped her fingers in sudden recall. "You need a couple other things. Come on."

She led me upstairs to Hal's suite, where she purloined gold-and-sapphire cuff links from a posh yacht club in the Bahamas and a tie tack with a half-carat diamond. She started to take one of the three watches but put it back. "No, I'm going to buy you one," she said. I took the gifts, but I had vague misgivings. I didn't expect material things. She'd always indicated that she wanted to help me help myself, and that was what I expected and wanted. The clothes and the apartment, they were generous and I appreciated them—but what I hoped for was that she would make introductions and open doors.

On the way out she stopped at Hal's closet, which was twenty feet long behind sliding mirror panels. The shelf above the hangers was stacked with sweaters in plastic bags. She pulled down several. "You like cashmere? Here."

It was a simple V-neck in navy, but the label said: BERGDORF-GOODMAN, and the feel was the incomparable softness of cashmere.

She was singing as we went back downstairs. In the Blue Room she took a cigarette from a box and a wooden kitchen match from another. Instead of using the striker, she pulled the match along the wall. It ignited, but it also left a long streak on the wall. "What the hell, it belongs to the board of education."

It took a few seconds for me to get the humor and laugh, although her humor and my laugh were tinged with sadness, for this Monterey Colonial with its shaded grounds and lush lawns had the serene beauty of a cloister. Because she had always been a clown and comic, it would take repeated bizarre incidents over several months before I realized that something was wrong.

STANDARD PROCEDURE FOR THE PAROLEE IS to visit the parole officer—now known as the parole agent—the day after release, where he is given the rest of his "gate money." I was shopping with Louise the day after release; then came the weekend, so it wasn't until Monday that I met my parole officer, a small man with a flat-top haircut and a tiny mustache. Even then it was not at the parole office. I was at Wallis Farms, in the Blue Room, with me seated next to Louise Fazenda Wallis—on the wide armrest of her overstuffed chair, my other arm extended along the top of the chair back. She played gracious lady as well as Katherine Cornell. Would he and his wife like to see the studio? "Not on one of those tours. I'll take you behind the scenes. You have a wife and children?"

Ah yes, she played him beautifully. It wasn't manipulation with ulterior motive. It was to make him forget about me. He had more than a hundred parolees under his supervision and could keep track of very few. I wanted to be ignored, and that seemed the message he gave me when I walked him out to his car. He stopped and looked back and up at the house and around at the property. "Well," he said laconically, "I'm pretty sure I won't pick up the paper and read about you in a shootout with the LAPD."

"What about a car? Can I drive?"

"If you have a license."

We shook hands and he drove around the circle and down the road toward the front gate. I felt great. A car. I was going to have a car—as soon as I had a driver's license. I was bobbing and weaving and shadowboxing as I went back inside the house.

Louise saw me and laughed. "Feel good, huh?"

"Couldn't feel better. He said I could drive . . . if I had a license."

"I've been thinking about that. Can you pass a driver's license exam?"

I was dubious and it showed. I'd gone on joy rides in stolen cars and on couple of high-speed chases that ended in wrecks, but beyond knowing what red and green meant on a traffic light, I was totally ignorant of the traffic laws.

"No matter," she said. "I thought about it. We'll get you some lessons. When you get a license you'll need a car. Nothing new or fancy, but I put some money aside from the house. I had no reinvest nearly all of it or give it to the government. Taxes, you know. We can get richer and richer—in fact, we have to get richer and richer or the government will take it."

"It looks to me like you're doing okay."

She laughed in a way that felt like an affectionate hug.

▪ ▪ ▪

THE FOLLOWING WEEK I STARTED WORK at the McKinley Home for Boys. My duties sort of evolved. At first I filled in at different places. At the swimming pool my job was closer to scarecrow than lifeguard. Every boy could swim, and everyone ten or older could swim better than I could. I was charged with maintaining order, keeping horseplay to a minimum, and stopping the running around the poolside. When a busload of boys went somewhere, say the *Times* charity game between LA Rams and the Washington Redskins, I was the second man, the one who kept them from yelling out the windows and made sure nobody was separated from the group. When the fall school semester started, I tutored in study hall three evenings a week. After I got a driver's license and a four-year-old Ford convertible, my main job was taking boys to appointments with doctors, dentists, and psychologists. Within a month I would have won a popularity contest as the staff member best liked by the boys. That was partly because my position didn't require me to enforce much authority, but the primary reason was because I had been raised in places like McKinley, although none so good. I knew what it was to be a child raised by strangers, to be without a family to turn to. I could not fill that emptiness, but I was friend and adviser and I never judged. I wanted to help them find their footing in life. Some were hard to like, the whiners and crybabies, and I was ashamed for not liking them, for they had the greatest need for attention and understanding. Among the hundred and twenty were a handful who were beyond help. The warp was already too great. A pair of these broke into a hi-fi store in Van Nuys and stashed the loot in my car. I yelled, "Oh God! Oh shit!" when they told me. It could mean a trip back to San Quentin as a parole violator. The adult authorities would treat me like a twentieth-century Fagin. Yet I could not countenance turning them in. Although I had no intention of ever committing another crime, I still had an unquestioning acceptance of the criminal's number-one rule: thou shall not snitch, not even on a snitch. "Get that shit outta there," I told them. "Right now."

Naturally they were caught the moment they went to school and started flashing their booty. I held my breath, but my name was never mentioned. They'd been in trouble before, and this time Mr. S. sent them to juvenile hall and the juvenile justice system. It saddened me because it was so much like my own childhood, one thing leading to another and eventually to prison. A decade later I ran into one of them in the penitentiary.

Nobody at McKinley except Mr. and Mrs. S. knew I was an ex-convict, nor did they know of my special relationship with Mrs. Wallis. She lived so close that it was easy for me to visit. When she wanted me to meet someone, she sent for me.

Hal was gone, and somehow I got the impression that he was on location with *Gunfight at the O.K. Corral*. Their son, Brent, was a lieutenant in the army or air force, stationed in Northern California. He came home on the weekends, where I finally met him on a blistering San Fernando Valley afternoon. He had a moderately powerful physique. He had worked out with weights since his early teens. From the books lining the walls of his room he was obviously well educated, well read, and interested in ideas. Many of his books were in Spanish. Louise said she had lost him when he was about twelve years old. She had taken him with her as she followed Hal to trysts with mistresses that he maintained quite flagrantly. Brent's reaction, according to her, was to dislike his father and turn cold to her. "He's got armor thick as a battleship's," she said to me. He had a Ph.D. in psychology, and she thought his choice of professions was because of his childhood. He intensely disliked the movie industry, she said.

When I met him, I wondered what she'd said to him about me. Of course he knew I had been in prison while he had been at one of the prestigious Claremont Colleges. I had no idea which one. Did he see me as an interloper?

I found him as inscrutable as the proverbial Asian. Brent was so well mannered that I was unable to read him. His courtliness I would have expected among the English aristocracy rather than in the scion of Hollywood *nouveau riche*. Louise thought it was from his being raised by European governesses. He had the best manners of any man I'd met so far. He introduced me to the first imported beer I'd ever seen, Heineken. It was markedly better than Lucky Lager and Brew 102, which teenagers in the poorer sections of Los Angeles drank to get drunk. What other reason was there to drink beer?

When he drove me back to McKinley in a Mercedes 190 SL roadster, it was the first time I'd ridden in a sports car. The feel on curves and corners was an almost erotic sensation. It felt totally different from other cars. It was fun. I wanted one. I wanted a lot of things.

Although he had been gracious and friendly, I had no idea what he thought or how he really felt. I didn't want him thinking that I was exploiting his mother. I would never take advantage of her, although there would come a time when I wished I had done so. I wanted her to do what she had said from the beginning: help me to help myself. That began to change. She began to give me money far beyond what I expected or wanted, and when I tried to tell her that, she waved me away: "Never mind. We've got more than we ever dreamed of having. I just made two million." Indeed, they had purchased the estate of a millionaire in Chatsworth. It had a sprawling house, a bunkhouse, stables, and a timing track for the racehorses Hal had raised. As it was zoned for agriculture, Louise planned to raise alfalfa and write off the losses against other income. Two months after they completed escrow on the property, the zoning was changed so it could be subdivided into tract homes. Its value doubled from $2 million to $4 million. When you're rich, she said, you keep getting richer with very little effort, as long as you don't intentionally throw your money away. How could I protest when she gave me a few hundred dollars? Once I gave her back a thousand dollars; the next day it arrived at McKinley in the U.S. Mail.

Not knowing what else to do, for certainly I wasn't going to hurl it into the street, I deposited it in my checking account. I could use it; there was no doubt of that.

Near the end of summer I met Hal Wallis for the first time. I'd gotten a flat tire about a quarter mile from the gate to Wallis Farms. I called Louise and she told me to come over and call the Auto Club on her membership card. That way I wouldn't have to pay for towing. I'd made the call, she had given me her card, and I was getting ready to walk back to the car to meet the tow truck when we heard the front door open, followed by male voices.

Hal came in, followed by Brent and another youth who I believe managed the actual agriculture of Wallis Farms, which actually grew something somewhere. They'd been at a preview screening of *Gunfight at the O.K. Corral* and carried stacks of audience reaction cards.

"How are they?" Louise asked.

"I think the best I've ever seen," Hal said. "And I've seen plenty over the years."

Gunfight starred Burt Lancaster and Kirk Douglas, both of whom Hal had discovered. Louise once told me that he was poorly educated and poorly mannered when she first met him. He was working in the publicity department of National Studios, which became Warner Brothers. One day on a set she saw him from the rear and, thinking he was someone else, grabbed him from behind. They got married and three years later he was executive producer in charge of production at Warner Brothers, the same job Irving Thalberg had at MGM. Hal's training: typing and shorthand at a Chicago business school. But he had two natural talents. He saved many thousands of dollars through an unerring sense of what should be cut from a script before having to wait until it was on film. He also had a perfect feel for whom the public would love. His very mediocre autobiography, *Star Maker,* which he would write twenty-five years later, scarcely did more than list his films. He was certainly a mogul from Hollywood's Golden Age who deserves a good biography, as does Louise Fazenda Wallis.

That night Mr. Wallis didn't notice me. I studied him, though. When young he had been handsome, she said, but now his hair was thinning, and he combed it straight back, which gave his face a sharpness. He was average-looking, at best, although his clothes glowed with the expensive good taste of an *Esquire* spread. He was cordial, but for a moment I saw his eyes unveiled. He saw life in terms of manipulation and combat, so how else would a twenty-two-year-old ex-con appear to him? I could understand his attitude. Ah well, but it would have been great to have his favor. He could open doors in this the capital of nepotism, oligarchy, and connections. Being a success in Hollywood took skills, but even more than skills, except in the technical end, it took connections. The easiest way to be a movie star is to have parents who were stars or directors or producers. As the children of movie people grow up, they see up close how the game is played, and they know the players, fathers of friends with whom they grew up. There is just enough new blood to keep it percolating.

"You'd better go," Louise said. "Or you'll miss the Auto Club truck."

I walked down the driveway to the electric gate and then along the side of Woodman toward Chandler Boulevard, named, I assume, for the founding family of the Los Angeles *Times*. Once upon a time they'd had estates with orange groves and children rode their horses along the roadside, which had neither curbs nor sidewalks. Now the orange groves were few, although I could smell their blossoms and jasmine in the night. Everything was the American Dream of the moment: three bedrooms, two baths, in a ranch-style tract home. A popular song proclaimed the joy of making the San Fernando Valley one's home.

As I walked along the roadside, footsteps crunching, occasional headlights flashing over me, crickets sounding in the night, I knew that Hal Wallis was nothing like his wife. She'd told me that he was a cold and ruthless man (married to Hollywood's Angel), and anyone cold and ruthless had to be very suspicious. It went together like mustard with a hot dog. While I wanted to be a writer and proclaimed it loudly, back then I specifically wanted to write screenplays, which I kept quiet about. If I had Hal Wallis as an ally . . . I had tried to pull him toward me, but there was the obstacle of hostile suspicion.

As I neared the car, the Auto Club tow truck pulled up. Its driver could hardly believe that I was unable to change a flat tire. It wasn't part of the reform school curriculum, and I'd had no chance to change a tire in San Quentin, so where would I learn? It was an explanation I kept to myself.

HAL DEPARTED CALIFORNIA FOR SOMEWHERE, and Brent went back to the base. Hal's sister, Minna Wallis, was in town, but she saw little of Louise. Minna had never married and some in Hollywood, according to Louise, spoke of her possessive mental incest toward her brother. She had gotten her brother his first job at the studio. "She was even jealous of me back then," Louise said. It was also said that Minna had forced an English actor, a poor man's facsimile of Ronald Colman, into being her lover in return for Hal renewing his contract. She saw Louise infrequently in the normal routine of the day. I was the one who saw Louise deteriorate, but not having been around her very much until now and because she was, after all, a professional clown, I attributed much of her bizarre behavior to her nature.

One afternoon I went to visit and found her whacking a house wall with a sledgehammer. All I could do was grin and shake my head. On another occasion, we spent a futile two hours telephoning around the world in search of a priest to whom she wished to speak. It was 3:30 A.M. in Austria, where his order had their headquarters. He was somewhere in the Holy Land, but they had no way to contact him. The mynah birds were flying around her room, and there were little spots where bird shit hit something and couldn't be totally washed away. Those spots could be immaculate otherwise, but a trace of stain remained. "I just wish the sons of bitches would say something," she said.

One afternoon I got a message at McKinley to call Mrs. Wallis. She was excited; she wanted me to come to dinner. Tennessee Williams would be there. Hal was negotiating for film rights to *Orpheus Descending,* a play that he had written specifically for Anna Magnani. Hal Wallis had a several-picture deal with her.

I arrived in a navy blue shirt and a necktie. Tennessee Williams was in black-and-red-check Pendleton, half-drunk, unshaven, and with perceptible body odor. By the time we sat down, he was totally drunk. Halfway through the soup, he said he felt sick and excused himself.

Every Saturday evening the latest movies were screened in the Blue Room. A screen rose out of the floor, and across the room a painting came down from an opening for a projection booth. The projectionist was hired from the studio. When Hal was home, his friends came. When he was gone, which was much of the time, Louise's friends were the guests. I liked languishing on an overstuffed chair while watching Elizabeth Taylor running through the jungle ahead of a herd of rampaging elephants or Jack Palance as a movie star who was simultaneously beloved by the multitude and under the thumb of the movie mogul. Having a private screening was a great way to start Saturday evening, and in the incomparable LA nights there were always adventures to be had until the sun rose on Saturday morning.

THE SUMMER OF '56 came to an end. The only change was that afternoons in the Valley were 82° now instead of 102°. I stayed away from most ex-convicts and former friends, but my vow of rehabilitation never included that I would stop smoking pot. That necessitated keeping a connection with my childhood partner, Wedo. When I went to see him, I found that during my five years in San Quentin he had married his girlfriend, fathered two children, and turned into a junkie who peddled on a street level to maintain his habit. He was on probation for illegal possession and on bail for a second case. Within the month he was going to court for sentencing and it was a cinch he was going where I had just been.

Through Wedo, I met his brother-in-law, Jimmy D., who was married to Wedo's wife's sister. Jimmy gladly procured me pot if I gave him some of it and a few dollars. Although we were in the same age, my five years in San Quentin gave me status. Jimmy was lean, powerful, and handsome, but he was oblivious to his appearance or his clothes. I once gave him an expensive suit. He put it in the trunk of his car. Five months later I saw him open the car trunk. The suit was there, now mildewed and ruined. Jimmy was too lazy to work and had become too scared to steal. A couple of years later he drove the getaway car while I heisted a bookmaker. When I came out, the car was gone. I had to make my escape on foot, down alleys and over fences in an area I knew poorly. I got away and, when I confronted him, he said that a police car had circled the block so the officers could give him special scrutiny, so he had driven away. At the time I gave him the benefit of the doubt, but when he later folded up en route to a score ("I can't do it, man; I just can't do it") I changed my judgment of the earlier episode. I used it as a basis for a sequence in the movie *Straight Time* two decades later.

I had no close family. I did have some second cousins, although I hadn't seen any of them since my parents' divorce, when they were adolescents and I was four. Bob H., then twenty-nine, ran one of several departments at Channel 4, the local NBC affiliate. He was a handsome man who sang well, but not quite well enough; he was an even better painter, but again not quite enough better. Or perhaps he could have been fulfilled in either endeavor but lacked enough tenacity to overcome. Either way, he wasn't what he wanted to be. He had converted to Catholicism and wanted to be a priest. I don't remember why that never reached fruition. At first I thought he was gay. His mannerisms appeared to me like those of a queen in the penitentiary. As a convict said, "I ain' never seen no man act that way." After a while, however, I reached a different opinion. I think Bob was asexual. Psychologically I believe he was far closer to being gay than being a male warrior, but the thought of male-to-male sex would have been physically repulsive.

Bob had a girlfriend, Patty Ann, although it was a weird romance. He had kissed her just once. She was *sui generis* as far as I was concerned. Twenty-six years old, slender, pretty, well-educated, vivacious, intelligent—she was a virgin. That was something I wouldn't learn for some time. Although it was still the uptight fifties and she was a nice Catholic girl, it was hard for me to believe that any twenty-six-year-old outside a nunnery was a virgin. I met her on a Saturday afternoon at Channel 4, where I went to see Cousin Robert about a party he was giving that night.

Patty Ann and I had an immediate affinity. By the time the party ended it was long past midnight. We walked through Hollywood until dawn, talking about all kinds of things. She'd never even met anyone who had been in jail. That, too, was hard for me to believe.

Within a week we were seeing each other regularly, and whatever idea we might have had about romance at the outset, it quickly became obvious that we were too different for anything more than a great friendship. However, we did share a love of books and writing. She gave me encouragement and advice. Of all the people I've known in my life, I think she has the best attitude toward life. She is as happy as anyone can be without being psychotic. She was a benefit to my etiquette, and when I started to think or act in the manner taught by my background, she would pinch my cheek and say, "No, no, poochie. You can't do that anymore. You're a writer now." She could always make me feel good.

Mrs. Wallis thought Patty Ann was wonderful and let us use a cabana at the Sand & Sea Club, the mansion that Hearst had built for Marion Davies on the beach at Santa Monica. The original colonial pillars, facing the ocean, were as big as those on the White House. The swimming pool, with a bridge across it, was of Carrara marble. Much of the original was gone, and a double deck of cabanas had been constructed. Each was a single room plus a bathroom and a shower, opening onto a wide terrace overlooking the sand and sea. Each cabana had furnishings appropriate for the beach: a sofa of bamboo and water-resistant cushions, a glass-topped table in an alcove, a cabinet with a bar and closet. It also had a card table. On occasion I would play the role of writer, moving a card table and portable typewriter onto the terrace and then posing with a tall drink while looking down at the unwashed masses running around below. For me it was a fancy way to go to the beach.

Meanwhile Louise's behavior became more irrational, although I still didn't see how irrational it was. Saying offhandedly that she had never really liked it, she gave Patty Ann a diamond-and-sapphire brooch. I had no idea of its value, nor that Louise had been dispensing her jewelry and other possessions almost willy-nilly. She changed toward me, too. Where she had once been generous but not excessive, and stressed helping me to help myself, now she began giving me more than I expected, wanted, or felt good about. I traded in the Ford convertible for a used XK 120 Jaguar, planning to make the payments myself. She said I was impatient and to slow down and how hard it was to ask someone to help me when I arrived in a Jaguar. Still, when I made a payment, the loan had been paid in full. It was great, but not what I wanted. When I pressed about those things, she waved me aside and said I didn't need to worry. It was easy to do, but I knew it was transitory. It wasn't a permanent lie I could hide behind. But it felt wrong.

Realization of the situation's gravity came at a Saturday-night screening. Usually I ate dinner at the house if I was invited to a screening, but for some reason Patty Ann and I dined at the Sportsman's Lodge on Ventura Boulevard, which was then fairly new and somewhat fashionable.

When we reached the house, dinner was finished there, too. Brent Wallis was on hand with a friend named Henry Fairbanks. Three or four Catholic teaching brothers from nearby Notre Dame High School were waiting for the movie, plus a young woman from the neighborhood with whom Brent had grown up and her husband, who worked for the Bank of America.

When we reached the Blue Room, Louise was drunk. The jacket of her white pants suit was unbuttoned down the back. Apparently a young woman had been protesting Louise's excessive generosity in giving them the mortgage to their home, which she held. That conversation was winding down because of our arrival and because everyone started settling in to watch the movie. The painting over the projection booth opening came down, the screen rose from the floor across the room, and people began to find seats. Louise sat on the right-hand side of a sofa at the rear, under the projection booth. She motioned Patty Ann to sit next to her. "And you there," she said to me, indicating the space on the other side of Patty Ann. My attention was caught by a conversation across the room, the content of which I no longer remember. Then Louise's voice, shrill with alcohol, cut through: ". . . take this and marry him. He needs you. He said he wanted me to get him Anita Ekberg. He was joking, but. . . . He doesn't want an actress. He just thinks he wants an actress. They never see anything outside the mirror. He needs a good girl. He's going to be rich . . . gonna make him the richest man in the San Fernando Valley." She noticed me paying attention and waved for me to turn away. "This is between us," she said. In her hand was a ring with a diamond I would have thought was fake if it were not being waved about by Mrs. Hal B. Wallis. It was somewhere between three and five carats.

The intercom buzzed and the projectionist notified Louise that all was ready. She told him to start the movie.

The lights went down and the beam of dancing gray light cut through the cigarette smoke and threw images on the screen as, simultaneously, the music rose. I was glad for the anonymity it gave, for my face was fiery with embarrassment and Patty Ann was nearly in tears.

As the credits rolled, Louise continued on Patty, repeating the phrase: "Do this little thing for me. Please do it for me." The movie sound was drowning Louise out. She pushed a button on the armrest, and the sound went off, although the movie continued to run, silent in the darkness. The only sound was Louise's drunken voice pleading with Patty Ann to take the ring and marry me.

Brent and his friend got up and left the room. I followed them into the entry hall. I forget what I said, but it was some kind of combination apology and disclaimer of responsibility. Likewise, I cannot recall Brent's reply, except that it was brief and gracious. They went out the front door.

I turned back toward the Blue Room. The sound was back on—thank God, I thought—and just then Patty Ann came out, shoulders shaking, arm over her face. When she raised her eyes to see where she was going (even mortified, she didn't want to crash headlong into a wall) I could see two black streaks of runny mascara. She was distraught and I could feel empathy for her. Nevertheless, the streaks of mascara somehow went beyond anguish into soap opera parody. Neither death nor jail was at stake. There was not merely pain, but pain's humor, and, despite myself, I started laughing.

After several seconds of increased tears, she suddenly stamped her foot on the floor. "Shame on you, Ed Bunker. You don't know how to comfort a girl." Then she, too, perceived the absurdity and began laughing while crying. I rubbed her back and debated returning to the Blue Room. Through the open door down the hall came the flashing gray light and sound track—but only for a moment. Then the movie stopped and the room's lights came up. I could have handled the darkness, but the particular kind of chaos likely to transpire was not what my life had prepared me for. And Patty Ann certainly didn't deserve further harassment, no matter what the motive or anything else.

"Come on; let's go." I guided her to the door.

My car was not far from the front door. As we got in, the Mercedes roadster with Brent and his friend went by. We were close behind as they went out the gate, but when they turned left, I turned right. I didn't want them to think even momentarily that I might be following them.

I drove up winding Beverly Glen to Mulholland Drive, which ran along the top of the line of hills, or short mountains, from Cahuenga Pass in Hollywood to the Pacific Coast Highway beside the ocean. Mulholland was curves and switchbacks. Sometimes the San Fernando Valley was visible, clustered lights with darkness in between. Soon enough it would become a carpet to the next line of mountains. We spoke little. The scene in the Blue Room was still with us, perhaps more so with me. All of Louise's earlier comedic behavior now had darker meanings. Something was wrong with her, and being drunk was only the catalyst exposing it.

ON MONDAY MORNING I CALLED PARAMOUNT and tried to contact Hal Wallis. He was out of town, and the woman wouldn't give me his number without my giving details of what I wanted. I wasn't ready to do that. I could have called Minna Wallis, but I didn't know her. Finally I called the Hacker Clinic in Beverly Hills. I knew Louise had once undergone therapy from Dr. Hacker. He listened to my story, but his response was noncommittal. Several days later, Dr. Frym called to tell me that I'd done the right thing. Someone had told Hal, who had flown back to Los Angeles and also called Dr. Hacker. Their telling him that I'd already informed them might lessen his suspicion of me. Dr. Frym emphasized two things: "Don't take any money from her, and don't drink with her. When someone has as much money as she does and starts giving it away, they'll take the right away from her."

Several days later, without warning, she was admitted to Cedars. Over that weekend they moved everything from the house in the Valley to the larger mansion at 515 Mapleton Drive in Holmby Hills. Dr. Hacker thought that losing the house in the Valley, which had been her sanctuary for many years from Hal's flagrant infidelity, was part of her problem. Over that weekend, I got a message at the McKinley Home to call Mr. Wallis. He wanted to see me. The move was in progress when I arrived at the house. He told me that she had given away a considerable amount of money and all her jewelry: "I know you didn't get that much of the money, but what about the jewelry?" All I could account for was the brooch she had given to Patty Ann. I retrieved it and returned it to him at the Hillcrest Country Club. The conversation lasted but a few seconds, but it ended with his saying that maybe he could help me.

When Louise exited Cedars, it was to the new house in Holmby Hills. Minnie and her husband, who were loyal to Louise, were replaced by a couple hired by Hal's sister. When I went to visit, I had the feeling that they were watching me. Always before I'd felt that Louise and I were together, in a kind of nonmalicious conspiracy. Now, however, she had manifestly experienced some kind of breakdown. Dr. Hacker still visited her every week. Under those circumstances it was impossible for me to talk with her as I once had. I couldn't add stress to her situation.

I had given her the half-finished manuscript to my second novel, about a young drug addict who becomes an informer. It was missing after the move. This was not a family unfamiliar with scripts and manuscripts. Nobody would throw it out without at least knowing what it was. I had no doubt that its loss was due to some malice from someone, but there was nothing I could say or do about it. The novel was probably unworthy of publication, as my next four were found wanting, although the last of those will soon be published in England, and perhaps in America with some judicious pruning and polishing. It was a kind of a Jim Thompson noir story, unlike the realism of my other work.

I'D BEEN OUT OF SAN QUENTIN for about a year, and it was time for me to move on from the McKinley Home for Boys. Because of my voracious reading and aspiration to the literary life, it seemed reasonable to try for a job in the story department of one of the studios. Louise thought the same, but she also thought it inappropriate for her to call Mervyn LeRoy. Minna Wallis, being an agent, dealt with people at the studios and would make the calls, although it would be behind the scenes at Warner Brothers, where mention of Hal Wallis would send Jack Warner into apoplexy. A "story analyst," or "reader," would be given a book or article and write a very brief, no more than a page, comment on its viability as a movie and then a three- or four-page synopsis of the story. I was given *The Nun's Story*, which Warner Brothers had already bought, and with Patty Ann's help did the job, which Louise read and thought quite good.

I'd gone through four studios when the head of the story department at Paramount told me that while Minna had arranged for the meeting, she had also said that she and Hal preferred that he not hire me. "I don't know what it's about," he said, "but don't think that she's your friend.

As I crossed the parking lot to my car, I was certain who had taken and destroyed my unfinished novel. I wasn't even angry. This confirmed my belief in human nature. And so much for Hal Wallis's throwaway line about helping me.

I had a first-class wardrobe and a Jaguar sports car, although it was evident to me that it was a lemon and the used-car lot had clipped me. It was constantly in need of frequently expensive repair. I had a $2,600 check that Louise had given me and I had never cashed. I knew how she handled such matters. A man she had put into business with a janitorial service that now serviced several downtown buildings was a bookkeeper. Once a month he came over and took care of her accounts. He would bring the unusual check to her attention, for in 1956 that would equal at least ten times as much as it does on the eve of the twenty-first century. Although not a king's ransom by the standards of the time, it was certainly an amount to be queried about. She would simply make it disappear. That I knew.

The clutch went out on my Jaguar. I cashed the check and forgot about it. I had not gotten it by subterfuge or deceit. It had been given me. And there had been no question of her competence at the time, not that I knew about. I will admit a slight sense of unease before doing it but no sense of having done wrong.

A few weeks went by. Without warning, she went into Cedars and had an "extremely serious" liver operation, as Dr. Frym phrased it. "The liver is always serious surgery."

I called Cedars, and they denied having any Louise Wallis or Mrs. Hal Wallis or any Wallis or Wallace or Fazenda. And by then the switchboard operator was abrupt and irritated.

I considered calling all the hospitals in Southern California, but the list was too long, the possibilities too many.

She was under another name, of course. The name of a character she'd played in some obscure movie.

She called me in about a week. It had been touch and go, or so I'd been told, but she sounded both strong and funny.

She stayed in the hospital another week, during which period the checks for the various personal accounts had come back. She told me immediately when I first visited her when she was convalescing at home on Mapleton Drive that Hal had gone through them. For a moment I felt as if I'd lost something—but I knew that I'd lost nothing. Hal Wallis was never going to help me unless he could profit from it, and that was unlikely, although he would have gotten a loyal friend without avaricious intent or duplicity for the deal. I would have wagered then, and now, that he could never have pointed to three men and sincerely proclaimed them his friends.

It was also obvious that I could no longer count on or conspire with Louise. She had given me so much that I fairly ached, near tears with gratitude for what she'd done, and only partially realized at the time that her main gift was letting me look from the outhouse into the mansion, and I was far too wise about too much to accept the future that the past wanted to mandate for me. Maybe she would help me sometime in the future, but for now I needed a plan for my current situation. Obviously I wasn't getting into a studio story department. I might have been able to get an office boy job at the *Herald Express,* as the afternoon Hearst newspaper was then named. Vanity of vanities, I could not see myself as an office boy, thank you.

Yet I needed a job of some kind, both to pacify the parole officer and to make a living. I had clothes, a nice apartment without rent, and a Jaguar roadster, but no cash flow. I applied for an insurance salesman job. They were enthused by my manner and appearance, but I never heard from them again after they discovered my background.

When I realized how slickly the used-car salesmen who had sold me the Jag had taken me off, me who thought I was half-slick, I decided it was a game I should learn. I became a used-car salesman. My first job was with a Chevrolet dealership on Wilshire Boulevard in Beverly Hills. They hired anyone who walked in the door. It was all commission, so what did they care? The idea was to sell to your mother and father, brother and sister, friends and lovers. Bring them in and turn them over to a closer. In about three days I understood that this was no way to anything.

Then I spent a couple of months at a dealership that sold Nashes and Ramblers. I don't recall if it was then called American Motors or something else. It was now 1958, a terrible year for car sales, and what we sold was the opposite of the swept-wing yachts then in vogue. I made a little money, but not much. I did, however, learn the game.

I finally went to work for the English mechanic who worked on my Jag. His business was on Second and LaBrea. He fixed foreign cars, especially English, and sold used sports cars of all varieties. It was the age of the Austin-Healey, Jaguar, MG, and bathtub Porsche. He only had two salesmen. We worked hours that I liked. I would come in at noon and stay until 9:00 in the evening. The last three hours I was alone. The next day I would open up at 9:00 A.M. and work until noon, when the other salesman took over. Then I was off until noon the next day. I had unlimited free use of a telephone, and anyone could visit me about anything in the privacy of my small office with the loud little air conditioner in the window. I could dress in jacket and necktie, and no grime got under my fingernails. It was the conservative fifties, long before anyone even heard of grunge as a style choice. Even beatnik poets were neat and stylish, albeit with individualized flairs. Another fringe benefit was that every other evening when I locked up, I could use any of the two dozen or so foreign sports cars on the lot. A bathtub Porsche one night, an Austin-Healey, Jaguar, or Mercedes 190 SL the next. The owner did take in a gull-wing 300 SL Mercedes, which he asked me not to take. "I wasn't thinking about it," I told him.

"And why not?" he asked.

"It's almost empty of gas." For although Richfield premium was about twenty cents a gallon, I almost always took a car whose gas tank was full or nearly full.

In the argot of the underworld, a car salesman's job proved to be a good front. . . .

9

THE RUN

PROFESSIONAL THIEVES RECOGNIZE that playing the game means doing time. They measure success not by the certainty of eventual imprisonment, but rather by the length of imprisonment *vis-à-vis* the length of a run he has and how well he lives before being incarcerated. Although the subculture of the professional thief depicted in Dickens, Melville, and Victor Hugo was first eroded by Prohibition's organized crime and their turf wars, it was destroyed by drugs and the drug underworld. Until today, when a young criminal's crime skills are limited to shooting somebody and dealing crack. Back in '57 there were still enough adherents so I could find righteous thieves, safecrackers, boosters, players of short con, and burglars. My initial parole officer had said, quite correctly, that he never worried about picking up the morning newspaper to read where I shot my way out of a supermarket or a bank. He had over a hundred cases, and others needed his attention far more than I did. After about six months without trouble, I saw him no more. The only requirement was that I send in monthly reports. That put no strain on my resentment of authority. I could do that.

Without Louise Wallis the movie business was closed to me in 1957. The Biz was a fraction of the size it is today, and the boss of one of the top three agencies, sister of Paramount's number-one moneymaker year after year, had shown her dislike of me. She had gone out of her way to salt me down and slide grease under me. Once I would have told Louise and we would have plotted something together. That was now impossible. She was suffering from borderline schizophrenia—or clinical depression aggravated by alcoholism. I couldn't be sure that her telephone wasn't monitored "for her well-being," and it was like visiting somebody in jail when I went to see her. Ideas of writing screenplays had to wait. I took the attitude that if I couldn't have it, I didn't want it.

It wasn't my true milieu anyway. I was more comfortable in Hollywood's dark side, amid call girls, vice and drugs and nightclubs that glittered in the night.

The thief's underworld, which is different from that of the mafiosi, gang bangers, and racketeers, has many adages and observations. If you can't do the time don't mess with crime is the best-known. Another is: A thief's nerve is in direct proportion to his financial condition. Or: Hard times make hard people.

I started with the advantage of a classy apartment, a nice wardrobe, and an XK 120 Jaguar roadster, which still had panache despite a dented fender and a bent front bumper. I was under no pressure for a quick score to get out of some problem. Many crimes are committed because of traffic tickets or child care payments. I wasn't confronted with such problems. I could take my time. Thinking back, I cannot recall a moment when I decided to return to crime as a way of life. I was simply trying to get by and live well in the world that I found.

For confederates, I went to neighborhoods and *barrios* east of the LA River, where I had friends and a certain amount of reputation and respect. In Beverly Hills a Jaguar was just another car, whereas in East Los Angeles Jags were seldom seen. As a criminal you might say I was a jack-of-all-trades rather than a specialist—and there were crimes I balked at committing. I did not burglarize private homes or steal from the old and the poor. They didn't have anything to steal anyway.

My preferred victims were insurance companies, and I sought nonviolent crimes with profit, although I despise confidence men. Books and movies depict them as handsome, suave, witty and likable, but the truth is that con men are despicable in most cases. They prey upon the old and the weak. They lack loyalty, for they see everyone as a potential sucker. I liked armed robbers better. Most were fools acting from desperation. When they needed money to pay rent or a ticket or to get a fix, all they knew was to put a gun in somebody's face and say, "Give it up." Most of them cruise around until something looks easy, a small market or a liquor store. Then they park around the corner and go in, never knowing what they will find. If they have been doing it regularly in the area, they could well run into a stakeout, the shotgun-wielding brother-in-law of the owner, or a policeman hidden behind a curtain. Finally, robbery was always an offense the law looked harshly upon. There have always been three strikes and out for the armed robber, it was called the habitual criminal statute. I would consider a robbery, but it required there be a substantial amount of money, a minuscule chance of having to shoot, and a situation where I could mask my face. I would never commit a robbery where a witness could point a finger from the witness stand and say, *"That's the man."* There are only two ways to be convicted for robbery. One is to be caught on the scene; the other is for the victims to make a positive, in-court identification. The police, even today, will coach a witness to make an identification if they are certain and the witness is not. They tell the witness, "We *know* this is the man, but if you don't identify him, he will get away to rob again." The only way to counter that is to make it demonstrably impossible that an identification is made. An over-the-head rubber mask of Frankenstein does the trick. Even with the best plans and all that protection, I still hesitated a long time. Too many things could go wrong. It had too many *x* factors.

However, I wasn't against planning robberies and selling them to others to commit. This is how this all came about.

Far up North Main Street in the Lincoln Heights district, home of the city jail, general hospital, and juvenile hall, was a beer-and-wine joint called Mama's. Mama Selino owned the license, cooked the tastiest pasta, and loved the hoodlums who hung out there. Her son Frank, an erstwhile Van Gogh, ran the place. Frank's paintings were on every surface.

Mama's was a great hangout, but Frank didn't invite new business. Once a new patron wandered in on a hot afternoon and Frank was having a bad art day. After ten or fifteen minutes the customer coughed and tried to get his attention. Instead, Frank threw a bottle of Heineken's at him and the fool ran out the door. Needless to say, the clientele in Mama's was very limited.

The LAPD from the Highland Park Division knew about Mama's. They often parked in front of a hot dog stand across the street. Its owners told the police about the comings and goings until one late night the hot dog stand burned to the ground.

Mama Selino had come from Salerno with her husband in 1920, prospering during Prohibition until he was gunned down a decade later, leaving her two small sons. She loved "her boys," not just sons Frank and Rocky. "Her boys" included the hoodlums and thieves she fed pasta and ravioli on credit. They paid her with interest when they made a score. Frank, the older son, was as tough as he could be. He and Gene "Dizzy" Davis had done one term together at San Quentin for robbery. Her second son, Rocky, was a taxpaying upstanding citizen who had a small construction company. Frank now did nothing but paint. The bar provided a meager living. The law said that bars had to quit serving at 2:00 A.M. Mama's sometimes stayed open until the sun came up.

It was in Mama's that I ran into Dizzy Davis. We had known each other in San Quentin, but had spoken just once or twice. He was over average height and moderately good-looking, with wavy blond hair that lay close to his skull. His nose was aquiline and his eyes a wet blue. He'd been out about two months after serving nine years. He had no family, although he was one of Mama Selino's favorites. Someone had given him a pistol and he had been sticking up small businesses for survival money, enough for a motel room, food at a fast-food counter, and to sit in a bar with a drink on the plank. Worst of all, he was giving someone half of what he got just to drive him. The driver picked Dizzy up two or three blocks away.

He knew better. "I feel like a fool," he said, but he didn't know what else to do. He personified something I'd noticed about criminals. Many of them knew how a crime should be committed, but they were driven before the wind of circumstances to take risks they knew were stupid. They could not wait; they could not plan; they needed money *now*. Indeed, many of them didn't commit a crime until they saw themselves in desperate straits. God knows how many felonies have been committed to pay a traffic ticket or child support or the bail bondsman.

I wasn't rich, but I had enough to rent Dizzy a furnished room by the week, one of those with a frayed carpet and a toilet and shower down the hall. There was a sink in the room that caught a lot of piss. I made sure he had a few dollars for meals and cigarettes and promised to find him a good score. He listened to me. My confidence gave *him* confidence.

Finding and planning robberies was relatively simple. I sought out places that handled cash and where control of that cash was under one person's authority. This was before double-key drop safes that managers could not open without the armored car guards, so supermarkets were the best, although nightclubs and steak houses were also possibilities. I would simply drive around until I saw something that satisfied the preliminary requirements. Then I would go in and ask for the manager. When he was pointed out, I might even approach him about something. All I wanted was to be able to recognize him. I also tried to get a look at where the money was kept, often a safe in the office. On the way out, I made note of the establishment's hours.

When the place closed, I would watch the employees come out. Invariably the manager was last. I watched what car he got into. Sometimes I followed him home, but usually not.

The next night, I brought Dizzy and pointed it all out to him. The next night after that, he simply waited in the parking lot, grabbed the manager at the car, and walked him back to open the safe. On the first score, a market in Burbank, I parked across the street and watched Dizzy march the manager across the parking lot and back inside through a side door. I took 20 percent. Dizzy and his driver split the remaining 80 percent. It was pretty good money, and I was far in the background. Concerning evidence against me, there was none at all.

This plan was good for three fine scores and a misfire. Dizzy grabbed the butcher instead of the manager. Everything went downhill from there. Still, three out of four successes is a good percentage for a predator. I lost him late one afternoon in Lincoln Heights. Several of the fellas were in the parking lot of Le Blanc's, on the corner of Griffin Avenue and North Broadway. Most were known ex-cons; the others were Italian and liked to gamble, so were presumed to be affiliated with East Coast or Midwestern mobsters. One or two might have been "made" men. Dizzy was in the group. A pair of young uniformed officers out of the Highland Park Division, driving a black-and-white, passed by the parking lot and saw the nefarious group. The officers continued around the block and appeared without warning: "Hold it! All of you!"

After a few minutes of checking identification to make sure nobody had outstanding warrants, or "wants," and writing down all the names, most of which they knew, the officers were ready to leave. But an incident a month earlier in El Segundo had created a ripple that changed a lot of lives. Two police officers had stopped someone, and suddenly he had killed them both. No weapon was found and they had not taken a license number immediately on deciding to stop the vehicle, so there was no way to trace the car. For many years there would be a composite drawing in every precinct and jail of the suspected cop killer. All the hundreds and thousands of those arrested were compared to the composite drawing. This parking lot scene with Dizzy was before the California Supreme Court case *In re Cahan* and the decision from the Supreme Court of the United States, *Mapp v. Ohio,* both of which held that all remedies had to be tried to make police comply with the Fourth Amendment, the right of the people to be free of "unreasonable searches and seizures," including the application of civil and criminal penalties, which juries would not enforce. After a century of futility it was time to take from the police the motive for their unconstitutional behavior, i.e., the evidence they seized, plus evidence that the primary illegality led them to. That was "fruit of the poisoned tree" *(Wong Sun v. U.S.).*

Mapp v. Ohio was still a couple of years away. The uniformed officers decided to pat Dizzy down. The gun they found was lawful evidence. They put him in lineups. Before I had taken him under my wing, in addition to the liquor stores and neighborhood markets, he had robbed the teller of a Wells Fargo bank. The teller pointed a finger from the witness stand and said, "That's him." The jury said, "Guilty." The judge said, "Eighteen years." *Sic transit gloria,* Dizzy Davis.

Although I kept a few capers on file and sold them from time to time, my days as a planner of robberies were essentially over. It was just as well, because I had another thing going. A friend of the Hernandez brothers in Tijuana would supply three sets of identification, mainly a California driver's license backed up with other things, and a hundred payroll checks for $1,000. I would get the identification in common Mexican names—Gonzales, Cruz, Martinez—and their description was "Five-eight, with black hair and brown eyes." My first batch of checks was on the Southern Pacific. Lots of Chicanos worked for the railroad. A fellow I knew named Sonny Ballesteros found three willing youngsters from the neighborhood. We gave them three checks apiece. When those were cashed and the money handed over, I gave Sonny the remaining ninety-one checks. I don't know what deal he made with them, but I was happy with what I made—and again I was out of harm's way. The check scheme worked three times; then my connection in Tijuana was shot and paralyzed. I had enough money for several months and another plan.

To anyone morally outraged by my schemes and lack of apparent remorse, let me say that I only had to justify myself to myself, which is all that anyone has to do. No man does evil in his own mind. I thought, and still think, that if God weighed all I have done against all that has been done to me in society's name, it would be hard to call which way the scales would tilt. I only stole money and stopped doing that as soon as I sold a novel. I refused to accept the position to which society relegates the ex-offender. I would rather risk going back to prison than accept a job in a car wash or a career as a fry cook. Nothing is wrong with either, but they're not for me. I'd already heard too many heroic tales and raged to live. I had no family to constrain me with shame, and I owed society nothing, as far as I could determine, and considered most of its members deserving of whatever happened to them. They were classic hypocrites, proclaiming Christian virtue but at best living by older, meaner ideas and violating even those if it was expedient and they could suck up their courage. They did not live in good faith with the values and virtues that they professed, explicitly or implicitly. I had no misgivings about stealing their money. They might have gotten it legally, but not by creating anything, doing anything constructive, or otherwise contributing to the commonwealth or to human freedom or anything else save, perhaps, their immediate family. The Salvation Army and Franciscans were real Christians. They didn't make their domicile in the greatest palace on the planet, amid riches and art greater than those of any two museums on earth; they were out on the street trying to help. There were others, real Christians, persons of good faith, but they were a minority. One thing that gave me unique freedom was my lack of concern about what they thought of me or what they could do to me. I was more concerned with the truth—and having as much fun and as many adventures as I could find. What I liked I would do until it became boring.

Every morning (actually closer to noon), I sallied forth in search of adventure. Schwab's drugstore on Sunset where Crescent Heights ends and Laurel Canyon begins (and, legend has it, Lana Turner was discovered) had a counter with a great breakfast. Next door was Sherry's, a cocktail lounge frequented by bookmakers, gamblers, fringe gangsters, high-powered call girls, and their pimps, although they took umbrage at the term *pimp*. They called themselves players. Outside Sherry's, somebody ambushed Los Angeles's famous gangster Mickey Cohen. He was unscratched; his bodyguard was slain.

I was brought to Sherry's by a woman who used the name of "Sandy Winters." Raised in an LA suburb, as an adolescent she had been big and shapeless. Her friends in high school were the dope smokers and delinquents, a few of whom went on to serious crime. Her boyfriend went to reform school for car theft. While he was gone, she lost the baby fat, revealing the body of a Las Vegas showgirl, with full breasts, a narrow waist, and big hips and thighs, closer to Jayne Mansfield than Jane Fonda. Ann "turned out," becoming a high-priced call girl for a pimp (excuse me, "a player"), but she was his "second store" (number-two girl), and she disliked giving him all her money, even though he bought her clothes from Bullocks and gave her a Coupe de Ville— but kept the ownership certificate. The pimp/player was the kind who rules by terror, although careful not to bruise her where it showed. After a few months Sandy packed up and went home to the San Gabriel Valley. She took a copy of her "book," a green ledger with several hundred names and phone numbers.

Coded marks behind each name indicated what each paid, what he liked, when last seen—and sometimes notations ran down the margin. Among the names were those of movie moguls and movie stars. Why would Mitchum frequent a call girl? Because there would be no repercussions, although some hookers recently had been feeding things to the notorious scandal rag of the hour, *Confidential.*

Sandy stopped turning tricks and started work as a secretary, although she was not adverse to playing weekend courtesan if someone she liked wanted to buy her diamonds and drape her on his arm. Although not the most beautiful of women, she had the sexiest walk I've ever seen, and she did turn men's heads wherever she went. After the weekend in Vegas or New York, she invariably had another piece of jewelry and what amounted to a month's wages to deposit with her stockbroker.

Sandy and I were introduced by Jimmy D., brother-in-law of my childhood partner, Wedo, whom I've mentioned earlier. He had been awaiting sentence to prison when I paroled. Now he was gone. Jimmy was married to the sister of Wedo's wife. Although we were the same age, Jimmy had a fraction of my knowledge, academic or street. At twenty-two I'd graduated with honors after a nickel in San Quentin. Jimmy did know young women who liked to get high and party and where to do it. I had the money and the Jaguar sports car, which was rapidly accumulating dings and dents and had a headlight that threw a skewed beam toward the sky. One night he called me with excitement in his voice: "Ah, man, I'm gonna cut you into this big redheaded stallion. She's so *fine* . . . me oh my . . . she likes to get high."

It was before seat belts, much less seat belt laws, so all three of us squeezed into two bucket seats. "So what're we gonna do?" I asked.

"It's on you, baby," Jimmy said to Sandy.

"I want to get loaded," she said. "I called my connection. He's holding."

"Where is he?"

"On the east side . . . near Brooklyn and Soto."

We were on Sweetzer just north of Santa Monica Boulevard in the Sunset Strip. It would be renamed West Hollywood when it incorporated as a city, but in '57 it was still a "strip" of county territory surrounded on three sides by the City of Angels and on the fourth by Beverly Hills. The Strip was home to most of the flashy clubs, vice, and gambling. A hooker busted in county territory got a $100 fine. In Beverly Hills she would get ninety days the first time, six months the second.

"East LA is a long way," I said. "I know somebody a mile from here."

"A connection?"

"Uh-huh . . . a friend of mine."

"A drug dealer in Hollywood?"

"Uh-huh."

"He must be the first one."

It was true. Until then anyone who wanted drugs had to go east, at least to

Temple Street just west of the Civic Center, or to the Grand Central Market on Third and Broadway, where drug dealers stood around with tiny balloons of drugs in their mouths—like chipmunks. If the narcotics officers jumped out of a doorway, the street pusher simply swallowed.

I called my friend Denis Kanos, Hollywood's first resident drug dealer, from a pay phone in a Richfield station. He was on his way out, but because we were so close he agreed to meet us in the parking lot of a Smokey Joe's, a coffee shop with legendary hamburgers at the intersection of Beverly and La Cienega Boulevards.

We arrived first and got out of the crowded car to wait. I spotted Denis's new two-seat Thunderbird as it turned in. He parked some distance away. Not knowing Sandy and Jimmy, Denis had no desire to meet them, a standard precaution for the cautious drug dealer. As I walked up, he was looking past me at Sandy. "Damn, man, that sure is a big fine redhead. You didn't tell me what you wanted."

"Just a couple of caps." In those days heroin, at least on the streets of Los Angeles, was sold in small #5 gelatin capsules. A cap was still potent and two nonaddicts could share one, but the practice of cutting it with lactose was beginning. Every hand it went through put another cut on it. In a couple of years it would be a fraction of what it had been, and eventually they sold grams in balloons.

"I didn't think you slammed," Denis said.

"I've tried it a couple of times. It feels so good that I don't wanna fuck with it. I can see how somebody gets hooked."

"Yeah . . . and when you've had a good jones, you're hooked for the rest of your life. You *always* crave it."

He fished out two white capsules and dropped them into a cigarette pack's cellophane and twisted the top. They would melt if carried by hand.

"Thanks, D. What do I owe you?"

"A favor sometime down the line."

"Damn, who ever heard of a dope dealer giving anything away?"

"We do it all the time . . . especially to kids . . . until we get them hooked. Then we make them turn tricks and steal the family TV." He said it flatly, his face expressionless; it was his idea of humor.

"Did you cop?" Sandy asked when I returned.

I opened my hand so she could see the cellophane pack, and we stuffed ourselves back into the Jaguar.

"So where do we go?" she asked.

"What about that spot at the beach you told me about?" Jimmy said.

My apartment was closer but less impressive than the private cabana Louise had authorized me to use at the Sand & Sea Club on the Santa Monica beach. Jimmy had a good idea, for although I had never been obsessed with girls (or sex) to the same extent as my teenage friends, on occasion the serpent of lust would bite me—and it bit me now. I wanted to spread this big redhead's legs until it caused pain in my crotch. And although I lacked experience in the games of seduction, I sensed that Sandy sneered at men who were too obvious. Such men were tricks to be manipulated and not respected. A whore is often more difficult to seduce than a good, God-fearing woman, not unless money is involved, at which time the man becomes a john or a trick, deserving only disdain. It was important to hide how much lust I had.

As I expected, the parking lot was empty and nobody saw us push through a gate and circle the swimming pool to where the stairs rose one flight to a long balcony that fronted all the cabanas. The crash and whoosh of surf further masked our presence. Although I was authorized to use the place, I had no key. During the day the manager opened the door for me. It was a sliding glass door, and I had rigged it to slide open without a key.

I shook my head when it was my turn to fix. "I'm seeing my parole officer tomorrow. I think he's going to test me with nalline."

"You're on parole?" Sandy asked. Was it with new interest or was it my perception of new interest? In some worlds, instead of a stigma, a prison term was a cause for respect.

"Yeah."

"He did five years," Jimmy said.

"Not quite five."

"In San Quentin," Jimmy said.

"I thought you were a little rich boy," she said.

"That's my dream, but it's sure not the reality."

"He knows Flip," Jimmy said.

"Do you really know the legendary Yvonne Renee Dillon?"

"I'll never forget her."

Sandy laughed and nodded agreement.

With the drapes pulled shut over the glass doors and the ocean smacking the beach and whooshing up the sand, they fixed.

"Good junk," Sandy said, her voice slurred and full of gravel, meanwhile rubbing her eye and nose with the back of her hand. "Real good," she added, her head slowly falling to her chest, then snapping erect. She was fighting the nod and feeling a euphoria that went through her entire being, physical and emotional. It was a total absence of pain. This wasn't a time to pitch at her or even to talk very much. Someone full of junk wants to stay in one place, eating ice-cream cones and smoking cigarettes. Junkies do have a high percentage of cigarette fires. On the nod they burn a lot of upholstery. But I could see how good they felt, how they became sufficient unto it, including the ritual, and it scared me.

Sandy didn't want any more conversation for the present. I went out onto the balcony and smoked a Camel while watching a big moon low on the horizon. The wide beam of moonlight stretched across the sea like a path that could be walked. The wind was mild and the night comfortable. When the surf finished each crashing roll and rushed up the beach, it left a pattern like white lace that lasted a few seconds before disappearing as the broken wave receded.

Such scenes as these always triggered inchoate longing, or perhaps epiphany, in me. More than anyone I knew, I liked being alone with my thoughts in certain settings. This was one of them; so was trekking through the dark, sleeping city in the hours after midnight when all was quiet and empty. Good pot would unlock the doors of perception. I was disappointed that Sandy had zonked herself to heroin oblivion. I wanted to know her better. No doubt her body with its high, full breasts and big, tanned thighs stirred my desire, but there was also her personality. Jimmy said she was like one of the guys. In a way it was true; she was as much a man's woman as any I've known, comfortable among the roughest of men. Knowing what they wanted, the primal lust she aroused in men, gave her power she recognized, yet hidden beneath that was hunger to be the small, helpless female that is looked after, protected, and loved by men. Sometimes she thought she had found it, but so far it had proved a mirage when the masks were taken off and the face of truth exposed.

Those insights would come over time as I knew her better. At the moment she had me thinking of Flip, whom I hadn't seen for more than five years, although I had certainly thought about her many times in the darkness of my cell, remembering how beautiful she had been, the alabaster skin, the perfect butt, the way she could fuck. Although I could not claim wide sexual experience, she made all others seem limp bodies who simply stretched out and opened their legs. Back then the power of her beauty intimidated me. On graduating from a nickel in the House of Dracula, I was no longer intimidated by anything less than a twelve-gauge shotgun two inches from my head. Surviving five years in San Quentin will do wonders for self-confidence.

SEVERAL DAYS LATER MY TELEPHONE RANG. Sandy was on the line. "I got your number from Jimmy," she said. "I hope you don't mind."

"No. What's up?"

"Flip remembers you. She wants to see you."

"I want to see her, too. What about tonight?"

"No. She said Thursday. She's not doing real good right now."

"What's wrong?"

"The guy she was with cut her loose. She had everything in her car. She went to score out in East LA and somebody threw a brick through the side window and stole her clothes—all her clothes. It's hard for her to work without a front."

"Why does she need a wardrobe to lie down first and get up last?"

"She doesn't . . . but she needs to look like Bloomingdale's to walk through a fancy hotel lobby on a date."

Yes, that was understandable. The difference between a whore on the corner and a call girl in a penthouse was often no more than a facade. Take the former to a hair stylist, put her under a sun lamp, dress her from Neiman Marcus, and put her in a plush apartment—and her price for the same services goes from $20 to $200 for twenty minutes and from $200 to $2,000 for the night.

IN 1957 PARAMOUNT STUDIOS did not extend out to front Melrose Avenue, as it does now. It was back a block on a street called Marathon. On the narrow street that ran between Melrose and Marathon was a three-story apartment building of lathe and plaster in a *faux* Tudor design. Each third-floor apartment had a window opening to a fire escape that overlooked the DeMille gate, that studio landmark somewhat less famous than the snowcapped mountain logo. The window faced west and caught the sunset full on.

Flip liked to sit in the window next to the fire escape and drink Scotch whiskey during the magic twilight hour. She would muse on what might have been had she not been so hell-bent on personal destruction.

When Sandy led the way through the apartment's front door, I didn't get a good look at Flip until we were in the living room. She closed the door and turned to us. I don't think I reacted visibly, although perhaps the flesh flinched between my eyes. The idealized image of perfect sexually potent beauty was dashed. Five years of Scotch and heroin had defaced the perfect sensual beauty God had given her. Her face was still unusually beautiful, and with a little makeup she would be stunning, but her body showed the flab that came from kicking habits.

"Hey, sweetmeat," she said. "You've grown up. I'll bet you shave now."

I think I blushed; at least my face felt hot.

"I haven't got much time," she said. "I'm sorry. I got an unexpected call for a date. A regular. Scott Brady."

"The actor?" Sandy asked.

"Uh-huh," Flip said. "Wait here."

An exposed stairway went up the side wall to another floor. Bathroom, bedroom, and a door to the hallway were up there. "It's a good place for a working girl," Sandy said. When I didn't understand, she explained, "It can stand traffic. A john leaving through that door up there"—she indicated up the stairway—"doesn't run into a john coming in that door." She indicated the front door. Then I understood.

Flip came down the stairs. She had combed her hair but had done little else and was several levels scruffier than my expectation for a high-powered call girl. "Look here," she said to Sandy. "Do me a favor and give me a ride to his house."

"We're not going to wait for you," Sandy said.

"No . . . no . . . that's fine. I'll get back on my own."

Scott Brady lived in a small white house perched on a flattened bluff somewhere up Laurel Canyon. A swimming pool covered all the property not taken by the house. It was one of those where you can hold onto the rim of the swimming pool and look down and out over the vast plain of either Los Angeles or the San Fernando Valley. When she got out, Flip handed me a slip of paper with her phone number. "Gimme a call. I'll cook you a steak and baked potato."

As we drove Laurel Canyon's tight turns toward the Sunset Strip, Sandy joshed me, "Damn, baby, looks like you caught the absolutely fabulous Miss Yvonne Renee Dillon of Palm Springs and Hollywood."

"The question is, how much trouble is she? They don't call her Flip for nothing."

"She is Flip . . . but she's still a moneymaker. Her book has over a thousand numbers, and she's got some regulars who won't see another girl."

"No . . . uh-uh . . . I'm no pimp. In fact, I despise pimps. I like whores . . . but not pimps."

"Some aren't so bad. They look after their old lady . . . don't let her shoot the money in her arm. A lot of girls can't trick unless they're loaded."

I could understand. Being high would buffer them from the unpleasant realities of sucking a strange prick. "They do have a lot of money," Sandy said, "and they don't go to jail. Not very often, anyway."

At the time of the conversation my attention was primarily focused on the intermittent flash of brake lights on the car ahead of us. What she said registered without being examined. Sometime within the next couple of days, an idea came to mind: I would make these pimps pay me for protection. I would, so to speak, play Lucky Luciano and organize them. The main selling thing was to convince them they needed protection. All kinds of things could happen if they didn't have protection from vandals and maniacs. They owned jukeboxes and cigarette machines that could fall over or suffer an accidental sledgehammer blow. Didn't what's his name own a nightclub on Santa Monica Boulevard? It could burn down. The wives of their tricks could be called and told about their whoring husbands. The pimps could have an accident somewhere along the line. Wasn't it worth 10 or 15 percent to feel secure and protected? Eighty-five percent of big money was better than a hundred percent of nothing but trouble.

To make it work, it had to be a *fait accompli* at the moment they heard about it. The first move had to be checkmate where killing me would bring about the deaths of everyone they knew. Actually, they only had to *believe* that killing me would result in madmen they couldn't identify kicking down doors to slaughter them and their whole family.

Of course I wasn't that capable. It was a game with me, backed up with a vicious Sunday punch and a mouth that would make anyone believe I was ready to murder him at any moment. My eyes rolled, my hand was steady, and I was telling them that I wanted to go to the —— and the muzzle of a twelve-gauge was ten feet away. Nobody ever told me, "Go ahead, asshole." God knows what would have happened in such an event.

Several bona fide madmen were loose in Los Angeles. I could enlist their help. The problem was, could I control them afterward? Maybe I could use some of Joe Morgan's boys to stand in the background and look mean.

The protection idea was still floating around in the undecided part of my brain several days later when I called Flip to see if her offer of a steak and baked potato was real. That very night was fine. Six-thirty? Fine.

It was still twilight when I parked at the curb and got out. Flip was perched in the window and fire escape, glass in hand. She saw me and held it up in a salute. When she opened the door and I stepped in, she pulled me close and gave me a wet, sloppy kiss. Then she said, "I'm gonna cook you a big steak and fuck your brains out." She smelled of Scotch whiskey and was already drunk. After she poured me a drink and freshened hers, the bottle was empty. "Why don't you go get a pint while I cook?" she said. "There's a liquor store right around the corner on Melrose."

"Sure," I replied. The least I could do was get her a pint of whiskey if she was going to fuck my brains out. If past is prelude, she was certainly capable of it.

By the time she finished cooking the steak, long before the potato was done, she was too drunk to move the meat from the frying pan to plate. It fell from fork to floor with a splatter of hot grease. She laughed and I joined her.

When she bent over to retrieve it, she got the fork in and was lifting it; then she lost her balance and fell down. This time the meat flew through the air. If the first mishap was funny, this was hilarious. "I wasn't hungry anyway," I said, reaching for her. She was compliant enough, but I quickly realized that I didn't want her either, not in a drunken near-stupor.

During the next few days, I visited Flip several times, invariably bringing her a pint of Black and White, which was what she liked. Next to getting high, her favorite activity was talking. She reviled the pimps to whom she had given so much money before they threw her out. From Flip I learned about the beach house one owned in Hermosa and the partnership that owned the Regency Club in North Hollywood. I had a photocopy made of the "book." This was before Xerox and therefore the copy was white print on black background instead of black print on white paper. One afternoon we were in a beer joint on Santa Monica Boulevard and she mentioned that the pimp Richie owned the jukebox. "Do you know other places he's got them?" I asked.

"Uh-huh. A few."

"What about cigarette machines?"

"Yeah . . . at least some of them. Why do you want to know anyway?"

Being young and vain, plus believing she despised them, I told her about my plan. I was unaware how much she feared them and had no idea she had told them of me until I pulled into an underground garage off Sunset Boulevard. A pair of goons imported from Las Vegas were waiting. As I got out of the car, one called me to "wait up." Not expecting anything, I waited for them—until they were twenty feet away and I saw one of them slip on a pair of brass knuckles.

I jumped as if touched by a live wire. I ran between cars, then jumped on hoods and ran on top of cars to a partially open window. The pursuit was half-hearted, their threatening curses ringing in my ears. "Better run, you fuckin' punk," was the epithet I remembered. Although I cannot recall exactly what they said, I knew who they represented. Flip or Sandy had told me the Hollywood pimps were Mob-connected in Las Vegas.

Of course I was frightened at the moment. Brass knuckles are terrible weapons. They easily crush facial bones. But once I was out the window and down the street, the fright gave way to a weird excitement. It wasn't anger. It was an exhilaration. This was my best game. It was a level of excitement that my metabolism thrived on. My whole life had conditioned me to such situations. They would think they had conjured up a demon.

I walked to Sherry's, at Sunset and Crescent Heights. Among the many underworld characters who frequented Sherry's was Denis Kanos. He was not there. I called him from the pay phone and told him I would be walking on the south side of Sunset Boulevard. There was a chance the two goons would come to Sherry's.

I WAS GRINNING WHEN DENIS pulled to the curb and honked. I got in and we pulled away, east on Sunset toward Hollywood.

"You bring me a piece?" I asked.

He pointed toward the glove compartment. "In there."

"Can they trace it?"

"Not to us. Did you know Richard Eck?"

"I met him." Richard Eck had been killed running from a burglary a couple of years earlier.

"I bought it from him. I think he got it out of a prowl."

The glove compartment divulged a small automatic with WALTHER along its barrel. About firearms I knew very little. This looked light enough to carry without disheveling my clothes, but it both looked small and was an automatic, so I had questions.

"Are you sure it's got enough punch?" I asked.

"Oh yeah. It's what German officers carried in World War II. They're expensive."

"I saw somebody shot with a little twenty-five Beretta and it didn't even slow him down. He beat the shit out of the guy that shot him." Actually, I hadn't see the futile shooting; this was a tale related to me in a Big Yard bull-shit session.

"No, no, it'll stop 'em."

It fit in my jacket pocket. Good. Nevertheless, I would have preferred a .38- or .44-caliber revolver. Automatics were better weapons if one was firing many shots. You could simply drop out the magazine and ram another in. It took a couple of seconds, assuming you had a spare magazine. A revolver, however, had to be reloaded by putting individual bullets in the cylinder. An automatic held eight to a dozen bullets, a revolver five or six. I still preferred the revolver because it was far more dependable. Leave a loaded automatic in a drawer for a couple of years and the springs might weaken and fail to shove a new cartridge into the firing chamber. They tended to jam. I'd been target shooting with a 7.6 Beretta and it happened on the second shot. I'd never even heard of a revolver jamming.

I remained silent about the pistol preference, grateful for anything for the moment. A few days later, I bought a snub-nosed .38 Smith & Wesson and left the German automatic at Flip's apartment. When I confronted her with having warned them, she admitted it and said, "They'd have somebody cut my face up. You're nuts, man. That shit you're talkin' is something out of the movies." It was obvious from her speech patterns that she had spent some time with black men, although her last pimp—and the several who controlled the call girls of the time and place—happened to be white.

I suppose they thought I would shit in my britches and hide because they had imported some supposedly Mob-connected muscle from Vegas. It was they who got their ideas from movies. Instead of hiding, I went hunting. Although I could have used the thousand phone numbers in the book to destroy their business, it would have been a Pyrrhic victory. By hassling the tricks and their wives, I would pull it all down—but then they would have no way to pay me for protection against extortion, and so forth.

I didn't know where they lived, but I did know a trick pad, an apartment on Sweetzer below Sunset used by one pimp's second store. I knew the routine, too. Call girls, unlike streetwalkers, do most of their business during daytime business hours. Their johns, men able to afford high-priced call girls, were not chained to a desk or a schedule. Nobody raised an eyebrow if these men were gone for a couple of hours in the afternoon. It was more difficult to get away from a wife at night or on the weekend. Most of time the call girl finished work by early evening. That was when the pimp came to get *his* money. "All she made belonged to him" was the cardinal principle of the relationship between whore and pimp. During the day while she sold herself, he played pool and flashed his Hickey-Freeman suits and diamond pinky ring. After another hard day, he picked up his women and took them to dinner at some of the city's best restaurants, where they looked like anything but whores with their pimps.

It was during this dinner hour that I jimmied open the apartment's kitchen door and went inside to wait. I used a tiny penlight to navigate into the living room, where I sat down to wait for their return, giggling as I envisioned his face when he turned on the lights and saw me seated on his living room sofa.

Tick tock turned the clock. They seemed gone for a long, long time. I finally found a closet and opened the door. The tiny flashlight revealed empty space, no clothes. Hmmm.

I swept the penlight around the room and couldn't be sure of what I saw. I flipped the switch beside the door. Sure enough. It was an empty furnished apartment. They had bailed out, and I had to assume it was because the pimp had anticipated me.

For the next few days I spent much of my time on the east side, in Lincoln Heights, East Los Angeles, Bell Gardens, and other, poorer districts where ex-cons were more likely to be found. I had one ally whom I trusted and heard names of men I knew who were plenty tough, but they were also too wild to control. They would want to rip everything off, including the women, most of whom were far more beautiful than any of the tattooed junkies who were their girlfriends. Denis and I discussed burning down the nightclub and bashing in some jukeboxes, but by themselves such things wouldn't accomplish my purpose. Flip had fouled my plan by telling them before I was ready to move.

Out of nowhere the number one pimp died in an automobile accident between Palm Springs and the Salton Sea. He and his main store (number one girl) went over the middle line and hit a Greyhound head-on. Even though it was impossible for it to have been a murder, around the Hollywood underworld it was whispered that I had taken them out. All of a sudden it was impossible for movie moguls and others to get a date with a call girl in West Hollywood. The pimps had loaded their women into their Cadillacs and left town. Sandy and Denis thought this was hilarious.

Around this time I had one of my more bizarre experiences. After midnight during the week, my phone rang. I was living in my apartment on Ninth and Detroit. Flip was on the other end. She was drunk. "I have to see you, Eddie."

"It's late, baby. I'll see you in the morning." I hung up.

The phone rang within seconds. I answered.

"If you don't come, I'll kill myself."

"I'll be right there, baby."

I drove to her apartment building in the shadow of Paramount and parked on the narrow street in front of it. When I rang the buzzer for her apartment there was no response. Had she killed herself? I doubted it, but still . . . (In fact, she did commit suicide within three years.)

Walking around the building, in the alley I spotted a hallway window open a few inches for ventilation. Beside it was a heavy galvanized drainpipe, strong enough for me to go up it to the window. Once inside, I moved on crepe-soled shoes along the hallway and up the stairs to the third floor.

Nobody responded to my knock. Not wanting to pound and wake up the building, I went downstairs and out the front door, propping it open with a throwaway newspaper. From my car I took a jimmy bar, then went back inside and up the stairs to the third floor. At the end of the hallway the window opened onto the fire escape, which extended over a few feet to her kitchen window. A little tap followed by tinkling glass, and I reached in and unlatched the window. Through the arch I could see part of the living room. It was flooded in green light, which she liked to use when entertaining.

In the living room, I found Flip flopped on the sofa in a rumpled black teddy, passed out and snoring. I shook her and got one eye open. "Where's my pistol?" I had left a pistol there a couple of days earlier.

"Don' hurt Michael."

"Michael! I'm not gonna hurt Michael."

"Don' hurt Michael."

Shit. Then I saw him, also passed out, on the bottom landing of the stairs that led up to the bedroom and bathroom on the fourth floor. He was in his skivvies, one of those Italians with a mat of black hair that covers his chest and, to a lesser extent, his shoulders. He was a friend of Johnny Stompanato, who had been killed by Lana Turner's daughter. Michael worked as a bartender in a cocktail lounge, the Playboy, a block away on Melrose. He wore a ducktail with a Tony Curtis curl falling down over his forehead. He fancied himself a ladies' man extraordinaire. Flip had "pussy whipped" him, which she could do if any woman ever could. He was in love with her, and, being an Italian stallion and stud, he hated it—that she was a whore and that he loved her was hard for him to handle, especially when she played a mean game of tormenting him. When the phone rang and Michael was there, she would stare at him while telling the trick what she was going to do to him in bed. Michael got drunk and slapped her around. He cried. She loved it, and afterward they had great sex.

No matter how I protested, she refused to believe I wasn't going to hurt Michael. After I shook her awake a couple of times, I gave up that tactic and decided to find the pistol on my own. How many places could she hide it in such a small apartment?

The first place I looked was behind the cushions of the sofa where she lay. Reaching down between them, I felt something and pulled it up. A butcher knife. What the hell was it doing there?

I carried the butcher knife into the kitchen and put it on the table. Then I began to search, and in about twenty minutes I found the pistol in a broiler pan inside the oven. I pocketed it and went home.

I slept until about 11:00 A.M., and then spent an hour or so taking a bath and getting dressed. Through the window I saw the newspaper boy delivering the afternoon paper, Hearst's *Herald Express*, to my neighbor. As was my frequent practice, I opened the door and went out to get the newspaper. I always put it back when I went out for the day sometime in the afternoon.

At this time Los Angeles was hunting for one of its fairly common serial killers. They have had all kinds of names, such as the Night Stalker and Freeway Killers. This time the killer was labeled the Hollywood Prowler. He had been invading the apartments of single women around Hollywood and Hollywood Hills, often by cutting a window screen or using some similar mode of entry. He had killed at least one, as I recall.

I carried the newspaper back to my apartment, poured myself a cup of hot coffee, and opened it. The big headline across the top said: "**PROWLER'S FINGERPRINTS FOUND.**" To the right below the headline was a four-column picture of a butcher knife. The ensuing article began: "Latest victim of the Hollywood Prowler, actress/model Yvonne Renee Dillon . . ." It was hard to read because my hands shook. It did say that she was alive. Thank God for that.

I was instantly at the window, and within a minute I was going down the outdoor back stairs with shirt unbuttoned and shoes in hand. My car was at the curb. I paused, hidden by bushes, trying to see if it was staked out. It seemed all right. I got in and took off. Where should I go? I headed up Highland Avenue toward the Hollywood Freeway. At a traffic light I looked in the rearview mirror and saw a black-and-white police car pull up behind me. Either they didn't have the license number or they weren't paying any attention. When the light turned green, I accelerated slowly, fighting the urge to stomp the gas pedal. That surely would have gotten undue attention.

On reaching the freeway, I decided to go east toward El Monte. I had friends out there. The Hollywood Freeway became the San Bernardino. I turned on the radio. The lead story of the spot news was about the prowler's fingerprints being found at the scene of his latest crime. It also mentioned that the police wanted to talk to an ex-con. Imagine the sinking feeling in my gut. At least my name wasn't mentioned.

On Valley Boulevard near Five Points, I checked into a $1.50-a-night motel, sans telephone or air-conditioning, then walked the half-mile to where Jimmy D. lived with his wife, child, and in-laws, including the wife's sister and her two children. Her husband was in San Quentin. Jimmy wasn't there. His wife wasn't sure where he was; she suspected he had gone to the barrio with Japo, the nickname of a Chicano with vaguely Asian features. I'd known Japo since juvenile hall. I didn't tell Jimmy's wife of my situation; fear of her husband getting into trouble might cause her to call the police. "I'll call him," I said, then began my trudge through the afternoon summer heat back toward the motel. As my feet kicked up puffs of powdered dirt with each step, I alternately felt sorry for myself and laughed aloud at the absurdity of the whole thing. The more I thought about it, the more unlikely it seemed that I would be charged as a serial killer or rapist. I even remember thinking that someday I would write about these particular happenings. Proust they were not, but entertaining they had to be.

Back on Valley Boulevard, I used a gas station pay phone to call Sandy. She answered in her mellifluous call girl voice, but with bemused challenge: "It's your dime," she said.

"It's me," I said, rightfully confident that she would recognize my voice. I quickly told her of the situation. When I finished, she said, "Oh my God! That's crazy!"

"Do me a favor. Call Flip and find out what happened. Don't tell her you talked to me. Tell her you read it in the paper. I'll call you back in half an hour."

When I called back, Sandy had the story. Early in the morning, when Flip and Michael woke up with hangovers, he began to slap her because she was a whore and he was in love with her. She told him, "Michael, Michael, after what I went through to protect you." She then showed him the broken window and told him a story of being raped. He reached for the telephone. Now I was a suspected serial rapist and murderer.

For two days I hid out in El Monte, wondering what I should do. Actually, I was less concerned with the possibility of being charged with murder than with the matter getting to my parole officer. I had a good parole officer (that would change soon enough), but something like this could arouse too much heat.

After the one headline there were no more newspaper stories. Sandy convinced me to talk to a sleazeball shyster lawyer who was one of her special johns. He called the homicide detectives. All my concern was for nothing. By the afternoon of the first day they had known it was a hoax. Yvonne Renee Dillon had several arrests for a law called vag addict. It was then a misdemeanor to simply be an addict in California, a law the Supreme Court would soon declare unconstitutional. She also had some prostitution arrests. She'd even been in Camarillo. They didn't even want to talk to me, and nobody had notified the parole department. So the desperate drama had ended not with a bang but with a fizzle.

OTHER UNDERWORLD ADVENTURES CAME MY WAY in the next seven or eight months. I can no longer remember clearly the sequence of these things, nor even when they occurred relative to modern history. I think I recall standing outside the Broadway Department Store at the intersection of Vine Street and Hollywood Boulevard, looking through the display window at several TV sets, all of them turned to a news broadcast, behind which pulsed a dinging sound as the Soviet Union's *Sputnik,* the first man-made object to reach space, orbited Earth.

My friend Denis once called me and said he needed help. "And bring a pistol," he had added. Unlike most of my friends, he was someone I'd met since getting out. Of Greek descent, he was classically handsome. He was a couple of inches shorter than my bare six feet and had dark hair, aquiline nose, excellent teeth, and skin with the hint of an olive tint. In Denver, where his father owned a restaurant, the police had given Denis a "floater." They had told him to permanently vacate Denver or they were going to bury him in prison or a grave and, if they couldn't get him right, they would frame him. He followed Horace Greeley's advice, going west, and set himself up as a drug dealer, which he would remain all the days of his life except when he was in prison.

So here I was, a .38 in the hip pocket of my pair of Levi's, its butt hidden by the tail of the bottom of a charcoal tweed Ivy League–styled sport coat. It had the abundant buttons of Ivy League garments.

His red-with-white-trim two-seat Ford Thunderbird appeared. A car waiting to park kept him from jockeying into the curb lane. I made sure the pistol was snug. I didn't want it to fall onto Hollywood Boulevard at eight in the evening. I slipped between cars onto the street. He leaned over and opened the passenger door, and we were already moving when I slammed it shut.

"What's up, brother?" I asked. "You don't have me in a killing squabble, do you?"

"I dunno. We gotta go see."

He drove south on Vine and east on Fountain past Cedars of Lebanon, where I was born. He parked on Fountain and we walked down an alley and up an exterior stairway to the door of a small apartment over a garage. The door was covered with sheet metal and had the type of lock usually found on the back door of a liquor store endangered by burglars. A small black man of undetermined years with a pinched face and exaggerated femininity let us in. The left side of his face was grossly swollen and discolored. "Oh, man, I'm so glad to see you. That fuckin' nigger Pinky," he began, then sniffled as if ready to cry.

"Awww, man," Denis said, "freeze on that shit and tell me what happened."

"He bought a gram, man. A couple of hours later he come back with some other gutter ass black motherfucker an' say the stuff was no good and he wanted his money back. I told him if it was bunk why in Mary's name did he shoot it all? He said he wasn't gonna argue . . . he wanted his money. I told him no and he started punchin' on me. He put a knife on my throat an' said he was takin' everything . . . money . . . smack . . . everything. . . ."

"What'd he get, Dixie?"

"Shit . . . he got it all . . . everything."

Denis shook his head. "Goddamn it's hard to make any dough. Do you know how to find him?"

"I don't know where he lives, but he's got a white girl works as a cocktail waitress in that . . . uh . . . hotel . . . Roosevelt Hotel right on Hollywood Boulevard. One night we had to wait for her to get off work so he could get money to score. I'll bet you can nail him through her."

"Do you know her name?"

"I think it was Elaine . . . a little bitty blonde with a country accent."

"Let's go check it out," Denis said to me.

"Hey, D., can you do something for me? I don't have anything for a getup. I'm gonna be sick in the morning."

From Denis's pocket came a bankroll that would choke a horse. This was before the age of credit cards, when cash was still king. Denis tore off a couple of twenty-dollar bills and handed them over. "You know where to score, don't you?"

"I gotta go down to the ghetto."

"Better'n being sick. Get outta this place first thing in the morning."

"Can you front me an o.z. so I can get back on my feet."

"Call me when you get moved. Let's go."

We went to the Roosevelt Hotel on Hollywood Boulevard across the street from the Chinese Theater with the world-famous outdoor lobby of footprints and handprints of the most famous movie stars. The club off the Roosevelt's lobby was the site of the first Academy Awards, but in the subsequent decades the hotel had gone downhill; so had its club.

Denis was a step ahead of me as we crossed the lobby toward the club's open door. As we reached it, he stopped and I bumped into him. "Get back." He pushed away from the open door.

"What's up?"

"He's in there with her."

"The guy we want?"

"Yeah—Pinky."

"You know him, huh?"

"Not really. I've seen him coming down from Dixie's when I was makin' a delivery."

"Does he know you?"

"I don't think so."

"Would he recognize you?"

He shook his head, but it was less than emphatic.

"Let me check him out," I said.

"I'll wait out front."

He went out and I entered the cocktail lounge. It was dim and nearly empty. Two men were together at a table; two more, each by himself, were perched on bar stools. I took an empty table near the entrance and thought to myself that Denis had made a mistake. There was no black man in here.

The cocktail waitress delivered drinks to the pair at the table, then came to me. Her name tag said: ELLIE. That was close enough. "Gimme a shot of bourbon and mix another one in 7UP for a chaser."

She nodded and went to tell the bartender, then she stood beside one of the men at the bar while waiting for the drink. The seated man put a possessive arm around her waist. I got up and went over to the bar and handed the waitress some money. "Here. I'm going to the john. I'll be right back." The seated man turned to look at me. His skin was at least as white as mine, and only in America would he have been considered black. Yet his features, especially the wide, flat nose, declared that some of his ancestors had taken the Middle Passage to come to America. He swung his gaze past the girl onto me. I winked, but his reaction was coldly blank.

I walked out, but instead of crossing the lobby to the rest room, I headed down the short hall to the door onto Hollywood Boulevard. Pedestrians were moving back and forth; a tour bus was disgorging tourists in front of the landmark theater across the street. I looked around.

Denis came out of a doorway. "That's him all right." The sidewalk was full of pedestrians, the street with cars—and a black-and-white went slowly past.

"We can't do anything here. Too many witnesses. We'll wait for him to come out and see where he goes. Maybe come back later."

"Like six-thirty in the morning." I liked early-morning jackups. The suckers often staggered to the door rubbing their glazed eyes.

"Right," Denis said, then: "There! Freeze!" It was soft but sharp. I froze.

A figure passed us from my rear. The scent of men's cologne. Denis had seen him coming. He grinned at me. "Sometimes even a blind dog gets lucky. Come on."

Pinky walked along in front of the hotel and turned right at the corner, going along its east side. We followed at some distance, far enough so he was unlikely to look back and get suspicious. I was going along with this, but my heart wasn't in it. It wasn't my trouble; I wasn't angry. Pinky was big, too, probably six-three and a couple hundred rangy pounds. No doubt Denis and I in tandem would kick Pinky's ass pretty quick, but it was also probable that he was tougher *mano a mano* than either of us. In short, I guess, my adrenaline wasn't pumping enough yet.

I expected Pinky to continue to the parking lot behind the hotel. Instead he stepped between cars at the curb and crossed the street at an angle, then turned into an alley running parallel to the boulevard.

Denis was ahead of me. I expected him to stop and wait for me. Instead he sped up and entered the alley. When I made the turn, Denis was calling, "Hey, Pinky! Wait up!"

Pinky looked back and stopped. Although his face was shadowed, his body was ready to run. Before he could decide, Denis had closed the distance to him. I stopped a few feet away.

"Yeah, what?" Pinky asked.

"I'm not lookin' for trouble . . . but you owe me some dough."

"*Some* dough? Who the fuck are you?"

"I'm the motherfucker that owned that shit you took off little Dixie."

"I don't know you . . . an' I ain't got shit to say to you."

Pinky's hostile scorn now had my anger rising. Who'd he think he was fucking with? I stepped forward. "You sure have a . . . bad attitude, man." I had to catch my breath in midsentence. My temper used to interfere with my conversation, causing a half-stutter I lost when I was a little older and less prone to excessive temper. I moved around so we had Pinky boxed between us.

Pinky's head turned to look deeper into the dark alley. It made me glance that way. A figure got out of a car parked thirty yards away and started walking quickly toward us.

"What's happenin', man?" this new man wanted to know.

I was closest to him. He was the size of an NFL linebacker and outweighed me by about eighty pounds or more. I eased the pistol out of my back pocket with my left hand, using my body as a shield so neither black man could see it.

"These peckerwood motherfuckers be tryin' to muscle—"

The big man was upon me, sticking his finger in my chest. I could see he was older, with a shiny head bald except for gray around the ears. He still looked like a grizzly to me. The alley was dark, and neither of them saw the small black pistol in my hand "Little white motherfucker," he said.

I said nothing. This was no time for me to talk. I raised the pistol close to my body and shot across my stomach. I could feel the heat of the muzzle (and later found powder burns on my shirt) as the barrel spit fire. I deliberately aimed downward (I didn't intend to kill him), and the bullet hit him just above the knee. It went through and kicked up sparks on the concrete. He yelped in pain, grabbed his leg, and went down in a kneeling position. I stepped back. I wanted to be clear enough to shoot him good if he lunged for me. He didn't. I turned to Pinky. "You want some?" He was waving his hands, shaking his head, and backing away.

"I want my dough, asshole," Denis said.

I didn't want anything but to get away from the scene. It was a block from Hollywood Boulevard. To me the shot had sounded like a howitzer going off. "C'mon . . . c'mon," I said. "Let's get outta here."

Denis and I turned and ran. When we got to the car, he started laughing. "I thought we were in big trouble with those bucks. I forgot you had that piece."

Denis never got his money back. Pinky left the area. Ten years later, in 1967, I was in Folsom and the big black man came in on the Department of Corrections bus. I recognized him immediately, a recognition confirmed by his limp. While he was still locked up on fish row, on the fifth tier of #2 Building, I sneaked up to his cell and talked to him. I told him who I was and that I didn't want any trouble . . . but I would try to kill him if I got the idea that he wanted any revenge. He said it was forgotten; he had a parole date seven months away—and Pinky was a stool pigeon anyway. It was a mistake to back a stool pigeon no matter what his color. This made me grin; his was the attitude all outlaws should have.

A YEAR HAD PASSED without an arrest. Of course for nine months I hadn't done anything besides smoke some grass. I didn't feel the wheels that were starting to shake under me. Life was too exciting. The tide started turning against me on a typical LA night, which is cool no matter how hot the day, when I went to meet Joe Morgan at the Club El Sereno on Huntington Drive. An old-style cocktail lounge with big booths of red leather, wood-paneled walls, and soft light, it was a hangout for the high-rolling Chicano drug dealers of the era. On this night it had a full house of various kinds of *Angelenos* all attracted to Art Pepper's trio. Pepper was perhaps the best white alto sax man of the time. Like his idol, Charlie Parker, Pepper loved junk, smack, ghow, heroin. . . . In the argot of a certain underworld, he was a "hope-to-die dope fiend." But he sure could play the saxophone.

The club was full and quiet. Pepper was blowing "Body and Soul." He could play the soul of the saxophone, and his audience was rapt.

Of course not entirely. The owner was at the rear on the phone, and in the most distant booth two couples were laughing. Not seeing Joe, I found an empty space at the bar, and when the bartender arrived and leaned toward me, I did the same and ordered a shot of Jack Daniel's backed with a bourbon and 7UP. I downed the shot and sipped the highball. It seemed a good way to drink at the time.

I knew several people in the room. The cocktail waitress was an exotically beautiful Eurasian girl who was most attractive. She was also quick-witted and hip. I was very interested until I found out she had two children. I wasn't ready for that, so what had been a pursuit of lust for a few days was now simply flirtatious banter while she delivered drinks. Jimmy D. was there with his wife. She must have held a gun to his head, or least raised hell, to make him take her out. He traveled alone; he liked new adventures and new pussy. I could understand all that. Alas, he had two very young children. He often complained that life weighed a ton, ". . . and my old lady . . ." He shook his head. His pain was on his face.

At the front end of the bar stood Billy the Bouncer and Russian Al. They were both about fifty, and neither had done time for twenty years. They were expert safecrackers, back when the safecracker was the most respected of thieves. It is nearly impossible to convict anyone of burglary unless he is caught on the score, and that happens rarely. Russian Al had gone to prison once back in the thirties. He had been staying in a third-rate hotel across the street from a small department store in Modesto. Between Saturday night and Sunday morning, he entered the store, opened the safe, and took almost forty thousand dollars, a fantastic score at the time. He returned to the hotel and changed from the clothes he was wearing into an expensive suit. When he came off the elevator, two detectives were in the lobby investigating a report of a drug dealer in the hotel. They spotted Russian Al in his expensive clothes, stopped him, and asked what was in the suitcase he carried. They were looking for narcotics, but they were happy with what they found. He did nine years for "burglary with explosives," a special category of burglary. An acetylene torch had been deemed to fall within the statute. They hadn't touched him in fifteen years.

Billy the Bouncer had served one county jail sentence for the misdemeanor offense of possessing burglary tools.

I felt the spreading warmth of two drinks. That called for two more, again throwing one down and sipping the other, meanwhile watching each time the rear door opened. Joe was still a no-show when Art Pepper's trio finished the first set and went out into the parking lot for a cigarette or, more likely, a few tokes on a joint. I'd been waiting more than an hour, and if it had been anyone but Joe Morgan, I would have left after half an hour. Joe, however, was different. I gave him the utmost respect.

Pepper was halfway through his rendition of "When Sunny Gets Blue" in his second set when the cocktail waitress came down the bar, touched my arm, and pointed to the club's owner at the rear. He was holding a telephone, and when he saw me look toward him he extended it toward me. I had a phone call. I went to see what it was about.

It was a female voice: "Are you Eddie B.?"

"I dunno. Who're you?"

"Big Joe told me to call you."

"Uh-huh. What's up?"

"They came and got him."

"Uhh . . . who . . . who came for him?"

"FBI. They wouldn't tell me what it was for. When they were taking him away, he said 'Call Eddie B. at the club and tell him.' So that's what I did."

"Thanks." I hung up. The feds. It wasn't about Joe's drug operation. J. Edgar Hoover didn't let the FBI do narcotics busts; there was too much temptation for corruption. It would be several years before I saw Joe again. He was initially charged with bank robbery, but the government never took it to trial. They had no evidence. Instead the Department of Corrections sent him back to prison as a parole violator. The violation was for leaving the state of California; they had a record where he had rented a car in Las Vegas. But these were events that would unfold in the months to come. That night I only knew he was busted.

Half-drunk from six drinks in two hours, I went out to my car, a 1955 XK 120 Jaguar, with a Dodge Red Ram V8 under the hood, instead of the stock Jaguar six-cylinder engine. The Jags of that model were long and sleek and beautiful. Alas, it was less than three years old and was already frequent trouble, including tonight. The starter turned, but the engine refused to kick over and catch. I opened the hood and fiddled with the wires even though I had no idea what I was looking for. I found nothing I recognized.

The pay phone was in a short corridor to the rest rooms. I was calling the tow truck when Billy the Bouncer passed by en route to take a leak. On his way out, he stopped and waited until I hung up. "You need a ride?" he asked.

"Yeah . . . but you know where I live?"

"Out near Hollywood, don't you?"

"Near Wilshire and LaBrea."

"We're goin' pretty near there . . . so if you don't want to pay that cab fare . . ."

The cab fare from where we were to where I lived would cost plenty. Taxis are not economically viable in Southern California. The streetcar would take a couple of hours, first to downtown; then I'd need to take a bus. I was happy to get the ride.

While rolling through the city, they told me they were going to Beverly Hills to check out a score. "We're not doing anything," Al said. "Just gonna look at a couple things."

In Hollywood, we stopped at Tiny Naylor's, a big and bright drive-in restaurant on the corner of Sunset and LaBrea where I knew one of the waitresses. She was Betty by name. She got off work in about two hours, at 1:00 A.M., and a musician friend had told her about an after-hours jam session down on Forty-second and Central Avenue. Did I want to take her? We could use her car. It was decided that I would come back in two hours. I would go with Russian Al and Billy the Bouncer—they weren't going to do anything tonight— and they would drop me off on the way back. If a little early, I could sit inside and eat a piece of pie.

Santa Monica Boulevard was less gay than it is today, but the sidewalks outside the clubs were crowded.

Beverly Hills was not. Its skyline was low, with almost nothing over three floors, and it had an aura of quaint wealth displayed in Southwestern and Mediterranean architecture. Restaurants were few, nightclubs nonexistent.

Billy was driving. He turned into an alley behind Beverly Drive. In midblock he turned into an empty parking space and stopped. They got out and I remained in the car as they stood and talked.

The glare of a flashlight illuminated the interior of the car as its beam highlighted the two figures. I sat up and turned to look. A policeman. Oh shit!

Then the flash of fear disappeared. We weren't doing anything.

"Turn around. Come here," the officer ordered. I leaned back and closed my eyes. Whatever happened, I would claim to be the drunk in the backseat.

The flashlight tapped on the side window; the flashlight beam was directly on my face. I could see the glare through closed eyelids. I opened one eye at a time. "Wha . . . what's happening?"

"Step out of the car."

I got out. "What's the problem, Officer?"

"Over there. Let's see some ID."

As we each showed identification, Billy wanted to know what this was about. It seemed that the officer, walking a beat, had seen us turn the wrong way into a one-way alley. "What're you doing back here?"

"Taking a leak," Billy said.

"I dunno," I said. "I was sleeping in the backseat."

"Let's take a walk," the cop said.

We walked from the alley along a street. My instinct was to run. Although I was always notoriously slow, the policeman had a potbelly that said he wasn't a sprinter, either. If I ran, he would face a dilemma: if he chased me, they would get away. What kept me from running was the fact that I hadn't done anything.

He unlocked a call-in box and picked up the phone. We waited until a sergeant drove up and then drove back to the alley. En route the sergeant asked what we were doing in the alley. I said I was asleep in the backseat. The others repeated that they had been taking a leak.

The sergeant flashed the light around the car. "Open the trunk."

Billy unlocked the trunk. The sergeant trained his flashlight inside—and there we saw a portable acetylene torch, with straps so it could be carried on the back. Inside a bag was a drill and a bit, a handsaw that could cut circles, a jimmy bar, several freshly sharpened chisels and a small sledgehammer, and other tools. "You're under arrest," he said, pulling his weapon. Now it was too late to run.

As soon as we were being booked, I began demanding a telephone call. The booking officer said I had to wait for the detectives to approve it. "No, I don't. I've got a right to a phone call."

"You've got a right to an ass kicking."

That temporarily silenced me—but as soon as I was in the cell, I began to yell, "I want a telephone call!" Everyone who passed outside the cell or within earshot heard my cry for a phone call. I had to get out on bail before Monday morning, when the parole officer would learn that I was in jail and automatically put a parole hold on me. The earliest I could hope for release was after the charges were settled, whatever they might be. If I was convicted of so much as a misdemeanor, I would likely be returned to San Quentin as a parole violator, and the parole board could refix my term at the maximum. The misdemeanor would constitute a parole violation, as I was in company with *known felons* and *persons of ill repute*. I had to get a phone call. I was booked on suspicion of burglary. A lawyer could go to a judge with a petition for *habeas corpus*, and the judge would issue a show cause order and set bail. A bail bondsman would take 10 percent as his fee, plus a lien on something like a house for the whole amount. It would go down to a misdemeanor and a lower bail on Monday, but I could not wait for Monday. "My mother's got thirty million dollars and *I want a phone call!*" I yelled through the night.

The detectives came in on Saturday morning, their day off. They drooled at the chance of putting the two wily old safecrackers into prison. They called me first, knowing my story about sleeping in the backseat was bullshit. "You're on parole, Bunker; you can go back that fast." He snapped his fingers. "So? You know those guys were starting to break into one of those stores. You help us and we'll help you."

"I'd like to . . . but you don't want any lies, do you?"

They looked at each other and then at me with eyes of dislike.

"Go back to the cell. We'll talk to you later."

As they walked me back to the holding tank where a jailer would let me in, I asked them in front of him, "Tell this guy to let me make a phone call."

"Let him make a call," the detective said.

The jailer nodded as he opened the gate and slammed it shut behind me. Twenty minutes later, he took me out to the pay phone. "Go ahead."

"I need a dime."

"You don't have a dime?"

"Man, you guys took my money when you booked me."

"I didn't book you. I wasn't here."

"How am I gonna make a phone call?"

"Without a dime, I don't know."

My face was aflame when he put me back in the cell. I swung on an emotional pendulum between indignant fury and a bolt of despair.

An hour later, an old Chicano, a trusty in khaki with COUNTY JAIL stamped across both knees, the breast pocket, and the back of the shirt, came down the runway outside the cells. He was pushing a broom.

"Hey, man, *ese!*"

The trusty looked around to make sure no jailer was watching. "Yeah?"

"Hey, man, I need a fuckin' dime to make a phone call."

He made a face of pain. He was torn between fear of the jailers and desire to help another prisoner.

"Please, man."

When he reached my cell he put a quarter on the bars and kept going.

"Jailer! Jailer! My mama's got thirty million dollars and *I want a phone call!*" I punctuated the cry by shaking the gate as hard as I could. It banged loudly.

"Shut the fuck up down there, Mr. thirty million motherfucker."

"Fuck you, and your mama, too. *Officer! Jailer! I wanna make a phone call!*"

On Saturday night the detectives began taking us out at roll call. That is when the shift of officers changes. They meet in the muster room. After checking the roll and assigning cars, they are told about recent crimes and other things they should know about. The burglary detectives marched us downstairs and paraded us in front of the graveyard shift. Our pedigrees were announced. ". . . two of the best safecrackers in California . . . and this one looks young, but don't be fooled. This"—he shook several pages of yellow paper—"is his rap sheet. . . ."

We were taken again when the day shift came on. As I stood under the hot lights, I called out, "Do I get to make a phone call or not?"

"Didn't they let you make one already?"

"No."

When they took us back, a different jailer took me back to the pay phone. "Go ahead," he said.

As I stepped up and dropped the quarter into the slot, I watched the jailer's face—and his surprise was almost neon across his mug. I dialed Louise's private number, to her phone in her bedroom. "Hello," she said.

"Hello, Mama, it's me. I need help . . ." I explained what had happened and what my situation was. I had no one else to call. I told her what had to be done and even gave her the name of a shyster mouthpiece who would take care of it.

It took until Sunday evening to get the writ and post the bail. While I was out seeing the bondsman, Billy the Bouncer was out seeing his lawyer. He wasn't going to bother with a writ. Tomorrow they would be charged with a misdemeanor and have a misdemeanor bail. It was about one-fifth of the felony bail I had to post today. He didn't have a parole officer to worry about. He laughed with bad teeth and told me the detectives were angry. They'd hoped to match the tools in the car trunk with tool marks on several open safes. Alas, all the tools had been freshly ground down and sharpened. They were so clean that they didn't even have fingerprints. "How the hell can they get in a car trunk without being touched by a human hand?"

I walked out into the Beverly Hills night, palm trees blowing in a Santa Ana breeze. Louise waited, her presence unexpected. She drove me to my apartment on Ninth and Detroit. I told her exactly what had happened, and in my view I was innocence personified. I was, indeed, the drunk in the backseat. Whether she believed me or not, her voice and manner registered disappointment, partly for the trouble and partly because I had almost stopped coming to see her: "You went to see Marion last week. Why didn't you visit me?" True enough, one afternoon I had stopped by Marion Davies's house and had a gin and tonic with her. She drank a lot of gin.

The writ was returnable in the Beverly Hills Municipal Court in ten days. I was to be there at 10:00 A.M. with counsel. I marked it on the calendar and forgot about it. I had other things to think about. This meatball case could be stalled for many months, quite possibly until I was off parole. Then a misdemeanor conviction would be inconsequential. I would gladly serve six months in jail if I could get rid of the parole leash that was choking me.

As expected, all they could charge me with was several misdemeanors. Instead of entering a plea, we motioned for a month's postponement to study the arrest and investigation reports. My lawyer, an old man who taught criminal law and knew the judge but was long of tooth for trial wars, combat by words, was able to get us five weeks' postponement to study the reports. The city attorney objected; he was young and feisty. The judge ignored him and set arraignment for a Monday, at 10:00 A.M., five weeks away. We would probably enter a "Not Guilty" plea and have a trial date set for ninety days away. Even if we went to trial and a jury found me guilty, during the appeal of a misdemeanor conviction the defendant has an absolute right to bail. An appeal would last a minimum of eighteen months. In other words, if all things went bad, the earliest I had to confront fleeing the country or going to jail for a few months was over two years away. That was eternity relative to the pace I was living.

IT WOULD TAKE TOO LONG to recount all my adventures at twenty-three. As I had read Aldous Huxley's *The Doors of Perception* and *Heaven and*

Hell, when a magazine article did a piece on magic mushrooms in Mexico I happened to have $9,000 and a willing companion in Bill D., Jimmy D.'s brother. We drove old Route 66 through Arizona and New Mexico and turned south to pass through El Paso into Juárez. We drove through Mexico, and twice when stopped by soldiers and asked for a visa we paid fifty dollars and drove on. We got some mushrooms from an Indian. It was a strange high. Three weeks later we went back to Los Angeles.

I also discovered Las Vegas. Sandy took me there the first time, but after that I would go for two or three days almost on a whim. I loved to gamble. No, not gamble exactly, but rather I loved to play poker. Although the casinos of the era seemed the ultimate in wealth and glamour, they were virtually insignificant compared to the gigantic gambling palaces of today. I liked to cross the casino pit and have a pit boss tell me, "Table open, Mr. Bunker. . . ." I was twenty-three years old; it made me feel like a big shot.

One funny thing happened. As I said, I had a Jaguar sports car. My insurance had been canceled, so I had a crushed-in bumper and a few other dings and dents; plus it was a world of trouble mechanically. Half-humorously I told a youngster that I'd give him a couple of cans of grass if he would get me a car that looked like mine. At the used-sports-car lot where I had the front of a job, I learned that Jaguars have their numbers on a plate screwed into the fire wall. What was screwed in could be unscrewed and screwed in somewhere else— like on a better car.

The following Sunday morning I awakened at Flip's apartment next to Paramount and for some reason called the neighbor who lived in the bottom apartment of the main house. The neighbor said, "That kid made a lot of noise when he brought your car here last night."

My car! At home. "Wait a second," I said. I went to the window and looked down onto the street. There sat my car. The one the youth had brought was not mine.

We went to look at it. It was an exact duplicate, including skirts along the rear wheel well. In perfect condition, it was a jewel.

My problem was to dispose of the old one. With Flip in tow, I went looking for help. I wanted Jimmy D., who knew the scrap metal business, and Jack K., who was a machinist and had access to a cutting torch from his father's machine shop. They would help me cut up the Jag. Its body was aluminum; Jimmy could have that for scrap. Jack was into engines; he could have the Jaguar six, already a legendary piece of work. The Jag engine was always great; it was everything else, especially electricity, that made them deteriorate so quickly for so many years. We don't know how good they are today; it will take a few years. They do depreciate swiftly.

The day was hot, the asphalt parking lots soft. I found Jimmy and Jack together, coming out of the dim coolness of a bar. They were game for the plan. Jack went to get the acetylene torch. We would chop the Jag up in the garage of Jimmy's father-in-law, whom I had known since I was caught sleeping in his garage when on an escape from juvenile custody. His eldest daughter was then my girlfriend. Now she was married to a man in prison, who had been my running partner in youth. The second daughter was married to Jimmy, and he disliked being married except for his two sons, whom he adored. He had a physical revulsion to routine and was psychologically incapable of getting to a job on time. He might stay up partying until six-thirty, so how could he get to a job at eight? Cutting up a car on a Sunday afternoon was another matter.

The house with the garage was in El Monte. It had a deep backyard, so what we were doing in the garage should not have disturbed the family barbecue. We would make one cut through the body and peel it off in two pieces. While Jack put on the goggles and wielded the torch, Jimmy used his considerable muscle with a crowbar to dig and pry.

More and more family members and friends walked by the garage to the backyard barbecue. Everything might have been all right, except the torch had set rubber insulation on fire, or at least smoldering so seriously that smoke poured through a broken window at the rear of the garage and billowed out across the yard. The acrid black smoke filled the garage, too. We had to raise the garage door to let in air. The air blew even more smoke through the broken window in the backyard of coughing and choking Italians.

Flip, wearing white hot pants, white blouse, and white headband (the look of Lana Turner in *The Postman Always Rings Twice*), stood in the garage doorway and laughed until she was in tears.

Soon enough the dispute began: Jimmy would get the aluminum body and Jack would take the engine, but who would get the chassis had not been considered. I told them to finish cutting it out and then we would decide.

When the body was peeled off and all that remained was a chassis, four wheels, and two bucket seats, I took the license plates, the plate we had unscrewed from the fire wall, and the car keys and departed the scene with Flip.

Forty minutes later I screwed the plate with the vehicle identification number, engine number, and the rest onto the pristine black XK 140 convertible. I liked it better than the 120 because it had windows that rolled up. The 120 had side panels that snapped into place.

To make it look normal, I inserted the key to the old Jag into the ignition of the stolen one. With a tiny jiggle the key turned and I pushed the starter button, which was separate from the key. It kicked over and roared, the sound hypnotic to the sports car enthusiast, in which category I qualified.

A few days later I discovered that Jimmy and Jack had taken the chassis with four wheels and two seats—but no body, no windshield, no headlights, no license plates—out onto the San Bernardino Freeway, Interstate 10, and driven it to Riverside. They said it was the fastest thing on the road. By some miracle the Highway Patrol didn't spot them and test their speed claim. They sold the engine to someone who put it into a boat.

I drove the new Jaguar for about a year and once had it impounded without anyone discovering that it really belonged to a Van Nuys car dealer. Even when I became a fugitive, I put out-of-state license plates on the Jag and drove it for a few months. One night I parked it on one of the steeply sloped streets off the Sunset Strip. While I was gone the brakes gave out and it rolled downhill into the front door and entryway of an apartment building. It had been towed away when I came out. *C'est la vie le* Jaguar.

SANDY MOVED BACK TO the Sunset Strip, to a sleek apartment on Sweetzer between Sunset and Fountain. Late one afternoon she called me and said to come over: "Somebody wants to see you."

"Who is it?"

"No. No. It'll be a surprise."

When she opened the door, she said, "You'll never guess who's here."

On the living room sofa sat Ronnie H. Sandy was right; I never would have guessed. I had no idea he was out. I hadn't seen him since San Quentin. He was from Sandy's neighborhood; she had known him before he went to prison. Actually, she was friendlier with his sister, who would later be murdered in the desert by an escaped convict, who was sentenced to die, although I cannot recall if he was actually executed or got a commutation when the Supreme Court ruled the death penalty unconstitutional as it was then being applied. Ronnie H. had been a good convict, although no killer. In prison lexicon, he was a *regular*. He grinned gape-mouthed, showing a missing tooth. "Hey, Eddie B. We heard you had it all going for you, a Jaguar and all that."

Behind my affability was jealousy. Although Sandy was not my old lady and, in fact, we had not even gone to bed together, I felt a kernel of jealousy, which increased as she told me that Ronnie had lots of money from hanging bad paper and they were going away on a long trip together: "I always wanted to live awhile in New York."

"That's great. When are you leaving?"

Ronnie answered, "In a couple days. I gotta pick up some money that's owed me." When she went out of the room, he lowered his voice: "Bill D. said you could get blank payroll checks. I need some."

"How many do you want?"

"I dunno . . . as many as you can get, I guess."

"No, I don't think you want *that* many. You can only cash about a dozen a day."

"I got some other people cashin' 'em, too. What about a hundred . . . maybe a hundred and fifty? How much is that?"

"How's six grand?"

"That sounds fair enough."

"Okay . . . what's tomorrow?"

"Friday."

"I'll get 'em tomorrow night. You'll have my money?"

"Oh yeah . . . sure . . . as soon as I see these guys that owe me."

"No, no . . . I don't want to wait."

"No, you won't have to wait. If I don't see them, I'll give it to you out of some other money I've got."

"Okay, good. When I get the checks, where do you want me to reach you?"

"Reach me here at Sandy's."

As I went back to my car, I was laughing at myself because I had felt something unusual for me, jealousy. I hadn't known how much I wanted Sandy until it appeared as if she was leaving.

I had a dozen Southern Pacific Railroad checks and nine from Walt Disney, all made out. Not enough. I knew where to get more, from a machine shop in South Pasadena. It was an easy prowl; there was no burglar alarm. It had security bars on the rear window, but they had been cut so an air conditioner would fit on the window ledge. Wearing gloves, of course, I bent the bars, lifted out the air conditioner, and climbed in. In a couple of minutes I had a big checkbook. The checks could not get hot until Monday. That would give them two days before they were on any kind of hot list.

I called Sandy from the machine shop. "Hey, baby, is he there?" I asked.

"He went out somewhere . . . I think to see those guys about the money they owe him. He'll be back in a little while."

"Hold him. I'm on my way."

"Did you get them?"

"Yes, ma'am."

It was still dusk when I turned down the ramp onto the Pasadena Freeway, but when I exited the Hollywood Freeway at Highland Avenue, the city's lights were biting into night. I followed Highland to Fountain, went west to Sweetzer, and found a parking space at the curb.

The apartment building was from Southern California's architectural heyday, around 1940. It was a two-story stucco with red-tile roof. Entering from the street required passing through the gate of a walled courtyard with lush ferns and a fountain.

When Sandy opened the door, she let me know that Ronnie was in the apartment.

"Has he got my money?"

"I dunno. Talk to him."

He was in the living room watching a football game on TV. As soon as he saw me and stood up, I knew without a word that he didn't have the money. "They were supposed to meet me," he said.

"Uh-uh! No! That's bullshit. That's got nothing to do with me. I need my money."

"I know you do," he said. "I'll pay you out of these checks—right off the top."

"Look here, Ronnie; you and me are all right . . . but I don't commit felonies for free. I want my money tomorrow, and I want fifty dollars a check instead of forty."

Ronnie nodded before I finished. "Sure, man. Thanks, man. Fuck, I'll even cash some tonight and give you the dough." He looked toward the door to the bedroom, where Sandy was packing up. "Can you get me a check protector?"

"I don't know. Maybe."

"Let's go get some money," he said. "We'll take my car, but you drive. Okay?"

It was fine with me. Then I could keep track of my money. We went to my apartment to type a name on the checks. It was then I learned that Ronnie lacked phony identification. "We'll use my ID," he said. "Why not? I mean . . . what the fuck . . . I'm gonna be a fugitive anyway. What's the difference between a parole violation and a new check beef?"

His logic had some validity. I wouldn't have done it, but the truth was that he might serve about the same time for hanging paper as for a parole violation. He'd gone down the first time for armed robbery. The parole board might think he was improving if he came back on a forgery.

When he came out of the first market and handed me the money, he said, "Don't tell Sandy about this."

"About what?"

"About using my own identification."

"Yeah . . . sure."

"I'll get the rest tomorrow," I said.

"Yeah, sure. It's going good, huh?"

I nodded. "You better get all the money you can . . . because the more you have, the longer you can run."

"That's right. We'll have plenty when we pass the rest of that paper."

THE NEXT MORNING IT FELL upon me to evacuate Sandy from the apartment. What she wasn't taking with her was going to the garage at her parents' home in the San Gabriel Valley. When I arrived at the apartment she was in a heated argument with the landlady, who refused to return the security deposit because Sandy was leaving before her lease expired. "C'mon," I said, almost dragging her away. Sandy was a big girl, and although she dressed like a socialite, she had been raised on mean streets and was not adverse to punching the landlady in the eye. I didn't want that to happen. As I pulled Sandy to the car, I said, "Take it easy. We'll get her. I'll come back and clean it out." Which I did several nights later, carting away everything that would sell, including a rug that, by itself, brought twice the security deposit. The landlady was a shrewish bitch, but she did have good taste.

After leaving everything except two suitcases at the small but neat tract home, we went to a house in Alhambra. It was a frame house situated far back on the lot built before the Depression. The unpaved driveway had two grooves from the passage of countless cars. Once there had been a front lawn; now some patches of grass remained, and it was obviously a common practice to park in the front yard. Two cars sat there. I recognized neither. Ronnie's wasn't there, nor was his crime partner's. R.L. was in on the forgery scheme. In fact, he was supposed to pay me the rest of the money. He drove an old maroon Cadillac convertible. It predated the rear fins, which by 1957 had evolved to their maximum flamboyance.

I let Sandy out and went around the block to park. It was unlikely that the police would arrive, but it was possible. If they did pull up in front, I would have a chance to go over the rear fence. If that happened, I didn't want to leave my car. It was always my practice to park some distance away when I was doing something wrong.

Sandy was alone in the living room when I entered. "Who's here?" I asked.

"R.L.'s old lady and some teenage chick." She gestured toward the archway into the kitchen. There I found the wife, called Charlie, and a neighborhood girl named Bonnie. Charlie was feeding a baby in a high chair. Piled on the kitchen table were sacks of groceries. Somebody had been cashing the checks. Hanging paper in supermarkets, which was the place to cash them, created a by-product of many groceries. I would give them to Jimmy D.'s sister-in-law, whose husband was in San Quentin. She could use it all, especially the baby food.

Charlie's greeting was cold, and when I asked the whereabouts of her husband, she made a face and a sound of disgust. "I don't know. I don't care. Here." From beneath a magazine she produced a stack of greenbacks. "We still owe you six hundred," she said. "Get it from him."

To Bonnie, I made a face intended to be a humorous reaction to Charlene's manifest anger. Bonnie didn't respond, and on closer scrutiny I could see that she had been crying.

The sound of the front screen door banging shut brought me back to the living room. R.L. had returned. He was grinning at Sandy with drunken stupidity. "How ya doin', ya big, fine . . ." Then he saw me. "Hey, big E.B. Damn, you dress sharp. Where's that baaadass Jaguar of yours?"

Charlene came past me. "Well . . . ?" she said.

"Well, what . . . ?" R.L. responded.

"Did you pass any?"

He shook his head. "They won't take 'em from me."

"Lyin' bastard," she said, then snorted and went back to the kitchen.

R.L. looked to me as the appeal judge. "I don't know why, man. I swear, they won't take 'em from me."

Fifteen minutes later we pulled R.L.'s Cadillac into a parking lot beside a supermarket on Huntington Drive. While we were driving there I had told R.L.

exactly what to do. He got out and I waited. Five minutes later he came around the other corner and hurried to the car, shaking his head even before he got in. "I told you. They just won't."

It was obvious that he had simply walked around the market without going in. When we stopped at the next market, I accompanied him. It was a huge Safeway. "Get a cart," I said.

He pushed the cart and I piled it high with groceries. I went with him to the checkout line. When he was one customer from the cash register, I went around and stood by the door. He handed over the payroll check. The checker called the manager, who looked at the driver's license and initialed the check. The groceries were bagged and loaded back into the cart while the checkout clerk counted out the change and handed it over.

"That was easy," R.L. said when we were back in the car.

I held out my hand.

"Oh yeah, I owe you," he said, handing me the wad of bills.

I took him through the same dance twice more, loading the cart, leading him to the checkout line, and patting him on the back before stepping to the sidelines. "Man, it's easier than I thought," he said as he handed me the money. It was all he owed me. "Let's get a couple more before we go back."

At the next market, as we neared the front door, Ronnie H. came out pushing a cart of groceries. "Don't go in there," he said. "The manager was a *little bit* suspicious. Let's go back to the house."

When we got back, I had all the money owed me. I had wads that bulged both pants pockets and the inside pocket of my jacket. I got my car and loaded it with the groceries to give away. Ronnie was taking a temporary rest before going out again. He knew that it didn't matter if he cashed ten checks or two hundred; he would serve the same amount of time when caught. The more he cashed, the farther he could travel and the longer he could stay out of danger. *Give me enough money and it will be impossible for the authorities to catch me,* he figured.

Sandy was still waiting on the sofa. Ronnie looked at her and said, "You're the smartest one of all. You're getting everything without doing anything."

"No," she said. "I'm not the smartest. He is." She nodded toward me.

I was at the screen door. "Good-bye and good luck to one and all."

"I'll call you tomorrow," Sandy said.

"You're leaving town."

"I'll call you from wherever I am. You'll want to know how I am, won't you?"

"Of course. Later."

I gave them all a salute and walked out into the late-afternoon light, humming a song and snapping my fingers. "I'm the king of everything . . . gotta have a joint before I swing."

I got in the car and fired up a fat joint called a bomber.

▪ ▪ ▪

WHEN THE PHONE RANG late the following afternoon, I knew it was Sandy. When I picked up the receiver, I said, "Hi, baby."

"How'd you know it was me?"

"ESP."

"Wanna go to a movie?"

"Sure."

"Pick me up at my mother's."

"What time?"

"Whenever you get here."

That evening we drove to Pasadena, where we saw Frank Sinatra play the Prohibition era comedian Joe E. Lewis in *The Joker Is Wild.* It seemed a good movie, although my memory thereof is less clear than for some I've seen. I lost track of the movie while thinking about Sandy's body beside me. I'd played a waiting game, hiding my lust for many months, certain of her contempt for a man she could lead around by his sexual desire. Now she was ready to be my woman. The idea was dizzying. She was the perfect female for me, streetwise yet educated. That she had been a call girl was great with me. I had no use for a square john chick who, if I was in jail, would come to the visiting room and cry on the glass. I wanted a partner who could, and would, trick the bondsman to raise me on bail. She was fine, too, five-nine, with an eye-turning shape and long, gleaming red hair. She had the most sensuous walk I've ever seen on a woman, with long, tanned legs that were shapely, although her thighs were bigger than is fashionable today—but just what I like. So do most men.

Although visions of having her on white sheets with those legs spread wide filled my mind, I knew it would come to pass, but this wasn't the right time to bring it forward. A lot of things were communicated wordlessly. "We can be a great team," she said and, after a pause, added this: "Incidentally, I hear well. . . ." I said nothing; I even liked that she said it, for it validated my dominance in the relationship. Why tell her that the very idea of hitting a woman was anathema to me?

A WEEK LATER WE HAD an apartment on Sunset Boulevard near where Holloway Drive intersects. I remember standing on the balcony, high on pot, looking out over the plain of city lights, with Ella Fitzgerald's voice singing *The Rodgers and Hart Songbook.* I was waiting for Sandy to get ready for dinner. The whole world was spread at my feet. I was king of all I surveyed.

10
THE SHIT
HITS THE FAN

THE PHONE RANG. I picked it up. "Hello."

"Edward Bunker."

I didn't recognize the voice, but warning bells rang in my brain. "Who's calling?"

"Who's this?" he asked.

"I asked first."

There was a pause. "I'm his parole officer . . . and he's in big trouble."

Oh shit. "He's not here right now."

"Who're you?"

"I'll tell him to call you." I hung up. My shirt was wet from sweat.

The phone rang again. I let it ring.

The next morning I put a handkerchief over the phone, affected a slight southern accent, and called the parole officer. I was put through to Harry Sanders.

"I got a message you wanted to talk to me."

"I'm your new parole officer. Who do you think you are, driving a Jaguar?"

"I had permission to get a car."

"I can't find any *written* authorization in your file."

"Well, my old parole officer gave it to me. You can ask him."

"He isn't here anymore. Besides, it's supposed to be in writing."

I said nothing. What could I say?

"You haven't even tried to do this parole."

"I've got a job."

"You've got a job selling cars. That's a con game. You're supposed to be in jail right now with those charges pending in Beverly Hills. I don't know how the hell you got out."

Again I was silent.

"Get down to this office right now."

"Are you going to put me in jail?"

"We'll decide that when you get here."

"I just wanted to know if I should bring a toothbrush and clean underwear."

"You're a smart-ass, too."

"No, I'm not . . . not really."

On hanging up the phone, I debated flight. In my opinion, it is better to be hunted than caught, and it was obvious that a new day had dawned in my relationship with the Division of Adult Paroles. With great misgivings, I got in my car and drove down to the parole office. It was downtown in the office building above the old Million Dollar Theater. Once you entered, the receptionist had to buzz the door for you to get out. The cubicles used as offices were down a narrow passageway, very much like a vision from Kafka. A door opened, a head appeared, and a hand beckoned me.

"Personally, I'd put you in jail right now," was Harry Sanders's first sentence. He was in his thirties, fat, and unattractive, with jowls hanging over shirt collar. They vibrated when he moved his head. "My supervisor said to wait."

I was sure the supervisor thought I still had the patronage of Mrs. Hal Wallis. He wasn't going to make any rash moves.

"I'll tell you one thing," Sanders continued. "You're getting a different job."

"What's wrong with selling cars?"

"Too much temptation . . . too many con games played on the public."

I wanted to argue, but I knew the newspapers were full of a scandal lately involving H. J. Caruso, one of the largest car dealers in Southern California. I shrugged and kept my mouth shut.

"And that Jaguar. You get rid of that car. Who the hell do you think you are, a parolee driving a Jaguar?"

I dropped my eyes in subservience, but I was envisioning how I would like to have him off somewhere without witnesses. When I got back to the car, I realized that my hands were trembling. As you must know from what you've read, I am not a man easily shaken. I wanted to kill Sanders, for I knew, contrary to popular belief, that murder is perhaps the easiest felony to commit and get away with if the perpetrator follows a simple script. First, trust nobody. It is too much weight for others to carry, especially if they come into a situation where they can trade it for their own freedom. Too many people seem compelled to trust somebody, to pour it out. Murder weighs so heavy on the soul. It shouldn't, but it does. The second step is finding a place to catch the victim alone, in the driveway, a parking lot, or a subterranean garage. Step up and shoot him, preferably between the eyes or behind the ear; the heart is okay, too. *Make sure* you fire killing shots and that nobody can identify you. Dispose of the weapon where it can never be found, and make sure that it cannot be traced to you if it is found. Then this is a crime without evidence or witnesses. Even if the police believe you did it, that is not evidence they can put before a jury. If questioned, don't lie. Say nothing except: "I want to see my lawyer." Say it to the arresting officers; say it to the booking officer; say it to the detectives who interrogate you; say it to every officer who passes by; say it to the nurse passing out medications; say it to the janitor: "I want to see my lawyer."

I could get away with it, but I didn't have it in me to murder in cold blood. In self-defense, yes. If someone was a threat to my life, I would take him out quickly. Harry S. might fit into that category, but *might* was not enough to take his life, worthless as he was. I would try to ride it out, go along with what he said, and try to placate him. It was contrary to my nature, but it was the only chance I had to win. My parole had nine months and twelve days remaining. The state had put a leash around my neck when I was four and they made me a ward of the court. Ever since I had been on parole or probation. If I could ride it out, I hoped he then would have other cases to attract his attention. If I could hang on for a year I would be discharged and truly free.

I quit selling cars and took a laborer's job at the Disney studio, moving scenery on the back lot in the burning sun. After two weeks I couldn't take it and quit. The brother of an ex-con friend owned a strippers' club on Seventh Street near downtown. He gave me a front, writing a check that I gave back; plus I paid the tax deductions and Social Security. The parole officer would disallow the job next month when I sent my parole report. After that I would simply claim that I couldn't get a job. He would have a hard time getting me for violating my parole by not working when he'd made me quit two jobs.

Another thing that bothered Sanders was women. "How come you have so many girlfriends? Who are these women?" He wanted to see them. I had Flip see him using Patty Ann's name.

To comply with his order to get rid of the Jaguar, I simply put it in Sandy's name with an appropriate bill of sale. He wanted to know who she was, and when I told him that she was someone who had called when I put a FOR SALE sign in the window, he demanded her name and number. I couldn't say that I didn't have it. When I told Sandy, she said, "What an asshole." My sentiments precisely. When he called, saying he was a parole officer and wanted to know about the car, she told him to see her lawyer. Instead, he called the bank (because the loan had to be transferred), got the information on her credit application—and called the movie producer who covered for Sandy when she needed a reference. Sanders interrogated the movie producer. "Who is this girl? Did you know . . ."

As soon as the parole officer hung up, the producer called Sandy, demanding to know, "Who is this Edward Bunker?"

She stroked him verbally and calmed him down, but at the end, he still said, "I don't know if I can keep on being your job reference. Let me think about it."

As soon as he hung up, Sandy was on the phone with me: "That parole officer is fuckin' nutty. Do you know what he did?"

"Nothing would surprise me."

"That sadistic bastard called my producer friend and—ohhh shit! Double shit!"

"I'm sorry, girl. Really. . . ."

"Fuck it. It's over. No use snivelin'." She paused. "You know what, I think that parole officer has some kind of sexual hangup . . . probably can't get any."

"He's got an ass like an elephant."

That made Sandy laugh but made me feel no better. "Forget him," I said. "Where do you want to go eat?"

"What about the Captain's Table?"

"That's fine with me."

"I'll be ready in about fifteen minutes."

While Sandy dressed and put on her face, I put *Ella Fitzgerald Sings Rodgers and Hart* on the hi-fi record player and stepped onto the balcony to smoke a joint and look out at the plain of lights beginning to glow in the growing night. The music and the lilting, perfect voice came through the open door. Screw Sanders. I was king of everything—or at least the pot made me feel that way—and my city was spread out as far as I could see. I popped my fingers to the music and laughed into the dusk. Oh man, for a twenty-three-year-old state-raised ex-convict I had life by the balls. Should we take my Jag or her Cad? How many twenty-three-year-old state-raised ex-convicts had that choice? In retrospect, I should have had less hubris.

It came time to appear in the Beverly Hills Municipal Court. The police had originally booked me on suspicion of burglary, a felony, but all they could file were several misdemeanors. My lawyer, retained by Louise, was an old man who taught at Loyola. He was no lion in court, but he did know a lot of people in the legal system. The judge had been his student. The city attorney prosecuting the case would drop everything except one misdemeanor vagrancy—if I would plead guilty. And they would not argue for any time if the judge wanted me to pay a fine. "They couldn't care less about you. They want the other two."

"You guarantee it?"

"I can't *guarantee* it, but if the prosecutor doesn't oppose it, I've known this judge a long time. If we go to trial, the judge might find you guilty of everything and he could give you six months in jail on each count. As soon as they find you guilty, he's going to rescind bail, sure as the sun rises. If you plead guilty, he'll leave you out until the day of sentencing . . . and if you get a fine—"

"How long before the sentencing?"

"Six weeks . . . two months . . . and pay a fine."

With hesitant misgivings, I nodded acquiescence.

In the courtroom devoid of spectators, I entered a plea of "Guilty" to one count of vagrancy. The judge set a date for probation hearing and sentencing seven weeks away. He referred the matter to the probation department for a report.

On the way out, the lawyer squeezed my shoulder and said that he would call the chief probation officer. "Don't worry about it."

Don't worry about it. Was he crazy? All I would do was worry, or so I expected. By that night, however, six weeks was far away, and every day was a fresh experience. Sandy knew things that I didn't know—about sex and how to have fun. It was before the era of the hippie and dawn of sloppy dress, so we were stylish when we went to dine at such restaurants as Perino's, Romanoff's, Chasen's, Edna Earle's Fog Cutter, and Don the Beachcomber's, and after that we went to hear Francis Faye at the Interlude, above the Crescendo. We caught Billie Holiday at Jazz City on Hollywood Boulevard near Western. Billie was obviously half-sick from withdrawal, so during the break between sets, when she went to the ladies' room, Sandy followed her. There was no chance to take a fix, but Sandy offered her a toot—and when she sang her next set, her voice was husky and deep and at its unique best. It is phenomenal how fast a little toot of smack will take away the agony of withdrawal and most other kinds of pain. What it cannot take away it makes meaningless. You may still have a broken arm, but somehow it doesn't matter so much. The same is true for angst and anxiety. Toot instantly wraps up your troubles and throws them out the window. It cancels pain so hidden that you were unaware of its existence until it disappeared.

After the regular clubs closed, we often went to the after-hours clubs around Forty-second and Central Avenue, where the whiskey you ordered was poured from teapot into teacup, the lights were low, the cigarette smoke was thick, and some legendary musicians came after their regular gigs to jam until the dawn.

The presentencing interview and report went well enough. The probation officer was overworked and indifferent. He accepted as real the facade of a job I gave him, and there was, in fact, some question as to whether I had been involved in the safecracking scheme. Even the police report said I was apparently asleep in the backseat when the officer walked up to the car. After reading the probation report, my lawyer talked to the judge, "kind of unofficially . . . and he thinks it calls for something like a hundred dollars or fifty days. . . ."

"Fifty days!"

"No . . . no. It's fifty days if you don't pay the fine. Two dollars a day."

I stopped worrying and continued devouring hedonistic pleasures. The days ticked away. Finally came the day circled on the calendar.

It was an afternoon appearance and I was late. I don't remember why. I do remember meeting my lawyer in the corridor outside the courtroom. He was upset: "They already called you. The judge was ready to issue a bench warrant." While speaking, he ushered me through the courtroom door. The courtroom was uncrowded but still had plenty of business. The judge was hearing arguments on another case, someone seeking a bail reduction. My lawyer had two seats on the aisle. When we sat down, he handed me some papers. "Jesus, why didn't you warn me?"

I read: "Department of Corrections, Parole and Community Services." Oh God! It was *him,* my elephant-assed *bête noire.* I read in snatches, my mind jumping too much for continuity: *". . . LAPD has suspected him of two murders . . ."* Was he nuts? What was he talking about? A long time later I would realize that he was referring to the Hollywood Prowler fiasco—but I never did find out what other murder he was talking about. *". . . involved in drug trafficking and exploiting prostitutes in the Sunset–Beverly Hills area. . . ."* Had he been in the courtroom and I had a pistol, he would have been shot dead in front of judge, bailiffs, deputy district attorney, and God Almighty. I was going to jail on this bullshit. *Murder!* What kind of shit was that? *Exploiting prostitutes!* That was crazy. I was a whore's best friend. I *hated* pimps.

If I had just known about this . . . "I'm gonna take a piss," I said, intending to leave and not come back.

"The People versus Bunker, number five six nine six dash five seven. . . ."

The judge gave me ninety days in the county jail, and the bailiffs closed in and took me to the bullpen beside the courtroom. When one bailiff unlocked the heavy door, I was met with the combined stench of unwashed bodies and a stopped-up toilet. Like most courtroom bullpens, it was crowded. All the benches were taken; so was most of the floor. I was by far the most elegantly dressed. All the others had come from a precinct house, where they'd slept for two or three days in whatever they were wearing when arrested. Nearly all were poor, and it showed in their clothes. I found space near the wall, took off my camel-hair sport coat, and used it for a pillow. If my past experiences were any indicator, it would be a long wait before we went anywhere.

At about six-thirty, the deputies arrived with the chains. The bus waited outside. From Beverly Hills we went to Inglewood and picked up more prisoners, and from there to Long Beach. It was long after midnight when we were disgorged at the old Hall of Justice at Temple and Broadway. A new central jail had been planned for a landfill over a dump behind the Union Station, but it was a couple of years away. It took eighteen hours to go through the booking process, most of it spent waiting somewhere in the building. The visiting room was used after visits were over, ditto for courtroom bullpens downstairs during the night. Once a fish was dropped into the processing hopper, not even God could find him until he came out the other end, his body sticky with DDT sprayed on after a shower, wearing rumpled, ill-fitting jail clothes and carrying a mattress cover bedroll.

It was Friday afternoon when the judge sentenced me. It was about four in the morning on Sunday when the jail tank's gate crashed shut behind me. The runway outside the cells was wall-to-wall mattresses and mostly sleeping bodies. One or two men were reading paperbacks by the light coming through the outer bars from the jailers' walkway. I was able to stretch out on the concrete without a mattress and use the folded mattress cover for a pillow. Despite the discomfort, I quickly fell asleep. I'd gotten less than an hour the night before, and that, too, was on a hard floor.

On weekdays at 4:00 A.M. a deputy with a clipboard would start calling names for court. Because it was Sunday, it was 6:00 A.M. when the lights went on and the tank trusties came out of the first cell and began waking up those sleeping on the runway. Around the jail the gates were beginning to open. The runways were being cleared of mattresses and bedding so breakfast could be passed out. I struggled hard against the awesome weight of needing sleep. The runway was rapidly getting emptier as prisoners rolled up their mattresses and carried them into cells. This wasn't the same as high power, which always had room. This was five men to each two-man cell. I turned toward the first cell; the tank trusties would assign me to a cell.

"Bunker! Eddie Bunker!" The speaker was in the doorway of the first cell. He wore a blue tank top that matched the India ink blue tattoos covering both arms and every other spot of exposed flesh, including a line around his neck with the words: CUT ON DOTTED LINE. It was the full beard, which wasn't allowed in San Quentin, that made me frown, because I didn't recognize the speaker for a few seconds. He recognized the origin of my frown. "Jimmy Thomas, fool!"

Sure. Skinny Jimmy. I hadn't seen him in several years. "Hey, man, what's goin' on?"

"I'm fightin' a robbery beef. Me and Buddy Sloan. Bring your gear in here." He beckoned me into the first cell. No matter how crowded the rest of the tank, Cell #1 had just two occupants for the two bunks. Nobody even slept on the floor unless invited—and they invited me. Indeed, from here onward it was impossible for me to enter a jail or prison on the West Coast without knowing several (if it was a jail) or many (if it was a prison) of the occupants.

The other trusty from the first cell appeared in the doorway, all six-foot-four of lean muscle and shaven head. "You know Bobby Hedberg?"

"I sure know who he is." I extended a hand. "Eddie Bunker."

"I know about you, too . . . crazy motherfucker."

"Not crazy as you." It was true, Bobby Hedberg was a bona fide crazy man. He seemed to be sane and rational in his conversation—he made sense when he talked—but he did some things so wild that my adventures were minor by comparison. Had I done what Bobby did over the course of his criminal career, I would have spent my entire life in prison rather than a mere eighteen years in three jolts. Bobby was an anomaly. His father, R.B., for whom Bobby was named because he was the oldest son, was rich from building tract homes in the San Fernando Valley when World War II ended. R.B. was a tough, strict Irish Catholic, and everyone to him was either a nigger, a spic, a greaseball wop, a kike, a Jap, a king-worshiping English sonofabitch, a guinea bastard, or a fuckin' Protestant. He disliked everyone but the pope, and he was suspicious of John XXIII for being too goddamned liberal. Bobby was the oldest son, and Bobby broke his father's heart by being a hoodlum. Bobby was no rich boy having an adventure on the other side of the tracks; he was a hard-core tough guy to the bone. He would do outrageous things over the next two decades, in prison and out. Being pursued by the California Highway Patrol once, he crashed through the U.S.–Mexican border in a hailstorm of bullets and surrendered over there. Another time, a parole officer managed to lock Bobby in an office on the ninth floor of a downtown office building. He threw everything out the window onto downtown streets, his own ticker-tape parade made up of inmate records. He finished the scene by taking Ronald Reagan's picture off the wall and throwing that, too.

I went to see him one time in West Hollywood. When I reached the high-rise condominium it was cordoned off by black-and-white sheriff's cars. At a nearby pay telephone I called him. Sure enough, it was Bobby they had surrounded, although now I can't remember why. His voice was slurred with a heroin high. We talked a few seconds, and he said he had to go. Months later I learned that he had packed as much heroin as he could into condoms tied in tight knots and stuck up his butt that he doubled over. Then he fixed until he nearly overdosed. When they kicked in the door, he was unconscious on the middle of the floor. He didn't even know he'd been arrested until he woke up in the jail ward of the general hospital.

Another time he was in the county jail and he conspired with one of the Manson girls to kidnap a Central American consul general to force his release. The FBI curtailed the plot and never took it seriously. I would have gotten forty years, Bobby got two—and they ran concurrently with the term he was serving in San Quentin.

Bobby overdosed himself to death when he was forty or so but that was in the future. When we met in the jail, Bobby said, "Man, I've been hearing about you since I went to juvenile hall."

The tank was packed four and five to a cell, except for the first three cells, which held two, three, and three, and the men in those cells passed out the food, swept and mopped the runway, assigned cells and bunks—and maintained order with boot and fist. I moved into the first cell with a mattress on the floor.

It was Sunday and slow. No court appearances, no visits, no vendor wagons selling things except for Oscar's newspaper and magazine cart. Oscar had the jail concession for decades; selling thousands of newspapers and paperbacks every day made him a wealthy man. I slept on Bobby's bunk through the day. After the evening count, I played poker for something to occupy my mind so I wouldn't dwell on my troubles. There was nothing I could do except worry. Better to concentrate on the cards coming off the deck.

Finally, it was lockup and lights out. I went to sleep quickly to escape thinking about my situation.

Late the following morning, I was called out of the tank and told to go to the Attorney Room. As I checked in with the deputy on the desk, I looked around the room and saw the parole officer. Walking between the tables toward him, I saw the malicious glee in his little pig eyes and the corners of his mouth.

"You know you're going back, don't you?"

I nodded, not trusting what would come out of my mouth. Sheer willpower kept me from diving across the table and smashing him in the face. It wasn't the consequences that bothered me. It was that in seconds they would pile on and pull me off. If I'd had even two or three minutes I would have assaulted him. I'd be lucky to get fifteen seconds, and that wouldn't have provided enough satisfaction for the beating they would inflict on me, the stint in the hole, and the addendum to his parole report. Actually, he was merely confirming what I already knew. It was standard policy that any parolee sent to jail for anything went back to prison; then the adult authorities reviewed the matter. Nobody was ever reinstated on parole. Some men did more time on the parole violation than on the original conviction. I'd been trying to maintain hope despite what I knew. That was over.

As I walked back through the corridors to the tank, I was resigned to seeing the Big Yard. Now my biggest hope was that the paperwork go through quickly so I didn't have to spend a couple of months in the county jail.

When I reached the landing outside the tank, Bobby Hedberg was waiting inside the gate. He had my meager gear in hand. "Who was that?"

"The parole officer." I turned my thumb downward; the gesture said it all.

"They called you for roll up to the farm."

"To the farm."

"Yeah. Right after you left."

The deputy who ran the four tanks on the landing came up to unlock the gate and let me in. Bobby told him, "This is Bunker. Here's his gear."

The deputy unlocked the gate, and Bobby handed out the mattress cover.

Half an hour later I was on a sheriff's bus heading north through the San Fernando Valley. I wore no handcuffs. The county farm was minimum-security. As the bus rolled, I realized that the jail bureaucracy, which always needed space in the downtown jail, saw me as someone eligible for the farm. The parole officer had not yet put the detainer on me when the roll up was called.

As the bus turned off U.S. 99 at Castaic and went through the gate into the farm, I prayed silently that they wouldn't be waiting for me.

The bus pulled up. A sergeant was waiting. He called off names and assigned each of us to a barracks. "Bunker, Barracks Eleven, Bed Fifteen."

I walked into the barracks, walked past Bed Fifteen, went out the back door, sucked up my courage, and leaped high on the fence. The fence shook, the sound vibrating along its surface for some distance. I kept climbing. It had three strands of barbed wire at the top. I got a leg over it, the barbs hooking my pants and gouging my leg. I tore loose and kept going, oblivious to the cut. It was far riskier jumping the fence in daylight than at night. Any passing deputy or one of the supervisors for the many work crews constantly laboring on the reservation might spot me. At night, darkness would cloak me once I was over the fence. Alas, I didn't have the choice of waiting for night. The teletype could come at any minute.

I dropped onto the dirt road that ran along the other side of the fence. A sharp pain ran up from my ankle. I'd twisted it enough so that I limped up the first slope. It was bare desert earth with a few dry desert plants. As I neared the summit I was high enough so anyone in the compound could see me. I got lucky. Nobody sounded the alarm. I went over the summit of the low ridge and was out of sight. Now the odds were in my favor. I began telling myself: *"I'm gonna get away! I'm gonna get away!"* It was a chant that matched my pace. Gone was my depression. Now there was excitement. Somewhere down the line, in a month, two months, or two years, they would catch me. That I knew. But right now it was better being wanted than caught. Better a fugitive than a convict. LA, here I come again.

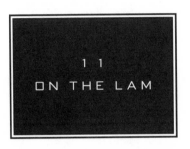

1 1

ON THE LAM

IF THERE IS AN APPRENTICESHIP to bring a fugitive, I began serving it in early childhood with all of the runaways from foster homes and military schools. I polished these skills in the escapes from juvenile hall and reform school. I assumed the authorities would do the usual for a parolee at large or a walkaway from a minimum-security institution, which means they simply wait until the fugitive is stopped for a traffic violation or arrested for some minor offense, then nab him. In most instances he cannot produce false identification. He has either none or his own. He hands it over and prays. It's the computers that nail him. Or else the authorities have a neighbor call them if he goes around the family home. It surprised me when they put forth effort to catch me. They tried to pressure Sandy into giving me up. When she refused to rat ("I don't know where he is," she said. "Let me call my lawyer."), they arrested her for suspicion of burglary, hoping to intimidate her. Instead she went from the substation to the Sybil Brand women's facility in a sheriff's bus, eliciting whistles and cheers from the male prisoners. She was the only female in the special wire cage at the front. She wore a tight leather skirt and tighter sweater (it was the era of outstanding breasts in upstanding bras) and opera gloves.

The sheriff's department really got angry when a lawyer arrived two hours later with a writ that set bail for Sandy, followed by a bail bondsman who put it up. The real effect was to make me far more cautious than I would have been otherwise. My false identification would withstand anything except a fingerprint check. That could be done then only in the station house. It took three days to come back from Sacramento or Washington, unless there was an urgency call attached to it.

A fugitive, like everyone else, is confronted with making a living. Social

Security and the computer make legitimate employment unavailable unless you want to do something like herd sheep in Montana. From my earlier check-passing schemes I still had several partial batches of payroll checks. They had cooled off in the intervening months, and it was easy to find people willing to go around cashing them. It was safe and lucrative.

I rented an apartment in Monterey Park, a community in Los Angeles County east of the central city. The apartments were on two levels, with a balcony running around the upper level. It was shaped like a horseshoe and had a swimming pool in the center. One night I returned to my apartment, turned the key, and opened the door. Facing me was a pair of detectives, one of them with a pistol. Instantly, even before he could speak, I made a right pivot and took off along the balcony.

"*Stop! Stop!*" someone yelled as I reached the end of the balcony and vaulted the rail to the stairs and landing. I hit them wrong and fell the rest of the way to the bottom, stopping my fall with my hands. I sprained both wrists and scraped off the skin to the meat, something I didn't notice at the time.

"Stop!" he yelled again. I ignored the voice and headed for a low wall at the rear.

Three shots rang out, the last one as I went over the wall. I saw it kick up sparks as it angled off the concrete. I was now in the parking lot, but I ignored my car. It would take too long. I kept going and spent the rest of the night lying in low bushes in front of a house while police cars cruised back and forth through the neighborhood, their roof lights glowing and their spotlights illuminating driveways and other possible hiding places. The bushes where I hid were so low that I had to lie flat. They were so unlikely a hiding place that they got only passing scrutiny.

As the sky turned gray with first light, it began to rain. I'd once gotten a sort of thrill at playing fugitive, but on this particular dawn I was a wet, miserable wanted man. They gave up the search when it was time to change shifts.

Someone had fingered me. Perhaps half a dozen people knew where I was staying, but I had no idea who was my Judas. Maybe that person had confided in someone else and the confidant had dialed the phone. I now had lost my car, clothes, typewriter, and another partial draft of my second attempt at writing a novel. I had a soggy $300 in my pocket. Using a hundred, I bought a '46 Ford. Another hundred went for a .32 Colt semiautomatic pistol and a double-barreled 12-gauge, plus a hacksaw to shorten the barrel and cut off the handle. It looked like an eighteenth-century pirate pistol, complete with double hammers. The last thing I did was rent a furnished room near Seventh Street and Alvarado, a mile west of downtown. It cost a preinflation twelve dollars a week.

Not knowing who had ratted me off, I trusted none of them thereafter except Sandy and Carlos Guitterez, aka Boonie. It wasn't Sandy; she had already gone to jail rather than rat me off. I trusted Boonie simply because of his integrity. He was a mediocre criminal, mainly because he wouldn't do anything unless he was broke and desperate for money. Indeed, as I said before, most crimes are acts of desperation. Of course the single overwhelming cause of desperate crimes is the need for money to buy drugs. Hard times make hard people, and nothing makes anyone harder than heroin addiction or the madness of craving cocaine. At the start of a cocaine run, nothing, not even religious ecstasy, will provide the same joy, but soon the craving becomes obsession, the high a keening paranoia, and then it is as awful as the depression. The black dog in the white powder consumes the whole soul.

Most thieves steal or rob only when poverty is fast approaching or is already at hand. I tried to avoid that mistake. When I was a thief, it was a profession practiced twenty-four hours a day. My eye was always looking for money or something that could be turned into money. I never owned a Rolls-Royce or even a fancier-model Mercedes, but I usually managed to keep a fat bankroll—if not a bank account—and a credit card or two, even if they were bogus or stolen.

AFTER NEARLY A YEAR on the run, they almost got me again, although they had been waiting for my pal Denis Kanos. We were going to meet twin sisters whose claim to fame was having done a *Penthouse* photo spread. They were both kind of gaunt from shooting speedballs. We were to meet them at a motel on Sunset near the Silverlake District. Although Denis had the virtues of loyalty and generosity, which I value more than the others, he was habitually the latest person I ever met. If he was to meet you at seven, he might arrive at eleven or midnight. I stopped paying attention and went on about my business even if he was late. On that night, however, I was with him. He was supposed to be at the motel around five-thirty. As darkness fell on that December evening, it was 9:45 when we turned the corner and saw several black-and-whites, roof lights spinning bright. As we drove by, we saw the sisters in handcuffs with a female officer. We later learned the police had staked out the motel for Denis. They waited and waited and got tired of waiting, so they kicked the door in. Denis's excessive tardiness had kept us from walking into a trap.

A couple of weeks later, Denis and I played police detectives and arrested a Compton drug dealer. It was a nice score.

I decided to leave Los Angeles. My only trips outside California had been several visits to Las Vegas, which was really no more than a distant suburb of the City of the Angels, and to Tijuana, Mexico. I wanted to see New York City and all the country between the two oceans.

It was February when I started east on Route 66, reversing the sequence of the song. San Bernardino was first instead of last. Arizona seemed starkly of another world at twilight, its flat mesas rising to golden orange at their summits while the deep purple of night slowly climbed their sides. I had to drive slowly enough to appreciate the sight, for the Arizona highway back then was one axle-busting hole after another.

New Mexico's portion of Route 66 was equally rough. Albuquerque had a stretch of "motor courts," seedy bungalows, some cheap facsimiles of a hacienda and one a cluster of lathe-and-plaster Indian tepees, something I'd expect to have seen in the Los Angeles of my childhood.

I stayed one night in Albuquerque looking around the town. Nothing attracted me to remain longer, so before first light I was on the highway, pedal to the metal. I passed without stopping through part of the Texas panhandle and pulled into Oklahoma City, and it did look mighty pretty. I ran into an LA musician at an all-night coffee shop, and he knew some people around town so I stayed three weeks before pushing on.

I should have listened to the weather reports, for between Oklahoma City and Joplin, Missouri, the wind rose and the snow began to fall slanting across the road. I had no chains and skidded more than once. The cold began to seep inside despite the car's heater. The radio said it was snowing all the way to St. Louis. I was alone in the storm at night in the middle of America. My clothes were for Southern California's gentle clime, where a sweater and jacket are all anyone ever needs. I didn't own a muffler or a pair of gloves or a hat or anything like that. I pulled to the side of the road and put on another pair of pants, another shirt, and a sweater over that. My hands were still freezing on the steering wheel. I traded off, using one on the wheel and the other down between my thighs. Needles of freezing wind came through cracks in the car I didn't know existed. The road froze in spots, first on the occasional bridge because the cold could work on bridges from both top and bottom. Ahead were red flares and a figure waving a flashlight. The traffic was inching past a giant tractor trailer that had jackknifed and fallen on its side. There were several police cars with flashing lights alongside the road, and an ambulance arrived from the other direction.

I slowed even more, creeping along at fifteen or twenty miles an hour, going tense whenever I felt the tires lose grip and the car begin to skid. Each time, it straightened out. I shivered every inch of the way.

In Joplin I saw a red neon sign: HOTEL through the snow. It was a cheap hotel over a bowling alley. Although I was on the fourth floor, I could hear the crashing rattle of tenpins below me. At least the room was warm, with hissing steam heat, and it had a TV set. The late movie was about ancient Egypt, starring Joan Collins, who was a ruthless, scheming bitch. She could have schemed on me and I wouldn't have cared, as fine as she was.

The snow had stopped by morning, but it blanketed everything. I went out to eat and buy some warmer clothes. In a J.C. Penney, the salesgirl recommended long underwear. I thought only old men wore long johns, but I bought them, plus gloves, a hat, and a heavy coat. I carried the packages back to the room and changed.

Now warmly dressed, I wanted to look around Joplin. I'd stashed most of my money in the crack of the room's armchair. I stuck my hand down and felt around. Gone! No, it couldn't be gone. I felt around again. I searched the mattress, knowing it was fruitless even while doing it.

The despair was replaced by my standard rage. I remembered the desk clerk's face when I went by. It had something on it, something imperceptible at the time, but now I recognized it as acknowledgment. *I oughta shoot him,* I thought, imagining my satisfaction at his cry of pain when I shot him through a kneecap. But I couldn't do that. Although I'd used an alias, the license number was real. That could lead them to me. My fingerprints were everywhere. No, I wouldn't shoot him, but he damn sure deserved to be shot—or at least experience a thorough ass kicking.

My guns were in the car trunk. Thank God for that. Wherever I was, Joplin, Chicago, Rome, Italy, or Timbuktu, I could always get some money if I had a pistol. I didn't even need to speak the language. The pistol muzzle was in universal language: *Gimme da money!*

I half-grunted a laugh, while inside I wanted to cry. What bad luck.

In the winter darkness with Christmas lights and decorations filling the store windows, I walked around downtown Joplin. Everything was closed except a movie theater. I walked some more and came upon a bank. It was a couple of blocks from the hotel. A bank robbery! Good God. They would bury my young ass if they caught me robbing a bank. But I needed money. I couldn't get a job. I didn't even have a Social Security number. Plus I didn't know how to do anything that anybody would pay me for.

On my way back to the hotel, the movie theater's box office was just shutting down. The marquee lights were turned off. The manager was counting money with the cashier. I knocked on the window. "Can I buy a ticket?"

"It started ten minutes ago."

"That's okay."

He motioned me to enter. In the flickering gray light, I lost myself in a mediocre story. Rock Hudson is the handsome, straight farmer in Kenya, battling the Mau Mau uprising. In retrospect, the movie seemed to promulgate the racist views of civilized European farmers versus the Mau Mau "savages," who wantonly slaughtered white women and loyal native servants with big knives called *pangas.* At the time I made no analysis of the political or historical implications. It was just a story and the viewpoint precisely the expected one. Thirty years later it would be equally predictable, the heroic rebels versus the racist oppressors. We went from the cliché of Stepin Fetchit to the cliché of Mr. T., both stereotypes at the opposite end of the spectrum. If another movie was made about the Mau Mau, they would be the heroic freedom fighters against the white oppressor. But at least the movie relaxed me without making me think.

Back at the hotel, I was glad that a different clerk was on duty. I fell asleep easily.

In the morning, as I walked by the main desk, the clerk said I was overdue one day. I told him that I would be back with what I owed and that he should get my bill ready because I was checking out.

Without the pressure of being broke, I might not have had enough guts to rob my first bank. As it was, I froze on my first pass. I went in and stopped at the counter away from the tellers, where I began to fill out a deposit slip. I looked around, conscious of the weight of the pistol in my waistband. A man in a business suit was talking to a bank executive; somehow I thought he was a cop. I froze and walked out.

An hour later, fortified by three shots of Wild Turkey, I walked back to the bank and to the assistant manager's desk and told him that this was a robbery. I opened my jacket enough to display the pistol butt. To stifle my fear I spoke with fury until I saw the fear on his face. We walked behind the two tellers' cages and he scooped currency from the drawers and put it in a bag. The tellers looked confused, but one of them recognized what was going on when the assistant manager handed me the bag. I could see that teller wanted to say something or sound the alarm, until I shook my head and put my hand inside my jacket.

The distance to the front door seemed to stretch out like a road in a Salvador Dalí painting. Then I hit the door and stepped out. God, the brisk winter air felt wonderful. I walked along the sidewalk in front of the bank window. At the end of the building was the alley, and when I turned into it I broke into an all-out run. As I neared its end, I looked back. Empty. Nobody was following me.

Entering the hotel lobby, I choked back my heavy breathing as I passed the clerk, giving him a little wave. I started to wait for the elevator and then instead went up the stairs beside it.

With my door locked, I dumped the money on the bed and began to count it. It came to slightly over seven thousand dollars.

Twenty minutes later, I was driving out of Joplin. At a coffee shop several miles out of town, with big trucks with trailers parked in front, I stopped for breakfast, bacon and scrambled eggs. I knew I was in the South because I had the choice between home fries and grits. A newspaper was on the counter: "JFK TO THE MOON." I skimmed the story. The handsome young president had committed the United States to landing a man on the Moon and returning him to Earth within the decade. The weather said the storm had stalled in the Ozarks. It also said that parking enforcement was suspended until the roads were cleared of snow.

Later as I sped down the black ribbon of highway between fields of white snow, I was initially elated; I'd gotten away with heisting a jug. I was from so far away that nobody would think to show my mug shot to the victims. This robbery slipped into the annals of unsolved crimes, and the statute of limitations expired decades ago.

Soon, however, my elation slipped into something like the blues. It wasn't guilt, for my life experiences had diminished that capacity. It was sadness, loneliness, and the desperation of my days. It was always a question of choice, but *how* one would choose, now there was the rub. I had to heist the bank because I was a wanted man unable to work and without any money. If I could have gotten money without a pistol, which was my preference, I would have done so, but I knew nothing of Joplin and if I stole something salable, I had nowhere to sell it. It seemed to me that circumstances had funneled me into the bank robbery. What else could I do? Give myself up. Yeah. Right.

Of course, looking back, I didn't have to jump the fence at the county farm. I could have waited until they took me back to the central jail and ridden the bus back to San Quentin as a parole violator. That was contrary to my nature. I was incapable of lying down without a fight. I had to struggle. If I hadn't taken that ride with Billy and Al to Beverly Hills on that summer night, all this wouldn't have happened. A square john wouldn't have known a pair of safecrackers, or if he knew them, he wouldn't have known what they were. I wouldn't have known them if I hadn't been to San Quentin. Had I been to Harvard, I would have known an entirely different class, but that had been foreclosed when the sapling was bent by the winds of fortune, or misfortune, so very long ago. Everything in life stands on what has gone before. You do this or that because, at the moment, it seems what to do. You are faced with this or that because of what happened somewhere earlier in your journey of life. What happened earlier depends on what went before that. Who would dispute that nobody stands in a void or a vacuum?

MY HEADLIGHT BEAMS WERE BITING into the gray light before me. It was a sunless winter day where the hour could have been high noon or dusk. Two hundred miles northeast, the night rose up and swallowed the land. *"Onward, onward, rode the six hundred."* I turned on the radio and tried to find some music I liked. Darkness made for clearer reception. Maybe I could pick up Chicago or St. Louis. What I got was country and western. I preferred jazz, blues, and some classical, especially Mozart, because that was all I knew. In juvenile hall and reform school, most of the wards were city boys, whatever their skin color, and there was a bias against country boys as corn-fed fools. In prison, however, that prejudice disappeared. The toughest convicts I know are offspring of country people who poured into California from the Dust Bowl of Middle America during the Great Depression of the thirties.

Although my preference in singers leaned toward a quartet of black females: Ella Fitzgerald, Dinah Washington, Sarah Vaughn, and Billie Holiday, when Patsy Cline's twangy voice filled with lament came over the speaker, I stopped turning the dial and listened. She had what they had—soul.

Somewhere in Missouri I made a wrong turn. I found myself in Cairo, Illinois, where the Ohio River joins the mighty Mississippi. I crossed into Kentucky. My car began throwing oil. Somewhere east of the Mississippi I bought a case of forty-weight, and I stopped every hundred miles to pour in another quart or two. It was messy on the undercarriage, and when I came out of a coffee shop a thick pool of oil was on the ground. But as long as I kept pouring it in, the engine kept running.

I was a few miles outside Paducah, Kentucky, when suddenly the engine stopped. I rolled to a stop on a long, slight grade, the kind that giant trucks and trailers race up if they have gathered momentum. The last thing any driver wants to do is stop for some fool standing beside a stalled car at 4:00 A.M. on a freezing night. It was *cold* out, but now I had some warm clothes. The ground was barren black, but where it was shaded by bushes or tree trunks there were white patches of snow. The air was icy and clean—and the sky was filled with more glittering stars than I'd ever seen before. A shooting star arched for a few seconds and went out. I had a thought I've had many times since. How reasonable was our idea of God when the tiny blue marble of Earth was, compared to the universe, less than one grain of sand on the beach at Santa Monica? If we could see galaxies of a billion suns each 2 million light-years away, how could it be that God spoke personally to Moses or had a son named Jesus? The Bible did have some truths and insights, the most obvious one being ". . . all is vanity."

When the sun came up, a pickup truck stopped. The driver took me to a gas station with a mechanic on the edge of Paducah. I thought the fuel pump had gone out. The gauge said a quarter-full, but the engine wasn't getting any gas. A tow truck was sent to bring it in. A new fuel pump was installed, but the engine still wasn't getting any gas. The mechanic put a stick down the gas tank. It came up dry. The problem wasn't the fuel pump. It was that the float in the gas tank had gotten stuck. I was sure the mechanic had known the truth and had, by not checking before installing a new fuel pump, taken advantage of me. I envisaged his consternated terror if I put a pistol in his face and took all his money. I figured it wouldn't be worth the heat I would bring on myself, so I choked back my anger and paid him, remembering the con man's adage that if you're going to be a sucker, be a quiet one.

In Paducah I rented a room in a three-story brick residential hotel. It cost fifty dollars a month and it was a respectable establishment. Its residents were bachelor salesclerks or otherwise employed. One was a recently graduated law student. He was working in Paducah's most prestigious law firm and preparing for the bar exam. Another was a bartender. The hotel arranged for me to rent a TV from a nearby furniture store, owned by the same people who owned the hotel. I told them I was a writer but acted mysterious when asked what I was writing. I was actually working on my second novel, the same for which the manuscript had been lost in the Wallis house move, and also a journal of my travel as a fugitive, much of which I sent in letters to Sandy via another address. One of the residents commented that he heard my typewriter when coming in late one Saturday night.

As I had been born in Southern California, where anything older than forty years was positively decrepit with age, Paducah was the oldest city I'd ever seen. Paducah seemed all dark brick with abundant wrought iron. In a cocktail lounge near the river I met a whore named Jetta. She was from Detroit, and her old man was doing six months in the local jail for playing a con game called the Pigeon Drop. She knew the meager extent of Paducah's fast life—and we both needed companionship. I told her a little, but not too much. She could probably have traded me for her old man if she knew the truth. I told her that I was hiding from an ex-wife who wanted child support. "I'd pay it," I said. "But I don't think the little rug rat is even mine. Kid looks more like her goddamned boyfriend."

Within a week, Paducah grew boring. I'd seen all the movies, some of them twice, and, because it was so cold, I spent lots of time in my room. I got some work done on the second of what would become six unpublished novels. In Paducah I made another mistake of hubris, which, as you know, is one of my many character defects. I sent the parole officer in Los Angeles a postcard: *"Glad you're not here. Ha ha ha . . ."* I mailed it the day before I left town.

I planned to drive to New York City, which always had a fascination for me. I knew it as well as anyone could who hadn't been there. I'd read Thomas Wolfe's symphonic descriptions of Penn Station and Park Avenue—and of walking the city at night. I'd been on top of the Empire State Building with Cary Grant and Deborah Kerr in *An Affair to Remember* and in Harlem with Richard Wright's *Outsider*. I knew about the Cotton Club and the Fulton Fish Market. I'd never seen a play or a Broadway musical, but I knew I could find both near Times Square. New York was somewhere I wanted to see more than anything else.

Instead of taking a highway that angled northeast, I wound up on U.S. 40, heading due north toward the Windy City: Chicago. I knew my mistake within a few hours when I saw the signs. What the hell, I might as well see Chicago, too. What did Sandburg call it: *"hog butcher for the world . . ."?* I knew Chicago, too, from Nelson Algren and Willard Motley's great novel, *Knock on Any Door*, which made me cry late at night in the county jail as Nicky ("live fast, die young and have a good-looking corpse") Romano went to the electric chair. I don't remember if he saw his son before he died. It was a story that I really identified with. It would be okay to see Chicago, too.

By morning I was approaching the South Side of the great city. As I was born and raised in Southern California, where flowers bloom for the entire year and the worst slums are single-family bungalows with front yards, Chicago's South Side was a bleak revelation. The recent snow had turned to a filthy sludge mixed with rock salt. All the buildings seemed to be three-story brick with wooden stairs and porches attached to the rear. It was poverty unlike anything I had ever seen. I wanted to get out of Chicago—but I ended up going north along the lakeshore, and it wasn't until I neared Northwestern University that I realized this was the wrong way to go around Lake Michigan. I'd have to go through Canada to head east that way.

I turned around and was glad when I crossed into Indiana, where for the first time on this journey I got a road map. From Chicago to New York City the highway was wide, flat, and straight. The only time I had to stop was at a state line and for gas—and oil. Lots of oil.

Outside South Bend, I checked into a motel. By morning more snow was falling, and there was a lake of oil beneath the car. It refused to start. I unloaded it, removing the license plates and throwing them into a drainage ditch behind the motel. A taxi took me to the Greyhound station. The bus took me to Toledo, my father's birthplace, or so I thought, and still think, even though I cannot remember where I got this idea. I did know that he and my aunt had been raised in Toledo, so I assumed they had also been born there. I knew, too, that my paternal ancestors had come from France in the eighteenth century and became fur trappers in the Great Lakes region, including Canada. There is a large Bunker Family Association whose members gather yearly from all over America. I subscribe to their newsletter, but that Bunker family is from Anglo-Saxon forebears who settled first on Nantucket and in New Hampshire. I doubt that I am one of them or that they would even want me. I know nothing of my paternal grandmother, neither her first, nor her family name, although I *think* her first name was Ida. I also *think,* albeit more confidently, that my grandfather's name was Charles. I was told that he was a captain or officer on a Great Lakes sailing vessel and drowned when my father was quite young. It is meager knowledge about a family history that might be interesting, seeing as how it spans America's history, too. When I arrived in Toledo, I thought about the stories I heard from the turn of the century when my father had seen the Dempsey-Firpo fight. Firpo knocked Dempsey out of the ring. It was one of the most furious heavyweight fights of all time.

I stayed in Toledo at a motel until the weather cleared. It was still cold, but it was at least bright. From a classified ad I saw in the Toledo newspaper I bought a '54 Olds Rocket 88, a hot car of the era. When the weatherman predicted bright sunny days for the rest of the week, I continued on my journey. I'd now decided that I would eventually arrive in New York, but before that I would take my time and look at the countryside. I wished that I had done that instead of burning up the highway at the outset. I had recently read Bruce Catton's *Stillness at Appomattox* and knew that major Civil War battlefields were within a few hundred miles. Pennsylvania had Gettysburg. I wanted to see that. I wanted to see many things. I had time and money, so why not drive where my whims dictated?

I saw Cincinnati, then crossed the river back into Kentucky. America has transcending beauty in incalculable quantity, but the serene loveliness of Kentucky's bluegrass country, mile after mile of white fences—I imagined feeding horses beneath shade trees in verdant pastures with the brick colonial or Federal house in the distant background—that to me was it. If I had my choice of living anywhere, this area would get a long, hard look—but so would Paris,

London, Capri, Martha's Vineyard, Roxbury, Connecticut, or eight months in Montana and four in Los Angeles. Still and all, I loved the bluegrass country.

Memphis in June was all right, too, although the days were now getting a little hot and sticky. The nights were wee balmy and beautiful. I was planning to stay a few days, but I met a girl at a Dairy Queen and stayed almost a month. This was before the sexual revolution, and although she would neck and pet until I was crazy, she wouldn't let me fuck her. I figured it was time to move on.

I put off going to New York. They said it was at its worst during the midsummer—too hot, too humid. Those who could afford it departed in the baking months.

After a few days of driving around the South, staying a night here and a night there, I found myself in Fulton County, Georgia, where I pulled into a motel of neat frame bungalows that were arranged in a horseshoe, with the space in the middle being paved with gravel. It had no landscaping, and the office was equally bare and excessively prim. When the clerk or proprietor or whoever he was came from the rear, through the open door I heard opera. I think it was Wagner.

Later after checking in, I took a drive and passed a tiny cluster of businesses—gas station, coffee shop, and store—less than a mile up the road. When the sun started to set, I took a walk to get something to eat and a pack of Camels. When I came out of the tiny convenience market a state trooper with his lights flashing went by. I turned down the road and watched him. The flashing lights went out before he reached the motel driveway and turned in. Uh-oh!

My first thought was, *At least I have my money.* The truth was, that was all I had. Clothes, car, guns, typewriter, everything else was in the car or in the room. Could I get some of it back, maybe the guns? They were all in the car trunk, and I had the keys.

I set out down the road, remaining in the shadows and keeping my eyes on the spot ahead where I would see headlights. About two hundred yards from the motel's driveway I veered into the woods. The greenery was wet with dew, and the ground was uneven. I saw the lights again, and when I reached the edge of the woods I now saw two state troopers' cars and uniformed men with wide-brimmed hats. They were at the open door of my bungalow and around my car. One of them was looking inside the car with a flashlight.

It was time to run.

Rather, it was time to start trudging through the night. I had no idea how much manpower was mustered to catch me in the area. I saw nobody; then again, I stayed off the roads as much as possible. I passed farms and aroused barking dogs. At every pair of headlights I hid myself until they were gone. By morning I gave up hiding and walked beside a narrow state highway with my thumb out. A black man in a pickup truck gave me a ride to a hamlet, the name of which I cannot recall. It had a Continental Trailways bus depot with a waiting room and a coffee shop.

At the window I asked the price of tickets to New York, to Miami, and to Los Angeles. The young woman quoted the prices.

"Which one leaves first?"

"A bus to the south leaves in twenty minutes. For Miami you have to change in Jacksonville."

"That leaves first?"

"Yes."

"Give me a one-way ticket."

"You really want to go *somewhere*, don't you?"

"How can you tell?"

"Psychic powers."

Soon I was riding south. I found that I could get off wherever the bus stopped and catch another going the same route. I got off in Jacksonville and rented a hotel room and bought a cheap pistol. The next afternoon I robbed another bank. Rather, I tried to rob another bank. When I handed the note to the teller, she looked me over. Seeing that I had no weapon in view, she dropped down out of sight and began screaming, "Help! Help! *Help!*"

Even if I'd drawn my pistol and had it at her head, I would never have fired—but I might have punched her. I spun, tucked in my gun, and walked, swiveling my head with a frown, as if I, too, were looking for the cause of the screams.

Everybody was looking around. My eyes locked with those of a young man in a business suit behind a desk. He was focused on me. Had I been moving faster, he would have yelled and pointed a finger. Instead he hesitated—until I was two steps from the front door. My hands were raised to push it open when I heard: "There he goes!"

I hit the revolving door and spun out onto the sidewalk at a dead run, straight across the street. Brakes squealed as a driver stomped them, followed by the crunch of cars hitting other cars. I kept going without a glance. On the other side of the street I went around the corner and down a side street. An alley ran behind the storefronts. Halfway down the alley I looked back. In hot pursuit were three or four high school students. I pulled the pistol and fired a shot over their heads. The leader stopped. Those behind crashed into him. They all went down in a heap.

I fired another shot and they retreated. Around the corner of the building I took off running again. The bus depot was a block and a half away.

I dripped sweat through soaked clothes and fought to breathe as I climbed the steps onto the bus. As I did so, I could see down the exit ramp to the street. A police car sped by. I flopped on my seat and closed my eyes. A few minutes later my body declared that this had all been too close for comfort. My body began shaking, and the fear I stifled when things were happening went through me in waves. Jesus Christ, a fugitive ex-con firing shots in a bank robbery. They would bury me in Leavenworth. I'd be fifty when they let me out again.

12
ADJUDGED
CRIMINALLY
INSANE

ALTHOUGH I OCCASIONALLY PULLED an armed robbery in my lengthy criminal career, it was never my first choice among the various methods of thievery. Firearms created a situation too inherently volatile. There was always the chance of something going wrong. Guns had explosive consequences. Similarly, the authorities considered armed robbery far more serious than forgery or even safecracking. At the end of the day, I would say that I was primarily a merchandising burglar. I didn't burglarize homes, but beyond that you could say that I stole whatever I could sell. The best things were cigarettes and whiskey, of course, and I have stolen those in abundance, but I have also stolen a truckload of outboard motors, 2,000 paintbrushes (which sold quite rapidly, believe it or not), a roomful of cameras, the contents of a scuba-diving store and a couple of pawnshops.

ON A RAINY WEEKEND an old professional thief named Jerry and I took off a cocktail lounge in the Rampart district of Los Angeles. It was ridiculously easy to enter. The door had a burglar alarm, but it also had a transom without an alarm. Jerry boosted me on his shoulders. I put masking tape over part of the transom above the latch, then hit it with a fist wrapped in a towel. The glass cracked without falling. I peeled back the tape with the glass stuck to it except for a couple of shards that fell with a tinkle.

Seconds later I dropped inside the lounge, landing softly as a cat. I listened for a couple of heartbeats; then I unlocked the door for Jerry to enter. The rainstorm covered for us. Jerry had a Buick Roadmaster. We had taken out the backseats and filled every inch of space with cases of whiskey. I also found a shotgun and a few other things worth money. In the desk was a checkbook. I tore out several pages at the back of the checkbook and returned it to the drawer. From a pawnshop I could get a check protector machine. I figured the bar owner might not notice checks missing from the rear.

A Hollywood club owner was waiting for the whiskey. We unloaded it through the back door on a wet Sunday afternoon. The next morning I took the other stuff to a fence who owned a small car wash on Venice Boulevard a mile from downtown Los Angeles. While we were negotiating prices his telephone rang. The fence answered it and his side of the conversation was grunts and monosyllables: "Uh-uh. . . . Yeah. . . . Uh-huh. . . . Yeah. Right." Then the fence said, "Tell this guy." He handed the telephone to me.

"What's up?" I said.

"Look here," said the voice of a black man. "I'm down here on Western. I've got all kinds of stuff out in the alley behind an electronics store. I can't get my car running and I need a ride."

"Where are you?" It was down Western in the seventies.

"I'm tellin' you, man, it's a taxi job."

It would cost me nothing to look, and I was intrigued. In retrospect it was crazy, but I had a fascination with crazy once upon a time.

On the corner of Western and the cross street he gave me, a skinny black man with the haggard face of the hooked junkie met me. He had me go around the block and turn down the alley. Sure enough, covered by a blanket in the parking space behind a shop was a pile of stereos and television sets and a thousand LPs that sold for a dollar and a half apiece on the hot goods market. It wasn't Fort Knox, but as he said, it was a taxi job.

I turned in and stopped, bending down the license plate as I got out of the car—in case someone came by. We began piling stuff in the back of the Buick, which still had its backseat removed. In less than two minutes we were rolling.

The fence bought everything except a full-length woman's coat. It was cashmere except for a mink hood, collar, and label. The label said: BULLOCKS. The fence offered less than I knew I could get from a cocktail waitress on Sunset Boulevard. Even if she gave me less, I preferred letting her have it. In fact, if she was friendly enough, I might make her a gift.

My new crime partner, whose name I didn't know, was simultaneously sweating and shivering and yawning. "You're *sick*, huh?" I asked. The term *sick* on the street meant sick from heroin withdrawal.

"Like a dog, man. You use, man?"

I shook my head. "I'll smoke some grass."

"Would you drive me to my connection?"

On impulse, I agreed. Actually, I had to drive him to two connections. The first one wasn't home; the second one wanted to know who I was. We were so far from a white area that we might as well have been in Nairobi.

It was dark when I took him to his home near Manchester and Western. It was a nice bungalow on a residential street. I went inside to use the telephone. I wanted to tell a barmaid that I'd be late and not to make another date.

While I was in the house, someone knocked on the door. My new crime partner's girlfriend went to answer it. I heard voices that had an unfriendly timbre. It was time for me to go.

"I'm gone," I said to my associate, heading toward the front door.

The newcomer was actually a pair of young black men. Both of them were six-foot-three or more. As I squeezed past and stepped outside into the darkness, I could feel their eyes burning me.

Down the walk and out the gate, my car was at the curb thirty feet away. As I reached it, I heard the gate squeak. I looked back. The two young black men were following me. I got in and opened my knife just as they arrived. One came around to the driver's side. He suddenly reached through the back window and grabbed the mink-trimmed coat: "That's my mother's coat."

As soon as he spoke, I understood the whole thing. My "crime partner" had burglarized someone he knew, someone who suspected him as soon as the crime was discovered.

He reached to open the driver's door. I swung the knife and he jumped back. I turned the key and punched the gas. The big Buick fishtailed and burned rubber.

I turned a corner and another, meanwhile constantly looking in the mirror. I saw a pair of headlights. Were they following me? I couldn't tell. I turned a corner and hit the gas.

Suddenly a car behind me announced it was the police with flashing lights on its roof.

Here we go again. I pushed the accelerator to the floor and the car jumped forward. The scream of the siren filled the LA night.

I had to abandon the car. I was out of my area and didn't know the streets. But first I had to get around two corners—and then bail out. I could just imagine the chase. The radio was being cleared, and the car in pursuit was giving them a running account: "South on Budlong, turned west on Forty-third. . . . South on . . ." Other police cars were coming to join the chase.

I came down a side street toward a boulevard with a traffic light ahead. Both lanes were blocked with waiting cars. I spun the wheel to the right, half-jumped the curb and driveway into a gas station, hit the brakes, and swerved. My back end swung around and smashed into a signpost. Over the curb onto boulevard. Punch it. The speedometer climbed. They weren't around the corner when I turned the next one. Halfway down the block, I stomped the brakes. The tires screeched and the car skidded to a halt. Before it stopped, I was out and running in a line across the street and down a driveway beside a house. Behind me the police car came around the corner. Had they seen me? I couldn't tell.

I sprinted through a backyard, hands extended. Before everyone got washers and dryers for their laundry, clotheslines in backyards were a menace to fugitives running through the darkness. I'd once hit one across the forehead while running full tilt. My feet kept going and went right up into the air. I came down on my head, lucky that I didn't break my neck. It cut me in a line to the bone, and blood flowed copiously down my whole face. That is how the face bleeds.

Through the backyard, over a fence that teetered beneath me I ran. Out the next backyard, out a driveway, and across the next street, praying in a silent scream that another car didn't turn the corner at that moment. One didn't. I had a chance if they spread out like water in all directions from the site of the abandoned car.

I crossed a front yard and down into the darkness of another driveway. It had a gate. As I reached for the latch, a snarling Rottweiler leaped up, snapping at my hand, its breath hot on my face. *Shit!*

Without a moment's hesitation, I doubled back. I would go down the driveway next door. I came out and cut across the lawn.

Across the street, from where I'd come, appeared a dark uniform. *"Halt!"*

I ran faster.

A shot sounded. The bullet kicked up sparks on the driveway ahead of me. I tried to run faster. Ahead of me another gate. Please, God, no dogs.

I tried to hurdle it. My foot hooked. Down I went. Headfirst. My foot still hooked.

The bobbing flashlight was followed a second later by a dark, looming figure. A .357 Magnum leveled on me. "Don't *fuckin' move!*"

Another dark uniformed figure, panting hard, arrived. Lights in both houses were going on. One policeman was trying to open the gate while the other held flashlight and pistol trained on me. "Just stay right there."

A window went up. "What's goin' on out there?" The voice had the telltale sound of the African-American.

"Police business! Stay inside!"

They got the gate open and the handcuffs on, then began half-pushing, half-pulling me down the sidewalk. A couple other cops arrived. They were pumped up and fairly vibrating from the hot pursuit. One kicked at my stomach, but I managed to turn and raise my knee enough to deflect it. "Ixnay . . . ixnay," said one policeman. I remember it clearly because it was a term I hadn't heard since grammar school. *Ixnay! What kinda shit is that?* The reason was the witnesses. Several of the neighbors had come out onto their porches to look. It was a black middle-class neighborhood.

An alley ran from street to street, so they didn't have to take me all the way around the block. Now there were four cops and two more came charging down the alley from the other side, crashing into me like charging linebackers. "Okay, sonofabitch! We'll teach you to run, fuckhead . . . shit-for-brains bastard. . . ."

It has always been de rigueur for cops to kick some ass at the end of a chase. It's all part of the game. I expected it and felt no indignation but, in fact, a little gratitude, because half a dozen were trying to get in their licks. A cluster of bodies rolled down the alley to the next street where several police cars sat with lights flashing. The Buick filled the middle of the street with the driver's door still open. A crowd of neighbors was at the curb. They were all black, and over the other noises I heard a voice say in surprise, "It's a white man! Goddamn!"

I was shoved into the back of a police car. A sergeant came over and opened the door. They had taken my wallet. He was holding up the three driver's licenses in three different names from three different states. "What's your name?"

"I'm John McCone, CIA. I tried to warn them—"

"Warn them? About what?"

"In thirty-six, I told them the Japanese were going to bomb Pearl Harbor."

"What the fuck have you been taking?"

"Will you get me to Washington?"

Another policeman came over and peered in. "He's loaded on something. Fucker thinks he's in the CIA."

"Who cares if he's the queen of May? Let's book him so we can go home."

They took me to the infamous Seventy-seventh Street precinct house, where I was the first white man they'd booked in two years. They beat on me awhile for being white. By now I was into it. When they booked me, I signed the booking card as Marty Cagle, Lt., USNR, and gave my birth year as 1905. The booking officer showed it to the sergeant: "Put it down. Who cares?" They booked me as "John Doe #1."

They threw me in a cell. There was no way to make bail. I was a fugitive and a parole violator, ineligible for bail. They were going to have to drag me back to prison. There would be skid marks all the way up the highway. They'd wondered if I was crazy since I was ten years old, so I decided now I would be nutty as a fruitcake. Let the games begin. The bravado covered an inner emptiness bordering utter despair.

One would assume that a situation such as this would have me climbing the walls. Instead an all-powerful drowsiness washed over me. Sleep is an escape from depression. I slept with the stink of the jail mattress in my nose.

IN THE MORNING, A UNIFORMED OFFICER unlocked my cell gate. A detective waited to interrogate me in the standard windowless room with a table and three hard-backed chairs. He looked at me with cold, hostile eyes. "Sit down, Bunker."

They knew my name already. Damn! They had pulled out all the stops, or so I thought for a moment. "He's dead," I said. "I am number five. Who are you?" As I spoke, I leaned to the left and looked at the ceiling, slowly moving my head as if watching something crawl across.

The detective's face maintained its studied impassivity, but his eyes narrowed ever so slightly, and he did glance at the ceiling.

"You know who they are, don't you?" I asked.

"What?"

"Catholics. They've been trying to put a radio in my brain, you know."

"What I want to know about are these burglaries. We found those checks in your hotel room."

Hotel room! How did they . . . ? The hotel key. Damn. It was in the car.

"I don't know about a hotel. It's the Church. . . . It's all of them . . . all of it. Don't you see?"

My words had a stridence that stopped him. He'd assumed I was high on angel dust or some other hallucinogen. He was a handsome man, well tailored. He also had a cold demeanor. Most wizened old detectives have seen so many human foibles that they are bemused most of the time. In many instances an old cop and an old thief will have more in common than either has with a newcomer of either persuasion.

He broke off the interrogation and sent me to the cell. I had to walk in front of half a dozen cells. Each had four or five young blacks. It was the age of the Afro hairstyle, which they created by using a hair pick to fluff it into an upstanding bush, the bigger the better. Alas, the booking officers took away their hair picks, so after a night in jail their hair looked like wild explosions of countless watch springs. As I went by a cell, one of them said in disbelief, "Hey, man, they got a white dude in the back."

"White dudes break the law," said another.

"I ain' ne'er seen one in Seventy-seventh."

The uniformed officer escorting me said, "He's no white man. He's a white nigger."

Back in my cage with graffiti on the walls and the striped mattress shiny with the sweat and smell of previous occupants, I sank into the pit of despond. What a life. What had I done to deserve this? The question had its own answer, and I laughed at my moment of self-pity. One thing was certain: I would give them one helluva fight before San Quentin's gates slammed shut behind me again.

In late afternoon, with the light coming through the small barred windows across from the cell turning gray, the outer door opened and two sets of feet sounded out, coming down the runway. "Hey, man . . . hey . . . hey . . . *hey, motherfucker!*" screamed a brother down the tier. The jailer failed to acknowledge the summons.

The jailer, a beefy black man in a dark LAPD uniform, still had exasperation on his face when he reached my cell and opened it. Behind him was an older white man. We'll call him Pollack, because his name was Eastern European, I think. He was seamed and rumpled; he had been around.

I was led back to the interrogation room. Pollack, the handsome detective, waited for me with some files in front of him. I sat down.

"Your parole officer says you're faking," the detective said.

"Man . . . he's part of the Church. Don't you see that?"

It sent his eyes rolling, and a barely audible: "Shiiit. . . .

"Look, Bunker," said Pollack, pulling forth his wallet and extracting a card. "I'm not a Catholic. I'm a Lutheran. Look. . . ." He extended a church membership card.

I leaned forward and peered at the card with great seriousness, then sniffed. "Forged," I said.

So it went. They asked about Gordo. *Where'd they get that name?* Many months later, reading a police report during a courtroom proceeding, I learned that he had called the hotel and left his name.

ONE DARK NIGHT, BRIGHT WITH LIGHTS, they took me out to the scene of a safe burglary. A woman living next door to the bar had seen a car drive up beside the back door. A man stepped out, she said, crossed the sidewalk, and entered the car. She was about thirty yards away and saw him at an angle partly from the rear. Could she identify me?

I had to get out of the car I was in and stand beside it. One detective stood beside me, while the other brought the witness to the curb fifteen feet away. We exchanged no words, but I saw her shake her head and toss her shoulder. No identification. It hadn't been me anyway. I had been driving the car in that heist.

The next morning the detective and his partner took me from the cell at the Seventy-seventh to the Municipal Court in Inglewood for arraignment. There I would be served with the complaint. They locked me in a bullpen next to the courtroom. It held several others scooped from the streets in the last day or so. All of them were going before the judge for the first time.

During the wait, I got into costume. I tied Bull Durham sacks to my shirt like a row of medals. I put a towel over my head and tied it with a shoelace. I had my shirttail out and my pants rolled up above my knees. To the court, I looked like the craziest fool they'd ever seen, although the deputies paid no attention. They had seen many crazy fools pass through.

Before court convened, we filed into the courtroom and sat in the jury box. This was the arraignment court. It buzzed with activity, with lawyers and bondsmen, clerks and arresting offices, and abundant spectators in the audience.

The clerk entered and announced that the Municipal Court of the City of Inglewood, County of Los Angeles, was now in session, the Honorable James Shanrahan presiding judge.

When the judge came through the door, I came out of my chair, screaming at the top of my lungs, *"I know him! He's a bishop! Lookit the robes! Help! Help!"*

Bailiffs came running, their keys jangling; chairs crashed. Spectators jumped up, some to see, some to flee. Chaos reigned in the court.

They carried me out, screaming maledictions, feet waving. I even lost a shoe that never got returned.

In an adjacent office, a young district attorney asked me a few questions, such as how long I'd been in jail. A hundred and six years seemed appropriate. After a few more questions and similar answers, they took me back into the courtroom before the judge. I was flanked by two burly deputies. The young district attorney made a motion under Section 1367, California Penal Code. With a vacant expression, I paid no attention and looked around the courtroom. Actually, Section 1367, California Penal Code, stops the proceedings and refers the matter to a department of the Superior Court for a sanity hearing to determine if the accused is competent to stand trial. Although it does not deal with guilt or innocence, it can be considered with other evidence.

As they led me from the courtroom, I looked at the handsome detective who had conducted the investigation. He was seated in the row inside the railing, and his displeasure was written large across his face. I wanted to wink, but that would have been too much of an insult, and somewhere down the line he would have to testify. Besides, what did I have to wink about? I was caged and he was free. All my machinations might, at best, slice a tiny fraction from how long I would be imprisoned.

AFTER COURT, I WAS AMONG those called for the first bus back to the jail. It was a new jail, having opened while I was away, and it was already notorious as a place where the deputies busted heads and had killed more than one prisoner. I remembered a friend, Ebie, telling me that some drunk Mexican being booked in had thrown a trash can through an interior window. They had dragged him away. It was when they were away, in a room without witnesses, that the guy slipped on a banana peel and broke his skull on the bars. It was part of the criminal ethos to expect an ass kicking as part of the game if you did certain things, mainly threatened them physically, either by word or deed. In some places a little mouth could bring the goon squad down on you. All places of incarceration have a goon squad, although it may have been called something more politically correct than goon squad, something like reaction team.

In the LA Central Jail it took nothing to get jumped and stomped, maybe teargassed and thrown in the hole—and maybe charged with a new crime, for the best way they had of getting away with administering a savage beating was charging the inmate with attacking them. It was their collective word against his individual word.

The module where they placed me happened to have single cells. When the gates opened for chow, I saw many familiar faces coming through the serving line or seated at the tables. The food was barely edible; I could force down a few bites and eat the bread and drink the hot, sweet tea at night. I lived on oranges.

A few days later they called me out to court at 5:00 A.M. We were fed eggs in the mess hall and sent downstairs to the "court line." Our civilian clothes were given to us if we wanted them for court. It mattered not to me. I was in costume and the jail blues helped.

The sanity court was held over at the general hospital. A deputy public defender came to interview me. I made no sense to him. The court appearance lasted about thirty seconds. The clerk called the case. The judge peered at me, the poor, demented creature with strips of toilet paper stuck in his ears, shirt worn inside-out with Bull Durham sacks attached like medals. The judge had seen many crazies in his time, and the figure facing him was classic. With everyone stipulating, he appointed two psychiatrists to conduct an examination and submit a report.

When the deputy public defender tried to talk to me, I babbled nonsensically. He gave it up and wished me good luck. Riding the bus back to the jail, I visually devoured the city at night, as I always did on such journeys. So today I remember, as if it were yesterday, a sight thirty years in the past: an open door of a cantina with the sounds of mariachis pouring onto the sidewalk. Incarceration at least has the beneficial aspect of letting a prisoner see the world with fresh eyes, the way an artist does.

The next day I was called for the busload being transferred to the old county jail above the Hall of Justice. We were herded like cattle into a bullpen. Who was assigned to a particular jail was determined by where they went to court. Those kept in the new central jail were going to outlying courtrooms in Santa Monica, Van Nuys, Pasadena, and elsewhere around the vast county. Those going to court in the Hall of Justice were those arrested in the central city; hence blacks were the majority being transferred.

The deputies yelled and bullied the prisoners. We were jammed together—and I smoldered. A couple of trembling old winos were on the bus.

On arrival at the Hall of Justice, we were taken to the shower area. It was the same place I had cut up mass murderer Billy Cook more than a decade earlier. "Listen up!" yelled a deputy. "Strip to your underwear and throw your clothes in here." He indicated a wheeled laundry basket.

As outer clothes came off, the stench of unwashed bodies came up. I breathed softly through my mouth, thinking that mankind must have really smelled until recently.

Everyone was hurrying except me and an old wino shaking from age and booze. Having a hard time maintaining his balance while stripping down, he stumbled and reflexively reached out to steady himself, inadvertently bumping a black youth. The youth turned and saw it was a trembling old man. "Fucking old grape," the youth said. "Get the fuck away from me." Using both hands, he shoved the old man, who slipped on the floor and went down hard. Nobody moved to help him. They walked past him to throw their clothes in a laundry hamper and stand naked in line. The little display of racial hatred grated on me, but it was none of my business according to the prison code.

I hung back. Let everyone else go first. I wasn't in a hurry to get into another set of jail denim. There was plenty to go around.

"Move it, man; move it." Pressing behind me was another young black. He was taller than me but slender.

"Take it easy. We'll get there."

He said something. The words I didn't decipher, but the sound was hostile. It has been my experience that young ghetto blacks huff and puff and bump chests together before getting it on, a sort of male dance of intimidation. While he was huffing, I put a short left hook into his solar plexus. His grunt was surprise and pain. No white man was supposed to fight. That wasn't what he'd been taught. I swung another left hook and missed, wrapping my arm around his neck. Down we went on the tile floor. He was on the bottom.

Within seconds the deputies were there, dragging us apart. Off to Siberia we went. Siberia was a tank of regular cells stripped of amenities, including mattresses, and devoid of all privileges.

It was time to add to the record of insanity: an old-fashioned suicide attempt for later use, if it became necessary. It always helped. The light fixture was recessed in the ceiling and covered with mesh so the prisoner would not reach the bulb. When they brought the meal, I kept the Styrofoam cup. I filled it with water and threw it onto the hot bulb. Pop! It broke and I had shards of sharp glass. Using a shirt sleeve as a tourniquet around my upper arm, I chopped at the swollen vein at the inner aspect of my elbow. At first I was tentative. It may be physically easy, but it is not mentally easy to cut yourself. The skin parted, exposing white meat and the vein. It took several chops. Then it opened and blood shot up about three feet. I quickly grabbed the paper cup and let the blood run in there until it was about an inch high. I added two inches of water. Then I poured that slowly over my naked shoulders and chest until it covered my torso. Then I began spinning and swinging my arm. The blood splattered around all the walls and dripped from the cell bars. It made for a gory mess. Finally, I partially filled the cup with blood and water and poured it outside the cell, so it ran along the floor on the runway. "Hey, next door!" I called. "Look over here . . . through the door."

"Goddamn! Oh shit!"

"Call the bull."

The bar shaking and screaming began: *"Poo-leese! Officer! Help! Help! Man down! Man down!"*

In seconds, it was a chorus from all the cells.

It took several minutes before I heard the outer gates opening. At that point I stretched out in the pool of blood on the floor. The cell looked like a slaughterhouse.

The jangling keys, then the startled voice: "Jesus Christ! Call the clinic. Get a gurney!"

The gurney rattled loudly as they came on the run. As they wheeled me past prisoners looking through their bars, I heard voices: "Aw, man, that dude's dead." "Shit, man, that's fuckin' messy." "Chump killed hisself." Someone passed judgment: "Sucker gotta be weak to do that. . . ."

Down the elevator, into an ambulance, and out the tunnel for a siren-screaming ride to the general hospital several miles away. They sewed me up, washed me off, and took me to the jail ward on the thirteenth floor. When the doctor asked why I'd done it, I said the Catholic Church had a radio in my brain and told me to. He wrote it down. Thank you, Doctor.

The jail ward in the hospital was so overcrowded that beds overflowed the rooms and lined the big main corridor. Late that night they discharged me back to the central jail. I was put in a room with three beds in the jail infirmary, left ankle and right hand chained to the bed. The middle bed was occupied by an old diabetic. Next to him was a husky young Chicano who had one foot cuffed to the bed frame. He sat up, rocking back and forth while saying his rosary over and over, sometimes mixing in Acts of Contrition. The nurse who passed out medication said he was having a reaction to angel dust. She gave me two brown pills that I recognized as Thorazine. I feigned taking them.

It was in this hospital room that I saw something so grotesque that it remains etched in my mind as if burned by acid. "Jesus Christ!" exclaimed the old diabetic, then jumped up and began pounding and kicking the door. For a moment I looked at him, and then I turned my gaze to the Chicano on the other bunk. He was sitting up, still rocking and muttering prayers. His right eye socket opened and shut—but it held no eyeball. It stared up from the white bed sheet. His left eye dangled back and forth below his chin, held by some kind of tendon. He had used his thumbs to reach into both eyes and pluck them from his head. My heart bounced and my hair stood up. It was horrifying. More than a year later, I came back to the central jail and saw him being led to court. He was totally blind, but they didn't drop the charges. Oh no, he wasn't going to get off that easy. I don't know if they sent him to prison. It wouldn't surprise me. After all, he had stolen something.

When the jail doctor came to talk to me, I told him that the pope had assassins waiting to murder me in the Hall of Justice and that I couldn't be in a cell with anybody else because I could see lights floating over their heads. I hoped to be put in the "ding" tank here in the central jail. I wanted to avoid the Hall of Justice, mainly because they would immediately put me back in Siberia when I returned. He wrote it down on the chart and told me not to worry; I wasn't going back to the Hall of Justice.

The next morning, needing the space, another doctor discharged me. I was put in a section of one-man cells in the central jail. That suited me fine.

Two days later, the deputy called out, "Bunker, roll 'em up!" It was for transfer to the Hall of Justice. It was a transfer determined by the numbers; nobody looked at any files. When the deputy opened my cell and called for me to step out, I went to the front. He was at the control panel, in a cage behind bars, busily throwing levers and calling names. Other prisoners were being transferred or called out to see their lawyer or parole officer. He was a fresh-faced kid, and he had been told at the academy that all prisoners were liars and con men, scum wanting to take advantage of him. So when I approached the bars and said, "Hey, boss," which according to my education was a sign of respect, he thought it was some kind of disrespect and responded with suspicious hostility. He wasn't receptive when I told him that I wasn't supposed to go to the Hall of Justice, according to the jail doctor. "Don't tell me," he said. "Tell the deputy in the control booth in the hallway." He pushed the button that buzzed open the lock to the second-floor hallway. It was long and wide. Prisoners had to walk along the right-hand wall. Next to the doorway to the escalator was the control booth. The deputy sat up high behind reinforced glass, so he had a clear sight of everything in the corridor.

I walked up to the window. "They called me to roll up to HOJ, but I'm not supposed to go."

"You're not? Why not?"

"The doctor said—"

"Tell the deputy running the court line downstairs," he cut me off.

I went down the escalator and followed the painted line on the floor to the doorway into the large room filled with cages, each about fifteen feet square, with a sign over its gate designating an outlying courtroom. In the morning, long before daylight, the cages were packed with prisoners waiting to take bus rides. It was less humane than the stock pens in railroad yards.

It was late morning now. The buses had gone and would not begin returning until late afternoon, continuing through the evening. The cages had been swept and held prisoners being transferred to other facilities, including the Hall of Justice.

A deputy sat behind a table that had lists of names Scotch-taped to its top. As prisoners gave their names, he directed them to cages. Even before I stepped up and started my story, I knew that the deputy at the module, who had sent me to the booth, and the deputy at the booth, who had sent me here, had been playing a game: to move me another step closer to the bus.

"I'm not supposed to go to the Hall of Justice."

"What's your name?"

"The doctor wrote it in the medical records."

"What's your name?"

"Bunker."

"Cage Six."

"The doctor—"

"I don't give a shit about the doctor. Get in Cage Six."

"Would you check with the medical department?"

"I'm not checking with anybody. Get in the goddamn cage." He stood up to add threat to his order. Cage Six was directly across from the table. I stepped inside and he slammed the gate shut.

"Look here, Deputy," I said. "Can I see a senior or a sergeant?"

"No. You can't see anybody."

"Okay . . . but let me say something—I'm not going."

"Not going! You're going on that bus if I have to put you in chains and throw you on it."

I decided I might as well add more insanity to the record. I was carrying an empty cigarette carton with my meager personal property: comb, tooth-brush—and Gillette razor blades.

I unwrapped a new razor blade, put it on the bars, and took off my shirt and the bandage around my arm. I twisted the sleeve around the bicep, pumped up the vein, retrieved the razor blade, and began to chop. It was much easier than with the piece of lightbulb. Two whacks and the blood squirted. I kept the homemade tourniquet tight and held my arm close to the bars. Blood sprayed across the space and began to rain on the lists fastened to the table.

The deputy had missed what I was doing until the blood rained down on his paperwork. Even then, it took him a couple of seconds to wake up. "What the hell. . . ." He jumped to his feet. He tried to grab the paperwork, but it was Scotch-taped to the table. He ripped one sheet in half. Blood splattered across the rest as I moved my arm and changed the trajectory.

The deputy yelled for assistance, and deputies came running. While they reached for a key to open the gate, I moved my arm back and forth, spraying blood on their uniforms, which made them cry out and curse as their wool olive twill uniforms sucked up my blood.

The door came open and they swarmed over me. I must admit that they only punched and kicked me a few times. I expected worse from the sheriff's department. Three or four of them carried me, facedown, along the corridor to the infirmary. I saw the deputy who had said he was putting me in chains. "I told you I wasn't going," I said. He said nothing, but I think he would have siz-zled if someone threw water on him.

An hour later I was back in the hospital ward with the three beds. After a couple of days the doctor put me back in a regular cell. This time there was no doubt that I wasn't supposed to go to the Hall of Justice.

The psychiatrists appointed to examine me came one at a time. When I was called down to an interview room in the hospital area I was ready. I sat rocking back and forth, looking at him with narrowed eyes; then I looked down at the floor. He asked me what the voices were telling me. I told him it was too dirty and I couldn't repeat it. Then I asked him if he was a Catholic. When he assured me that he wasn't, I told him that the Catholics had been after me for years.

"What do they do?"

"You know what they do."

"Can't you tell me?"

"They talk to me through the radio and TV . . . call me bad names . . . tell me I'm a queer. I ain't no goddamned queer."

"Of course not."

After about ten minutes the examination was over. There was no suspicion of my feigning because, strictly speaking, the provisions of Section 1367 and 1368 did not constitute an acquittal by reason of insanity. They simply said I was incompetent to stand trial at this time. As soon as I was adjudged competent, I would be put on trial. People may commit a crime years hence and be sane and responsible when it happened, but when arrested and charged they may be totally out of their minds. How can a defendant be brought to trial, or punished, while crazy?

The second psychiatrist was a *café-au-lait* black man with a French name, probably with ancestors from Louisiana. I put on the same act, but he seemed to be observing me very closely—so I suddenly yelped, overturned the table, and ran out of the room. Down the jail corridor I sprinted, deputies in hot pursuit. They tackled me and dragged me back. I sat trembling in the chair. The examining psychiatrist told me his decision without knowing that he did so. He said, "You can go back to your ward." It was an obvious Freudian error. *Ward* means hospital, and that's where the sick go.

Both psychiatrists said I was "an acute, chronic paranoid schizophrenic, suffering auditory hallucinations and delusions of persecution, is and was legally insane and mentally ill." It was as crazy as you can be. Back at the sanity court, the judge determined me "insane within the meaning of Sections 1367 and 1368, California Penal Code." He committed me to Atascadero State Hospital until I was certified as competent to stand trial.

I was ready to stand trial forthwith. I had my defense. Although being incompetent to stand trial doesn't mean someone was insane at the time of the crime, it is admissible evidence a jury can consider. The arresting officers would testify, unless they lied, that I had claimed to be en route to Dallas with new evidence about the Kennedy assassination. The precinct booking records had me claiming to be ninety years old. The investigating detectives had to testify, again unless they lied, that I had claimed that the Catholic Church had a radio in my brain. The jail's hospital records had two suicide attempts and other irrational behavior. Finally, if the psychiatrists said I was insane two weeks after the crime, how could I not have been crazy when the crime occurred hours before the arrest? How could a jury not find me insane? Moreover, it was highly unlikely that the district attorney's office would fight very hard. It was routine burglary. Moreover, I wouldn't really beat the system, for it would take at least six months to a year to get back to court, and no matter what happened there, the parole board would take me back to finish my first term. I would serve three or four years at a minimum, which was all the crime deserved. My only gain would be getting rid of another parole, or perhaps I could escape. A state hospital was not a prison. It might have bars, but it had no gun towers. A friend of mine once led a breakout from Atascadero. He and several others had used a heavy bench as a battering ram to get through a rear door.

One thing I was unaware of at the time. My rap sheet would forever list the following: "Adjudged Criminally Insane." Anyone who saw that without knowing the truth would expect a raving maniac.

LOCATED HALFWAY BETWEEN LOS ANGELES and San Francisco, Atascadero State Hospital was as close to maximum custody as a state hospital can be. The majority of its patients were under commitment as mentally disordered sex offenders, commonly known as pedophiles or child molesters and in convict parlance: short eyes. I'd been taught convict values, and by convict values a child molester is a maggot to be reviled, spit upon, and persecuted. In prison, anything done to a child molester is acceptable. Anyone sent to prison for child molesting does his best to hide the fact. Nobody admits to that despicable behavior. The usual defense, which I've heard more than once, is that a vindictive wife orchestrated a false accusation.

In Atascadero, the short-eyed child-molesting majority looked down on the criminally insane thief minority. They were sick; we were criminals—that was how they saw it. The cherry on the sundae was that the institution had a "patient patrol," complete with armbands, which to my way of thinking was no more than a license to snitch. I remember someone in Folsom saying that child molesters were as bad as stool pigeons, and someone else said, "Not as bad . . . the same thing. I've never seen a short eyes who wasn't a rat, have you? They go together like a horse and carriage." The observation was greeted with grunts of concurrence.

Atascadero was boring. Patients were not allowed to lie down during the day. They had to sit in the dayroom, watching soap operas on TV, or maybe they went to OT (Occupational Therapy), where they made clay ashtrays or painted pictures, neither of which interested me. OT was too much like the second grade. The dayroom had a poker game (thank God), and I went through it like a dose of salts. I acted perfectly rational except once, when an attendant came over to the game and asked how I was feeling. I told him I was fine except that I'd seen a priest in the hallway, ". . . and I could tell by the red light over his head that he was after me."

When we wanted to go anywhere, perhaps to the commissary, the nurse had to write out a pass. We weren't supposed to wander around. I, however, was looking for a hole, a way out, a place where I could climb or cut and escape into the surrounding hills. What the officials had done, however, was make note of all the weak places and then either reinforce them or assign a member of the patient patrol on duty to watch them. That was how I got into trouble. I was looking around backstage in the auditorium when a child molester with an armband asked what I was looking for. He didn't recognize me, but I recognized him from years earlier in the county jail. He had been awaiting trial for molesting his niece. I recalled that it had started when she was three and continued until she was seven and told on him. I was remembering as he was asking my name and what ward I was on. . . .

I dipped slightly left for leverage, then sank my left fist in his stomach just like I was in a gym at the heavy bag. Any prizefighter will appreciate how wicked that can be if unexpected. He gasped and doubled over, then toppled sideways onto the floor, moving his legs as if on a bicycle. It was really wanton violence, a displacement of my frustrations and anger and how much I loathed Atascadero. Good God, I'd rather be in the penitentiary than turned into a vegetable and treated like a child in a state hospital, which is what seemed to be happening.

Nobody had seen the punch. I departed the auditorium and went back to the poker game and put it out of my mind. Atascadero had nearly three thousand patients. What were they going to do, have a lineup of three thousand? Besides, the fool would be fine once he could breathe again.

Without realizing it, I'd cracked three of his ribs. That evening as I went through the serving line in the mess hall, I looked up and saw him standing in the kitchen doorway with the white-clad attendant in charge of the watch. The molester tugged the attendant's sleeve and then pointed his finger directly at me while his mouth worked energetically. In the argot of the jail, he was tellin' it. . . . He was still tellin' it when the attendants took me to the office.

The third watch wrote a summary of the incident and referred it to the day watch, when doctors and administrators were on hand. I didn't expect anything to happen. I'd already seen several dingbats blow their tops and swing on somebody. At most they would be locked in a side room for a few hours until they calmed down. Unknown to me, the Department of Corrections report on A20284 Bunker had arrived that morning. Instead of a side room, they put me on the special locked ward, reserved for about two dozen of those considered the most volatile patients. Among them were three ex-cons whom I knew from prison. One of them, Rick, really qualified as a paranoid maniac. When I first entered San Quentin, I met Rick in the reception unit. Rick had words with another inmate in an orientation class. The inmate was a bit of a bully, and he gave Rick a dose of fear, a bad thing to do to a paranoiac. The only weapon Rick could get on short notice was a short-bladed but razor-sharp X-Acto knife. That evening in the mess hall, Rick saw the wanna-be bully carry his tray from the serving line and sit down. Rick walked up behind him, pulled his head back, and cut his throat. Blood spurted ten feet in the air. Anywhere else in the world the victim would've died. In San Quentin, doctors specialize in the endemic disease of knife wounds and they managed to save his life. Rick did his whole sentence in administrative segregation, the psych ward, and the prison medical facility in Vacaville, when that opened. When his prison term was finished, they committed him to the state hospital. Now, here he was, happy to see me. The other two I knew less well. One was a tough young Chicano whose mind seemed a little out of focus but whose precise malady escaped me.

The ward of twenty-two patients had eight attendants on duty at all times except for the graveyard shift, midnight to 8:00, when they had just three. The ward consisted of the dayroom, with wicker chairs and padded cushions, two hallways with regular side rooms where we slept but were not allowed in otherwise, and a final short hall behind a heavy, locked door. There were a total of fifteen rooms all used for maximum lockdown. It was called being in seclusion, but the hole is the hole no matter what nomenclature is applied. At the end of that short hall was a door to a road around the institution. Rick told me that it was the very same door that my friend Bobby Hagler and his pals had battered through several years earlier with the heavy bench. Since then the door had been reinforced, the heavy benches had been removed, and several more attendants had been added. We discussed the possibility and decided it was impossible. Alas, someone heard it and told it—and suddenly there were twenty white-clad attendants crowding the dayroom. The three of us were stripped to undershorts and locked in short hall rooms.

It may have been called seclusion, but it was a strip cell to me. A state hospital can do things that would never be allowed in prisons. It had a hole in the floor for a toilet. The stench that rose from it was overwhelming. In prison the hole could be covered with a newspaper or magazine, but such things weren't allowed in seclusion. They might be disturbing. The room had a window (mesh screen and bars) so high that I had to chin myself with fingertips to get a brief look at the barren rolling hillsides outside.

A doctor arrived every afternoon and spoke in meaningless monosyllables. He had an accent that reminded me of my childhood experience in the nuthouse near Pomona. I asked him where he was from. "Estonia," he said.

"Weren't you guys allied with the Nazis?" I asked.

His face got red, his accent thickened, and I knew I was in trouble. Nevertheless, I stepped back, threw up a right arm, and declared: "Heil Hitler!" He really disliked that. Then again, I disliked him. He would have adapted well to concentration camp experiments.

Every day he made his rounds, peeking through the little observation window on each door, sometimes saying something, more often not. I asked him how long I was going to be locked up, and his reply was shrink jargon: "How long *do you* think it should be?"

In prison there were rules and regulations about such matters; in the nuthouse it was according to the whim of the psychiatrist in charge. It wasn't punishment; it was treatment.

After two weeks without seeing a chink in the status quo, my usual instinct toward rebellion took over. I began to agitate the thirteen patients in the other rooms. By nightfall they were worked up. Each of them broke the little observation window and used the pieces of glass to cut a vein. In an hour the superintendent was on the ward. He was upset, for although a prison warden can disparage whatever convicts do, it is a different matter when patients in a hospital protest conditions with self-mutilation. Something like this could cause some negative media coverage.

The neo-Nazi ward doctor then arrived. He knew immediately who was behind it. He and the superintendent came to talk to me. I told them our demands—mattresses and bedding instead of the rubber pads, books and magazines, and the right to write and receive letters.

The superintendent agreed to everything, but the phones and teletypes were humming. At nine in the morning, my door opened and several attendants told me to step out. They gave me a white jumpsuit to put on, put me in restraints, and took me out the back door to a waiting car. Three hours later I arrived at the California Medical Facility in Vacaville. The transfer was under a statute that allowed certain dangerous mental patients committed under criminal statutes to be housed in the correctional facility.

When I arrived, the prison officials only had teletypes about me. There was a lieutenant named Estelle, who I think would later head the Texas prison system and who knew me from another prison and for some reason had a special personal animosity toward me. He put me in S-3, the unit on the third floor of S Wing. It consisted of cells with walls of glass from about waist-height to the ceiling. The glass wall was both front and rear, causing the cells to be labelled *the fish bowls*. Some had the hole in the floor, and some had a cast-metal combination of washbasin and toilet. I was lucky and got the latter. When the water ran out of the washbasin, it ran into the toilet below. The drawback was that the bottom of the toilet was a fraction of an inch off the floor, and in the warm, wet darkness resided a million cockroaches, so many that some got pushed out into the light where they ran around looking for darkness. When I lit a piece of paper and pushed it under the toilet, they charged forth in their multitudes, so many that I stood on top of the toilet until they scurried back inside. I never bothered them again. To my benefit, the cell lights were never turned out.

I have no idea what papers or documents were teletyped or sent between the Department of Mental Hygiene and the Department of Corrections, but the latter somehow got the idea that I had gone to trial on the burglaries and had been acquitted by reason of insanity and now the state hospital had discharged me and jurisdiction had reverted to Corrections. I stayed a month or so in the goldfish bowl. Convicts on the main line sent me books from the library. I've always been able to make it if I could read. While on S-3 I first read Herman Hesse and Sartre. I think I also read *Anna Karenina* and *Lord Jim* while lying on the floor of the fish bowl.

Across from me was the man for whom the law authorizing transfers from mental hospital to Vacaville had been written. His name was Jack Cathy. He was from Los Angeles but had gone to prison in Arizona, where he had killed someone. He eventually finished that term and was paroled. In Hollywood he was arrested and charged with another murder. He was initially found incompetent to stand trial under Sections 1367 and 1368, California Penal Code, and committed to Atascadero, where he had stabbed four attendants, killing one. A court in San Luis Obispo again found him incompetent to stand trial but ordered that he be held in the California Medical Facility at Vacaville, which had a prison's security. A lawyer filed a petition for *habeas corpus*. In response the legislature passed the statute allowing his transfer—and mine. I was on S-3 for several months. Three times a week he was taken out of his cell and given a shock treatment. A convict said Cathy had been getting them three times a week for several years. In half an hour they brought him back and dumped him in the cell. An hour or so after he was returned, and he would call out, "Hey, man . . . you . . . next door . . ."

I would stand up so I could see him through the glass. Three times a week we would have the same conversation. He would ask where he was, and I would tell him. He would ask where I was from. I would tell him. He would ask if I knew Eddie "the Fox" Chaplick. In a day Cathy's memory would nearly return. He would say, "Oh yeah," and remember something else. It was always the same sequence of conversation. When his memory was almost back, they would take him out for another electric shock treatment. It went on for two months.

They let me out of S-3, put me in the parole violators' unit, and began preparing for a parole violation hearing. They sent to the field for a parole officer report, and when they gave me the parole violation charges, included were the same charges a court had ruled that I was incompetent to face trial for in a court of law with an attorney and all the protections of American jurisprudence. If I couldn't face the charges there, how could I face them in a parole violation hearing without any legal protection or even a record? I sensed that they had made a mistake and began studying law books.

The parole violator unit had several men I'd known in San Quentin and elsewhere, including one who would eventually tell me the story that is the basis of my novel *Dog Eat Dog*. My legal insanity became a running gag. Loitering in the long corridor in the parole violators' unit was prohibited. A guard would come along, telling inmates to move on—out to the yard or into the housing unit. As a joke, when he got about fifteen feet away I would turn and begin jabbing my finger at the wall and talking irrationally: "What? What? You better not say that. I'm tellin' ya now . . . now and now. . . . Stop it . . . freeze. Vroom . . . vroom . . . vroom. . . ." And I would punctuate the last words with a pantomime of shifting gears in a car, which I would throw into third, make a hard pivot, and take off walking while making engine sounds. The guard would look consternated, and my friends would choke back their laughter.

In the mess hall serving line, the new arrivals assigned to ladling the food were scared of me. I would look at them wild-eyed and shake my tray in front of them. They would overload it, although I did this more for the fun than for the food, which was usually hard to eat in a regular ration, much less in extra portions.

About this time I received a letter from the daughter of a psychiatrist I met during court proceedings of the assault on the correctional officer. Every so often there is a newspaper account of some apparently middle-class woman falling in love with some seeming human monster who had committed a passel of grisly murders and was awaiting execution. Most people simply shake their heads in awed distaste; it is beyond their range of experience. Actually the infatuation is not with a real person but with someone created in fantasy, someone the woman can visit periodically, as a patient does with a psychoanalyst. The convict behind bars suddenly has all the attributes for which she yearns. She gives them to him. She creates an *imago* and loves it as if it is a fully realized person. She can come every week or every month and sit across from him for several hours, pouring forth the torments of her soul and psyche until the inevitable transference transpires.

I could see that this was what was happening here. I was very ambiguous about the relationship. I'd been accused of being manipulative and exploitative, especially of women. In all candor, it was a judgment I thought erroneous. Where were the facts? Mrs. Hal Wallis? I had not taken advantage of her even when she was having a breakdown and would have given me anything. Nevertheless, I was still very conscious of the accusation—even though the whole world was arrayed against me and I needed at least one ally.

This woman named "Mary" was not merely willing; she was enthusiastic. She said she had been in a cocoon since she was a teenager, "and now I'm a butterfly flying free." Frankly, she scared me. If she got hurt in my world, the other world would blame me. I was unconcerned about most of them, but Mary's father had befriended me. However, this was a war for survival, and anyone close could get hit by shrapnel. Alone save for some scruffy convicts, I was desperate for allies. I let her into my life.

Her letters became fiery and voluminous. Mail was pushed under the cell door before morning unlock, on the assumption that it would start the convict's day with him in a good mood. The assumption was correct. Mary wrote every day, but with the vagaries of the U.S. Mail and the prison mail room, some mornings nothing was beneath the door and on others, usually Tuesday, her letters would literally cover my floor.

Then she came to visit. She was no drop-dead beauty, but she radiated a powerful sensuality from the toss of her thick raven hair to the bounce of her hips as she walked. She bore some physical resemblance to Elizabeth Taylor, with a great upper body and legs a little too short for perfection. Although I have always been a connoisseur of legs and derriere, with only minimal interest in the female breast (a nearly un-American attitude), I found Mary to be sexually attractive. Her most attractive characteristic, however, was not physical; it was her moxie. She was dying for adventure. She would get plenty before it was over.

When she left, she went to the county seat of Fairfield and retained a young lawyer, who came over and asked, "How do you treat him?"

The prison official replied, "We treat him like everyone else."

"That's the point. He isn't like everyone. He's a mental patient."

The lawyer went to check the law books for remedies. The Department of Corrections decided to throw the hot potato. One day without warning, the public-address system called out: "Bunker . . . A-two-oh-two-eight-four, report to Receiving and Release."

I thought maybe it was a clothing package or they needed some fingerprints. The last thing I expected was that they would throw me a white jumpsuit and tell me to change. Fifteen minutes later I was rolling out the back gate in the backseat of a seven-passenger van.

When we reached Atascadero, the state hospital was taken by surprise. They didn't want me. I told them that I would leave immediately on foot if they were serious. The prison psychiatrists certified that I was returned to competency.

After three hours of waiting, they took me in and let the driver leave. The neo-Nazi doctor was ready and waiting for me. Back to the same side room, as they are called. I noted that the glass observation windows had been replaced by metal plates with holes to look through. That was before they put me in "full" restraints. First the straitjacket, then they stretched me on the bed and tied bed sheets from my ankles to the bed frame and other bed sheets from my armpits to the top of the bed frame. The restraints were so tight and the old bed sagged so much in the middle that I was suspended over it. (No, that's an exaggeration, but barely.) The whole thing was topped off by a shot of Prolixin, the drug of instant, prolonged mental vegetation. The effect of a single injection lasts a week. As the attendant readied the needle, the neo-Nazi doctor stood grinning beside the bed. He'd taken my earlier insurrection of the insane very personally. Looking at me, he saw an outlaw, a criminal. When I looked at him, I envisioned a black uniform with swastika armband and death's head lapel buttons, and I would not have been surprised if he had once worked in a German hospital's eugenics program.

Reports were written, signed, sealed, stamped, and sent in record time to the Municipal Court, City of Inglewood. In three weeks the sheriff's department bus came through, dropping some off, picking some up. I was among the latter.

WHILE I WAS IN VACAVILLE, Denis, my drug-dealing friend from Hollywood, came through the Reception Center on a parole violation. He'd been approached for help by the pimps when I was extorting them. Denis told me that a certain well-known shyster lawyer named Brad Arthur could get my parole warrant lifted. How did he do it? Denis wasn't sure, but it could be done. I had immediately sent Mary to see Brad Arthur to ascertain if he could do it and, if so, what it would cost. "But don't give him any money until I tell you. . . ."

Within days of that instruction, I was transferred back to Atascadero State Hospital. There, wearing a straitjacket, tied to a bed, and turned into a vegetable, I was allowed neither visits nor letter writing. The necessary pencil was considered too dangerous for me to handle.

Mary, who knew California Supreme Court justice Stanley Mosk through her father, called him up. Although he didn't appreciate the imposition and probably found her request borderline improper, he called Atascadero's superintendent and made an inquiry. Coming from a State Supreme Court justice, this was enough to get her and Brad Arthur through the fire wall of the neo-Nazi doctor. I was to be returned to Los Angeles within the week. Although attendants and the doctor hovered around us, I was able to tell Mary and Brad to "take care of the parole hold."

I had no idea if it had been done when the sheriff's department bus arrived at Atascadero, dropping a couple off, picking some up. For the next several days we traversed the highways of Central California, stopping at county jails to pick up prisoners wanted in Los Angeles and delivering others wanted in San Luis Obispo or Monterey or Bakersfield. When we reached the bus unloading yard of the LA Central Jail, it was past midnight. LAPD buses and vans were disgorging young black men by the score and by the hundreds through the night. The air was filled with anger's ozone. The police wielded nightsticks, poking and prodding and slapping them in their palms as threats, while yelling, "Move it! Move on in!" I did not know it at the time, but it was the first night of the Watts riot. While I was being booked, notice came that bail had been posted. I knew the critical moment would be when I was at the last stage of release, when the booking clerk called me to the window to check my armband and compare my fingerprints.

"When the door buzzes, push out," said the deputy.

The gray paint was worn off where countless thousands of hands had pushed through ahead of me. The door buzzed, I pushed, and the door opened. Mary was waiting outside, and dawn was coming up over the City of Angels. We went forthwith to a motel on Seventh Street where she had already rented a room. We watched the Watts riot on the tube. Thank God I wasn't in jail when the thousands of angry young blacks were dragged in.

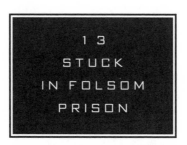

THE SUMMER OF LOVE in San Francisco, '67, '68, or '69, I'm not sure which, for I was stuck in Folsom Prison and had lost all track of time. Even then, California had prisons the way General Motors had cars—in a range of models and styles and performance. It had them with ramps for the geriatric thief in a wheelchair doing a sentence as a habitual criminal and medical facilities for the sick and the crazy. It had tough prisons for the predator and soft facilities for the weak who could not make it in other prisons. Some prisons were ancient and some so modern that the paint color was chosen by a psychologist. There was just one designated maximum-custody, and that was Folsom, postmarked *Represa*.

Twenty miles east of Sacramento in the belly of Gold Rush territory, Folsom covers 400 acres, though the walled area is smaller. It has just three walls. The fourth wall is across a yard made by flattening a hilltop, and is a gorge through which the American River millraces and foams. One fool convict made himself into a human submarine complete with breathing tube and weighted pockets but misjudged his buoyancy and sank to the bottom and drowned. The chances of reaching the river are small, for the lower yard is bordered with double fences topped by concertina wire and watched by towers with machine guns. A maximum-custody prisoner isn't allowed near the lower yard. Getting that far means another gun tower and another fence topped with concertina.

The surrounding countryside had been peeled bare in the mad search for gold. It never fully recovered, an early environmental disaster. The one view from the prison is across the river to a rolling land of sunburned scrub, hills that have a two-week fling of green each spring before returning to the usual desolate landscape. When a prison was proposed for the site in 1864, a doctor doubted that it was a healthy location. That convinced the legislature to order construction. By 1880 enough buildings were ready to receive the first prisoners. Soon the convicts took over the work, hewing the granite that still makes up much of the prison's incoherent architecture, one that is so strange that sometimes huge granite blocks fade seamlessly into poured concrete in the same wall. It is a weird symbiosis.

Folsom's history is blood-spattered and brutal. Straitjackets, bread and water, and tricing up by the thumbs were standard punishments well into the twentieth century. Hangings were common. Ninety-one men were topped on Folsom's gallows before California went to the gas chamber and first used it in San Quentin.

Folsom has had bloodbath breaks, the largest led by "Red Shirt" Gordon in 1903 (called Red Shirt because incorrigibles were made visible to the gun towers in that color). He and a dozen more rushed the Captain's Office, stabbing to death a guard who tried to stop them. Gordon's group took several hostages, including the warden and his nephew, the captain, and two turnkeys. On their way out of the prison they stopped at the armory and helped themselves to an arsenal of weapons. In the open countryside a few broke away from the main band and were captured. A hastily formed posse, including some militia, overtook the main band. The fugitives made a stand. Two troopers were killed, and several citizens were wounded. The prisoners left one dead. The rest got away. Six were never recaptured. Of those who were caught, two were hanged; the others were eventually released to become upright citizens.

Folsom's bloodiest day was on Thanksgiving, 1927. Armed with a revolver and knives, six convicts planned to take over an indoor area adjacent to the administration building and kidnap the warden. They took the first area but couldn't locate a crucial key. Frustrated, they turned back and tried to go through a different gate, one leading not outside the prison but to a lesser security area. A guard saw them coming and slammed the gate. He was shot in the leg. A second shot missed him but killed a convict gate tender. The now-berserk escapees were trapped in the inner prison. They rushed to the recreation hall, where a thousand men were watching a movie, the last movie shown until *Mr. Smith Goes to Washington* a dozen years later. They hacked a guard to death at the door, took others hostage, and sought refuge in the multitude. The militia, complete with machine guns, came from Sacramento. A thirty-six-hour siege ensued. Ten prisoners were killed and half a dozen more wounded before the desperadoes surrendered. They were quickly tried and hanged.

Their execution failed as deterrent. Ten years later another group tried to use a warden as their ticket to freedom. It was a Sunday and Warden Larkin was holding interviews at the Captain's Office. A long line of prisoners waited outside, beyond a wire fence and under what is now #16 Gun Tower. Seven of the waiting men had knives on their bodies and more than interviews on their minds. One had previously broken out of the Kansas penitentiary. Another was serving time for smuggling pistols into San Quentin, where they were used to kidnap the entire parole board.

When the gate was opened to let other prisoners out, the seven rushed in. Their audacity kept tower guards from seeing what was before their very eyes. The convicts quickly overpowered Warden Larkin and Capt. Bill (The Pig) Ryan, who *demanded* the nickname. A couple convicts wanted to stab Ryan, but the leader called them off. A wire noose was thrown around the warden's neck. Two guards rushed in to attempt a rescue with their lead "canes." They were stabbed and driven off. One died.

In a tight group with the warden and captain in the middle, the prisoners went outside. The warden ordered the guard at the closest gun tower to send down a rifle. Guards were standing at a distance, unable to move. One guard in a different tower saw his chance and pulled the trigger. He killed two convicts with two shots. Then guards in other gun towers started shooting while the remaining frenzied prisoners began stabbing the hostages from all angles until more guards ran forward and caned them down.

Warden Larkin died of his wounds. The convicts who survived the rifles played opening night at the gas chamber. Bill Ryan survived and was still Folsom's associate warden when I arrived.

This holocaust prompted the legislature to pass a law that no convict is to be allowed to escape through the use of hostages. Guards are forbidden by law to heed orders from the warden, or anyone else, in such circumstances. In 1961 a church choir was making an appearance at the Folsom chapel. It included several young women. They were taken hostage by three prisoners, all of whom I knew quite well. An intervening convict was stabbed to death (he got a posthumous pardon). But the gates of Folsom remained shut and there was no thought of opening them. Every convict knows the law and knows it will be enforced. That is one of the first things they are told on arrival.

UNLIKE ALL COUNTY JAILS and most prisons, Folsom comes awake quietly, without clanging bells or buzzers. The cell house surrounds the five-tiered cell block like a large box holding a smaller one. Countless baby sparrows, pigeons, and blackbirds in crevices and eaves have been crying raucously for hours, but convicts sleep until cell tenders are heard ramming huge keys into cell locks, a hard sound, each twist wrenched with an exquisite pause: *cla . . . ck, cla . . . ck. . . .*

Folsom's cells have the same dimensions as San Quentin's, being eleven or twelve feet long, four and a half feet wide. As in San Quentin, I had a table just wide enough to support a typewriter with a pile of manuscript paper beside it. I'd finished my third unpublished novel and was now embarking on my fourth. This time in prison I had nobody outside. If I'd been murdered and buried underneath the cell house, nobody in the world would have asked what had become of me. *Esquire* magazine had done a large piece on the New York literary world, which included literary agents. I wrote to Armitage (Mike) Watkins, whose mother was one of New York's first literary agents and had represented many well-known writers of an earlier era. I didn't think someone who was red-hot would be interested, but from the literary quality of the clients, I thought he might at least read my manuscripts. I wrote and said that I had no money for a reading fee and would pay the postage by selling a pint of blood. Would he read what I had? He wrote back and said he would. I sent him two novels. He sent them back. He said I had some talent and that he would like to read anything else I wrote in the future. I was already writing another, and so I continued.

The sudden sound followed by the ragged volley of myriad cell gates indicated that the tier above had been opened and another day at Folsom had begun. Trash began cascading down as the convicts above trudged down the tier toward the center stairway. What was being opened was "behind the screen," the close custody section of #1 Building. My tier was next. I pulled up the blankets without really making the bed. While buttoning my shirt, I was kicking trash toward the front of the cell, to be pushed out when the security bar went up. Nobody would care, I thought. Not about one day. A convict known fondly as the Flea (when the public-address system called, it said: "Flea, report to . . .") sleeps in his clothes in inches of tobacco grounds on grime-coated bedding with trash a foot deep on the floor. Once a month or so the guards clean him out. The Flea complains that they are taking his "personal" property. My half-made bed won't offend anyone's sensibilities in Folsom as it might in one of the new showcase prisons.

Through the cell bars, two indoor fences, a set of larger bars on a narrow window, and yet another layer of wire, I can dimly see the granite block retaining wall at the base of a steep hill, on top of which is another fence with barbed wire and a gun tower, while out of sight beyond that is another wall with more gun towers.

Crash. The bars go up. I push the gate open and carry my shoes onto the tier. Cons are going by. Of the thirty men on this tier, at least half are doing life sentences or have been deemed habitual criminals. All five tiers have the same ratio. Joe Morgan, a name that California convicts should recognize from legend, likes to rib me that I'm the only guy doing a second-degree burglary who is "behind the screen."

Indio goes by with a barely perceptible limp, a quick smile of greeting, and a pat on the arm. He spent several years on death row for killing a freeman in San Quentin who harassed him. Indio was already serving a term stretching to infinity, and he wished, and still wishes, to be left alone. He leaves others alone.

A tall Muslim with a permanently stern countenance goes past. His partner waits for him at the end of the tier. Like all Black Muslims, he is quiet and reserved, dresses neatly, and follows a moral code John Calvin would approve.

He, too, was on the row, but I do not know his crime and it would be an intrusion to ask.

Jerry O'Brien is struggling from his cell under the burden of half a dozen paintings for the Spring Art Show. He paints twelve hours a day and is rapidly becoming a good artist. It is a running joke that he is destined to become the Painter of Folsom, like the Birdman of Alcatraz, by the time he finishes his sentence. He killed a Torrance police officer in a robbery shootout (he was shot down years earlier while unarmed and on his hands and knees) and became the object of a vast manhunt. Captured in Utah and returned to Los Angeles, he was sentenced to die. On a penalty retrial, he represented himself and won a life sentence, no small feat for a layman. Yet his agony has just begun. Twenty-five or thirty years in prison is to execution like cancer to a heart attack, although a young man could serve twenty-five years and lead a good life thereafter. Tall and gaunt, he seems always in a hurry, which is unusual for Folsom, where everything is very slow. He hasn't slipped into the zombielike trance necessary to carry such a load of time. Occasionally his eyes glaze as he viscerally realizes that Folsom is his universe and the earliest parole he can *hope* for is decades hence. Even that cannot be expected.

Two young guards at tier's end are covered by a rifleman on the catwalk ten feet away beyond the two fences. All three are drowsy. The midnight to 8:00 A.M. shift exhausts itself in its dullness. The guards sit screening mail and listening to silence broken by clunking steam pipes.

The mess hall is in a separate building older than the cell house. It is joined to the latter by a solid-steel door, so there is no need to go outside in order to eat. The affiliation of buildings is not for convict convenience, but because of the fog that sometimes blankets everything.

In the Michelin Guide to California prisons, Folsom's food gets three and a half stars, although the quality has gone down in recent years since Pig Ryan retired. He thought the best way to keep convicts peaceful was fattening them up. A man with a full belly is usually peaceful. San Quentin has the worst food in the prison system, but nothing compares in gastronomic horror with the LA Central Jail, where it is literally impossible to eat for days at a time. I lost forty pounds there between April and September. The curious aspect is that the sheriff's department spends a lot of money for jail food, which may be why one went to jail years later.

Convicts in Folsom eat quietly in a relaxed atmosphere. The tables are four-man setups bolted to the floor. Stools are attached, so it's necessary to slip onto them. Tables must be used in order, but not filled up. Most men have regular eating partners. I usually ate with two friends, but one was in the hospital and the other had gotten off maximum custody and changed cell houses. It left a gap. The convict world is so intimate, so totally without privacy, that in the beginning one aches to be alone. Time erodes that need, and eventually the opposite attitude dominates, so one doesn't like to be alone.

That morning I ate quietly, anxious to get to the yard. The route out is through the cell house with its perpetually gray light. That is another thing to which one becomes accustomed. Cells on the bottom tier are the same as all the others, and yet men there have different personalities. Men will build the semblance of a world wherever they are and whatever the conditions. In Folsom there were no rigid rules about cell decoration. Elsewhere in the prison system, especially in the newer prisons, every cell was identical and had no decorations. But in Folsom it was said: "Whatever you get to the cell is yours, including the warden's carpet." This was an exaggeration tinctured with truth. Here's a cell stacked high with boxes of Colgate toothpaste, tubes of shaving cream, cans of pipe tobacco, boxes of candy bars, doughnuts, and cigars—a whole canteen neatly on display. Alas, all the containers are empty, a kind of pop art. Here's another cell so immaculate that the man takes off his shoes before he enters and doesn't sit on the bunk until time to go to bed. Another cell has dolls and a pink quilt bedspread. Some are as bare and unkempt as a furnished room. One has photos of Malcolm X, Elijah Muhammad, and Huey Newton.

I turned through a short, wide tunnel, following men through an open gate into the yard. Beside the gate is a granite gatehouse, a checkpoint with coffeepot. Guards are lounging around. They have recently been issued nightsticks, although Orwellian nomenclature now calls them batons. (A club by any other name hurts just the same.) Resurrection of the practice of guards carrying weapons (the lead-tipped canes went to the museum in 1940) came after guards were killed in various prisons, although not yet in Folsom. San Quentin had a serious riot a year earlier, and racial wars had erupted in Tracy, Soledad, and San Quentin.

In the bright morning light, I stop and look around. I don't want to stumble upon one of my few enemies. He might think it was a sneak attack and retaliate. The yard is mainly a square, though part of it wraps around #1 Building to a handball court, weight-lifting area, two outdoor television sets, and a marble ring. Marbles are gambled on like pool.

The square is somewhere larger than a medium-sized softball field, an easy comparison because a softball diamond takes up 80 percent of the space. Foul balls off the left field line crash into the domino tables and the pitted-asphalt basketball court in front of #1 Building. Out in deep right field sits #16 Tower, overlooking the yard and a fence with a gate outside the Custody Office. In #16 sits a guard called Tuesday Slim, and legend or myth says he is a champion marksman and can hit a sucker's heel at a hundred and fifty yards. An additional four gun towers overlook the yard from various positions. They are not to guard the prison's perimeter; they are to keep order within the walls. None has a shot longer than fifty yards.

Most convicts are already at work, up the hill at the license plate factory or down the hill the other way, but a couple of hundred numbered men still remain on the yard. Some pace back and forth along the left field line of the softball field. Other individuals or groups lounge against the Adjustment Center wall to bask in the warmth of morning sun. The motorcycle clique is together.

Most blacks are around the basketball court and #1 Building wall, more insular than they once were, as racial troubles from other prisons and the streets have crept into Folsom. But there is less tension here than in prisons for younger convicts. Too many men in Folsom have known each other since childhood. Motor (short for Motormouth) Buford is on his back in the middle of the basketball court, stamping his heels into the asphalt as he rolls from side to side, babbling and laughing too frantically for anyone to understand more than a fraction of what he's saying—but he makes them smile nonetheless. He has no enemies and many friends. He picked up a life sentence for killing Sheik Thompson, the most hated and most unbelievable man I've ever known. Sheik was some kind of throwback. If ever the term *animal* fit any human being, it had to be Sheik. When I first went to San Quentin, Sheik worked outside the walls at the rock quarry, making little ones from big ones. It was a mile from the walls, up a gentle grade—but still a grade. He jogged under a wooden yoke. When that got too easy, he put a hundred-pound convict on his shoulders. Sheik never weighed more than 170 pounds, yet on Labor Day, when San Quentin once held a track-and-field meet in the morning and a boxing card in the afternoon, Sheik would run the 440, 880, and mile in the morning. After lunch he would fight for the middleweight, light heavyweight, and heavyweight titles. Sometimes he won, sometimes he lost, but I cannot recall his ever being stopped. Sheik had no ears. They had been chewed off in a legendary fight. He and Albert Johnson, another black, had gotten into a fight behind #1 Building. Three gun towers began shooting at them (California is the only prison in America that shoots unarmed prisoners to break up fistfights the way you would use a water hose to separate fighting dogs) with 30.30s and 30.06s. Many shots were fired. They were hit several times apiece and kept fighting, kicking, biting, punching. Albert Johnson was hit in the testicles. He bit off Sheik's ears and swallowed them. Later, when the public-address system asked for blood donors, not one convict would give Sheik a drop. Albert Johnson had plenty of donors.

The abiding hatred for Sheik was not due to his animal physical abilities, but rather it was a response to his animalistic attitude. Every word he spoke was a challenge radiant with rage. He was both homosexual and informer and once put a prisoner on death row. The prisoner got off without being executed but ever after carried the nickname Death Row Jefferson. At slight provocation Sheik would spit on another prisoner, a truly awful insult in a world where machismo reigns. When Motor and Slim finally killed Sheik, they were marched across the yard from the Custody Office to the Adjustment Center just when all Folsom's convicts were lined up to go in for lockup and count. Every one of them clapped and cheered for Motor and Slim. Motor got life, Slim was sentenced to die, but Motor was seen in South Central in the nineties, and Slim was not executed.

To the unknowing, the Folsom yard would look peaceful and homogeneous, the convicts seeming to move as placidly as cows in a pasture. But beneath the somnolence and the guards' hawk eyes were deadly intrigues and murderous feuds. Men here had enemies they wanted to kill. The hostility smoldered like hot coals beneath gray ashes. Very little was needed to ignite a fire, maybe a glance or a word someone *thought* he heard. Men maintained a watchful eye for their enemies and stayed in areas where their friends lounged about.

When I approached Denis, Ebie, Paul, and Andy, the conversation was about the death penalty.

"How many they got up there now?"

"I dunno. A hundred and fifty maybe . . . something like that."

"And they add two or three every month, right?"

"Yeah."

"Sometime down the line, push is gonna come to shove. They gotta execute 'em faster than they arrive. Otherwise they're gonna have thousands. What're they gonna do then—have some kind of bloodbath?"

"I wouldn't doubt it for a minute," Andy said. "In fact, that's what I'd do to most of those worthless assholes."

"Yeah, but you ain't running for governor. Say they executed thirty or forty fools in two or three months. He'd ruin his political career."

"I wouldn't be so sure of that," Andy said. "It might make him president."

Denis asked me, "You goin' down?"

He meant to the library, where we were both assigned. He was the law library clerk, a job I'd relinquished in favor of being chief clerk, with a private office in the rear, behind the free librarian's outer office. Denis was my best friend. You may recall my mentioning him earlier as the first resident drug dealer in Hollywood. He was serving fifteen years to life, with first parole eligibility fourteen years and nine months from the date he began the term.

The loudspeaker crackled and a voice bellowed: *"The eight-thirty line is going in!"*

The tidal rhythm of pacing men and superficial homogeneity began breaking apart. The greater mass began to cluster around and funnel through the #5 Building gate. It was the sole route to the education department, hobby shop, and hospital. Denis and I went the other way, circling behind home plate along a walkway in front of the granite chapel, which looks more like a nineteenth-century power plant than a church. The Cat Man is outside the chapel, his jacket pockets filled with scraps of food and a couple of jars of milk. The cats are coming from around and beneath the building. One or two convicts lean on a rail, like spectators at a zoo. From a cardboard crate emerges Pinky, the patriarchal tomcat. His face is scarred and he is missing patches of fur, emblems of battles with other cats and the ground squirrels that thrive on the steep hillsides and live in the spaces of the granite retaining walls. The Cat Man feeds and cares for all of them. They are his friends in a cold, friendless world. A few months earlier the cat population exploded, and during the night two litters of kittens were taken away. The Cat Man was so distraught that they put him in the Psych Ward for a few days. Now he took Thorazine and fixed Pinky's meal separate from the others.

Denis and I pass through an inspection post and go down the walkway to the library. It is a low building of ocher plaster walls and gray roof, which rises and sags according to the supporting beams underneath. Originally built as an engineer's shack, it had a soft wood floor that became a plane of splinters; it was converted by simply adding some free-standing bookcases in one room and lining the walls with shelves. Very little had changed since the library came into existence. The largest of the three rooms is the Law Section, which the Department of Corrections wants to remove to help the attorney general. As usual, the law library table is full of convicts. Piled before them are the red books of codes, the cream-colored tomes of California Appeals Court decisions, the dark brown of the federal appeals courts—plus folders and scratch paper. Quiet prevails most of the time, although sometimes it gets loud when jailhouse lawyers argue the law with vehemence: "Fool, you don't know nuthin'. Read *People versus Bilderbach, Sixty-two Cal. second.* That applies the *Wong Sun* doctrine to the state of California."

Folsom convicts file twenty thousand petitions a year. Twenty years earlier that was unheard of and a convict seen carrying legal papers received scornful derision. Law was seen as a secret religion beyond comprehension by anyone except its high priests. To fight in the courts one needed an expensive mouthpiece who knew the judges. Caryl Chessman's twelve-year battle to stay out of the gas chamber changed the attitude of convicts. The ceaseless flow of petitions is Chessman's legacy. The Irish Sweepstakes are a better gamble, but for some men appeal is their only hope, no matter how faint, for resurrection.

Denis turns into the law library. I go the other way, through the librarian's office to mine through another door. I like the librarian. As usual, he is reading. At a nearby desk is Dacy, who answers the phone. He is serving "all day," life without possibility of parole. After a lifetime of petty crime, he made the big gamble, a kidnapping for ransom. He has gallows humor about his situation. He knows I am an aspiring writer and jokingly wants me to ghost his biography. The title would be: *How to Turn a Strange Child into Money,* subtitled: *My Thirty Years in California Prisons.* Alternately: *How to Lose Friends and Alienate Parole Officers.* His humor has been missing lately; maybe there's unfolding awareness of the true horror of his destiny.

In my office, I handle the library's clerical work, which is more than most convicts do, but still it takes a mere two hours a day. Nobody develops work habits in prison. I drink a cup of coffee. By 10:00 A.M., I am finished, and I go up to the yard to jog my twenty-five laps around the infield. I want to finish before the multitude begins jogging at the lunch hour, kicking up dust like a herd of buffalo. Only one other man, Merkouris, is circling the base paths in a trot awhile, walk awhile gait. Of medium height, with leonine white hair, he wears a white T-shirt over his spreading waistline no matter what the weather. He is in good shape for someone edging old age. Merkouris is a loner; he has no friends. He disdains convicts and is disdained by them. He is a man who obviously worked hard all his life and who possesses an inflexible, austere moral code alien to the prison ethic. A first-term prisoner, he has already served about fifteen years. In the early fifties, he was the lead actor in one of Los Angeles's most publicized murder trials. His former wife and her new husband, an ex-policeman, were found shot to death in their small business. The dead man's brother was a sergeant on the LAPD, which added petrol to the blaze. In the courtroom Merkouris was strapped to a chair, gagged, and put inside a glass booth. He still claims his innocence. He says he was the victim of the crime, that *she* had stolen all his money and shared it with her new man. Merkouris would never commit another crime, assuming he committed the first one, for he is no criminal and, in fact, despises criminals. He is lucky not to have been murdered in Folsom, for he tells the authorities if he sees anyone breaking the rules. I have nothing to say to him, and he would be suspicious if I spoke to him.

The early lunch line is going into the mess hall. I'm on the list, and I go in to eat with a friend who is being transferred to Chino the next morning. He has sixty days until parole. He's served nine years for robbing a Thrifty Drug Store. He doesn't say it in so many words, but he's afraid of going out. Another robbery conviction will bring a habitual criminal judgment. Thirty-nine years old, having served a total of fourteen years in two terms, he wants to change his life. His fear is that he won't fit, that so many years within the walls have maimed him. He will have sixty dollars and no friends except other ex-convicts or criminals. If he is unable to find a niche in society, a place with a little acceptance and self-respect, he will return to the world where he does have friends and acceptance and respect, even though it isn't what he really wants. He knows the probable result—the waste of the rest of his life.

The after-lunch work whistle goes off, exploding a cluster of blackbirds from a building roof. Almost as if it's a signal, half a dozen guards come from the Adjustment Center, leading a trio of prisoners in khakis (out-to-court clothes), handcuffs, and waist chains. Their hair is too long for them to be Folsom convicts. Someone calls out. One of them turns, grins, and gives a nod of recognition. The trio is being held in Folsom for security while being tried for killing a Sutter County deputy sheriff.

Back in the library, I drink tea and let time drift away in the trance in which prisoners learn to wrap themselves. It shuts out reality and lets daydreams rise. I stare out a window across the lower yard, the fences, the American River, and the arid hills to the white gauze clouds. Johnny Cash was lying; you can't hear any train from inside Folsom Prison.

So the afternoon goes, emptily. In Folsom a man becomes accustomed to the abbreviated day, so 2:00 P.M. is late and by 3:00 P.M. things are ready for lockup.

The lines of men begin gathering even before the lockup whistle. At a signal they trudge into the various cell houses, streaming up the steel stairs and along the tiers.

The bars drop, the gates are key-locked, and a guard comes by with the mail. He calls your name; you answer with your number. I don't expect him to stop; I never get any mail. This afternoon, however, the guard says, "Bunker."

I respond: "A-two-oh-two-eight-four." He puts an envelope on the bars. It is from New York literary agent Mike Watkins, who has agreed to read my manuscripts. I've sent him my fifth attempt at a novel. Over the years I have tried to write in various genres. This all began as a collaboration with Paul Allen. He was to come up with the story, and I was to write it. It was an attempt to write like Jim Thompson or Charles Williford, a short novel about a con man junkie who thinks everyone in the world is a sucker. Paul quit on me before we got very far. I finished it, making up the story, and sent it out. Once again the agent wrote: "You are improving, but this still falls short of our representing it. You might try someone else. We will hold the manuscript until you send instructions." The agent knew the difficulties I faced getting it out of the walls.

No, I wouldn't try another agent. I hoped the novel I'd already started would make the grade.

Minutes later the cell house filled with the sound of a rattle—a convict carried it ahead of a sergeant and a correctional officer. When the convict passed, you stood up. The sergeant and the guard have clipboards. They mark each empty space—one makes a positive count, the other a negative count, tallied by tier and total.

Fifteen minutes later the chow unlock begins. It is the same routine as the morning, except that after the mess hall it is back to the cell for another count. They count often in all maximum-security prisons. While it is still afternoon beyond the walls, the night routine has started in Folsom. For a few years it seems excruciatingly slow, but eventually it becomes preferred. Folsom convicts who are transferred to camps dislike dormitory living. The cell house is so quiet that it is hard to believe that the honeycomb of cages in this building confines several hundred men. Many stare at the small Sony they are now allowed to buy. The loudest sound is of scattered typewriters, each with a different speed and rhythm, from stilted uncertainty to an unbroken pulse, from petitions for writs of habeas corpus to the Great American Novel, for I am not the only Folsom convict who dreams of redemption via the literary life, of making a lotus grow from the mud. I doubt that I am the most talented. I will consider being deemed the most determined. I have written over a hundred short stories and five full-size novels without having a word in print under my own name—except in the Folsom Prison *Observer* and the San Quentin *News*.

When the security bar is down and the spike key has closed the steel bolt in the cell lock, I tune out the prison and immerse myself in books, reading them and writing them. I gave up writing on the typewriter. First drafts are in longhand. Every chapter I type, making changes as I go. If it is early, I usually read. It sounds absurd, I know, but I never seemed to have enough time to get in my reading. I believe that anyone who doesn't read remains dumb. Even if they know how, failing to regularly ingest the written word dooms them to ignorance, no matter what else they have or do.

At 8:00 P.M., a bell rings. Typewriters fall silent. Perhaps someone would ask someone nearby, "Did you get a score on the Dodger game?" There is no boisterous noise or prolonged conversations—not behind the screen in Folsom Prison where at least half the men would never see a day beyond the walls. Most wanted you to be quiet, and when push came to shove, they didn't care if it was the quiet of your grave—or their own, for that matter.

A decade and a half earlier, when my indiscriminate reading began to have some critical acumen, I focused primarily, though not exclusively, on American writers of the twentieth century. However, with Colin Wilson's *The Outsider* as a catalyst, I was now immersed in European writers, mostly French and Russian and some German, who dealt with themes of existence. Herman Hesse's *Steppenwolf, Siddhartha,* and *Magister Ludi.* Robert Musil's *Man without Qualities.* Camus's novels, plays, and essays. From Sartre I learned that understanding existentialism was visceral as much as intellectual and reaching visceral understanding required going through the nausea of existence. Reading Dostoyevski was like listening to someone foaming and overwrought as he told stories about the souls of human beings, and although I thought it was unlikely that someone would do as Raskalnikov did and go into the police station and confess a murder months or years after the fact because of conscience, I saw it actually happen twice with men I knew, Jack Mahone and Bobby Butler. Dostoyevski knew how guilt can chew at some men's souls. And there was the Italian Alberto Morovia, who could narrate with depth and clarity what went on in the minds of his characters. In my sixth novel I was trying to write of the underworld from the criminal's viewpoint. Many books are written about criminals, but the writer is always observing them and the world from society's perspective. I was trying to make the reader see the world through the criminal's perspective, what he saw, what he thought, what he felt—and why. I was also trying to write on three levels, first for the excitement of the story, second into the psychological makeup, and third so it promulgated a philosophical view. I was also trying to follow Hemingway's dictum that a writer should be as devoted to truth as a prelate of the Church is to God. Unlike most pundits and all politicians, I have never shaved a fact to fit an assertion. I sometimes end up positioning things that contradict each other, but we all know that a foolish consistency is the hobgoblin of little minds, which I read in the essay, not in *Bartlett's Familiar Quotations.*

At that time, all across America it was a period of disruption. Blacks rioted in the cities, and there were impassioned protests against Vietnam on college campuses. In other California prisons there had been some racial conflict and protests against the injustice of the indeterminate sentence law. Folsom, however, had been quiet except for the usual quota of knifings, although recently someone calling himself the Outlaw had been putting out fliers printed on stencil calling for a strike against the indeterminate sentence. A couple of days earlier I'd gone into the library rest room, where the janitor was ripping up a copy of the *Outlaw*.

"What's the matter?" I asked. "You against the strike?"

"Man, if they strike we won't get the weekend movie. Damn, man, it's *Bonnie and Clyde*. I don't want to miss that."

"I don't want 'em to strike."

"You don't?"

"No . . . I want 'em to riot and burn the joint down." Actually, I didn't care one way or another. It was true that the indeterminate sentence had been abused by the powers that be, but I doubted that anything convicts could do would alter anything. I was simply agitating someone I considered a fool. I seldom went to movies. While they were being shown, Joe Morgan and I were usually in the yard. It was the one time when I could get on the handball court.

I forgot the verbal exchange the moment I left the rest room, nor did I think of it during the main count lockup when a sergeant and a guard appeared outside my cell. The sergeant unlocked the cell gate and someone raised the security bar. "Let's go, Bunker."

The sergeant carried a white sheet of paper, the lockup authorization.

I made no protest. What was the use? I grabbed my denim jacket and mentally inventoried my pockets. No contraband. Good.

As we headed down the tier, I asked, "Who signed the order?"

The sergeant looked at it. "Associate warden."

The associate warden. Damn. That was unusual. A lieutenant commonly signed lockup orders. What could it be? "What's the charge?"

"Nothing."

"Whaddya mean, nothing?"

"Protective custody."

"Protective custody! Bullshit!" I stopped dead and everyone bumped into each other.

"Watch it, Bunker." They were ready to pile on. For a few seconds it was undecided. "C'mon, Bunker; don't make it worse."

"Yeah, okay." I started moving, but inside I was seething. It wasn't right. Nobody was locked up for protection unless he asked for it, and being locked up for protection made for a stigma hard to live down. I couldn't imagine asking for protection. If three mad dog killers were waiting for me on the yard, I wouldn't have asked for protection. *Never.* If I was really facing death, I might do something crazy to get locked up, but I would never ask for protection. I once had trouble with a known prison killer. He vowed to kill me as soon as we went to the Big Yard. It was during my first term. I wanted neither to die nor to kill him and go to the gas chamber or, more likely, get another sentence that would cost a dozen years in San Quentin. I saw him in the mess hall, walked up behind him, and busted his head with a stainless-steel tray. We were never on the yard together, and it added to my stature and reputation, although in truth I'd attacked from fear.

The sergeant and the guard marched me down the stairs and through the mess hall and kitchen. In a corridor between the two mess halls was the Adjustment Center entrance. One of the escorts pressed the door buzzer. A moment later a guard looked out, then let us in.

I could go through the strip search as if it were a minuet rehearsed for years. After they looked up my naked ass and down my throat, I put my undershorts back on. A guard walked me down the bottom floor in front of the cells. I was going to the strip cell in the rear. I seemed to always go to the strip cell in the rear. I glanced at the faces looking out at me. I thought about the big cats in the cages at Griffith Park. When I was about eight, I had climbed onto the bars roofing the big cats. The only one that jumped up to swipe at me was the mountain lion. The lions and tigers were too lazy. There was Big Raymond. I nodded and gave him a clenched fist. I'd known Raymond since I was eleven or twelve. We had been in the lockup in B Company in juvenile hall, the two strip cells that faced each other across an alcove. We tore it up, lying on our backs and kicking the sheet-metal-covered doors. The sound thundered. Nobody could sleep. The Man agitated several of the thirty boys in the company to jump us when we were let out to shower. We fought side by side in the combination washroom and shower. He was over six foot, skinny and strong as a steel cable, even then. In a melee like that, one seldom lands a punch with the leverage and accuracy of the notebook. Raymond did. Down one guy went. Another one, tussling with me, slipped and broke his wrist on the tile floor.

Raymond and I had known each other since then, so I nodded and showed respect, even though he was black. I'd heard that he'd transferred in from Soledad, but he'd gone directly to the hole, so this was the first time I'd seen him in more than a decade.

I could hear the control panel being unlocked. It was "maximum" segregation. One side was reserved for those they considered the hardest of the hard core. The majority had killed someone in prison or were considered likely to do so. The other side of the bottom floor was mostly for men serving a few days of hole time punishment for rule violations. Ten days for making home brew, a week for having two joints, plus referral to the local district attorney for possible prosecution, twenty-nine days for having a shiv, plus referral to the local district attorney for possible prosecution, five days for possessing football parlay tickets or for stealing sugar from the mess hall to make home brew. We came to the last cell gate; it was open and I stepped in. Five by seven, I knew it well. The escort signaled the front to close it. The gate slammed shut. The escort walked away.

Here I was with graffiti-etched walls to read, toilet bowl and sink in need of cleanser. I'd thought I had a good chance for parole at my next parole board hearing. Now it was in the air, depending on what they said I did and what their finding was.

▪ ▪ ▪

ON THE FOLLOWING FRIDAY, I went in front of the disciplinary committee. The hearing was conducted in the outer office of the Adjustment Center and was chaired by the captain or associate warden, flanked by a shrink and a flunky to keep minutes of the hearing. Today it was the associate warden, whom I'd known since he started as a lowly turnkey guard. He looked like an undergraduate student and had an affable demeanor over a lousy attitude. Still, he was better than Capt. Joe Campoy, who referred to the inmates as his "animals."

"You're charged with D eleven oh one, inmate behavior. Writing and distributing an illicit newspaper, the *Outlaw,* calling for a sit-down strike against the parole board.

"You're further charged with contraband, pilfering state supplies on which to create the illicit newspaper. How do you plead?"

"It's all bullshit."

"I assume that's 'not guilty.'"

"Not guilty as it gets."

"You also told an inmate you hoped for a riot where they'd burn the place down."

I instantly knew that it was the dingbat janitor in the rest room, the one who wanted to see *Bonnie and Clyde.* "I don't know anything about it. I barely read a copy of that . . . that *Outlaw.*"

"Bunker . . . Bunker . . . come on. I even recognize your literary style."

"What can I say . . . if you recognize the style?"

"Nothing."

The result was ten days' isolation and assignment to maximum administrative segregation, to be reviewed in ninety days—and every ninety days thereafter. The average sojourn in segregation was eighteen months.

Now that I'd been before the disciplinary committee, I was eligible to go to the exercise yard. Actually, the Adjustment Center had two exercise yards. As, like much of Folsom, the Adjustment Center was carved into a hillside, one exercise yard was on the bottom floor for the bottom-floor inmates; the other was level with the third floor and was used by the second- and third-floor inmates. The bottom, where I was assigned, was Max 4-A. There was no room for me at the moment, but I was allowed to exercise.

A guard appeared. "Wanna exercise?"

"Sure do."

Inmates were released from their cells one at a time. They came out in their underwear and walked to a grille gate where several guards waited. The inmates stepped inside and were searched and each given a jumpsuit without pockets folded around a pair of high-top shoes, which were kept in an open-faced locker. They gave me my jumpsuit and shoes and opened the door to the yard. It was formed by the walls of the Adjustment Center on two sides and the massive pile of concrete of #2 Cell House. The ground was all concrete. There were no guards on the ground, but high up on #2 Cell House was a rifleman with a cradled carbine. He kept order with his gun.

I had to move across a red line some distance from the door before starting to put on my clothes. I was the last of the dozen or so to be let out. I knew about half of the others: Red Howard, slender country boy and car mechanic, a good guy with a paranoid streak. He hadn't killed anyone yet, but he had cut up a couple, including Big Barry, a friend of Red's. There was Gene, a homicidal homosexual. Cornell Nolan was a black heavyweight prizefighter, tough and mean as he could be. His younger brother would be killed by a guard with a rifle in Soledad, the first death in a cause-and-effect chain that would leave dozens dead before it was over. Above all, Joe Morgan was in the yard. I'd known him since 1955, when he transferred to San Quentin from Folsom with a parole date.

As I put on the jumpsuit and sat on the concrete to slip on the shoes, I expected those I knew to greet me, for Joe, especially, to grin and say something funny. Nobody said a word to me. You cannot imagine the sudden total anxiety the silence aroused. Had somebody said I was a stool pigeon? Was Joe angry at me? Or Red or anyone else there? Should I go over to Joe and ask? Was he putting me on?

Suddenly, from peripheral vision, I saw a fast movement twenty feet away. A tall, skinny white guy had produced a weapon the size and shape of an ice pick (God knows where he got it) and was moving on an Indian, whose name I knew was Bobby Lee. He was a known troublemaker and general asshole. He wore no shirt and the first strike created a trickle of blood down his chest. It seemed superficial—but I didn't know how deep it was. Puncture wounds can cause internal bleeding even when they look superficial.

The white guy trailed Bobby Lee like a boxer cutting off the ring. I was hypnotized, still holding a shoelace half-tied.

The whistle blasted from above. Then again, followed by the sound of the mandatory warning shot. In the concrete canyon it sounded like a howitzer. I jumped and looked up. The rifleman, behind dark glasses, was drawing down on the pair. *Boom!* Shards of concrete jumped up. I could hear the ricochet. It might bounce anywhere in all this concrete.

Men were scattering. I followed Joe Morgan. He would know the best way to go.

Boom! Boom! Boom! Boom!

The bullets were kicking up the concrete around the white guy's feet. He never took his eyes of Bobby Lee, who was now darting back and forth.

The building door opened. Guards stuck out their heads. Bobby Lee fled to their arms and the door closed.

Joe Morgan looked at me, grinning, over his shoulder. "Another day in Four-A," he said. "I hear you're trying to start a strike on the yard."

"Ahhh, man . . . that's bullllllllshit!"

In another minute the door opened and a guard banged a key on the door frame. "Lockup." He looked at the white guy. "You first, Andy."

The slender white guy gave Joe a gesture of camaraderie and headed toward the door, clothes in one hand, shoes in the other. That was my first sight of Andy, who became a friend for all seasons—thirty years' worth. He was also an early endorser of my literary ambitions and gave me Strunk and White's *Elements of Style* and Lajos Egri's *The Art of Dramatic Writing.*

Back in the building, the authorities called us out for questioning one at a time. Those waiting to enter the office could tell how long anyone was inside. Convicts put a premium on getting out quickly. Without sitting down, before they could even ask a question, I gave my rote response: "I didn't see nuthin'; I didn't hear nuthin'; I don't know nuthin'; lemme go."

The associate warden made a sound like a fart with his mouth, looked at the ceiling, and jerked a thumb toward the door for me to leave. In record time.

That night in the shadowed cell, I looked out between the bars at the windows and thought, *I'm gonna be slammed in this cell for a year or more.* The thought fit the gloom of the world around me. "Ah well," I muttered, "when it gets too tough for everybody else, it's just the way I like it." After a few seconds, I added: "You're a lyin' bo diddy and your breath smells shitty." But the truth was that I could withstand whatever they did to me. If they killed me, I wouldn't know about it. I was mentally prepared to spend at least a year in the Adjustment Center.

EVERYBODY GETS LUCKY SOMETIME. About three months after this the wardens and superintendents of various California prisons met in Sacramento. It had long been a policy for wardens to rid themselves of trouble-makers by transferring them. They still did so from medium- and minimum-security institutions, but the policy had changed in high-security prisons. San Quentin, Folsom, and Soledad were required to handle whomever they had locked up. The wardens did make trades, and trades were on the Sacramento agenda. Locked up in San Quentin was Red Fenton. He'd killed a man in San Quentin fifteen years earlier and had been in the attempted breakout of Folsom in '61, when the visiting choir had been taken hostage. After going to court and getting a new five-year-to-life sentence and spending several years in the Folsom Adjustment Center, he had been transferred to San Quentin and given a chance on the main line. His reputation had preceded him. Weaklings were asking for protection by the score, so he had been locked up and remained locked up for two years. L. S. (Red) Nelson, San Quentin's warden, wanted to get rid of Fenton and was willing to take me in exchange. So Red Fenton came back to Folsom and I rode the bus to San Quentin, which was always my joint. Within weeks I had a single cell in the honor block and a new job where I could run around the prison until midnight.

1 4

PRISON

RACE WAR

IN THE CENTURY AND SOME SINCE a Spanish prison ship ran aground on the tip of the peninsula called Point San Quentin and a plank was run to shore to create San Quentin Prison, it has been the site of turbulent events. I cannot imagine how many murders have been committed there. In the age of the noose, it shared with Folsom in having a gallows, but with the gas chamber's advent, San Quentin stood alone as California's execution site. It has had violent breakouts (once the prisoners took the parole board; now the parole board meets outside the walls) and an escape or two when the authorities still don't know how the con got out. (I do.) It once headquartered a counterfeiting ring. The opposite side of the coin was that it was the studio for a coast-to-coast radio program (long before television), called *San Quentin on the Air,* which aired over the NBC Blue Network during prime time on Sunday evening. Convict #4242 sang the theme song: "Time on My Hands."

Nothing, however, was both so wild and so hilarious as the time of which I write. From the early forties through the fifties, San Quentin went from being one of America's most notoriously brutal prisons to being a leader in progressive penology and rehabilitation. Like other prisons, it was not ready for what happened when the revolution came to America. As drugs flooded the cities, likewise they flooded San Quentin. The racial turmoil of the streets was magnified in San Quentin's sardine can world. The polarization within can be illustrated by two events. In 1963 when John Kennedy was assassinated, it was lunchtime in the Big Yard. Everyone fell into a stunned silence. Eyes that hadn't cried since early childhood filled with tears, including those of the toughest black convicts. Five years later, when Bobby Kennedy was shot in the head, the response was different. Black convicts called out, "Right on!" "The chickens come home to roost," said the Black Panther newspaper. "Ten for one!" was the cry of black nationalists: kill ten whites for one black and they would win the revolution. The fiery political rhetoric was taken literally by unsophisticated men within the cage. In Soledad a rifleman in a gun tower fired three shots into a melee where five blacks had jumped two whites in the Adjustment Center yard. He killed three black convicts, one of them the brother of Cornell Nolan, who celled beside me in the Folsom Adjustment Center. That night in another wing of Soledad, a young white guard was thrown off the third tier to the concrete below. He died. Three black convicts, George Jackson, Fleeta Drumgo, and Clutchette, were locked up and charged with the crime. A Bay Area lawyer, Fay Stender, a socialist if not a full-blown Marxist, took George Jackson's case. She edited his letters, got Jean Genet to write an introduction, and had them published as *Soledad Brother.* The book made the three cause célèbres. She got them a change of venue to San Francisco and arranged for a transfer to San Quentin, where they were locked in the Adjustment Center. Because of the attention on the case, Angela Davis came to the courtroom. An avowed Marxist, Miss Davis lived in a different universe from the bourgeoisie. She saw a handsome, powerful black man in chains—and they did weigh him with tonnage. She became instantly enamored with the image and the fantasy, for that was all it could be. Nothing could come of it absent a miracle, and a sort of miracle came to pass, for Cluchette and Drumgo were eventually acquitted. Alas, George Jackson was pure sociopath and had the sociopath's characteristic lack of patience. Moreover, he had a worm's-eye view of the world and somehow believed the revolution was imminent.

A black inmate who was scheduled to testify against them for a parole was being held in the San Quentin prison hospital in a locked room with a guard at the door. Albert Johnson and another black convict managed to sneak into the hospital and make their way to the second floor. They murdered the guard seated outside the door, never imagining that the guard wouldn't have the room key. Poorly planned, one might say.

Another black inmate, Yogi Pinell, made a spear by rolling up pages of a magazine and fastening a stabbing device at the end. He managed to stab and kill a guard through the bars.

In the mess hall a black convict named Willy Christmas suddenly pulled a knife and went after the guard at the end of the steam table. It had one hilarious aspect. The guard ran through the kitchen screaming for help with Willy Christmas in hot pursuit, knife in hand.

For almost two decades no guard had been killed in a California prison. Then within a few months a dozen were killed in San Quentin, Soledad, and Folsom, all by blacks. Guards, who are invariably conservative and narrow-minded at the outset, heard the inflammatory rhetoric along with the murders and saw it as a direct personal threat. If they had been secret bigots, they now turned into outright racists.

For several years before the guards became combatants there had been a race war limited to Black Muslims and the self-proclaimed American Nazis. The Nazis had one copy of *Mein Kampf* that they passed around as if it were a Holy Bible. No one could really understand it. How could they? It borders on gibberish. Except for one or two, these erstwhile Nazis were skinny, pimple-faced kids who were afraid that someone would fuck them, but that fear didn't mean that several together would hesitate in stabbing someone. Indeed, most *wanted* to stab someone and get a reputation. My concern was academic. As long as they limited the murders to each other or, as my friend Danny Trejo said, "power to the people as long as they don't hurt my white old lady or dent my Cadillac," everything went by me. It was George Jackson who expanded the violence to the noninvolved. It started when several Muslims ambushed Stan Owens, the lead Nazi, and used him for bayonet practice. Anywhere else, he would have died, but as I said, San Quentin's doctors are the world's best with knife wounds. He lived—with one less kidney and a severe limp. Within the week the Nazis retaliated three times. One died; one survived as a paraplegic. The blacks in lockup thought the doctors deliberately let the black man die.

That was too much for George Jackson. He was not a Black Muslim; he was a racial militant. One day he pulled together a crew of three or four and at the after-lunch lockup, led them along the second tier of the South Cell House. There they stabbed every white on the tier, all of whom wore white jumpsuits, for they had just gotten off the bus and had no idea they would be attacked for being white. One died, and one who vaulted the railing to avoid the stabbing blades broke both his ankles on the concrete below.

Within hours all the assailants were in the hole, but none was indicted in outside court. George Jackson was transferred to Tracy, where he ignited another racial conflict. He got himself locked up and transferred to Soledad.

In prison movies it is a convention bordering on cliché that some super-tough convict within runs the show. In the days of Bogart and Cagney that kingpin con was white; now he was usually black. That notion may have validity in a small, soft prison in someplace like Maine or Vermont. But if someone really hard-core turns up in one of those joints, he is transferred under the Interstate Prison Compact. No convict runs the show in Leavenworth, Marion, San Quentin, Folsom, Angola, Jeff City, Joliet, Huntsville or other hard-core penitentiaries. Nobody of any color is that tough. Indeed, convicts do have little homilies such as, "tough guys are in the grave," or: "everybody bleeds, everybody dies, and anybody can kill you." Over the years I saw bona fide tough guys come to San Quentin or Folsom (usually San Quentin, because they don't last long enough to reach Folsom) and think they could take over on the muscle. One of them was a Bronx Puerto Rican who weighed about 120 pounds. He stabbed somebody within weeks of reaching the Guidance Center. He seriously believed that he was a killer and had everyone intimidated. He lasted eleven months. They found him in his cell with a piece of electrician's wire wrapped around his neck and eleven puncture wounds just under his rib cage, most of them directly in the heart. Someone gave a very terse eulogy: "Another *tough* motherfucker bites the dust."

With those parameters and constraints in mind, I think I had as much power and influence as any convict among the four thousand walking San Quentin's yard. Over the years I had assumed a code and attitude that mixed John Wayne with Machiavelli. I respected every man, including the weak and despicable, for it is better to have anyone or anything as a friend, even a mangy dog, rather than as an enemy. My friends were the toughest white and Chicano convicts. I maintained their loyalty by being loyal and their respect by being smart in several areas. One friend, Denis Kanos, whom I left in Folsom when I was transferred, had been granted a hearing in the California Supreme Court on the petition I had filed. Not only had they granted the hearing; they reversed the conviction. Denis, who had been required to wait fifteen years before being even *eligible* for parole, went free.

Within a couple of months of his release he was, as always, a kingpin drug trafficker again in Southern California. Every month or so, he would send me an ounce of heroin. Other men who got narcotics had to sell enough to pay for it. I paid nothing and was generous with my friends. It is difficult to convey what heroin is really worth in prison. Cocaine had almost no value, for convicts wanted what soothed them, not what made them crazier. A gram of heroin, a tiny fraction of an ounce, would, for example, easily purchase murder from many takes. When someone wanted to know who had heroin, they asked, "Who's God today?" Such was the power of the white serpent.

Although I played the game (it was the only game in town), I was really tired of it. I had prison under control, but I started thinking about when I would be free again. Without a miracle I would return to crime. It was the only way I knew to make money. God, if I could only sell a book. That, however, would be like hitting Lotto.

IT WAS 4:00 P.M. From my cell on the third tier of the yard side of the North Cell House I could look out the high window into the Big Yard. It was rapidly filling with convicts pouring in from their jobs. I had just finished typing a handwritten page of my sixth novel and was adding it to the extra-large loose-leaf binder. It was nearly finished. I had no idea if it was any good. It was, however, the first I'd written without self-consciously trying to follow a formula or a combination of formulas found in the "how to" books advertised in *Writer's Digest*. That manuscript would become *No Beast So Fierce*, my first published novel and, I think, my best all the way around.

Soon the Big Yard would be filled, the whistles would blow, and four thousand cons would file into the cell houses for lockup and count. That meant it was time for me to go out. As usual, the yard looked cold. Rain was predicted. I pulled a gray sweatshirt with Neiman Marcus across the chest over my prison shirt, then added two jackets, a black melton on the inside, covered by denim on the outside. In San Quentin it was a good idea to always take a jacket to the yard.

The North Cell House was one of two honor blocks. A convict tier tender on each tier had a key to the cells. As I went down the tier, I told him to lock my cell behind me.

I descended the steel stairway. To reach the yard I had to pass the cell house office. Several guards were around the doorway, getting packets of mail each would count for the tier. As I started past, the sergeant stepped out. "Bunker."

My first thought was a frisk, but the sergeant was extending an envelope. A letter. Who might write me? "Thanks." I looked at the return address: "Alexander Aris, 26 Main Geranium, Elbow, Texas." It was from Denis and the return address made me grin. It was a joke only a few would understand.

"I'm watching you, Bunker," the sergeant said.

"Hey, you know I'm a model inmate."

"It was your cell, wasn't it?"

Oh no, I thought. "No, oh no," I replied.

He nodded in a way that said yes, it was. A week earlier, several convicts had been fixing in my cell. I fixed first and left. Three were still in the cell cooking up, with a lookout (point man) standing on the tier. It was the middle of the tier and no guard could walk up unseen, but the outfit plugged up and the convicts in the cell were trying to unplug it, their heads huddled together. The lookout on the tier looked over his shoulder, got interested, and came inside. "Hey, *ese*. Put some water in the dropper and put a fire on the needle as you squeeze. It will swell up the metal and spit it out."

Just then the sergeant, who was walking the tiers on a routine patrol, happened to come down the third tier. When he reached my cell, he looked in and saw four of San Quentin's well-known sleazy convicts with their heads together like a football huddle. He walked in, put his head in the huddle, and simply took the outfit out of the guy's hand. Chaos. The sergeant blocked the door, and he must have been panicked, too. He managed to get their ID cards and walked them down to the office to call for backup.

Pretty Henry found me in the Big Yard right after that and told me what had happened. I told him to go back to my cell, put the stool away, straighten it up, turn out the light, and close the door.

Sure enough, the sergeant went back to the tier. He wasn't sure if it was the third or the fourth tier. He walked up and down, looking in the cells. He was unable to remember—at least not until late that night when I returned from work near midnight and he had to let me into my cell. Then a light went on. He told Lt. E. F. Ziemer, the third watch commander, but Ziemer told him that he didn't have a case. The next night Ziemer told me to watch myself: "He'd like to bust you. It would be a feather in his cap, and if he gets you dirty, I can't stop it."

"I always watch myself, boss," which wasn't quite true. When the day shift left at 4:30, Lieutenant Ziemer was the watch commander. He was the highest-ranking officer in the prison. If the warden or associate warden or captain came inside, whoever was on the gate would phone ahead. I had the run of San Quentin during those hours.

Before stepping onto the yard, I opened the letter from Denis. It said: "Twelve-page habeas petition mailed Marin County Court this afternoon." That translated: Twelve spoons, or twenty-four grams, of heroin had been sent to an address in Marin County. The address was that of Big Arm Barney's mother. She would deliver it.

There was one problem. The post office had gone on strike yesterday.

I plunged into the wall of noise made by the accumulation of several thousand voices in the pit formed by the cell houses. They made a churning lake of blue denim and faces. Right here it was all black. I veered left, along the East Cell House wall, past the hot-water spigot that steamed near boiling. It was for making instant coffee. As always, a few convicts loitered about, clutching plastic Tupperware tumblers wrapped in tape, steam rising. It was cold on the yard. Somewhere I'd read, perhaps in *Ripley's Believe It or Not,* that the San Quentin Big Yard was the only place in the world where the wind blew four ways at once. It did seem to swirl in every direction simultaneously.

I moved carefully through the mass of denim-wearing men, acknowledging those I knew with a nod or other gesture. Paranoia was too common in this milieu. Who could know what trivial slight might stir crazy thoughts? I was looking for Paul Allen and, to a lesser extent, the tough youngsters who were our partners and our backup. I found them gathered far down by the East Cell House wall. Paul, as usual, had the floor, while the younger men, T. D. Bingham, Wayne Odom, Blinky Williamson, Vito Rodriquez, Dicky Bird, and a couple more, listened with grins on their faces. Paul was telling a story: " . . . about fifteen of us in this jail yard when the guy got stabbed. It had one stall urinal off in the corner. They called everyone in for questioning, and the next day the newspaper said: 'Nobody witnesses stabbing. Fifteen prisoners using one urinal during incident.'"

Paul noticed my arrival. "What's up?"

I proffered the note from Denis. Paul read it, then grinned and pumped his elbows in a parody of the funky chicken. "Awright! We're in power again. Did you tell Big Arm?"

"I just came out the door. Don't get too happy. The post office is goin' on strike tomorrow. Right?"

The glee was wiped from Paul's face. "Awww . . . shit! I thought public employees can't strike. It's against the law, isn't it?"

"All I know is what I read in the paper. The *Chronicle* says they're gonna strike. We'll get it as soon as the strike's over."

"That's right," Wayne said. "Barney's ma ain' gonna shoot it up."

Suddenly a dozen police whistles bleated simultaneously. It was 4:30, time for the main count lockup. Guards moved along the domino tables, "Pick 'em up . . . pick 'em up."

I moved against the tide toward the yard gate, where a few stragglers were still coming in. I was on an out count, along with a couple of other convicts, at the Yard Office, which faintly resembled a modernistic hot dog stand. It had two rooms and a rest room. Except for the rest room it had windows all the way around. The former Yard Office had a closed back room that had acquired some notoriety over the years. Nothing could happen unseen in the new Yard Office. It had a cyclone fence and two gates across the road in front, one for vehicles, one for pedestrians. Directly behind it was the modern Adjustment Center, its door ten feet from the back door to the Yard Office. The Yard Office was situated so that anyone coming or going from the yard to the Garden Chapel, Custody Office, dental department, or other departments had to pass in front of the Yard Office. The bridge to the Old Industrial Building, which had contained the gym when I arrived, was in front of the Yard Office. Now all the upper floors were empty. Because the building was made of brick with lots of old, dry wood floors and other inflammable materials a convict was assigned as a "fire watch." This was known as a *bonaroo* job. Whoever had it had the run of the huge old building. It had many crevices and spaces where home brew could be made. One fire watch convict constructed a still for white lightning.

As I neared the Yard Office, I saw Bulldog hurrying across the Garden Beautiful, which was now nearly bare earth. He was about five-seven, with heart and a grin as big as anyone's. He was a talented athlete and could have been a professional golfer. He had certainly carried my clumsy ass on the handball court more than once. I waited for him outside the door, then walked a few paces with him back toward the yard. "Where you been?" I asked.

"Visiting room."

"I didn't think you got any visitors."

"Check this. C'mon."

I looked back over my shoulder. I had a minute and could get back before the count started. I walked with him toward the yard.

"You'll never guess who it was." He paused, then said, "That broad lawyer. Fay Stender."

"That radical, the one that's representing Jackson?"

"Yeah. He's out there now. He was waiting to see her after me, and he looked kinda hot 'cause he had to wait."

"Shit, 'dog, he's a celebrity. Damn near a star." I wanted to add that all it took was an act of suicidal rebellion, but Bulldog cut me off.

"You won't believe this, man, but you know what that broad wanted? . . . She wanted us, white dudes, to kill some bulls."

"Say what? She said it right out like that?"

"Yeah . . . well . . . like she said, how come the blacks are in the revolution and we're not helping 'em with the *pigs*?"

"I'd have told her there's no bull wantin' to kill me. She's nutty as a fruit-cake. What'd you tell her?"

"I told her she was nutty as a fruitcake. . . . No, I really told her that I'd talk to the fellas and blah blah blah. . . . Can you imagine . . . ? I want outta here.

Killin' a bull ain't gonna get me out . . . or put any money in my pocket. I ain't no cop lover, but I'm no cop killer, either. If I get in a spot and kill a cop, it's 'cause it was that or throwin' down my gun for a life sentence. Damn, killin' anybody is serious . . . double serious. Isn't that the craziest shit you ever heard?"

"Damn near." And it was. When we reached the yard gate, I had to turn back. As he hurried through, I could see that the yard was almost empty. The last of the lines were going into the East Cell House. Some vagrant sunlight got through the clouds and sparkled on the fifty-foot-high cell house windows. I remembered seeing this same view from the same perspective eighteen years earlier, and it now went through my mind that if I had known I would stand here eighteen years later, I would have killed myself. But I hadn't anticipated it and couldn't anticipate another eighteen years or anywhere near it. I turned and headed back toward the Yard Office.

Big was Yard Office officer during the day watch. He was just huge, neither particularly muscular, nor particularly fat. He weighed 310 pounds and was as playful as an eight-year-old. "What were you talking to Bulldog about?"

" 'Bulldog'! Who's Bulldog?"

"I'll bet you were makin' some kind of drug deal. You think I don't know?"

"No, Big, we were talkin' about you mama."

"Hey, hey, that's enough of that."

"Fuck you, Big."

He jerked open the bottom desk drawer and pulled out a nightstick. "Lemme smack you on the kneecap with this," he said. "I wanna see if it works." He slammed it down on the desk. It was a wicked sound. Nightsticks hurt. I can still feel the one that crashed into my back when I was fourteen years old and trying to sneak into a movie theater with the men's room down at the front.

"You sure do sound smart," I said with mocking scorn. Big liked all this. "Fuck around and I'll snitch you off . . . 'bout that medallion under your shirt." Big wore a heavy swastika medallion on a chain around his neck. He had gotten it when a guard was murdered in the prison hospital. Although Big had previously held racist views, having once told me, "I can't help it; I just think niggers on the whole are dumber than white people," he had been evenhanded in how he treated convicts. Now, however, there had been several long, hot summers of burning American cities and the racial murders in San Quentin. (He'd seen a Portuguese convict named Rios fight a black one on one in the lower yard. A mob of blacks attacked and stomped and beat Rios's head in with a baseball bat, until his skull was a flat as if an automobile had run over it.) Big's subdued bigotry had become nearly obsessed racial hatred. He had a peace officer's right to carry a pistol and repeatedly told me he was waiting for the right situation to kill a nigger and get away with it. I could understand how he felt, just as I could understand the streak of paranoid hate that ran through many blacks toward whites. I'd often thought that if I were black I would have made white society kill me a long time ago. I wasn't black, and I didn't intend to be a poster boy for black vengeance, either. I'd learned in juvenile hall and reform school that black racism is perhaps more virulent than white racism. Someone had once told me, "When we're racists, we just want to stay away from 'em. When they're racists, they want to kill us." It was true: black racists wanted revenge; white racists wanted segregation. Every black wasn't a racist, nor was every white. I really wished that everyone was oblivious to race and, absent that, everyone should be civil and respectful to everyone else. It is impossible to have a civil society without civility.

From the bridge-walkway to the Old Industrial Building Willy Hart appeared. I'd known Willy since he first came to San Quentin more than a dozen years earlier. He was an armed robber, but certainly not the public's vision of an armed robber. If someone had said, "No, I won't do that," and sat down with arms folded, Willy would have shrugged and departed. In other words, he wasn't going to hurt somebody—although if someone pulled a gun and started shooting at Willie, he would have shot back or shot first if he had to. This was his second time in for armed robbery. He had never had a serious moment during a decade and a half in San Quentin and Folsom. "Hey, Bunk, how the fuck ya doin' these days?" he asked as he crossed the road to the Yard Office. He, too, counted here, as did another convict, the lead man of the night yard crew. The moment the count cleared, the rest of the yard crew were unlocked. While the lines of convicts filed into the mess halls, the night yard crew used big fire hoses with bay water to wash away the phlegm and cigarette butts and the thousands of pieces of orange peel if oranges had been served. It was one of the better job assignments in San Quentin. The lead man was a holdover from the days when San Quentin functioned with con bosses.

As for Willy Hart, he'd first come to San Quentin on a transfer from a youth prison at Tracy, which had replaced Lancaster and filled the same niche, youthful felons from age eighteen to twenty-five. My first memory of him was his last night back then in Lancaster. He was in the showers with the rest of his tier. "Yeah . . . yeah," he proclaimed. "I escaped all these perverts. Nobody got my bunghole." His banter was boisterous and funny. He had one of the fastest mouths in the Department of Corrections, and it occasionally got him into trouble.

"Where you going?" he asked.

I replied with a gesture of eating. "Mess hall."

Just then the sally port opened. There were two guards with George Jackson between them. He was returning from the visiting room to the Adjustment Center, the door to which was fifteen feet from where we stood. He wore handcuffs. We watched him approach. I'd read *Soledad Brother.* It had been very successful without saying anything new. Eldridge Cleaver had covered the same terrain in *Soul on Ice* better, which was a few essays from *Ramparts* and more letters. Both books took a Marxist position on America, calling for armed revolution and a communist state. I think that George Jackson was introduced to Marxist rhetoric when he was discovered by white Bay Area Marxists, with

Fay Stender being first and foremost. Until then he had simply hated whites. I was already a veteran when he first came to prison, and was in a nearby cell. I heard him say that he didn't want equality; he wanted vengeance on the European race. This, however, was the first time I'd seen him for longer than a glance when he'd passed my cell. By any standard he was a handsome young man. I estimate he was six-foot or six-one and weighed 200 pounds, and he had the swagger of a warrior. He could see the two white convicts standing within a few feet of where he would pass. As he went by, he looked at us and made a head gesture that could be acknowledgment or challenge. I stared without expression. I could not acknowledge a man who killed people for no reason except that they were white, nor was it my style to say anything to him.

Not Willy, though, for just as George Jackson went by and the escort rang the entry bell at the adjustment center, a U.S. Air Force *Phantom* went by with a sonic boom. "That's mighty Whitey up there," Willy said, pointing to the sky.

I did not laugh, but I could not suppress a grin. Just before stepping through the door, George Jackson looked back with pure hate. When the door closed, Willy danced around and put up a hand for a high five. "I got off a good one, didn't I?"

"Yeah, I gotta give you a gold star for that one."

I FINISHED MY SIXTH NOVEL and, using a teacher who had befriended a partner of mine, I had it smuggled out and mailed to my agents, Mike Watkins and Gloria Loomis. Within a couple of weeks, Mike wrote back that he hoped and believed that he could get it published. It was only a hope, but it was still the best news I'd had in years. Indeed, it was the first letter I'd received in years.

One morning I was over by the Garden Chapel when I saw two blacks taken out of the Adjustment Center in chains; one of them I recognized, Willie Christmas. He had tried to stab a guard in the North Mess Hall. Now he was going to court in Marin County.

I thought nothing of it. Inmates were going to court in Marin County all the time. A few hours later I saw the captain run out of the Custody Office en route to the sally port, followed a moment later by a couple of lieutenants. Although it wasn't time for me to work, I went to the Yard Office to find out what was going on.

Big Brown was on the phone. The prison's tactical squad, known colloquially as the goon squad, was being called out. Brown was so excited that he stuttered.

"What's up?" I asked when Brown hung up.

"Christmas and that other nigger, they took over the courtroom."

"Took over the courtroom?"

"Guns! They've got guns and they've got hostages."

A couple of the goon squad with somber faces hurried by. The Marin County courthouse was a few minutes away. Would the law that forbid an escape from prison with hostages apply to this situation? That was something we would find out very soon. While Brown was on the telephone again, I headed toward the yard to share the news with my partners.

It was midmorning and the yard had more seagulls than convicts. A few were going to the canteen, and a couple were pacing the length of the yard, scattering a flock of pigeons and a few seagulls being fed bread crumbs by a convict. "I hope they shit all over you," I muttered as I went by. Over by the hot-water spigot on the East Cell House wall were a half-score of white and Chicano convicts gathered around Danny Trejo. From his intensity and their rapt attention it was obvious he knew about the events transpiring at the courthouse. It was a running joke that when anything happened, violent or scandalous, and anyone wanted the news, the word was: "Ask Danny." He was San Quentin's resident gossip columnist, speaking as I walked up:

" . . . some young rug stood up in the courtroom with an Uzi and said, 'I'm taking over.' He had a shitloadful of guns and passed 'em out to those crazy motherfuckers. They got the judge, the DA, the jury . . . *everybody* as a hostage. They might have God himself as a hostage."

"If they was in the walls, it wouldn't make no never mind. They'd blow 'em away faster'n God could get the news."

"Check this. . . . They got a sawed-off shotgun cocked and wired around the judge's neck. If the dude coughs, it'll blow his head off."

"Hey, Danny, you sure you ain't tellin' another goddamn lie. You know how you are."

"Yeah, I tell a good lie from time to time, *ese*, but this is straight shit, *carnal*."

"It's the truth," I said. "I heard about it in four post. The goon squad went runnin' out the gate."

"Damn," someone said, "them niggers is in trouble," which elicited nods of general agreement.

Willy Hart came through the gate and started across the yard. Seeing us, he veered over and approached, fairly vibrating with his excitement. "You guys hear what happened?"

"Yeah, we heard."

"It's all over now. They got out to the parking lot. I think the sheriff's department was backing off, but a couple bulls from the joint showed up. They shot the shit out of them fools. There's dead niggers and dead judges. There's bodies all over the place."

"Dead niggers and dead judges . . . how lucky can a peckerwood get? Ha . . . ha . . . ha . . . ha!"

I looked at the commentator, Dean Lakey. He aspired to be among the bona fide tough guys and would go far, but there was something mushy down deep, and he folded up down the line, when he faced someone tough and preferred to lockup. Once Lakey had crossed that barrier and was forever stigmatized, it was easy for him to go all the way to informant. He knew of several murders, including two where he was involved in a minor way, like standing point while the killing went down. When he made the aforementioned statement about niggers, judges, and peckerwoods, it resonated falsely. It was like someone trying to appear more racist and more *cold* than anyone could imagine who is not of this milieu. It was one of those, "methinks thou dost protest too much."

I wanted to know what had really happened. I would read the newspapers and talk to a black man who had been subpoenaed as a defense witness. When the madness broke out, they asked him if he wanted to go, and he said thanks but no thanks. He had a parole date within six months. He was doing what amounted to a drunk sentence. He was from the old school and much wiser.

What I learned that really went down was that the courtroom that day was nearly empty of spectators and none of the court personnel, judge, clerk, bailiff, deputy district attorney, noticed when Jonathan Jackson, George Jackson's seventeen-year-old brother, came in. He walked down the aisle and turned into a row of spectator benches. He carried a small duffel bag.

The only person who saw him was the defendant, Willie Christmas.

The others noticed him when he stood up with a pistol and said clearly, "All right, gentlemen, I'm taking over." I must say after careful reflection, whatever else the statement says, it has a certain *élan*. I think his brother had convinced him of the revolution's imminence.

Jonathan quickly armed Willie Christmas, disarmed the bailiff, plus took his keys, and unlocked the bullpen. Ruchell Magee was quick to arm himself. The convict I knew shook his head and stayed. The others left and he watched through the crack in the door. He couldn't see the whole courtroom, but he did see young Jackson put a wire noose attached to a shotgun over the judge's head and down on his neck. The primed shotgun was resting on his shoulder under his chin.

The convicts then gathered the hostages around them and made their way to the parking lot where a yellow van with sliding doors waited for them. The sheriff's squad moved with them but was afraid to take a shot.

They were getting in the van when one of the prison guards, using a big hunting rifle with scope sights, lined up the cross hairs and squeezed the trigger. The first shot dropped one convict. Then everyone else opened fire, the authorities pouring bullets through the thin van walls, the convicts shooting hostages. The judge's head was blown off; the deputy district attorney had his spine severed. He lived as a paraplegic and was later appointed to the bench of the Superior Court. The only convict who survived was Ruchell Magee. He was wounded but recovered. He was already doing a life sentence. That evening, the television news had film of the convicts' bodies being dragged from the van with ropes, like carcasses of beef. The authorities claimed a fear of booby traps, but I saw rage in their gesture. It would forever change how San Quentin convicts were handled in the courtrooms of Marin County.

It was revealed a few days later that the weapons used in the courtroom belonged to Angela Davis, the black communist professor. She fled before she could be arrested. A fugitive warrant was issued, charging her with being an accessory. It was several months before she was caught and brought back to America's most liberal city, San Francisco, for trial. She was represented by Charles Garry, the best trial lawyer in Northern California. His book on jury selection is a seminal work on the issue. After the trial, the jury not only acquitted Angela Davis but also gave her a party. I have no idea if she gave Jonathan Jackson the weapons or if he took them without her knowledge, but I do believe that she was in love with George Jackson. Big and handsome, he must have stirred deep feelings when she saw him draped in the white man's chains. To her he was no murderer, no matter if or who he killed. He was an enslaved black man in rebellion against his oppressors and therefore justified in all he did.

The Marin courthouse shootout made nationwide headlines and network news. The Soledad brothers became a greater cause célèbre. George Jackson was made a field marshal in the Black Panther Party. He was proud of his seventeen-year-old baby brother, who was pulled from the van with a piece of rope as if he were a side of beef. Fay Stender realized that talking of armed revolution was different game from judges getting their heads shot off, convicts being slaughtered, and a deputy district attorney being made a paraplegic. She gave up the cause and quit the case.

The Vietnam War rocked America's college campuses. Bombs exploded; white radicals became revolutionaries and robbed banks. Meanwhile the black ghettos in one American city after another burned in "long, hot summers" to the chant of "burn, baby, burn." In Mississippi the Klan murdered civil rights workers. In San Francisco a group of blacks prowled the night and killed whites they caught alone. These were called the Zebra Killings, and I thought it likely that black ex-convicts were involved (I was right), for only in California's prisons had I seen similar killings. Both sides did it, but George Jackson was the first. As with everyone, he did no evil in his own mind. All that matters is for the individual to justify himself in the mirror, and George did so with the four hundred years of slavery and then Jim Crow. Journalists came from around the world to interview him. He spent more time in the visiting room than his cell. Writers came from *Time, Newsweek, Le Monde,* the London *Times,* and the *New York Times.* It was the Department of Corrections policy to allow such interviews, and George got at least one, and sometimes several, every day of the week. The guards hated him and the "commie pinko bastards who took a hate-filled killer and made him a revolutionary hero." They didn't appreciate being called pigs and fascists, which none saw when they looked in their mirrors, although a few would wink when queried about racism, especially when they started being killed.

White convicts also resented being referred to as neo-Nazis and white supremacists, the villains of the plot, as it were. There were several race wars behind San Quentin's walls. In San Quentin there was so much racial paranoia that real provocation was unnecessary to evoke murder. Almost any excuse was enough to break out the shivs. One particular war began with events just lightly related to race.

It was a spring evening after chow, and the seven hundred convicts in the East Cell House straggled across the Big Yard into the building. The five tiers were crowded with some men waiting near their cells for the lockup, while others roamed the tiers, trying to hustle a paper of heroin, a tab of acid, a quart of home brew, or anything to soften the reality of the long night ahead of them. I lived in the North Cell House, but because of ex officio status, I roamed where I wanted. This evening I wanted to make a bet on the NCAA Final Four.

I ran up the stairs to the third tier, swung around the rail, and started down the tier. A humming roar of noise hung over everything, a sound so common and pervasive in the cell house that it ceased to be noticed when you became accustomed to it. It was the kind of noise that only attracts attention when it stops or its rhythm changes.

The rhythm changed. From a lower tier came the thud and grunt of struggling bodies, the bang as someone bumped against a cell gate and it hit the frame. Convicts nearby froze and turned, wary as animals at a sharp sound. Others on tiers above and below craned their necks to see what was going on. Tension spread like electricity through connected wires. Men forty yards away sensed within seconds that something had happened.

The gun rail guard, a rookie, ran back and forth, looking for the trouble. He saw something, a jumble of motion. His whistle bleated, repeated itself, and ended any trace of doubt that someone was being stabbed. San Quentin's convicts gave up fistfighting long ago to settle disputes. If it's not worth killing about, forget it. If you punch somebody in the mouth and let him go, he's liable to brood about it for a month or two and come back with a shiv.

There was suddenly silence throughout the cell house except for the scrape of running feet. More than one man was breaking through the crowd to get away. The guard leveled his rifle but was unable to shoot into the press of bodies. He tried to follow along the gun rail, still blasting his whistle in accusation, but the quarry disappeared down the rear stairs.

Guards on the cell house floor were too late to reach the scene. The assailants got away.

I decided to forgo my NCAA wager and get out of the cell house before the rotunda gate was locked. They might even ask *me* some questions. As I hurried back toward the front stairs, I looked down at the floor of the cell house. Four blacks were pushing a flatbed handcart used to move laundry hampers and metal trash barrels. Now it carried a "brother" who was being rushed toward the hospital. He was on his back, legs drawn up, denim jacket open, a red stain spread across his white tank top. The blacks who pushed the cart would have let a white man die, and a white convict who gave aid to a wounded black (unless the white was assigned to the hospital) would be ostracized by other whites, if not attacked. The first rumor was that he had been stabbed and thrown from the fourth tier. When you looked down, that seemed unlikely. The victim was on his back, legs drawn up, head raised. If he had been dropped forty feet to the concrete, bones would have been broken. He would have looked different than he did.

From the rows of tiers above, hundreds of convicts stared down at the exiting group. The question was who had stabbed him. If it was another black, it was between assailant, victim, and their partners. If it was a Chicano, so far that had not caused any widespread trouble, but if it was white on black or black on white, there would most certainly be trouble.

As I reached the rotunda door of the building, the sergeant was coming from another angle to lock it. In the background the public-address system was crackling and bellowing, *"Lock up! Bay side, lock up! Yard side, lock up!"* The sergeant raised a hand of restraint, recognized me, then let me slip out into the Big Yard night. Guards were coming on the double, holding their jangling key rings in one hand and batons in the other.

I started back across the yard. It was an Edward Hopper study in light and shadow, with several figures working. One wielded the nozzle of a heavy canvas fire hose, while another dragged the weight along behind. The powerful hose blasted the sputum and empty cigarette packs and made the thousands of pieces of orange peel dance to the water-running gutter next to the shed. Other convicts were sweeping up trash and shoveling it into wheelbarrows. Convicts made the yard a filthy mess every day. The night yard crew were all friends of mine. They couldn't get assigned without my wink to the lieutenant. Paul Allen was approaching, waving his broom. From the yard at night you could see into the lighted cell house. "What happened in there?"

"Some nigger got stabbed up on the fourth tier." Although I used the racial epithet, it was without animus. Although I would not have used it with any black, even joking with a friend, if I used anything different with Paul he would have commented.

"We got another war kickin' off?"

"I dunno who got him. He doesn't seem to be hurt bad."

Through the yard gate came Lt. E. F. Ziemer. A man in his mid-fifties, he had the gait of someone who had spent years on a rolling ship. In his case it had been a submarine. His hat was tilted rakishly to the side. He was sauntering toward the East Block rotunda. He was my boss and I gave him a half-salute. He stopped. "Hey, Bunk!" he called. "Keep yourself available. We're going to have reports to write tonight."

"I'll be around, boss."

"One other thing."

"What's up, boss?"

"They're supposed to gas Aaron Mitchell a week from Friday. It's pretty messy over there. I sent Willy Hart over to hit it with a mop. He wanted me to ask you to help him."

"He would."

"If you don't mind."

"Sure. How do I get in?" Keys to the execution area were kept in #2 Gun Tower over the Big Yard gate.

Just then a guard came out of the North Cell House rotunda, which provided entry to both the cell house through a steel door on the left and the overnight condemned cells through another steel door straight ahead. The guard was the runner, who picked up and delivered mail and memos and escorted convicts (say to the hospital) at night. He was heading toward #2 Gun Tower, obviously to return the key. Ziemer called his name and we walked over to meet him.

When the runner opened the green steel door, Willy was in the open gate of one of the two overnight cells. He had a broom in one hand and a grin on his face. Beside him was a bucket on wheels with a mop handle protruding. Behind him was an open green steel door, and two or three feet beyond that was the open oval door into the gas chamber, somewhat reminiscent of a diving bell. There sat two chairs side by side. I immediately thought of the story of Allen and Smitty, Folsom convicts executed for killing another inmate. A bull told me that when the door was closed and the wheel turned to seal it, they leaned their heads together and kissed good-bye, chair to chair. As I thought of it, I laughed. Willy had just said something funny, he was often very funny, and thought I was laughing at his witticism.

"Hey, Bunk, I see you came to help."

"I'll be back for you two in half an hour," the guard said. "How's that?"

"Sounds good," Willy said. "*We* should be done by then."

The guard closed the door and we were alone with the overnight cells and the gas chamber. I stood in the opened gateway of the first cell. One step out, one step to the right through the door. One long step (or two short steps or one skid mark of dragged feet) was the entrance to the gas chamber. Damn, it was small. It was painted green and shaped in an octagon, with windows from about waist-height up. Venetian blinds now hid the interior from the witnesses. They stood outside. The first row had their noses inches from the glass, and the doomed fellow was inches on the other side. A witness definitely witnessed things up close.

"Didn't Shorty Schrekendost paint this place?" Willy asked.

"I think so . . . 'bout ten years ago."

"I think he wrote his name under one of the seats."

"He wrote it everywhere else in the joint. Lemme check." So I flopped on the floor and rolled over on my back so I could see. I saw no graffiti, but I did see how death was administered, low technology, a lever with a hook where the gauze bag of cyanide pellets was draped. When the lever was moved, the bag dipped down into a bucket of sulphuric acid and gas was created. The seat bottom was perforated to ease the gas's flow upward.

I raised my head. Thinking about smells and stuff stirred a memory. "What about my outfit? Where's it at?"

"I got it stashed out there. As soon as we leave . . ."

"I hope you cleaned it so it doesn't stink." I was riding Willy as a joke. It was part of the relationship. If I acted otherwise, he would suspect some kind of put-on.

"It's clean . . . and oh, I've got a present for you, brother."

From a shirt pocket he brought forth a matchbook. Inserted so it stuck out both sides was a joint. "Well, fire the sucker up," I said.

So he did. We sat side by side in the gas chamber, passing the joint back and forth. It was pretty good pot, and we got high, laughing and telling stories until we heard the key turn in the outside lock. We jumped up and looked busy. Willy was swinging the mop, and I was swiping a rag across the witness chairs. I wondered how many pissed in their britches when the cyanide hit the pan and they were eyeball-to-eyeball with the dying man.

The guard was unconcerned with cleanliness, although he did sniff the air and ask, "What's that I smell?"

"I don't smell anything," Willy said. "You smell anything, Legend?"

"You put Pine Sol in the mop bucket, didn't you?"

Willy shook his head. "No . . . nuthin' but a little ammonia."

"That's what it's gotta be."

The guard sensed a put-on but didn't know what or why; he didn't recognize the smell. "C'mon," he said, and told Willy to bring the gear. "The lieutenant wants to see you *pronto*," he said to me. I went out with a grin.

WHILE WILLY AND I WERE MOPPING the execution chamber, Lieutenant Ziemer had been questioning convicts who had cells where the incident occurred. He had discovered very little, but he had to file a report of some kind. That was my job. All incident reports had the same form: "At approximately ——, on —— date, while on duty as ——, I observed, was told," etc. It was very ritualized, and I had it down pat:

> The victim, Robinson, B00000, suffered three puncture wounds from an unknown instrument in his right upper chest. (See medical report.) Subject claims he was assaulted by an unknown Mexican. It should be noted that Robinson was recently transferred to this institution following several disciplinary reports at the California Men's Colony. It should be noted that the subject has a hostile demeanor. The writer placed him on administrative lockup pending investigation and disposition of this incident.

Lieutenant Ziemer read the report and signed it. "Goddam I write a helluva report," he said, widening his eyes and gaping his mouth in feigned naïveté. "Big Red Nelson complimented me at the last staff meeting. He asked how you were doing."

"I'M GOIN' OVER TO THE CELL house," I said. "Unless you need me."

"Be around about eleven. Those officers working the East Block will have to file reports."

"I'll be here, boss."

When I reached the yard, where the yard crew was finished cleaning and putting away their equipment, Danny Trejo had the real news about the East Block stabbing. The altercation had begun in the education building where the Chicano and the black were both enrolled in literacy training, which means they had tested lower than the fourth-grade level and were being taught to read. Somehow they had exchanged stares, which became sneers and then a word or two: "So?" "So whatever." The bell then rang ending the period. Both existed in worlds where it was impossible to conceive, much less articulate, the senselessness of murder arising from locked stares and nothing more.

When word got around that it was Chicano and black, most whites relaxed, glad not to be involved. Some especially militant blacks plotted retaliation. As far as they were concerned, a brother had been stabbed and nothing else mattered. Chicanos anticipated possible trouble and readied themselves. Black tier tenders delivered knives from mattresses and ventilators. Chicano cell house workers did the same. Perhaps a dozen on each side actually armed themselves, taping large, crudely honed, but deadly knives to their forearms so they were easy to jerk from their sleeves. Or they poked a hole in the bottom of their front pants pocket, so the blade went down against their thighs while they held the handle out of sight in their pocket. It could be drawn in an instant. As in the Wild West, the quickest draw often decided who lived and who died.

The prison slept without realization that the tinder of black rage toward the white man had been ignited. No one could have imagined how hot the inferno would be or how long it would burn.

TWO GIANT MESS HALLS fed San Quentin's convicts. The larger of the two, the South, was divided into four sections, with murals of California history on their walls. It was like a high school cafeteria instead of the feeding place of robbers, rapists and murderers, drug addicts, and child molesters. Both mess halls together were inadequate to feed all of the convicts simultaneously, so it was done in shifts. The North and West Cell Houses ate first in the morning. After eating, the inmates could go out on the yard or back to their cell house until the 8:00 work call.

By 7:30 the last of the East and South Cell Houses were usually in the mess halls. Those first unlocked were, as a rule, already leaving for the yard. I never got up for breakfast, but this morning Veto Tewksbury (a San Fernando Valley Chicano despite the name, which came from an English squire who owned many thousands of acres in Arizona once upon a time) reached through the bars and shook my foot. "Get up, man. Shit's gonna hit the fan out in the yard."

I stood up and looked out through the cell house bars and the cell house bars to the Big Yard. Sure enough, it was more segregated than usual. As always, blacks were gathered along the North Cell House, directly below my window, but though they were usually joshing, laughing, and talking, this morning they were somber and silent. The line dividing the races was usually narrow and overlapping, with nobody paying real attention to the territorial imperatives, but on this morning the space between the races was at least thirty yards. About three hundred blacks stared balefully at two clusters of Mexicans; one cluster of about a hundred was partially under the shed on the blacks' right flank. Another hundred faced the blacks head-on across the empty asphalt. Behind the Chicanos, backing them, were a dozen young Nazis and a score of Hell's Angels. Sprinkled among the Chicanos were ten or fifteen whites ready to back their homeboys, or tight partners. One clique of whites was conspicuous standing on benches along the East Cell House wall. In the last black-versus-white race war, they had carried the brunt of the mayhem and had committed other stabbings and murders. It was the strongest white clique, but its numbers in the general population had been depleted by officials' locking them in segregation and transferring them. Though violent, the clique was not especially racist; that is, they would not start a race war. But its members, like me, had Chicano partners who backed us in a confrontation with a large Mexican gang, which would become La Nuestra Familia, mortal enemy of the Mexican Mafia, aka La Eme. In the Southwest, especially in Southern California but also in Arizona, New Mexico, and parts of Texas, it is far better to be an enemy of La Cosa Nostra than La Eme. On this particular morning, however, these gangs were still nameless embryos.

The guards were aware of the volatile situation in the yards and several were armed with rifles; one, a body-building sergeant, had an antiquated but effective Thompson submachine gun, and they were all lined up on the gun rail outside the North Cell House wall. It was easy to tell that most were lined up on the blacks. (It wasn't whites or Chicanos who had killed several guards during the last year.) One black guard, however, was conspicuously targeting the Mexican ranks. That was the racial situation in San Quentin. I was disgusted with the whole ignorant mess. It was beyond racism, race pride, or even revolution. It was something out of the tribal wars in the New Guinea jungle, complete with headhunting. No matter how insane it was, it wasn't something I could ignore. Too many whites, then still the majority, tried that tactic. It only invited aggression.

The standoff and stare-down continued for the next ten minutes as the mess halls finished disgorging prisoners into the yard. The ranks swelled. The riflemen watching from above anticipated an open riot, and tension was reaching an unbearable pitch.

From the sidelines a black and a Chicano appeared. The black, light-skinned and handsome, was a prizefighter so good that nobody within forty pounds of his weight would fight him. He did perform Ali's mantra of dancing like a butterfly and stinging like a bee. He was a dope fiend and disregarded racial lines to satisfy his craving. He was not known as a militant, although some suspected him of undercover agitation. I don't think he hated whites, but he was a proud black man and, like me, when the lines were drawn, he stood with his own. Nobody could blame him for that. The Chicano, who had recently returned to San Quentin on a murder conviction, wanted to be a "shot caller" in the prison firmament and had gathered a clique of about a dozen, whose members now stood with the throng under the shed.

When the two reached the center of the empty asphalt, the black prize-fighter motioned toward the mass of blacks. Two came forward, both tall and military in bearing, one with a head shaved and oiled like my own. It glistened in the morning sunlight. He had influence among the Black Muslims. The other wore tiny Ben Franklin glasses and a bushy Afro, the style favored by blacks at the time.

The quartet stood in a tight circle. The blacks spoke and gestured, tense with accusation and ire. The Chicano took over and held the floor, and the conversation went on while the yard gate was opened and the steam whistle blew the morning work call. Half the convicts in the yard streamed out, glad to avoid possible trouble. The faced-off warriors on both sides held their places. So did the riflemen looking down from the gun walk. The conference was allowed to continue because it might settle things without any further bloodshed.

The conference broke up. The black fighter shook hands with the two militants, and the Mexican walked back to his waiting crew. He said something and gestured toward the gate, leading his clique off the yard. The black spokesmen went back to their waiting throng. A dozen black warriors gathered around them and listened to what they said.

The public-address system blared an order to clear the yard. T.D. and Bulldog stepped off the bench along the wall and walked past me. T.D. held up a packet of canteen ducats. "I'm buyin' the spread." (He meant pints of ice cream that would be passed out and eaten with IDs, which were perfect for dipping into the pint boxes.) "Ain't nuthin' gonna happen."

"And everybody's glad," another voice said.

To which I thought, *I don't know about everybody, but I'm damn sure glad.*

The confrontation disintegrated, turning into individuals and tiny clots moving toward their assignments. Within minutes the yard was nearly empty except for a few night workers, our crew standing in a circle. The seagulls and pigeons that saw their chances descended to take them. T.D. handed me an open pint of Neopolitan. I had my ID card ready to dig in.

"I was ready to get it on," T.D. said, draping a meaty forearm on Veto

Rodriquez's shoulder. "Nobody was gonna hurt Mule." Veto was sometimes called Mule because of his large penis, and he really needed very little help to avoid being hurt.

"I wonder what they said out there," Paul said. "You think he apologized?" The last comment brought laughter but no further speculation. My thought was, *Who cares?* Days later, the truth was revealed: the Mexican clique leader had disowned the assailant, claiming that he was a Nazi, not a Chicano—hence there was no trouble between brown and black.

WHILE THE TROUBLE WAS BREWING between the Nazi Mex (he was, indeed, an admirer of the Nazis, especially the black SS uniforms, but as he was illiterate, how much could he know?) and the black, another fuse was burning elsewhere. Two burly white bikers had swindled a black for twenty papers of heroin with a counterfeit $100 bill. A wife of one of the bikers had smuggled him several bills in the visiting room. The black gave it to his own wife to buy more smack. She took their children to Disneyland, and the ticket booth cashier recognized the counterfeit. She was taken in and her children were taken away. Because she had no record and there was only a single piece of currency, the U.S. Attorney declined to indict. She, however, was mad as hell, which was quite understandable. She told her man that she was bringing him no more drugs. The black was enraged at being conned by a pair of "motorcycle-drivin', tattoo-wearin', bad-smellin' honkies. . . ." An hour after the standoff in the Big Yard, the victimized black and several friends caught the two bikers at the rear of the South Cell House and began swinging knives. The whites, both young and strong, managed to fight off being killed, but they were badly carved up and hospitalized.

The leading white clique, several of whom would later found the Aryan Brotherhood, knew about the burn behind the stabbing and decided not to get involved. "They brought that shit on themselves," was Bulldog's observation. "What'd they expect . . . they could burn the dude and nothin' would happen. Bullshit!" He emphasized his judgment by turning a thumb down, and that was the decision; he had great influence over the clique. Far more than I did.

Because my job assignment was four to midnight, my days were free. I seldom ate lunch, but during the lunch hour I frequently preferred my cell to the crowded yard. It was then that I typed what I had written in #2 pencil the night before using a pilfered flashlight that nobody cared I had. On this day, however, Paul Allen wanted me to shill in a poker game he was running. How could I refuse? We had no idea that the previous night's stabbing, aggravated by the one earlier today, had started the war in earnest. Men who lived in the North Cell House could come and go from their cells when they wanted. A tier tender on each tier had a key to the cells. He unlocked the gate when you asked.

While waiting for the poker players on the yard so we could take them to the boiler room where the game was being held, I tried to feel the tension on the yard. It was more than usual, but far less than earlier in the day. I put it down to something residual, for most convicts had no idea what was going on in such matters.

Guards then appeared, hurrying from several directions toward the North Cell House. Something had happened in the cell house or up on death row. Everything on the yard stopped except the whirling seagulls overhead. Everything was silent except the gulls with their raucous cries. All eyes faced the cell house door. Moments later, four white convicts rushed out of the cell house carrying a man on a litter. Two guards trotted along beside them. As the retinue crossed the yard diagonally toward the South Cell House entrance and the hospital beyond, a couple of the man's friends came out of the crowd and hurried along beside him. The escorting guards waved them away and were ignored. I could see the man on the litter talking and gesturing. When the litter reached the end of the building where the friends could go no farther, they turned back. The yard was silent. Three thousand sets of eyes were watching. The convict, whom I didn't know, threw his hands wide and screamed, *"Goddamned fucking niggers!"*

"I don't think we're playing poker today," Paul said.

A queasiness started in my stomach and spread through my limbs. This was so utterly senseless. Later, when I was summoned to type the reports, my misgivings were replaced by indignation. The wounded man would survive with some scars and diminished use of his right hand, because a tendon had been severed as he warded off knife blows. He was doing time for receiving stolen property and worked in the furniture factory. He'd never had a disciplinary infraction and had a medical lay-in. He was taking a nap with his cell gate open. Why not? He had no enemies. One black stepped in and stabbed him while the other kept lookout in the doorway. He had no idea who they were, and they didn't know him. He was selected because he was white and asleep. It could just as easily have been me, although I probably would not have taken a nap with the gate unlocked. Still, the black tier tender could have opened the gate for them.

Another voice yelled, *"You banjo-lipped nigger motherfuckers!"*

"Fuck you, honky!" was the retort from someone in the black crowd.

On the overhead catwalk appeared a guard with a bucket of tear gas grenades and a short-barreled launcher. Behind him, sweating and panting from the exertion, came a couple of guards lugging carbines. The convicts below, black and white, were confused. The shot callers had told them nothing. They had no idea what to do.

The steam whistle blew afternoon work call, and the convicts, like trained milk cows, began moving slowly toward their job assignments. I went back to my cell to continue reading a biography of Alexander the Great. Never in history did anyone deserve that appellation more than the Macedonian warrior king. I learned about the victory over Darius and the Persians, the burning of Persopolis, and the founding of the world's first great library at Alexandria by

Ptolemy, Alexander's general, whose descendants ruled Egypt to the time of Cleopatra. In a lockup somewhere, I'd had an argument with a semiliterate black who asserted that Cleopatra was a "black African queen with skin of ebony." It almost reached a physical altercation when I said that she may indeed have been black, but no reputable historian disputes that her antecedents were Greek—and that was an undisputed fact. Then came the ad hominem vitriol: *"White devils steal the black man's history."* I had not known of Alexander's fantastic march through the Kush and the Khyber Pass, conquering all who opposed him and tainting his golden image with what we would call war crimes. His will was indomitable, and he was often victorious through sheer determination. When he was my age he had already conquered the world and was both dead and immortal, whereas I was an outlaw and outcast serving time in a gray rock penitentiary. I had been born in the wrong era and under the wrong circumstances.

About two-thirty I had switched to Camus's *Reflection on the Guillotine*, perhaps the most thoughtful, and certainly the most beautifully written, essay on capital punishment. I stood up to unkink my back and take a leak. When I turned away from the toilet, I could see the yard through the windows. Convicts were trudging en masse toward the cell houses. No lines were being formed. It was an hour and a half until the regular lockup. Something was still going on, and I knew it was about race conflict. Had there been another incident?

Within a minute I could hear them begin to come through the rotunda door and trudge up the stairway to the tiers. A few passed my cell, moving too fast to stop and ask. Then Billy Michaels appeared. A tall, blond, handsome dope fiend—what is called a hope-to-die dope fiend—he was the kind that wants more than merely feeling good. He wants to keep fixing until his chin rests on his chest and he is oblivious of the world going on around him. Before I could ask him what was going on, he asked, "Lemme borrow your outfit."

"Whaddya got?"

"I ain't got nuthin', but Chente just came off a visit. His old lady gave him a taste. A couple grams. He can't get his back at the job because they're lockin' the joint down. I can slide in if I can get him a rig."

"I don't have it here."

"Shit!"

The tiers were rapidly filling with bodies. A voice on the loudspeaker said that all inmates were to proceed to their assignment for the main count. That meant me. "I can go get it and bring it back after the count clears."

"Oh, man, I'd sure appreciate that."

"I know I'm good for a fix."

"Oh, man! He ain't got but a gram or two."

"Two fixes is pretty easy—if he wants to get high tonight."

"I'll put it to him."

"What's this lockup about?"

"I dunno. Probably about all this race shit."

"Something else happen?"

"I didn't hear anything. I was cutting hair downstairs."

The cell house bell rang out. Security bars were raised and a thousand gates opened as convicts stepped in. I stepped out onto an empty tier of slamming gates and the inevitable straggler running hard to reach his cell before being locked out. Missing a lockup wasn't a disciplinary offense, but several misses could bring one. It tended to be the same convicts who missed lockups.

As I went through the yard gate, two groups of guards were hustling a pair of black convicts toward B Section lockup. I knew neither by name, but one had frequented the Folsom law library when I was the clerk. He was trying to find an error in his extradition. The FBI had kidnapped him from Mexico. Barely literate, he was one of many convicts who seemed to believe that if you find the right cases and repeat the citations like some kind of magical chant, the prison gates will fly open. I tried to explain the essential law: the Supreme Court said that it didn't matter how they got you before the court; the court didn't lose jurisdiction. He didn't like it. I remember saying, "Okay, okay, forget it. I was just trying to help you." His reply was laden with venom: "No white man ever helped a black man." It left nothing more to say, then or now. He had been Fanonized, even if he never heard of Franz Fanon. He sneered at me as he went by. Not to be undone, I sneered in reply, but inside I felt a keening ache. It was a sad, sad day.

When I reached the Yard Office, I found out what had happened. A fifty-year-old white convict who was being transferred wanted to say good-bye to a teacher. The classroom was up a stairway in an annex to the education building. Three blacks waited in the shadows on the landing to ambush whatever white appeared. It happened to be the man being transferred. They came out of the shadows while he was on the top stair before the landing, so surprising him that he fell crashing back down the stairway.

In the classroom, the teacher heard the ruckus and went to the door. As he opened it, the assailants were going down the stairs. The erstwhile victim cried out. The teacher began to sound the alarm with his whistle. Nearby guards came running. They caught two of the blacks as they ran out. As they were led away, one yelled, "Power to the people!" The elderly white convict had a sprained ankle.

That aborted assault was enough to bring the order to lock the prison down. The cons were sent back to the cell houses. On the tiers, paranoia ran high, for in the narrow space it was impossible to know when, or if, the long shivs would be pulled. Men without friends, those trying to quietly serve a term and get out, were in the worst predicament. They had no allies. Whites were indignant and afraid. Blacks were both jubilant and afraid, though they waited to yell their pleasure until they were locked in their cells and were anonymous voices.

That night guards and freemen began a search of the prison that would continue for days and reveal hundreds of weapons. Cell blocks were first. Personnel filed along the fifth tier without warning until two stood outside each cell gate. Riflemen behind them gave cover. Security bars were raised, and convicts were ordered to strip to their underwear and step out onto the tier. As soon as the convicts realized what was happening, knives were thrown between the bars, sailing down to clatter on the floor of the bottom tier. It was really unnecessary to discard the weapons, for the searchers were sadly out of shape, accustomed to sitting on their butts. Before finishing two cells they were panting, unable to do more than perfunctorily raise a mattress. Many just walked into cells and sat down.

On each tier behind the cells was a narrow service passage with plumbing and electrical conduits. Convict electricians and plumbers had access to the passages. Guards found two dozen knives and three roofing hatchets in the East Cell House passageways. The arsenal belonged to whites and Chicanos, as the plumber and electrician were a white and Chicano.

The only convicts out of their cells were essential workers—a couple of Captain's Office clerks, hospital attendants, the fire watch, the late cleanup crew in the kitchen, and me. I could wander almost wherever I wanted within San Quentin's walls until midnight. I went to the South Cell House. It was the skid row of San Quentin. The oldest of the big cell houses, it was divided into four sections, one of them the notorious long-term segregation unit named B Section. The rest of the cell house was quiet, but B Section was a cacophonous uproar until dawn; then the men slept the day away, rising up just for meals and an hour in the exercise yard. Many were now in segregation from the last race war. I don't remember all the details of that one, but after a cycle of stabbing, retaliation, stabbing, retaliation, the militant white convicts worked up a plan. Each of several really violent convicts would take a group of two or three or four to various positions, i.e., the library, the education building, and elsewhere. As soon as the afternoon work whistle blew at 1:00 P.M., each squad would attack and murder every black in the vicinity.

At 12:45 a fistfight broke out in the segregation unit exercise yard. The gun rail officer blew his whistle (no response) and fired the obligatory warning shot. That fight broke apart, but the rifle shot was heard throughout the prison. The white convicts waiting in the lower yard thought the general attack was under way. They drew their weapons and charged a group of unarmed blacks lounging around the gate into industries, men waiting to return to work after lunch. Unarmed and taken completely by surprise, they ran for their lives. There were two stragglers, gray-haired old men who failed to realize their mortal danger in time. They tried to run, but the pack of wolves closed on them swiftly. The leader sprang upon one's back. Down he went, disappearing under half a dozen more, the rising and falling knives red in the sun. The second old man reached the chain-link fence around the gardener's area. They tore him loose and fell upon him with the fury of wild dogs. The medical report said he suffered at least forty-two wounds that could have caused his death.

San Quentin was locked down for two months after all that. Daily buses rolled to Folsom, Soledad, Tracy. A couple of the craziest were sent to the

California Medical Facility at Vacaville and given electric shock therapy. That took away their aggression but also a few points of IQ that these guys couldn't afford to lose.

THE LOCKUP CONTINUED. The white clique and their Chicano partners managed to exchange a few words on the grapevine. The words were, "wait . . . wait . . . wait. . . ." They had been taken totally off guard by the series of attacks. They had no idea it was in retaliation for the black being stabbed in the East Cell House. That had been done by a Chicano. So what if he was a fan of Hitler's SS?

Nothing happened on the following Wednesday and Thursday. The lockup was too tight. Every convict out of the cell was searched several times. Even I got frisked by a rookie bull. On the weekend the West Honor Unit returned to normal schedule. A few other workers were pulled from the breakfast lines.

The associate warden had many inmates brought to his office. He wanted to know the mood of the prison. This associate warden, however, was both disliked and lacking in contacts with the right convicts. Those he called lacked prestige or influence in the yard. He appointed a committee of convicts to "cool" the situation, but those on the committee were without respect among their peers. The blacks, especially, had no juice. The very fact that they would even talk to the "chief pig" closed them off from their brothers.

A black program administrator summoned me and three other whites considered leaders. He wanted us to assure him that nothing more would happen. I told him that I didn't run anything and couldn't speak for anybody. Two others stood silent, heads down. The third flushed and stuttered, "They done downed five or six white dudes . . . old men and strays who didn't do nothin' to nobody. Next they'll want us to pluck our eyebrows and get a black joker. Me . . . I'm not promising anything." Nothing was resolved.

The plan of waiting for normal routine was gaining acceptance. Nazis and Hell's Angels backed away, claiming that none of their brothers had been hit and they would stay on the sideline until that happened.

The blacks weren't waiting for whitey. They continued on the offensive.

I happened to be on the fifth tier, standing outside a cell occupied by a couple friends of mine, when I saw two blacks appear around the corner and start down the tier. Luckily, my friends had a roofing hatchet in the cell. They passed it through the bars. The blacks saw it, stopped, and went the other way. It wasn't cowardice—but even if they killed me, I would surely inflict some wounds, and wounds would get them caught.

On the fourth tier, another white, a motorcycle rider, was in front of a cell trying to buy a tab of acid. He worked in the mess hall scullery and had just gotten off work. In fact, he was still wearing the heavy rubber boots from the job. The cell where he stood was in the middle of the tier. The same two blacks came down the tier from the rear. A third black walked along the tier below and climbed up near the front. The white was between them. He saw them and sensed danger, for he backed up against the rail, refusing to turn his back. Had I been in his situation, I would have climbed over the tier long before they arrived. The white convict spread his arms and rested his hands on the railing, leaning back so he could look up. He was probably trying to hide evidence of fear. A smart convict, white or black, would have climbed up or down without hesitation. This man probably thought he wasn't involved; he hadn't done anything to anyone. He was insufficiently afraid to save his own life. The black from the front arrived first. When ten feet away, he pulled his shiv and rushed forward. The white turned to face him and threw up his hands to ward off the blade. It went between his hands and plunged into his chest. An instant later the other two arrived from the rear. One knifed him in the back. The biggest of the trio grabbed him from behind and pinned his arms. The first black stabbed at his throat. The blade entered just above the collarbone and drove down through his lungs and into his heart. He continued struggling, but blood was spewing from his mouth and he was already dying. The second black kept stabbing him. There were no screams, just grunts and gasps and the horrifying sound of tearing flesh. Mirrors jutted between bars along the tier, periscopes of men trying to see what was going on. Whites began yelling and rattling the bars to drive off the killers. They were watching a murder and unable to do anything to stop it. Men on tiers above and below called out, "What's goin' on?" "Them niggers is killin' a motherfucker!" A black voice: "Gonna get all you honky motherfuckers."

The killers sprinted down the rear stairs as a score of guards arrived on the run. Only six blacks were out of their cells. All were taken into custody for investigation. A bloody knife was found beneath a blood-spattered denim jacket in a trash can. Neither item led to anyone. The next morning, following calls from the local NAACP chapter, the associate warden told the captain to release the six blacks because there was no evidence against them. Instead he ordered several friends of the victim to be locked up, the logic being that they might try to retaliate. Before they could be released, guards discovered traces of blood on the shoes of three; plus they told conflicting stories. The associate warden rescinded the release order.

That afternoon, word got around that guards would look the other way when whites struck back. Bias was long established, but outright license to kill was something new. The unholy alliance of white guards and convicts was not mutual love but shared hatred. Until recent years, most guards had been even-handed dealing with convicts.

The senseless murder in the East Cell House was the catalyst to madness. Even I, who had empathy for the anguish of the black man in America, now seethed with racial hatred. When the slow unlock for supper began, half a tier at a time, faces showed how things were going. White convicts were sullen and silent; blacks were laughing and joking. When the fifth tier of the East Cell House was unlocked, whistles suddenly began bleating. Guards ran up the stairway. They found two blacks in their cell, lying in their blood. One walked out, seriously wounded. The other was half under the bottom bunk, spuming blood from his mouth with each breath. That indicated a punctured lung. A gun rail guard had four whites covered, and blacks on the tier were pointing them out. Most guards were uninterested in investigating what had happened. Both victims lived. They claimed that two whites had run into their cell and started stabbing the moment the security bar went up, while the other two whites held everyone else at bay on the tier. The jocular laughter had turned to silence.

Seventy-two hours passed without incident except for a fistfight. The officials were considering a return to normal routine. Kitchen workers were already following the usual routine. The culinary department had a locker room and shower on the second floor. It could be reached only up a narrow concrete-walled stairway. More than one unsolved murder had occurred in the area, the last one of a stool pigeon whose jugular was literally torn from his throat. While officials were considering an unlock, half a dozen white convicts filed up the stairway, each with a knife in his belt. Five blacks were in the room, shaving, showering, rinsing their hands, or standing at the urinal, when the whites came through the door. One black saw the attack coming and ran into a wire enclosure where towels were stored. He held the door closed. The others had nowhere to go. Within seconds, blood was splattering the walls. Blacks were running in circles, followed by whites with knives. One husky black youth lowered his head and charged at the narrow entrance to the stairs. Two Hell's Angels waited. He got past the first one and crashed into the second. Both of them went down the stairs. The white broke his ankle. The black had several wounds, and a shiv was hanging from his buttock. He ran into the kitchen proper, where I happened to be standing next to Lieutenant Ziemer and the watch sergeant, both of whom were eating bacon-and-egg sandwiches. "I'm hit," the black convict said. Indeed, his white T-shirt was bloody and the shiv was dangling. It had a certain absurdity. The sergeant told him, "You're not hurt that bad. Wait over there."

The black who got down the stairs actually saved the lives of the others. The whites thought the alarm was given, and they fled before finishing off the remaining trio. One of the victims died. His spinal cord had been severed. He went into a coma and never regained consciousness. The other victims were never shown photos to identify. Higher officials were hamstrung by the hostile indifference of their sergeants and lieutenants. The plan to unlock the prison was put on hold. Cold sandwiches were pushed through the bars twice a day, except for the previously mentioned "essential workers." They were served hot meals. I was locked up all day, but when the shift changed I was let out. About 10:00 P.M., Lieutenant Ziemer went to Key Control and drew the keys to the kitchen's walk-in refrigerators. It was T-bone time for the favored few, me and the late cleanup crew. During the day I worked on cutting the novel and writing my first essay; it was about prison's racial troubles.

Gone was the laughter by blacks of the first few days, but blacks and whites who had known each other since childhood now passed with stone faces, without speaking or even acknowledging the other's existence. Friendships ceased. In a world absolutely integrated, each cell identical with every other cell, each man eating the same food and wearing the same clothes, racial hatred was malevolent and intractable. Most convicts lacked a sanctuary where they could relax. Even the cell offered no safety. An empty jar could be filled with gas and smashed against the bars, followed by a book of flaming matches. It happened more than once. Going to eat, even half a tier at a time, with two gun bulls fifteen feet away, required passing blind spots on the stair landings where an ambush could be laid. A group of whites or blacks could be waiting for someone of the opposite color, or maybe they were simply waiting for another friend—but someone of the opposite color wouldn't know why they were there and had to virtually brush against them while going by. A white was jumped that way, but he managed to get away. Ten minutes later in another cell house, a white lunged at a black but exposed his knife before he was in range. The black saw it and bolted down the tier.

The associate warden's committee of inmates was allowed to roam the cell houses at night, hopefully to talk to the militants and end the war. One white used the peacekeeping unlock to take a shower. A black caught him naked and wet and stabbed him in the neck. Miraculously he survived. Two black guards worked the cell house that night. They covered for the black assailant as the white guards had covered for whites in other situations.

The next day a friend of the latest victim lunged into a group of blacks with a knife. He stabbed one through the upper arm. Another black jumped on the assailant's back and pulled him down. Guards arrived and overpowered him. He would get a five-to-life for possession of the knife.

In the North Cell House the convicts reached a truce. No attacks would be made in the building. Outside the building it was still open season. Neither side entirely believed the other. No white or group of whites could speak for every other white, nor could any group of blacks speak for all other blacks. Yet the truce held as days became weeks, at least in the North Cell House.

In the rest of San Quentin a week went by, then two weeks. So many convicts were locked up that were four and five deep in the hole, and the buses were rolling. After another ten days, the prison was slowly returned to regular schedule. On Saturday afternoon the weekend movie was shown in the North Mess Hall. One of the blacks involved in the shower stabbing had not been picked up. He was in the movie. When "The End" flashed onscreen and the lights went up, the crowd started moving toward the exits. A white and his Chicano homeboy tried to stick the black, but someone yelled a warning and he got away.

Minutes later a hundred blacks were bunched under the weather shed, facing an equal number of whites and some Chicanos grouped next to the East Cell House. The Big Yard was totally silent. The convict disc jockey in the prison radio room then turned the country music full blast. I'll never forget the song: "The Eyes of Texas Are Upon You." I couldn't help laughing.

Only four or five of the white clique who did the killing were still in the general population. The rest were in segregation. Two of the remainder walked toward the blacks, as if going for a drink of water at the fountain amid them. One small black started to ease forward through the crowd, trying to move in from the rear. Several others moved with him. The two whites turned suddenly. One drew a roofing hatchet, the other a shiv the size of a short sword. The small black ducked back and discarded his knife, stopped by both the size and weaponry of the opposition and by the clacking sound of lever-action rifles being readied. It was the blacks that the white guards would shoot.

The whites near the East Cell House had started forward but now stopped. The two men in front got back into the crowd. A black guard kept one of them in sight, but the convict managed to drop his shiv and kick it into the crowd. Someone got rid of it.

Once more the prison was locked down. Two months passed before it was slowly unlocked. Now, however, guards carried nightsticks, the first time since the lead-tipped canes were taken away in 1940. Nobody was indicted or convicted of the stabbing and killings. Marin County didn't want San Quentin convicts in its courthouse.

DURING THE DAYS OF the long lockdown, I cut 20 percent of the book I was working on, *No Beast So Fierce*. Every extraneous page, paragraph, sentence, or word was considered. That was what Merrill Pollack at W. W. Norton & Co. said he wanted, and even if he couldn't offer me a contract in advance, his had been the most interest anyone had shown in seventeen years. Besides, what else did I have to do? When I sent it back, I included a story about the race war I've just described.

Two months later, I had a pass to see my caseworker to prepare the report for my yearly appearance before the parole board. Each cell house now had a row of cinder block offices on the floor. A young man fresh from San Francisco State, he had been a caseworker for several months. I knocked on the door.

"Oh yeah, Bunker. Come in. Let's go get your file." As we walked along the front of the cinder block cubicles to the first cell where records were kept in file cabinets, he said, "By the way, the warden's office called and authorized a phone call to New York."

"A phone call to New York? What about?"

"They didn't say."

He unlocked the cabinet and went through the manila folders. Most files or "jackets" were between a quarter- and a half-inch thick. The caseworker found mine and grunted as he pulled it out. It was about the thickness of a Los Angeles central telephone directory. While walking back to the office, he hoisted it to test the weight. "I've never even *seen* a file this big. As a matter of fact, this is *twice* the size of any file I've seen." We turned into the office, and he went behind the desk. "What's this?" He put on his glasses and looked at a slip of paper Scotch-taped to the outside of the folder, then burst into laughter. "Do you know what it says?"

I shook my head.

"It says: 'See file number two.'"

I saw the humor, but it was also sad. It was my life.

"Let's make this call," he said. He had the prison operator give him an outside line; then he dialed and handed me the telephone.

"Watkins Agency," a woman said.

"My name's Edward Bunker. I'm supposed to call."

"Oh yes, Mike wants to talk to you."

A voice one would expect from Victorian times came on the line. "Why, hello, Mr. Bunker, Mike Watkins here. I finally get to talk to you. Do you know what this is all about?"

"Uhhh . . . maybe . . . I dunno . . . I mean I hope."

He chuckled. "Merrill Pollack at W. W. Norton has made an offer to publish your book. The advance is small, but Norton is a good publishing house and I think we should take the offer."

"Oh . . . yes . . . sure . . . whatever you say."

"I was sure that was what you'd say. Oh, and one more thing. Louis Lapham at *Harper's* wants to publish that article you sent him about prison race war. He wants it for the February lead."

Seventeen years, six unpublished novels, scores of unpublished stories without seeing so much as one word in print. Writing had become my only chance to escape the morass of my existence. I had persevered even when the candle of hope had burned out. I had persevered from habit, because I had no idea what else to do. Now, in one day in one phone call, one of America's most prestigious magazines and a quality book publisher had agreed to publish my first essay and my sixth novel. Years before, when I first embarked on the path of becoming a writer, I had visions of what it would do for me. I would live a mixture of Hemingway, Scott and Zelda, and the then-famous Françoise Sagan, who had a smash international best-seller while a teenager. Writing a good book would open doors for me. The world would read the truths I would write. I would make a lotus grow from the mud. Those dreams were seventeen years old, fourteen of which had been spent behind grim prison walls. I was happy, of course, but time had taken the sheen from the dream. I had no idea what the future would hold beyond my continuing to write. I had already embarked on another novel.

That night in my cell I tried to conjure the same old dreams. They remained opaque and obscure. The truth of the subsequent two and a half decades would be greater, in most respects, than my visions of forty-five years ago. The dream was fulfilled—in spades. My four novels are still in print in nine countries, and the first, *No Beast So Fierce*, remains so twenty-five years after initial publication. A lotus definitely grows from the mud.

AFTERWORD

Paris Just Before Spring

I AM ALONE in Paris. My wife of nearly two decades has gone home to Brendan, our five-year-old son. I was invited here to play a small role in a small French movie, *Cameleon*, about a femme fatale who is definitely a chameleon. Benoit Cohen, the enthusiastic young director, is using both prayer and donated pieces of film stock to put his vision on the screen. My pay is minuscule, but it does cover most of my expenses—and who would refuse a free month in the world's most beautiful city? February has turned to March and the meager snow has disappeared except in the crevices the sun never probes. The tree branches are still starkly bare, but since I've been in Paris they're sprouting hard little buds that will soon become glorious leaves dancing in the breeze. God, I love Paris any time of year.

The Normandy Hotel is on the right bank near the Louvre, the Seine, and the Place de Concorde.

"Do you know where this is?" I asked the concierge. I had to pick up a week's per diem, the cash money for expenses that isn't taxed as income.

The concierge produced one of those convenience street maps for tourists, the kind that lists main boulevards and landmarks, but meager details otherwise. He pointed to a green spot designating a park. "It's right around there," he said, "four or five kilometers."

"I can walk it? Right?"

"Yes. It's a long walk . . . but it's a nice day."

He was right on both counts. I set forth up the Avenue de Opera. It is bright enough for sunglasses, but the morning chill is perfect coolant for a vigorous stride. I'm sure I can reach my destination if I find the park, and that should be easy. On the other hand, how long it takes is immaterial. I enjoy exploring cities on foot: New York, London, Rome, any city but LA—and Paris most of all. I recall Thomas Wolfe's nocturnal meanderings through the dark, empty streets of Manhattan while communing with his muse. His prose turned deserted streets into symphonies of description.

At the opera house (it sure is big enough to have a phantom wandering around inside), I turn right. I think it is the Boulevard Haussman. After another twenty minutes, I turn right again. Now I'm trudging up a fairly steep hill lined with chic apartments. Unlike the United States, where the middle class abandoned the central city to deteriorate in the care of the poor and minorities, in France and most of Europe, the affluent have stayed within the city. The poor have been pushed to the surrounding suburbs. Space in the city has increased in value. Apartments are small and expensive. It was one reason there was so much vibrant street life in Paris. In LA almost anyone might have a swimming pool in their backyard. In Paris only the rich have a backyard.

The park started a block from the hill's summit. It was bigger than I anticipated and I didn't know which way to go. Spotting a couple of men engaged in conversation, I waited for an opportunity to excuse my intrusion and extended the slip of paper with the address. It was a question that didn't require French. One of the men pointed back down the hill and up the next hill.

I started walking. I had gone about half a block when the sound of running footsteps made me stop and turn. A young man was gesturing for me to wait. I did so. He arrived, panting, and spoke in accented English: "I know you."

"You know me?"

He nodded. "Edward Bunker. I read your books." His grin was wide, perhaps in reply to my manifest surprise. He held up three fingers. That was how many I'd published at the time.

"There's another one due next year."

"I'll get it. What's the title?"

"*Dog Eat Dog.*"

"I'll still be waiting. That man—" he gestured back up the hill from whence I'd come. "He told you wrong. That street is that way . . . on the other side of the park. I saw a film crew over there."

"*Merci beaucoup.* That's what I'm looking for." I started to turn and stopped. "So how did you recognize me?"

"*Reservoir Dogs.* Mr. Blue, right?"

"Yep." The role had been minuscule, but *Reservoir Dogs* had been a blockbuster in most of Europe, especially France and England and, especially in the latter, had spurred sales of my books.

As I continued walking through the park that overlooked Paris, I found it hard to believe that someone would recognize me on a Paris sidewalk, six thousand miles from home, someone who had read all three of my books. I was still glowing within when I spotted the trucks and lights of the small film crew. The set was a cafe. When I arrived the cast and crew were having lunch. Without intruding, I paid my respects to Benoit Cohen, the talented young director, for he was going over a scene with the leads, Seymour Cassell and Chiara Mastrianni (I played his ex-con best pal), and it was poor movie protocol to interrupt such a situation. I found the production manager, who gave me a stack of francs, supposedly enough to live on for a week. She also had the "call sheet." I was scheduled to work the next day. It was at this location, and they were at the end of the scene they were shooting today. I was welcome to hang out and watch the scene being shot, but I had other plans for the afternoon. I wanted to see the Pantheon and Napoleon's tomb. He sure made some big noise for a little Corsican. They still have the Napoleonic "N" on bridges over the Seine.

As I waved good-bye to the director, one of the cameramen came up with two of my books in the French editions. Would I sign them? I drew my trusty felt tip, which makes for great signatures. Thick and dark, they look substantial. Ball-point pen signatures look too thin.

Before I finished with the cameraman, a line had formed. The crew was small as film crews go, no more than a score, but more than half had books for me to sign. Some were brand new, but many were books the owner had for some time. One said he'd taken the job because I was in the cast. Who would have imagined such things from my first forty years of life? It may not have equaled the metamorphosis of St. Augustine, but it was certainly unexpected. I never imagined this reality when I walked out of prison twenty some years earlier. Now I'd passed sixty, which I'd never thought I'd see. In recent years my body has shown evidence of mortality, bladder cancer cured by surgery ten years ago, antibodies for hepatitis C (I'm one of the 80% who remain inactive), a mild heart attack (if there is such a thing) treated with angioplasty, and a borderline case of adult diabetes that seems under control from half a pill and diligent exercise on a treadmill. I have never looked better and, with average luck, expect to live another decade to play with and educate my son. Still, whatever way I look at it, most of the game had been played and it seemed time to write about it.

Meandering in the direction of the hotel, I thought about the two decades since I'd gotten out of prison. Who would have expected me to stay out? Not me, for sure. The only decision in that regard was that I would not do anything stupid. Other than that, whatever happened, happened. Over the years I've been asked by interviewers why I've changed. My reply, and the truth, is that I changed as my circumstances changed. Being a published, and somewhat acclaimed writer was, of course, central to everything. Just when I got out, the movie based on the book was beginning preproduction. That introduced me to an entirely new milieu—and people that I liked. I also made my acting debut, playing a scene in a bar with Dustin Hoffman. It takes all day to shoot one five-minute scene. When the assistant director yelled, "That's a wrap" at the end of the day, the cast and crew applauded, which made me blush. Over the years I've appeared in a score of small roles, not exactly a living but enough to cover health insurance for my family.

The common belief is that having an ex-con on parole, as opposed to just releasing him, is beneficial to society. That may be true as a general principle, but with me the opposite is true. I reject the idea of *custodia legis*, that a parolee is still in legal custody. I gave up trying to do a parole after the first one. I would see the parole agent just once to pick up my "gate" money, and then I would find some false identification and disappear. The next time the parole agent saw me was when I was in jail. This time, however, I think I would have waited until the movie was finished, but after that I would have become a fugitive. By not being on parole, I was able to leave California, which seemed a wise move when a crony and former cell partner, Paul, escaped from the county jail and called me from the highway. I had to take him in and give him some help, at least for a few days. He began robbing banks, and because my name came up when his name went through the computer, the FBI came to see me on the movie set. My friend happened to be visiting me when they arrived—in Dustin Hoffman's trailer. He wasn't spotted; they weren't expecting him. They wanted it on record that I knew he was a fugitive, so if they found evidence that I had seen him and not reported it, they could charge me with aiding and abetting. Some weeks later, Paul was pounding on the door. When I let him in, he ran into the bathroom, kneeled down, and began dumping money on the floor. His pistol fell out of his waistband. He had barely escaped a bank robbery in nearby Santa Monica. Do you think the FBI would have believed my protests of innocence if they had been following him? It was time to bail out of LA when the movie was in the can and my second novel, *Animal Factory*, was in bookstores.

I stayed for awhile with an old girlfriend and her daughter in Chicago, but Chicago was too damned cold, so I went to New York. Dustin optioned the film rights to *Animal Factory*, not because he wanted to make it, but to help me out. My third novel, *Little Boy Blue*, was almost finished, and the first hundred pages are probably my best writing. Long before, I had recognized or decided that I either had to succeed as a writer or be an outlaw. By making such an unequivocal decision, I set myself on a path of perseverance, and only such determination, or obstinacy, would let me overcome this in the first place. Imagine someone with a seventh-grade education wanting to be a serious writer and accomplishing it without any help or encouragement. Indeed, the prison psychologist said it was another "manifestation of infantile fantasy." However, when my first novel was made into a movie, my second novel was published, and my third novel was nearly finished, I thought I was victorious. I wasn't prepared for *Little Boy Blue* to sell four thousand copies, despite rave reviews. It would have been hard to sell more, for my publisher had none in the stores, not even in LA when I was doing talk shows and on tour. At that time I might have returned to crime. I doubt that I would have robbed a bank, although I might have heisted a drug dealer or two, a crime I always liked because they couldn't go to the police. Most likely I would have grown some pot. It is easy to do, hard to get caught, and very profitable. While watching it grow, I would have continued writing. If caught growing pot it wouldn't have been a life sentence, not even for me. And back in a cell, I would have sharpened a pencil and continued writing. Now I knew I could, and likewise knew I couldn't do anything else—at least not anything legal.

The story has a happy ending solely because of Jennifer. She is my salvation. We met when I was first released. In the few weeks before the U.S. Court of Appeals for the Ninth Circuit reversed my conviction, I'd been in a halfway house. Jennifer was my counselor. She was twenty-four and looked like a seventeen-year-old personification of the California girl; tall, slender, blond, an upper-middle-class, University-of-Southern-California sorority girl. When my name was discussed at a staff meeting before my arrival, she said she knew of me from my essays in *The Nation*. I could scarcely believe it when this beautiful young woman introduced herself and said, "I'm your counselor."

Counselor! Unbelievable! The lamb would counsel the wolf.

It was a month until the court-ordered reversal came through. We became friends. She was interested in literature and philosophy. When I was out of the halfway house we twice met for coffee. When I left Los Angeles, I gave her my address and wrote one letter in two years. Romance never went through my mind. Not only was she married, but I can't imagine a metaphor to convey the difference in our backgrounds. I doubt that she'd ever met anyone who had spent a night in jail, much less eighteen years in America's toughest prisons, with much of that in the hole. As a teenager she had a horse; I had a fat rat running across my macaroni sandwich in the hole of the LA County Jail.

When I saw her again, she was in the process of getting a divorce, and romance did blossom. The difference in our backgrounds was the same, so I was pretty certain, although silent about it, that it was a star-crossed romance that wouldn't last. I would try to leave good memories, and I was sure I could play a sort of Pygmalion. She loved books and was a college graduate, but public schools, even in an upper-class enclave, leave vast gaps in what a truly educated person knows about history and literature and a myriad other things, gaps I could fill. On the other hand, she helped to civilize me, and was so obviously a nice girl that those who I might make nervous, or even scare, would look at us and think: "He can't be *that* dangerous if she is with him." I anticipated that this odd romance would last a year, perhaps two, before the glamour wore off for her or I got bored.

Neither came to pass, and after two decades it seems likely we'll be together until I die. Even more unlikely from my perspective, at sixty-five, I'm the father of a handsome, extremely bright and rambunctious five-year-old, my pride and joy. Who knows what he will think of his father, but the cards we dealt him are infinitely better than what fate dealt me. I could have played them better, no doubt, and there are things for which I am ashamed, but when I look in the mirror, I am proud of what I am. The traits that made me fight the world are also those that made me prevail.